Congressman Doc Hastings: Twenty Years of Turmoil

C. MARK SMITH

What Others Are Saying about
Congressman Doc Hastings

"I think Doc stayed around as long as he did because the people at home felt like he was there for the right reasons. He wasn't there for Doc. This wasn't about making him look good; this was about trying to change the government in a way he and they thought it needed to be changed. All of that is laid out in Mark Smith's excellent narrative. It's a first-class biography."

Lindsey Graham
Member of Congress (R-SC) (1995-2003)
US Senator (R-SC) (2003 to present)

"Mark Smith's book about Doc Hastings provides an in-depth look at Congress during the exciting but difficult years between 1995 and 2015. . . . Although he rarely sought the spotlight, his colleagues considered him a true legislator who thought government should be the servant of the people, and not its master, and who could be counted on to carry out difficult assignments when asked."

John Boehner
Member of Congress (R-OH) (1991-2015)
Speaker of the House of Representatives (2011-2015)

"Mark Smith's compelling, insightful biography of Doc Hastings introduces a statewide audience to an underrated Eastern Washington conservative with a conscience."

John C. Hughes
Legacy Washington Historian

"Doc was a mentor for me and an example what principled, conservative leadership is all about. He was a Ronald Reagan delegate to the 1976 Republican convention and remained true to the values of small government and free enterprise during his entire political career. . . . Doc was an influential leader on issues vital to our area: the cleanup of the Hanford Site, protecting the dams that provide electricity and irrigation, and improving forest management practices to reduce wildfires. . . . He came to know the complex House rules better than just about anyone. The Speaker could always turn to him when he needed a steady hand."

Cathy McMorris Rogers
Member of Congress (R-WA) (2005 to present)
Chair, House Republican Conference

Congressman Doc Hastings:
Twenty Years of Turmoil

C. MARK SMITH

BOOK PUBLISHERS NETWORK
Changing the World One Book at a Time

Book Publishers Network
P. O. Box 2256, Bothell, WA 98041
(425) 483-3040
www.bookpublishersnetwork.com

10 9 8 7 6 5 4 3 2 1

LCCN: 2017912638
ISBN: 978-1-945271-78-6
ISBN: 978-1-945271-96-0 (eBook)

Library of Congress Cataloging–in–Publication Data

Smith, C. Mark

Congressman Doc Hastings: Twenty Years of Turmoil / C. Mark Smith.
Includes bibliographical references and index.

LCSH: Hastings, Richard (Doc), 1941- | Legislators--United States--Biography.
| Politicians— United States--Biography. | United States. Congress. House. |
United States--Politics and government--20th century. | United States--Politics
and government--21st century. | Political culture--United States. | Washington
(State)--Politics and government--20th century. | Washington (State)--Politics and
government--21st century. | LCGFT: Biographies.

LCC: E748.H3867 S65 2017 | DDC: 973.92/0924--dc23

Manufactured in the United States of America

First Edition

Cover Photo: House Committee on Natural Resources
Cover design: *by* Laura Zugzda
Editor: Julie Scandora
Book design: Melissa Coffman
Production: Scott Book
Graphs: Matt Mathes
Index: Sam Arnold-Boyd. | *Printed and bound by Bang Printing. Brainerd, MN*

*This book is dedicated to the men and women
who devote their careers to public service
and to the interaction of their personal beliefs
and visions of America.*

*It is also dedicated to the notion
that those beliefs and visions
have the best chance of success
when our public servants listen to each other—and to us.*

*As always, it is also dedicated to my family
for putting up with a very focused author.*

Other Books by C. Mark Smith

Raising Cain:
The Life and Politics of Senator Harry P. Cain

Community Godfather:
How Sam Volpentest shaped the
history of Hanford and the Tri-Cities

In the Wake of Lewis and Clark:
From the Mountains to the Sea

CONTENTS

AUTHOR'S NOTE

I HAVE LIVED AND WORKED around the fringes of politics all my adult life. The subject of my first book was Harry P. Cain, the controversial former Tacoma mayor, US senator, and civil libertarian. He was a close friend of my father's and my first real role model and mentor outside my family. In my early thirties, quite by accident, I found myself serving as the regional director of the federal Economic Development Administration for the eight western states. I interacted daily with one or more of the eight governors, sixteen senators, and fifty-seven congressmen who represented the states in my region, as well as with presidential appointees in and out of my agency and the occasional member of the White House staff. That experience resulted in my forty-year career managing economic development organizations at the local, state, and federal level—jobs that were themselves never far from politics.

My second book was about Sam Volpentest, a legendary economic developer and community leader—in many ways the visionary behind the development of the modern Tri-Cities area in Washington State. Sam's success was the result of his tenacity and salesmanship, but it wouldn't have been possible without his longtime political connections and his adroit understanding of how to use them. I remember vividly the day I first met him in the mid-1970s. He was looking for a federal grant, and his visit to my Seattle office was followed almost immediately by a supporting call from our state's senior senator, Warren Magnuson.

Both Harry Cain and Sam Volpentest were gone when I wrote about them—something of an advantage for an author. Doc Hastings is very much alive, and our collaboration on this book has been an altogether different experience—one for which I shall be forever grateful. I say that because it has provided me with an opportunity to better understand, for better or worse, how the US House of Representatives—the "People's House"—works and the motivations and frustrations of those who know it well.

This is a book of biography and history—with a little commentary added for context when I thought it necessary. The thread that binds it together is the twenty-year congressional career of Richard "Doc" Hastings, the only member of Congress ever elected from Franklin County, Washington. For ten terms—twenty years—Doc represented a rural district that stretches from the Canadian border to the Columbia River, and the district he represented explains a lot about who Doc Hastings is as a person and a politician.

Doc was elected in the Newt Gingrich Republican Revolution of 1994 and served in Congress until January 2015. Many Congress watchers consider that 1994 "Contract with America" election as the modern starting point of the political polarization and governmental dysfunction that characterize today's political landscape.

The dramatic increase in political discord in our nation is the strong subtheme of this book. The 1995 budget crisis and government shutdown, the Clinton impeachment, 9/11, Hurricane Katrina, the wars in Afghanistan and Iraq, the Great Recession, the passage of the Affordable Care Act, and the budget crisis and fiscal cliff of 2013 played a role, but they were *events*. They occurred against a backdrop of cultural and technological trends, such as the increased use of social media, identity politics, self-segregation, and political gerrymandering that are described in more detail in my introduction to this book. As a result, the electorate was so conflicted that they voted to change the control of Congress in three major wave elections in 1994, 2006, and 2010. In addition, for most of that time, no party controlled both the legislative and executive branches of government at the same time. Doc's time in Congress has to be viewed against the backdrop of these events.

THIS BOOK WAS WRITTEN with the complete and much-appreciated cooperation of Doc Hastings, his family, and many of his friends and colleagues, but it is an independent work. I retained the final right of approval, and although Hastings and others read and commented on the chapters as they were being written, their primary contributions have been to help me better understand complicated political and procedural issues and to correct technical and factual errors.

I conducted more than fifty recorded interviews with Doc and his wife, Claire, at their home overlooking the Columbia River between January 2016 and August 2017. Claire contributed freely, occasionally corrected her husband, and provided numerous anecdotes. Obviously for the Hastings, politics is a team sport—and a highly partisan team sport at that. More than fifty others contributed through personal, transcribed, or email interviews including current and former members of Congress. Unless they declined to be mentioned, their names appear in the bibliography.

As always, I am indebted to many for their help. I particularly want to mention Kathy Rusk, who researched the Hastings' family history and made my job immeasurably easier. This is the third book in which I have collaborated with Tara Pegasus, a gifted editor and musician who again helped me in many, many ways. Again, I need to thank the research librarians at the Richland Public Library for their help with their veteran microfiche machine, which, like fine wine, seems only to improve with age. I am deeply grateful for the help of Donean Brown, the librarian for the *Yakima Herald-Republic*, and to Jack Briggs, Ken Robertson, and Bob Brawdy, denizens of the *Tri-City Herald*, for their critical help and advice.

Many people read the book as it was being written, too many to list here, but in particular I want to thank Tim Peckinpaugh, former staff aide to congressman Sid Morrison, and a partner of K&L Gates in Washington, DC, who has worked with Doc and our community on so many important issues; John C. Hughes, the former editor and publisher of the *Aberdeen Daily World*, the director of the Washington Secretary of State's Legacy Washington program, and my mentor on all matters of Washington State political history; Gary Petersen, former vice president of Government Programs for the Tri-City Development Council (TRIDEC), who worked with Doc over his entire career; and Tom Moak, a fellow

Tacoma native, former state legislator, mayor of Kennewick, and now commissioner for the Port of Kennewick, who, as always, was a great sounding board, asking me the questions I hadn't thought to ask myself.

Many of Doc's staff—again too many to mention—have provided me with great insight and valuable assistance, but I would like to single out one, Todd Ungerecht, for his particular help. Doc was indeed fortunate to have been served by such people, and I can easily see why they were considered to be one of the best congressional staffs in Washington, DC.

As with each of my previous book projects, my wife and family have endured—perhaps enjoyed—my many months behind the closed door of my office as I worked on this book. They will probably hope I find another project soon.

Finally, my appreciation goes out to Sheryn Hara and her Book Publishers Network team, who turned my scribblings into this book.

Many people are responsible for what is good about this book. I, alone, am responsible for what is not.

THERE IS AN OLD SAYING to the effect that if we saw how sausage was made, we wouldn't eat it. Lawmaking and governing are similar. It's hard work, and it's often not very pretty. There is a lot of sausage making in this book—arcane congressional rules and processes by which legislation is created and passed. If you find yourself getting bogged down in the details, move on. It's the result, more than the method, I want you to be aware of.

There is another old saying that voters love their congressman but hate Congress. Much in this book suggests that this is also true. Doc was routinely reelected by majorities of more than 60 percent while the approval ratings for Congress plummeted to as low as 9 percent. My hope is that this book allows the reader to become more familiar with what it's like to be a member of Congress and provides food for thought about what we can do as citizens to make the institution better.

INTRODUCTION

Doc Hastings was the first and only person to be elected to Congress from Franklin County, Washington—a wedge-shaped expanse of sparsely populated shrub-steppe extending north from the Columbia and the Snake Rivers in southeastern Washington State. Much of the low, rolling hills is covered with bunch grass, sagebrush, and dryland wheat fields. But irrigation water from the rivers and electricity from the hydroelectric dams transform the land into crop circles, orchards, and vineyards that change color with the seasons and produce an endless bounty of agricultural produce.

The residents of Franklin County are the sons and daughters of hardy pioneers—many originally from Scandinavia and Germany—who arrived on the Northern Pacific Railway before the turn of the century and lived in scattered farms and small towns with names like Mesa, Eltopia, and Kahlotus, The county's biggest city, Pasco, was created by the Northern Pacific Railway and incorporated in 1891.

Hastings represented the largely rural Fourth Congressional District, consisting of all or parts of eleven counties extending from the Canadian border to the Columbia River border with the state of Oregon. It had been created after the 1910 Census when the total population of Washington State was slightly more than a million people. Republican William LaFollette, the brother of the legendary Wisconsin Progressive congressman and governor, Robert LaFollette, had been elected to Congress from the Third Congressional District in 1910 and then represented the Fourth after it was created. The boundaries of the district changed twice due to reapportionment following the censuses of 2000 and 2010 (appendix A).

Its first two representatives had been Republicans, but that changed with the start of the Great Depression in 1932. The district and its voters certainly benefitted from President Franklin Roosevelt's New Deal. The Columbia River and Snake River dams provided electric power and irrigation water, and the government provided subsidies for farmers to grow wheat and paid others to keep their land out of production. Federal agencies created the vast national forests, funneled money into Indian reservations, and created federal payrolls at the Yakima Firing Center and the huge Hanford Site where plutonium was produced during World War II and the Cold War. During the war, the district slowly began to return to the Republican column, and only two Democrats have represented it since then (appendix B).

With few urban areas and a tiny unionized workforce at the time, 71 percent of the state legislators elected from Eastern Washington between 1933 and 1942 were Democrats. That percentage declined to 36 percent between 1943 and 1958 as the Republicans regained control after the end of World War II. Democratic Party representation increased to 52 percent between 1959 and 1966 during the Kennedy and Johnson years but dropped to 34 percent in the aftermath of the Vietnam War as the district's conservative farmers and ranchers became disenchanted with the Democrats over their positions on nuclear power, gun control, and controversial social issues. By the time Doc Hastings was elected to Congress in 1994, the percentage of Democrats elected in Eastern Washington had dropped to just 14 percent.[1]

EACH CONGRESSIONAL DISTRICT is unique. More than 40 percent of the Fourth District's roughly nineteen thousand square miles of land is in some form of public ownership. Most of Okanogan County consists of the Okanagan National Forest and the Colville Indian Reservation. Most of Chelan and Kittitas Counties are in the Wenatchee National Forest. The 2,185-square-mile Yakama Indian Nation and much of the US Army's 327,000-acre Yakima Firing Center are in Yakima County. The Atomic Energy Commission's 580-square-mile Hanford Site occupies large portions of Benton and Grant Counties. In addition, the Department of Interior's Bureau of Land Management oversees large sections of land throughout the district. The result is that much of the land in the district is not on the local tax rolls.

Most of the privately owned land is used for farming or ranching. By 2012, more than ten thousand of Hastings's constituents operated 16,600 farms and ranches, totaling more than 7.2 million acres. They were, arguably, his most important constituency. The number of farms and owners decreased each year, but their productivity and the market value of the crops they produced continued to rise dramatically. The income from the sale of crops, livestock, and poultry exceeded $6.1 billion annually, ranking it twelfth out of all 435 congressional districts in the market value of products sold.[1]

In Franklin County, the largest crop is dryland wheat. In the 1970s, as president of the Pasco Chamber of Commerce, Hastings worked hard to attract more farmers to its membership, so by the time he ran for Congress, he had a good understanding of a farmer's needs and philosophy of life. What he liked most about them was that none of their crops, with the exception of wheat, was subsidized by the federal government. His farmers took their chances with the free market, and he admired that. Believing that the best way to help them succeed was to expand the foreign markets for their crops, he became a strong supporter of free trade.

Another feature that makes the Fourth District unique is Hanford. Originally known as the Hanford Engineer Works, the original 670 square miles of mostly deserted shrub-steppe had been acquired by the US Army for the top-secret Manhattan project in 1943. Hanford's nine nuclear reactors produced the plutonium used in the nation's nuclear arsenal during World War II and the Cold War. By the time Hastings was elected to Congress, the process of cleaning up the nuclear waste at Hanford had begun but was progressing slowly, with much difficulty, and at great cost as the Department of Energy, its contractors, and the unions struggled to adjust their collective culture from nuclear production to cleanup.

Still another issue of concern was the impact of the 1973 federal Endangered Species Act on farmers in certain parts of the district, particularly in Grant County. The precious water that farmers needed for their crops was allocated to local irrigation districts by the Bureau of Reclamation. As technology improved, farmers could irrigate more land using the same amount of water. This led to more profits, but it also conflicted with the Bureau of Reclamation and other government agencies that were legally required to ensure that there was enough water to protect endangered salmon species and other fish runs in the Snake and Columbia Rivers.

In 1994, the Fourth Congressional District had a population of approximately 615,000.[2] More than 75 percent of constituents identified themselves as white. Approximately 2 percent were American Indians. Another 2 percent were Asian. Less than 1 percent identified as black or African American. More than 15 percent had been born outside the United States. Many of these identified themselves as Hispanic or Latino. Most had come from Mexico to work in agriculture. Some were recent immigrants, but most were descendants of migrant workers who had been working the fields and picking the crops of the Columbia Basin for at least six decades. By the mid-1990s, many of them had put down roots and owned small farms or businesses.

During the twenty years that Doc represented the Fourth District, its population grew by more than 14 percent to 704,000, but the number of Hispanics or Latinos in the district grew from 114,000 to 268,000, an increase of 135 percent. By 2014, Hispanics represented 38 percent of the district's total population.[3] They lived in all the district's heavily agricultural counties but were concentrated in Yakima and Franklin Counties.

In 1994, the median household income for a family of four in the district was approximately $31,500. That number would grow by the time Hastings retired to more than $50,000—but it was still less than the US average and more than $10,000 less than the average for the state of Washington. More than 13 percent of his constituents lived in what the federal government defined as poverty. Seventy-eight percent had completed high school. Nineteen percent had received a bachelor's degree or higher.[4]

Another unusual characteristic of the district is that while it is overwhelmingly rural in terms of land use, by 2014 almost 75 percent of its population lived in two urban areas, the Yakima County and Kennewick-Pasco-Richland Metropolitan Statistical Areas (MSA) consisting of Benton and Franklin Counties. The population of those two metropolitan areas had grown by 35.5 percent between 1994 and 2014. The Yakima County MSA grew from 208,950 to 247,600, but the growth of the Tri-Cities MSA was even more pronounced, increasing by more than 100,000 people from 1994 to 2014 to become one of the fastest-growing urban areas in the nation.

By 2010, the state's population had grown by another 830,000 people, requiring another redistricting plan. The plan transferred Klickitat County from the Fourth District into the Third District, moved Chelan, Kittitas, and most of the population of Douglas County into the Eighth District, and moved Okanogan County and Adams County into Doc's district.

Doc Hastings served in Congress during a time when it, and the nation as a whole, experienced a series of events that created nearly non-stop political turmoil. Partisanship had always been part of politics, of course, but prior to 1994, many moderate Republicans and conservative Democrats serving in Congress were willing to reach across the aisle and find bipartisan solutions to major issues facing the nation. Doc correctly notes that the vast majority of day-to-day congressional business is concluded in a bipartisan way. But there is no escaping the fact that both the nation and its representatives in Congress became more partisan and politically polarized during the twenty years Doc served in Congress. During that period, we have seen partisanship and political polarization inserted into the electorate's already existing cultural, racial, and religious divides to become an important—if not always welcome—part of our daily lives. Observers have noted a number of reasons for the change. Commentator Fareed Zakaria has called these dividing lines the four Cs—capitalism, culture, class, and communications.

One of Doc Hastings's primary motivations in running for office had been to stem the growth of government and return more freedom to its individual citizens. By the time he left office in 2015, Americans on both ends of the political spectrum believed their government had failed them. Many on the right believed the United States had become a socialist state while many on the left believed their government had favored the wealthy at the expense of the working and middle classes. Both sides believed their cultural and civil rights were in danger.

America's wars in Afghanistan and Iraq created trillions of dollars of new debt and helped lead to the Great Recession of 2008, multiple budget crises, a government shutdown, and the 2013 fiscal cliff. The greatest economy crisis since the Great Depression caused considerable suffering, and the slow pace of recovery led many to fear for their economic survival. Many still feel they are being left behind. Technology and regulatory changes have resulted in dramatic declines in manufacturing and natural resource-based jobs, while jobs in technology and health care sectors—requiring vastly different skill sets—have soared, challenging the preconceptions of generations of Americans who saw an assembly-line job as the path to middle-class success. In addition, they find themselves competing for jobs with a massive influx of immigrants seeking a better life in the United States. The growth of immigrant populations has increased the speed of major demographic changes that were already well underway because of the natural growth of existing minority communities.

As people became more politically polarized, they self-segregated themselves depending on their political views. Liberals moved to larger cities or to more liberal-leaning states, whereas the reverse was often true for conservatives. Rural residents resent what they perceive as the elitism of urban areas. Sixty percent of minorities surveyed in a 2016 Pew Research Center report believe that race relations are generally bad. Another Pew study reported that six in ten Republicans and Democrats actually *feared* the other's political agenda, a four-fold increase since the mid-1990s. Back then, Pew polling reported that 36 percent of Republican voters were more liberal than the average of all Democratic voters, while 30 percent of Democrats were more conservative than the average of all Republican voters. In 2014, when Doc retired from Congress, the poll suggested that just 8 percent of Republican voters and 6 percent of Democrats were more liberal or conservative than the other party.

As the public became more politically polarized, their views were reflected in the people they elected. Many state legislators and governors perpetuated their party's advantage by gerrymandering their congressional districts after each new census. They elected ever more liberal or conservative members to Congress, replacing their previously elected counterparts whose views often moderated after they discovered that once elected, you have to *govern* and that governing requires compromise. When those older members were replaced, Congress lost valuable institutional memory and leadership experience. New members often saw themselves as a member of a tribe whose primary role was not to govern but to *defeat* the other tribe.

Finally, technology and communications have also played an important role in the polarization of the electorate. C-SPAN, cable TV, political talk radio, and social media have created a 24-hour news cycle in which political news and commentary is instantaneously available. Technology has also made it easier for political operatives to engage in "identity politics," the use of voters' known views and preferences to raise huge sums of money to elect or defeat candidates.

The cost of technology and media has increased the expense of elections to the point where candidates are afraid to take positions that are at variance with their base or important donors for fear of being "primaried" in their next reelection campaign. Not surprisingly, most members of Congress spend much of their time raising money for their next election. And those elections have changed dramatically in how they are conducted. Traditionally, campaigns aimed to win the center. If you won the center, you won the election. Now, campaigns use technology to mobilize their blocks of voters rather than to try to sway undecided minds.

There was a time—not all that long ago—when most members of Congress lived in Washington, DC. With more time spent in the nation's capital, they got to know each other personally and became friends. That made it easier for them to negotiate and compromise. Today, Congress is often in session for only three full days a week, and its members commute weekly back to their home districts in order to prepare for their next election.

Doc saw this all play out during his twenty years he served in Congress. In the beginning, he had been something of a dissident himself—a Reagan Republican—and that political philosophy rarely, if ever, changed over twenty years in office. In the pages that follow, readers will have ample opportunity to agree or disagree with Doc's politics and his policy priorities. He should be held accountable to the answer he provided to the very first question he was asked at the beginning of this project: What is your political philosophy?

> My political philosophy is based on the notion that for one to have liberty and the freedom to pursue their individual goals, government should have a limited role in their individual lives. This is a logical extension of what our founders envisioned when they created a "government of the people" based on the rule of law and with the consent of the governed.
>
> I believe that history has proven that such a government, coupled with free markets, has been beneficial to its citizens and is what has made the United States exceptional among the nations of the world.[8]

CHAPTER ONE

Origins

★

DOC HASTINGS LOVED history as a student and remained interested in it for the rest of his life. Growing up in the small railroad town of Pasco, Washington, Doc was also aware of its colorful history. Many of those who helped to build the town were still alive when Doc first became interested in politics. His community helped to shape the conservative political philosophy that would guide him through the rest of his life. So that is probably a good place to start.

—

The Great Falls of the Spokane River attracted people to their rocky banks for centuries. The local Indian tribes gathered there to gossip, trade, and fish for salmon. The Canadian North West Company built a fur trading post there in 1810, and the first American settlers arrived in 1871. The Northern Pacific Railway arrived ten years later in 1881, bringing thousands of people from the Midwest and Northern Europe to find work in mining, logging, and agriculture. From a settlement of a thousand people in 1881, Spokane's population grew to twenty thousand by 1890 and then to thirty-seven thousand by 1900 when the second northern transcontinental railroad, the Great Northern, arrived. Fires ravaged Spokane's downtown in 1889 and again in 1910, but the city rebuilt each time and became the shipping and commercial hub of the Inland Northwest.

Doc's grandfather, Harold Hastings, arrived there 1895 under the most difficult of circumstances. Born in Cincinnati, Ohio, in 1881 (some documents say 1885), he was the oldest son of Charles E. Hastings, who had been born in Germany in 1846, and Emma Evans, who had been born in Kentucky in 1859. By 1868, Charles was working in Dayton, Ohio, as a marble cutter. He was just forty-four in 1890 when he was killed in a train wreck.

Emma headed west with young Harold and a second son, Roy, and ended up in a gold mining camp in Grangeville, Idaho, where she worked as a cook. In 1895, she died of amoebic dysentery when she was only thirty-six. Alone, fourteen-year-old Harold found his way to Spokane where he placed his brother in an orphanage. From that point on, he seems to have lived a hand-to-mouth existence, supporting himself with odd jobs. On Christmas Eve of 1903, he married Florence Seaman. Roy signed the marriage certificate as a witness.

Harold remained in Spokane working as a laborer or as a telephone battery man and renting rooms at a series of boarding houses and hotels. He is listed in the 1910 Census, now twenty-nine and divorced, working as a clerk in a hotel and living as a boarder in a house on East Bridgeport Avenue.

The following year, Harold married sixteen-year-old Mable Olson who had recently arrived in Spokane from the small farming community of Colfax, in Whitman County, Washington. Mable was one of twelve children born to Ole Olson and Marta Martinsdatter Olson between 1877 and 1896. Her parents had immigrated to the United States from Norway in 1881 and, like so many of their fellow countrymen, followed the tracks of the Northern Pacific to the Pacific Northwest.

Ivan Hastings, Doc's father, was Harold and Mable's first son, born in Spokane in 1912. A second son, Donald, was born there two years later.

Sometime before 1918, Harold and Mable moved to the small mining town of Northport in Stevens County, Washington. Located on a narrow stretch of the Columbia River called the Little Dalles, Northport was only seven miles south of the Canadian border. By the time Harold and his family arrived, the town was best known for its silver smelter, a very active tavern, and the fact that the town was the last stop before the Canadian border on the Spokane Falls and Northern Railway. A third son, Perry, was born in Northport in 1918.

Harold and Mable had a difficult marriage, and the couple moved from town to town before she left him and their three small children on April 18, 1924. Harold would later tell his grandchildren that he always remembered the date she left because it was Good Friday. Under the circumstances, Harold received custody of the three small boys. Now back in Spokane, Harold changed jobs periodically, supporting his family on a laborer's wages. In the 1930 Census, he was listed as a janitor. His oldest boys, Ivan and Donald, were eighteen and sixteen, respectively, and attended North Central High School just as the Great Depression arrived. Perry, the youngest boy, was twelve.

An excellent student in high school, Ivan was particularly interested in what was then called civics. The Great Depression provided students with lots of civics lessons. Ivan's oldest son (and Doc's brother), Roger, remembers finding a term paper his father wrote in his senior year that compared the advantages of capitalism to state ownership of wealth at a time when many different government philosophies were competing for America's attention. Ivan was exceptionally bright, and when he graduated from high school, he was offered a scholarship to the prestigious Whitman College in Walla Walla but declined it because he needed to work to help support his family.

The Great Depression hit the Spokane area hard. After the initial shock and loss of investment capital in the 1929 market crash, the impact of the calamity rolled from east to west across the nation. When it hit Spokane, the twin collapse of the local mining and agricultural economies was devastating.

By 1933, Spokane County's unemployment was at least 25 percent—not as bad as Seattle and Tacoma but bad enough to cause eight banks to fail and major downtown retail stores to close. The city's tax revenues declined to the point that the Manito Park Zoo closed and three bears were shot and stuffed. Clusters of squalid shanties sprouted in the ravines along the river below the city's bridges. A nearby brewery, closed since prohibition, provided a soup kitchen to feed the hungry residents.

At the Northern Pacific rail yards, passing freight trains disgorged hundreds of migrants and their families on their way west to escape whatever they had left behind. But Spokane was not the Promised Land. Spokane police regularly extorted sex, food, and money from the displaced farmers, workers, and their family members who arrived after hopping aboard the westbound trains. The scandal wasn't revealed until 1989 when Pulitzer Prize winning author Timothy Egan wrote about it in his book, *Breaking Blue*.[1]

Help arrived in 1933 in the form of an alphabet soup of New Deal programs. The Civilian Conservation Corps (CCC) provided jobs for ten thousand men in forty-nine camps built in the Inland Northwest. The Works Progress Administration (WPA) arrived a little later and built roads, public buildings, and sewer projects. They even blasted a new road to the top of Mt. Spokane. But the greatest help of all came in 1935 with the start of construction of the Grand Coulee Dam. By the time it was completed in 1941, it had provided jobs for twelve thousand people and electricity for the new Alcoa aluminum smelter and rolling mill plants that were being built near Spokane to help the nation arm itself for World War II.[2]

Ivan's decision to stay in Spokane was perhaps influenced by meeting the diminutive and attractive Florence Johnson in the early 1930s, probably while both were attending North Central High School. Born in 1914, she was two years younger than Ivan. It was far from easy to contemplate marriage in those early days of the Great Depression, and they conducted an extended four-year courtship before marrying on April 17, 1937. Almost everyone called her Flossie, but Ivan called his petite five-feet-two wife "Butch." The two were well suited to each other and complemented each other's strengths. He was hard-working and perhaps a little reserved, while she was a bundle of energy and fun.

Ivan's job at McClintock-Trunkey Company, Spokane's oldest wholesale grocery and supply firm, provided them with about one thousand dollars a year, and that was enough to buy a small house on Broadway Avenue in Dishman, a nearby community in the sparsely settled Spokane Valley.

Their first child arrived in 1939, a boy named Roger. Their second son, Richard, was born in Spokane's Sacred Heart Hospital on February

7, 1941. The family enjoyed nicknames and Roger, who was eighteen months older and learning to talk, repeatedly pointed to his new baby brother and said "Docka" over and over again. No one knew what he meant, but the name stuck. Richard would become "Doc" for the rest of his life. Later, after a series of miscarriages (all girls, Flossie claimed) two more boys were born into the family after the war—Robert in 1948 and Regan in 1953.

Ivan was twenty-nine when the Japanese attacked Pearl Harbor on December 7, 1941. With so many men away in the service, he received a promotion to salesman at McClintock-Trunkey in 1942. That allowed the couple to move into a recently built home with a daylight basement on West Courtland Avenue, not far from downtown, where they lived until the family moved to Pasco in 1947.

The United States drafted two hundred thousand men a month into the armed services during the war. Ivan received his induction notice in August 1945, just before the end of hostilities in the Pacific. He had dodged a different kind of bullet.

—

Flossie's mother, Gulborg Nettum, left Norway with her family in 1882. They first settled in Blue Earth, Minnesota, near the Iowa state line, but later moved to Stillwater and then to Hennepin, now a suburb of Minneapolis. Gulborg met her future husband quite by accident.

Charles Johnson was born in tiny Webster, Minnesota, on October 9, 1875, also of Norwegian immigrants. During the Philippine Insurrection, he served in Company K of the Thirteenth Minnesota Regiment. His tent-mate was carrying on an intense correspondence with a girl in Minneapolis who was one of Gulborg's best friends. She shared her letters, introducing Gulborg to Charles in the process. When he returned home, he looked her up; they fell in love and married on October 9, 1901.

Charles convinced Gulborg to change her name to Goldie because he thought it sounded more American. Their first child, Esther, was born later that year. She grew up to become a well-read, cultured, and altogether modern woman who operated high-end book shops in Birmingham,

Alabama, and New York City and wrote an unpublished "Family Chronicle" of her family and life experiences in 1976.[3]

Charles decided to move his family to the wide-open plains near Minot, North Dakota, and try his hand at farming in 1905. Esther wrote that they arrived at a "harsh and lonely" place and described their first house as "being so small that she thought it was a playhouse. It looked out over the low undulating hills just above Valley Street with a view of the railroad tracks and grain elevators."[4]

Not much went well for Charles. Farming didn't work out, so the family moved close to Minot, where he got a job with the Great Northern Railway. He lost an eye in a machine shop accident and, then after his recovery, worked a seasonal job threshing wheat. In 1911, the family moved into Minot, where at least they had running water from a city pump in the town square. Doc's mother, Florence, was born there.

In 1918, the family moved to Hillyard, located northeast of Spokane. Charles, by then forty-five, found worked as a boilermaker for the railroad. He passed away of pneumonia in 1927, leaving Goldie a widow with a large family. Goldie moved to Spokane with six of her eight children. Her parents, Ole and Marie Nettum, joined them there before Marie passed away in 1929. Goldie rode out the Depression living with various children but returned to Spokane sometime after 1940. From then on, she lived with different friends and relatives, visiting them for months at a time, until she passed away in 1970.

—

The end of World War II was followed by a painful peacetime recovery. There were wage and price controls and chronic shortages of just about everything. A series of strikes ensued as workers tried to make up for wages lost during the war. Ivan had worked for McClintock-Trunkey since 1937 and dreamed of someday owning his own business. He became active in the Spokane chapter of the Junior Chamber of Commerce, better known as the Jaycees.

Ivan had more reason to be optimistic than most. Unlike his father, Harold, who had almost no formal education, Ivan had been able to obtain a high school education—something only 24 percent of males in his age bracket had acquired by 1940—and had saved a little money during the war.[5] He had a white-collar job and, at thirty-five, enough ambition and ability to parlay his experience into starting his own business.

The paper and supply business in those days sold paper and paper products, like paper towels and cups, as well as janitorial supplies like floor polishes and finishes. It was not a competitive business as long as you were not in direct rivalry with a similar business in your community. National manufacturers relied on regional sales representatives to sell their products to local companies who then sold them to their customers. In smaller markets, one company generally controlled most of the local business.

Ivan talked with the company executives at McClintock-Trunkey and told them about his plans to find an underserved market and start his own business. They were understanding but sorry to lose him, realizing that his new company would not be a competitor. Ivan already knew many of the numerous manufacturers' sales representatives who regularly called on the business and was familiar with their products and pricing. His talks with company executives would probably have included such subjects as which lines to carry and whom to do business with.

The next question was where to locate his business. He looked at Yakima, Washington, and Missoula, Montana, only to discover that similar companies already existed there. One day he was discussing his plans with a friend in Lewiston, Idaho, who suggested that he look into the Tri-Cities. Ivan drove down and looked around, talked with a few people, liked what he saw, and decided on Pasco.

Through his membership in the Jaycees, he became acquainted with Lloyd A. "Bud" Simmonsen, a World War II army veteran about his age with what appeared to be a promising future. With some money the two men had saved—along with a little more borrowed from various members of Flossie's mother's family—the two men entered into an informal partnership, starting what became known as the Columbia Basin Paper and Supply Company.

Ivan sold his house in Spokane for $6,500 and bought a house at 1040 West Margaret Street in Pasco at the inflated price of $8,000. He was lucky to find a house at any price. His was one of about forty new homes that had been built in the early days of the war along Sylvester, Margaret, and Henry Streets on the western edge of Pasco. Miraculously, sheetrock and nails were still somehow available to the builder, but modern furnaces were not. The houses all had coal-fired furnaces. Flossie and the children moved down from Spokane in August 1947.

Ivan told a business writer for the *Tri-City Herald* many years later that his partnership with Simmonsen was based only on a handshake. "There was no legal paperwork, at least until [he] was getting a divorce," and Ivan was concerned that his own assets might somehow become part of the settlement.[6]

With buildings of any kind in post-war Pasco at a premium, the business operated out of a rented space located behind a gospel mission on the south side of Lewis Street, just west of the highway underpass below the railroad tracks that separated east and west Pasco. Doc remembered that they had to go through the mission to get to their warehouse.

Business friends in other communities provided excess inventory at reduced prices to help the new business get started. Doc and his brother Roger remembered driving to Lewiston as very young boys with their dad and Simmonsen to visit a business friend there. They would fill up the back of the van with boxes of paper towels and cups and drive them back to the store in Pasco. Florence recalled that she spent most of her time in the store while Ivan called on business clients. Their total sales that first week were only four hundred dollars.[7] Over time, the business prospered, and Ivan and his family became important members of the Pasco community.

PASCO WASN'T JUST ANOTHER RAILROAD TOWN. It was the essential central hub of the Northern Pacific Railway in the Pacific Northwest. The town was literally created by the railroad. Its antecedents began in 1879 as a raw construction camp named Ainsworth, which was located four miles away on the west bank of the Snake River where it empties into the Columbia River. The Northern Pacific had gone bankrupt after the Panic of 1873, and its new Portland-based owners chose that spot to restart construction, extending the rails to the north, south, east, and west.

The area's modern history began almost eighty years earlier at the nearby treeless, sandy point of land that jutted out into the confluence of the Snake and Columbia Rivers. The place was called "Kosith" by the local Wanapum Indians, meaning "Point of Land."[8] For centuries, members of the various tribes had come there to trade and fish.

On the afternoon of October 16, 1805, the American explorers Lewis and Clark and their Corps of Discovery landed there after paddling their dugout canoes down the Clearwater and the Snake Rivers, escaping potential death in the deep winter snows of the Bitterroots. They were welcomed by "great numbers" of curious Indians as they camped together for two days to rest before resuming their historic journey to the Pacific.

Clark described the place in his journal entry for October 16, 1805: "In every direction from the junction of those rivers the Countrey is one Continued plain low and rises from the water gradually, except a range of high Countrey which runs from S. W & N E and is on the opposit Side about 2 miles distant from the Collumbia."[9]

Almost six years later, on July 9, 1811, David Thompson of the Canadian North West Company fur-trading enterprise arrived at the very same point of land after navigating the Columbia River from the north and east on his way to the sea. He erected a pole and a notice claiming the country for Great Britain and stating the intention of the company to build a trading post at the site. Five days later, he discovered he had been too late when he arrived at the partially constructed Fort Astoria at the mouth of the Columbia River being built by the American John Jacob Astor's Pacific Fur Company. Almost seventy years later, a timeless description of Ainsworth and its historic surroundings was provided by Thomas S. Symons, a US Army surveyor who visited there in 1879. He described it as a "wild-and-wicked spot of sin" whose "streets were paved with broken whisky bottles and playing cards," and:

> one of the most uncomfortable, abominable places in America to live in. You can scan the horizon in vain for

a tree or anything resembling one. The heat through the summer is excessive, and high winds prevail and blow the sands about into everything. By the glare of the sun and the flying sands, one's eyes are in a constant state of winking, blinking, and torment, if nothing more serious results.[10]

Construction of a $1.3 million Northern Pacific railroad bridge across the Snake began almost immediately. Since the region was devoid of native trees, the massive bridge timbers had to be floated down the Clearwater and the Snake Rivers from Idaho. Until the bridge was completed in 1884, paddle wheeler steamboats, like the *Frederick Billings*, ferried freight and railroad cars from one side of the river to the other. After it was completed, the bridge connected the Northern Pacific at Ainsworth to the Oregon Railway and Navigation Company at Wallula, a town and rail junction located thirteen miles to the south, just north of the mouth of the Walla Walla River. Now it was possible to travel from St. Paul through Ainsworth to Wallula, and then west along the south bank of the Columbia and all the way to Portland.

In the fall of 1879, the railroad began laying track north from Ainsworth north to Spokane, where it arrived in 1881. By 1887, construction was underway on an even longer railroad bridge across the Columbia River, extending the railroad to the west through the Yakima Valley, across the Cascade Mountains at Stampede Pass, and on to Puget Sound.[11]

By 1884, the railroad had outgrown Ainsworth, and the town and rail facilities were moved to an open, grassy plain four miles to the west where there was ample room for new housing, a railroad station, rail yard, roundhouse, and shops. The new town, named Pasco, was incorporated in 1891. The town was named by Virgil C. Brogue, the principal engineer of the Northern Pacific's Cascade Division, who had earlier built a railroad across a similarly dry, windblown, treeless region of the Andes Mountains in Central Peru called Cerro de Pasco.

Because of the railroad, Pasco became an important steamboat hub and terminus for barge traffic on the Columbia and Snake Rivers. Then, as irrigation water became more available, Pasco became the primary commercial center for farmers and ranchers who found their way to the region. In the decade between 1900 and 1910, Pasco's population grew from 254 to more than two thousand. By 1920, that number had grown to 3,362.

The Great Depression hit Pasco and the surrounding area hard, depressing agricultural prices and putting many out of work. As an important rail center, it became a regular stop for hobos who rode the rails throughout the Pacific Northwest. They could be spotted around the rail yard, camping along the river, or living in nooks and crannies among abandoned buildings.

The town didn't change much during the Depression. It grew by only five hundred people during the entire decade of the 1930s, attaining a population of 3,900 by 1940. The developed part of the town fit within a square-mile area. Residents could walk anywhere in town in less than twenty minutes. The beautiful, copper-domed Franklin County Courthouse, built in 1912 for seventy-five thousand dollars, sat on the north edge of town. To the east of the railroad tracks that ran through town was a less developed area known as East Pasco, literally on the other side of the tracks, where the town's African Americans, Asians, and a few lower-income whites resided. As late as 1940, the majority of the town's streets were oiled but not yet paved.

World War II changed all that. In February 1942, the navy purchased 2,285 acres of land next to the town's small airport for five thousand dollars and relocated Seattle's Sand Point Naval Air Station, which was thought to be vulnerable to Japanese attack, to Pasco. Soon, a vast network of runways, hangars, and barracks were bulldozed out of the bunch grass and sagebrush. Originally used for pilot training, the Pasco Naval Air Station would later be used to transition experienced pilots into newer aircraft types.[12]

In May 1942, the army selected a 459-acre site on the Northern Pacific rail line just west of the former Ainsworth town site for a major depot to store and distribute engineering supplies and equipment, much of it Lend-Lease materials bound for the Soviet Union. Officially named the Pasco Holding and Reconsignment Depot, it contained more than

1.7 million square feet of warehouses. Workers unloaded up to 250 box-cars a day.

Then, in February 1943, the army began acquiring 670-square-miles of nearly vacant shrub steppe located along the Hanford Reach of the Columbia River, twenty miles north and west of Pasco, for the top-secret Hanford Engineer Works (HEW). The nearly two thousand people living there were relocated and told not to mention their moves to their sons serving in the armed services.

The government procurement specialists began showing up in al-ready overcrowded Pasco in early 1942. Because of the severe limitation of office and living space created by the war, they operated out of the basement of the Liberty Theater downtown and lived in people's garages.

Pasco was selected as the point through which all the workers and supplies would flow into the Hanford Site because of its existing rail and barge connections. While most white workers eventually were housed at a massive construction camp located on the site, black workers were required to live in deplorable conditions in East Pasco because of its ex-isting small African American community consisting mostly of porters, cooks, and other railroad workers.

Between March 1943 and the end of the war, DuPont built three plutonium production reactors, two chemical separation plants, and 554 other buildings, including a construction camp for 44,900 people, at Hanford. At Richland Village, located about twenty-five miles south of the reactors, it built administrative buildings, dormitories, a hospital, public utilities, services, and housing for 6,500 people.[13]

The B Reactor, the first of the three production reactors, began pro-ducing plutonium on December 28, 1944, and on August 5, 1945, the first atomic bomb was dropped on Hiroshima, Japan. Four days later, a second bomb, using plutonium produced at Hanford, was dropped on Nagasaki, ending World War II.

Neither Pasco, nor what became the Tri-Cities, would ever be the same again.

CHAPTER TWO

A Kid from Pasco

★

FOR DOC HASTINGS and many of his childhood friends, the most re-markable thing about growing up in Pasco after the war was just how un-remarkable it was. With the exception of the windstorms that propelled tumbleweeds through the air at the height of a car, Pasco was, for most at least, an idyllic community. The town was still very small. Children could walk or ride their bicycles from one end to the other in a half hour. Most people knew their neighbors. No one locked the door at night. The downtown streets were busy, and the schools provided a good education. In many ways, the town was like a Norman Rockwell illustration.

Life was less ideal for its African American, Asian, and low-income white residents who lived in East Pasco. The primary street access to East Pasco was through a narrow, two-lane underpass that had been built under the Northern Pacific's rails by the WPA in the 1930s that divided the town and reinforced its segregation. The Hastings family business was located nearby. East Pasco was in many ways a self-contained com-munity with its own grade school, black businesses, and black churches.[1]

Pasco's population had exploded to nearly nine thousand by 1944, with the influx of wartime activity and new jobs at the Army Recon-signment Center, the Pasco Naval Air Station, and the Hanford Site. New neighborhoods and apartments were built to the west as building materials and low-cost mortgage financing finally became available af-ter the war.

While its downtown still laid claim to being the region's shopping center, Pasco was no longer the area's largest city. That honor belonged to

Richland Village—later to become the city of Richland—located across the river. It was one of the three original "atomic cities" that included Oak Ridge, Tennessee, and Los Alamos, New Mexico. It served as the administrative headquarters of the sprawling 670-square-mile Hanford Site. In 1947, its permanent population was already fifteen thousand, and that didn't include the more than forty thousand construction workers who lived in a massive camp out on the site. No bridge or ferry crossed the Columbia River to Richland. The Atomic Energy Commission and its primary contractor, General Electric, owned all the land and buildings and denied access to those who didn't live or work there.

To the small-town residents of Pasco and Kennewick, the occupants of Richland were as strange as their town. Their relative affluence generated resentment, as did their superior attitude toward residents of their neighboring communities. Some called Richland's residents seagulls. "They're protected by Uncle Sam, they get everything for free, and they crap wherever they want."[2] But Pasco merchants enjoyed the money the Richland residents spent in their community because Richland's commercial district had not expanded from pre-war days. The army had never intended Richland to become a permanent community. Until the Uptown Mall was built in 1949, fewer than forty businesses were located there.

The city of Kennewick, located directly across the river from Pasco and southeast of Richland, also grew dramatically during the war. Its population was almost as large as Pasco's. Many Hanford workers who could not qualify for housing in Richland lived in Kennewick. So, too, did a growing number of businesses that provided goods and services to Hanford and its workers. With their separate and competitive high schools, the three communities developed distinctly different personalities.

On Memorial Day of 1948, the accumulated runoff from higher-than-average spring rains resulted in the worst flooding the three cities had ever seen. The flood forced more than a thousand families in Richland and Kennewick from their homes. The worst damage was in Kennewick, where much of the downtown business district was inundated.

The approaches to both sides of the narrow, two-lane Green Bridge, built in 1922, flooded. The only way to cross the river was on the

Northern Pacific railroad bridge, by boat, or by airplane. The fledgling *Tri-City Herald* chose the latter, printing its paper in Pasco and flying it across the river to the small Richland airport for distribution.[3] After about two weeks, the floodwaters receded, leaving fifty million dollars in damage and congestion at the local hospitals where children were lined up to receive their tetanus shots.[4]

While Richland and Kennewick rebuilt their flooded neighborhoods, Pasco focused its efforts on continuing its role as the region's most established community. With its well-established civic pride and commercial infrastructure, it was, as one long-time resident called it, "a happening place."[5] Farmers and residents from the other towns would go there to shop at J.C. Penny's or Sears, have dinner at a Chinese restaurant, and then drink and dance the night away at the Elks lodge or the American Legion hall. On a summer's night, the whistles of the not-too-distant steam engines filled the night air. Doc remembered the first time he saw Pasco. "There was a chain-link fence with tumbleweed piled so high that you couldn't see through to the other side."[6]

—

In September 1947, Doc and his older brother, Roger, began classes at Longfellow School, about six blocks away from their west Pasco home. Doc was in the first grade. The following year, the school burned to the ground, and they transferred to the new Captain Gray Elementary School, which had been rushed to completion. It was even closer to their house, about three blocks away.

Ivan acquired a 1948 Pontiac, and he and Flossie soon became the parents of a third Hastings boy named Robert. It was not long after he learned to speak that Robert became "Rabbit," a nickname awarded after the family noticed his habit of scratching the backs of his ears. "Why are you rubbing your ears?" they asked. "I'm trying to be a rabbit," he answered. The nickname stuck.[7]

Grandfather Harold would drive down from Spokane in his 1929 Ford sedan to visit, often staying for a week or two. Once Harold parked on the side street next to the Hastings house. Only the middle of many of Pasco's streets was paved in those days. The rest was graded but often covered with tack weed. Later, the boys discovered that two of his old tires were flat, punctured by the prickly weed. Doc recalled his grandfather's visits fondly. "By that time he was suffering from a little bit of dementia, but he could remember the details of what had happened years before really well. He had total recall of what happened around the turn of the century."[8]

Ivan and Florence ruled their household with a light hand. "Our dad wasn't around very much," Roger remembered. "Parents didn't engage then in their children's activities like they do today. They didn't need to. . . . Everyone knew everyone else, and the other kids' parents knew our parents. We knew that any misbehavior on our part would be reported."[9]

The Hastings home became a magnet for neighborhood kids. Some knew that within the Hastings family Ivan was known as "Baba," but everyone knew Florence as Flossie. LaMar Palmer, one of Doc's best friends, remembered her as "the most beautiful woman I'd ever known." Small, with petite features and long brunette hair, she reminded him of the 1940s movie actress Susan Hayward.[10]

At one time or another, most of the forty kids around the neighborhood visited the Hastings home, and many would become, and remain, Doc's lifelong friends. LaMar Palmer lived right across the street at 1039 West Margaret. The two were inseparable.

Though much bigger in size, Palmer was in awe of the Hastings boys. "They just *knew* stuff. Doc took after his mother—small hands, skinny—but he knew how to play marbles, and he was really good. He knew all about baseball, and later on, he taught me enough so that I could make the team and pitch. I liked being around them. They had savvy. At a time when most of us wore bib overalls, the Hastings kids dressed like city boys. They wore corduroy pants and cool-looking, long-sleeved pullover shirts with stripes."[11]

But the most distinctive piece of Doc's attire in those days was his stocking cap. One telling photo shows a group of neighborhood boys playing football on New Year's Day 1951 in the vacant lot where Pasco High School now stands. Doc is ten and Roger twelve. They are all lined up for the snap of the ball, but Doc has his trademark stocking cap on. In the background, not a tree or house can be seen in what is now a completely developed neighborhood.

In 1953, the Hastings family expanded again when Regan, the fourth of the Hastings boys, was born. In the following year, Ivan moved the family into a larger two-story home at 922 West Henry Street. Once again, the house attracted the neighborhood kids.

In addition to LaMar Palmer, there were the Thompson kids down the street, and Earl Martin. "He was one of the first kids I met," Doc said about Earl, "and we went all through school together. I didn't really have any best friends. Everyone was a best friend when we were in grade school."[12]

Another of Doc's special friends was a dog named Babe. Shaggy hair hung over her eyes and face. The rumor among the neighborhood kids was that if you cut her hair, she would go blind. She followed Doc everywhere.

From his earliest years, Doc enjoyed competition. As he grew a little older, it might be a game of poker or pool, baseball, or later yet, politics. In grade school, it was marbles. "I was a pretty good marble player in second grade," Doc said. "During recess at Longfellow, we played marbles out on the grounds. The rules were that you weren't really supposed to play for keeps. But I played for keeps. George Dyer was the principal of the school at that time, and he was a close friend of my mom and dad." One afternoon, Doc squatted, hunched over his shot, and "saw a shadow move across the ground. It was George Dyer. I can't remember if he told my parents or not, but we were busted."[13]

Ivan and Flossie made it a point to get to know the neighborhood kids. Janice Pope Ling had a close friend who lived across the alley from the Hastings family. The girl spent a lot of time at their house. "It was like Flossie was the girl's second mother. She called Flossie her *fun* mom."[14] Janice's husband, George, who has known Doc since they were in the ninth grade, remembered that Flossie was like one of the kids. She'd say, "'Well, let's go out to the river,' and she'd gather up whatever kids were there, and we'd just go. Some kids didn't have much of a home life, but they got one there."[15]

"Ivan was a standup guy," George recalled. "He'd always shake hands with Doc's friends when they would come over to their house. He was a little reserved, but you knew that you were always welcome there."[16]

Linda Yamauchi Atkinson lived at 106 North First Avenue, just west of Ivan's second business location at 129 West Lewis Street. Her aunt owned Eddy's Café across the street, and Linda helped out there. She thought that Ivan and Flossie Hastings were the best-looking and nicest couple who walked along Lewis Street. "I'd see Mr. Hastings walking along the street, and he'd give me a wave and say hello when most grownups didn't do that with kids."[17]

In 2014, contractors demolishing the two-story building that had once been the Yamauchi's home found an eight-by-nine-foot painted mural of a seascape and a large amount of Japanese yen dating from 1891. Linda Yamauchi's grandfather had apparently painted the mural as a backdrop for a Japanese language school for Japanese-American children that he'd intended to run in the 1950s.[18]

The story in the *Tri-City Herald* about the mural and the money reignited long-standing rumors of underground tunnels and meeting rooms used by Chinese railroad workers in the late 1880s. Linda Yamauchi remembered stories about one such entrance near the Lewis Street underpass.

—

Doc was eleven and Roger thirteen when construction began on the new Pasco High School in 1952. "We watched them build it every day and soon knew every nook and cranny of it," Roger said. "After it was built, we immediately learned how to gain access to the principal's office through the steam tunnel." They never did that, but they did figure out a few years later how to sneak into the gym and play basketball. "The janitor would catch us and kick us out, and we'd be right back the next night."[19]

"[Doc] had a great imagination and a curiosity about things," LaMar Palmer recalled. Part of their backyard had no grass. The boys would carefully rake the area smooth and spend hours building a town out of Popsicle sticks and little pieces of wood. Just before noon, they would turn on the water and flood the town. "But then, we became the engineers that had to save the town, and we'd build dikes and dams to try to save the town. But we could never do it. The water always won. Next day, we'd come back and do the same thing all over again."[20]

By the time Doc completed sixth grade, a new four-lane bridge was under construction west of town that connected West Pasco to the Kennewick Highlands. The Pioneer Memorial Bridge—everyone called it the "Blue Bridge" because of its color—was completed in 1954. The following year, Columbia Basin Community College held its first classes at the old naval air station.

In 1958, after several years of trying, Richland's residents incorporated their city and bought their homes and businesses from the Atomic Energy Commission. The city had continued to grow rapidly as a result of the Cold War, and its population grew to more than twenty-three thousand. Richland missed an opportunity to become the region's commercial center when its city council dithered about incorporating land for a proposed regional shopping mall. Kennewick seized the opportunity and became the center of retail trade in the region when the Columbia Center Mall opened in 1969.

Pasco's junior high school had taken over the former high school building when Doc began seventh grade there in 1953. His first venture into politics occurred when he was elected as his seventh grade homeroom president.

He also started playing sports. Although he enjoyed basketball, baseball held his greatest attraction. He played first base and threw and batted left-handed. He listened to the local Tri-City Braves and, when possible, to the major league game of the day on the radio. He soon knew the names and batting averages of his favorite players. Doc, LaMar Palmer, and Earl Martin, who had all attended elementary school together, now associated with new friends like Ron Grey, George Ling, Rich Beck, Ken Jacobs, and Dallas Barnes in junior high school.

Dallas Barnes arrived in Pasco in 1952 after being raised in an all-black neighborhood in St. Louis, Missouri. Dallas lived on the white side of the railroad tracks, but just barely. He had known Doc in grade school, but it was in junior high and high school that the two became good friends. Dallas was popular, self-assured, and an all-star athlete. He was quickly accepted into Doc's circle of friends.

Doc played on the same basketball team as Dallas in junior and senior high school, but Dallas was the star of the team. He went on to become an all-star guard and a member of the 1961 state championship basketball team at Columbia Basin College. "I don't know how many games Doc started, but he made the team. He was pretty good with his left hand," Dallas recalled. He also remembered something else. "He may have operated in the background, but I later learned that Doc had his fingerprints on just about every good thing that happened to me when we were going to school."[21]

The garage at Doc's house had an old basketball hoop attached to it. There was no net. George Ling remembers that they played hoops there for hours at a time. When someone would go to the rim for a hard layup and crash into the side of the garage, Flossie, who always seemed to be watching, yelled out the window, "Don't break anything out there!"[22]

If they weren't playing basketball, they were playing baseball. There were three ball diamonds in Pasco—one at Memorial Park, one at the new high school, and one at the junior high—and Doc and his friends played on all of them. His older brother, Roger, conceded, "He was a good baseball player. He could hit."[23] Some of Doc's favorite memories are of walking home on a warm summer evening after playing baseball until sunset. "The kids would just walk home, even if they lived across town, and think nothing of it," Roger said. [24]

And those weren't the only games the boys played. Flossie grew up playing poker with her family and continued the practice in her own home. She taught Roger and Doc to play at an early age. By junior high school, Flossie presided over a penny-ante poker game with a regular group of neighborhood boys that included Ron Grey, Stevens Stephens, John Rea, Larry Fogg, George Ling, and Clair Foley. The games started on a Saturday or Sunday afternoon but might last well into the evening. They would sit around the cloth-covered dining room table, playing free-wheeling games like seven-card draw with three wild cards or something called "pass the trash," with Florence speeding along the pace of play.

"Shut up and deal."

"Who's in and who's out here?"

"Who's light on the pot? Who's light?"[25]

Roger often kidded his mother about the games. Some of the players were barely teenagers, and they were playing for real money. One Sunday afternoon the police arrived at their front door in the middle of a game. Flossie jumped up and scooped up the cards, chips, and pot into the tablecloth and placed it out of sight just as the police rang the doorbell.

Roger knew the arrival of the police had nothing to do with the card game. The night before, he had been a passenger in a friend's car that had tried to outrun a Kennewick police cruiser. Although the night had ended badly for the car and its driver, Roger had been thrown from the car unharmed but lost his wallet. The police were there to return it and ask a few questions. He had some explaining to do to his parents.[26]

Ron Grey became another of the Hastings family favorites. He almost lived at the Hastings house. Flossie used to say that if she had another boy, she would name him Ron—the "fifth R."[27] During high school, Grey worked at the family business and was Doc's constant companion then, and later at Columbia Basin College, on a three-month road trip, in the army, and at Central Washington College.

—

The family business was becoming well-established, and in 1950, Ivan relocated it to a larger and more visible location at 515 West Columbia, just a block south of Lewis Street. He was easily recognized around town, driving his new red 1950 Studebaker with its distinctive bullet nose in the center of the grill.

Retired superior court judge Duane Taber knew Ivan well through their mutual membership in the local Elks lodge. As a prominent local lawyer, Taber was in a good position to observe Ivan and his business. "Ivan had a small business, but he was really sharp, and he handled it well. It didn't hurt that he was the only game in town, but he worked hard and grew that business. He was very reserved and pleasant. Wouldn't embarrass anybody. He was a unique person for this little town. He became a real icon here."[28]

Ivan's business was located across the street from the new Pasco Elks Lodge, a center of social activity in the Tri-Cities at the time. Doc was only nine, but he remembers seeing President Harry Truman when he stopped there long enough in the late evening of May 10, 1950, to dedicate the lodge and make a few remarks about Hanford. Doc didn't hear his remarks and was too young, in any event, to appreciate their significance. The government was in the process of expanding the facilities at Hanford to meet the needs of the Cold War, and the community—which largely depended on Hanford for its livelihood—was interested in its future. Truman must have been told of the citizens' concerns. "You need not worry about being abandoned. We have no such intention. We have never had any such intention." Then he spoke of the future:

> Installations like this cost money. It is easy for foolish people to say that we ought to slash national expenditures by cutting defenses. . . . The money we are spending at Hanford is also one of the soundest investments this Nation can make. At the present time and in the immediate future, it is providing the United States with a means for defense while international conditions remain unsettled.[29]

Almost exactly twelve years later, on May 9, 1962, Doc was able to get a glimpse of Vice President Lyndon Johnson, as he stopped at Fourth and Lewis to sign autographs on his way to the dedication of Ice Harbor Dam. Two years late, as president, Johnson would announce the phased deactivation of the plutonium reactors at Hanford.

Duane Taber was a lifelong Democrat. He remembered Ivan Hastings as a "behind-the-scenes, backdoor Republican. He had strong political beliefs, but he largely kept them to himself. I don't think I ever heard him make a speech."[30] Ivan was known, however, to talk politics with a neighbor who was a member of the ultra-conservative John Birch Society.

Ivan was willing to get involved in local civic and political issues. As early as 1946, he helped collect enough signatures to pass Initiative 14, a measure that guaranteed that every county in Washington would be represented by at least one state senator and one state representative. At the time, some smaller counties in Eastern Washington had no resident representative in the state legislature.

Some of Ivan's political beliefs may have come from his being an avid reader. His youngest granddaughter, Petrina, remembered him later in life "sitting in his recliner, smoking his pipe, and surrounded by books."[31] He loved to read history and studied the Constitution. Roger recalled that his father told him that he had been absolutely "fried" when President Franklin Roosevelt tried to pack the Supreme Court back in 1937.[32]

—

Ivan had been instrumental in helping the Spokane chapter of the Jaycees win the outstanding Junior Chamber of Commerce award in 1946. He attended the 1946 Jaycee National Convention in Chicago where he had been honored to meet Harold Stassen, former governor of Minnesota and a leading candidate for the Republican presidential nomination in 1948.[33]

He continued his involvement with the Jaycees after he moved to Pasco and helped make it a civic force in the community. He also joined the Pasco Kiwanis Club, enjoyed golf and bowling, and ultimately became the Exalted Ruler of Elks Lodge 1730 in Pasco. The back room of his store became an impromptu bar after work when the various salesmen who supplied him with products stopped by for a drink.

Doc entered Pasco High School as a freshman in 1955. His high school yearbook shows him as a skinny, handsome kid with a big smile and an engaging personality. He was president of his freshman class. He served on the student council all four years and was an officer in his junior year. He was assistant sports editor and then sports editor of the *Wasco*, the student newspaper, as well as a class officer, in his senior year.

Doc particularly liked Robert Gregson, the vice principal; Ed Banks, who taught history; and Tom Sullivan, who taught civics and coached the baseball team. Doc played baseball for the Pasco Bulldogs and lettered at first base from his sophomore through senior years. He was Prom Prince in his junior year and Senior Ball Prince in his senior year. Linda Yamauchi Atkinson suggested that he won the girls' votes "because he was considered to be a dream boat."[34] Either he didn't share this view, or he didn't let it go to his head. "He had lots of self-confidence, but he wasn't cocky," Janice Pope Ling said.[35]

People liked Doc, perhaps because he was interested in them. Many classmates used the same word to describe him—interested. "He was interested in everything," Judy Jump Mosebar said. "He was easy to talk to and a leader in so many ways. His real true goal was to be involved with what was going on in the school. He was quiet, not someone who pushed his way to be heard. He was kind of a 'steady-Eddy.'"[36] In all other respects, Doc Hastings appears to have been a pretty normal teenager. He experimented with cigarettes and alcohol but didn't become attached to either.

He dated, but his only extensive involvement was with a popular, pretty brunette who wrote across two pages in his school yearbook, the *Sinewesah*. It included the usual platitudes addressed to "Doc" and other nicknames by people who might never see each other again but also comments from friends like LaMar Palmer, Ron Grey, and Joe Mosebar who would remain his friends for the rest of their lives. He values those memories so much that he keeps his yearbook on a shelf in his living room for easy access.

After school or after sports, there was always time for fun in small-town Pasco. There were two theaters in town, the Liberty and the Pasco. "We played basketball in junior high on Thursday nights," Doc said. "The games were usually over by seven or eight o'clock, and several of us would go downtown and sneak into one of the theaters. I can't remember how we did it, but I remember that we didn't pay. What was remarkable was that by ten o'clock everything was closed up and [we] would just walk home and not think anything about it."[37]

The town's main intersection at Fourth and Lewis had two soda fountains—the Soda Shop and Crescent Drugs—located across the street from each other. Dallas Barnes remembers their counters were still segregated in the 1950s.[38] Both looked out on to the street, and Judy Jump Mosebar remembers the boys would drive their cars up and down the street and around town in a prescribed route, rev up their engines, and squeal their tires. For most of those who experienced life in Pasco, it was a special time in a special place.

—

Doc graduated from Pasco High School in June of 1959. That fall, he and some of his former classmates, including Ron Grey, signed up for classes at Columbia Basin College. Doc played on its baseball team and worked part time as a parts chaser for the local Buick dealership. He also sold shoes in a downtown Pasco shoe store. In the summers, he coached a Pony League baseball team. By his own admission, he was not a very good student and left after two years. "I was disinterested," he said.[39]

In September 1961, Doc and Ron set out on a three-month road trip in Doc's cream-colored, 1946 Chevrolet coupe. The trip can best be described as a classic rite-of-passage experience. They drove to Seattle and then stopped at Portland and Corvallis, where Clair Foley attended Oregon State University on a football scholarship. There they conducted a successful scavenger hunt, calling on the local fraternity houses to scrounge up what they needed for a cookout and "borrowing" half a bag of hazelnuts from an orchard that sustained them for much of the rest of the trip. Then they drove to Los Angeles, where they made a special point to visit Hollywood and Vine.

From there they headed east to Las Vegas, where Flossie was attending an Elks auxiliary convention, and on to Phoenix, where Doc's high school girlfriend lived. Next, it was off to Carlsbad Caverns, New Mexico, and then to El Paso, where they crossed the border to Juarez, Mexico. At a local bar, they ran into a group of visiting Norwegian airmen and had "a grand evening seeing and experiencing things we had never seen in Pasco, Washington."[40]

They drove across the oil country of West Texas to Dallas and on to New Orleans, where they met two German girls who were on an extensive tour of their own. The girls told them where to find a hotel just off the French Quarter. The room cost only seven dollars a week if you didn't mind walking down the hall to the bathroom or stepping over drunks to reach the front door. Ron Grey remembered that they took the girls to a bar where the famous jazz clarinetist Pete Fountain was playing. "The show cost ten dollars, and that included two free drinks."[41] The girls later sent them beer steins from Stuttgart in remembrance of the occasion.

Doc and Ron drove to Birmingham, Alabama, and then north through Nashville to Cincinnati, where Doc's Aunt Esther—the author of the Charles Johnson family history—lived with her husband, Wilmer, who ran a local school for the blind. Doc made sure they stopped at every road marker or historic site along the way.

They returned home by way of Springfield, Illinois, where Doc was able to satisfy his historical interest in Abraham Lincoln, and then drove west to Bozeman, Montana, to visit a former Columbia Basin College classmate attending Montana State on a basketball scholarship. Doc remembers that they almost froze on a cold November day in Montana and had to decide between listening to the radio and turning on the car's heater. The car wouldn't do both at the same time. They arrived home just before Thanksgiving Day 1961. Neither would ever forget their road trip. It had been a special experience. It was a time of bonding, of occasionally breaking the rules, and of finding themselves in unfamiliar situations and surroundings.

—

Not long after they returned to Pasco, they learned they were both likely to be drafted into the army. Bob Gregson, their vice principal at Pasco High School, was a lieutenant colonel in the army reserve and looked out for his former students. He was also on the lookout for new recruits. Two other former classmates, Steve Stephens and John Klundt, were in the same situation as Doc and Ron Grey. At Gregson's suggestion, they all signed up at one time so they could go through training together.

The four went into the service on August 16, 1963, and were sent to Ft. Ord, California, located on beautiful Monterey Bay in California. Basic training consisted of strenuous physical training and forced marches, but the sunny afternoons spent on the rifle ranges overlooking the bay or a weekend pass to Monterey or San Francisco, made up for a lot of other discomforts.

Fort Polk, Louisiana, where Doc and his classmates were sent for advanced infantry training, was another matter. Located in the swampy, piney woods of West-Central Louisiana, Ft. Polk in the summertime was one of the army's most disagreeable posts. Doc and the others were lucky to be there during the winter when it was only slightly less disagreeable. It rained all the time, and red mud clung to everything like glue. They received an unexpected shock when they were told President Kennedy had been assassinated and their unit was being placed on alert. It turned out that the alert was related to a stolen typewriter and not the country's presidential crisis.

One positive aspect of Ft. Polk's location, however, was its proximity to New Orleans. Doc and his friends went there on one of their first weekend leaves, and their graduation from advanced basic training coincided with the 1964 Mardi Gras weekend. Having been to New Orleans previously, Doc and Ron assumed they were familiar with the city. But they had never been there for Mardi Gras, and they were in for a surprise. Ron remembered that the experience "was the wildest thing I'd ever seen."[42]

Another unexpected benefit of their Ft. Polk experience occurred at the end of their training. As an experiment, their unit consisted of men from both the East and West Coasts to see if they could coalesce as a unit. One of the boys from the East was a recruit from Philadelphia, George Graves, whose father owned a summer home and kept a boat at Pompano Beach, Florida. Graves invited Doc and Ron to join him there after they completed training, and the three of them spent nearly a week in the sun before returning home in February 1964.

—

Doc worked for Ivan for a few months before deciding that he would eventually join the family business. But first, it seemed important to finish his college education. He enrolled at Central Washington State College in Ellensburg for the summer and fall semesters of 1964. In November, he cast his first vote for president, voting for Barry Goldwater who had won the nomination over the more moderate Nelson Rockefeller in a contentious, tension-filled convention.

Several of Doc's former classmates already attended Central. He took classes in government and business but had trouble applying himself. He took a part-time job at a local meat-packing plant, and after a four-hour shift of cutting fat out of beef livers, a cold beer and a shuffleboard game sounded better than studying for his classes. At the end of the fall semester, he left school and returned to Pasco just before Christmas.

Still not ready to settle down, Doc talked with his parents and decided to visit Ron Grey, John Rea, and Dennis Wanamaker who were living and working in Santa Clara, California, near San Jose. Doc and Daryl Idler, a friend of his from Burbank, joined them, and soon there were six twenty-something men living in the same apartment.

Doc moved out after he found a job at a local janitorial supply company. He was familiar with the work and the products because they carried the same line of cleaning chemicals, rug shampoos, floor finishes, and cleaners made by Multi-Clean Products that his father's store carried in Pasco.

It was not long before Jerry Klopp, the local Multi-Clean sales representative, tipped Doc off that the company intended to create a new sales territory in California's Central Valley. Doc got the job in the fall of 1965. He received his sales training and attended a national meeting in St. Paul during a cold Minnesota winter before returning to Sacramento in January. He spent the next two years building new territory up and down the Central Valley from Redding to Bakersfield and over to Reno.

Multi-Clean had a manufacturing facility in South San Francisco, and in March 1967, the International Sanitary Supply Association held its annual West Coast trade show in nearby San Francisco. Doc and Jerry Klopp manned the company's booth during the day and entertained customers at night. When it ended on a Friday afternoon, Doc drove back to Sacramento, not bothering to change out of his suit and tie.

In those days, Sacramento's east end was a haven for young singles looking to meet each other. Some of the apartment complexes sponsored singles parties in their recreation areas—usually just an informal "meet and greet" with a no-host bar to facilitate introductions. Doc stopped by a party at an apartment complex he had previously heard about. Not long after he arrived, he spotted an attractive girl across the room who, to his surprise, came over and introduced herself. Claire Hastings admitted later that she might have been attracted by his suit and tie.

—

Claire Marie Montmorency was born in Sheridan, Wyoming, on May 21, 1946, the youngest daughter of Arthur F. Montmorency and Jessie Irene Burke. Her father was the foreman at the roundhouse of the Chicago, Burlington & Quincy Railroad in Sheridan. Her mother was a homemaker who raised five children. Her father's family originated in Gibraltar. After coming to America, they lived in Iowa and then Omaha, Nebraska, where her grandfather was a freight agent for the Burlington Railroad. Her mother's family was originally from Sweden and Germany and had also moved to Omaha.

As a young girl, Claire attended St. Anne's Catholic School in Sheridan and found it humorous that her family lived on Works Street. She was eight when the family left Sheridan to escape the harsh winters after her father suffered a stroke. They moved briefly to Salt Lake City and then relocated to Tucson, Arizona, where she attended St. Cyril's Catholic School and Salpointe High School, graduating in 1964.

Claire enrolled at the University of Arizona but argued with her father over her curriculum. "He wanted me to take practical business classes, which I hated, and I wanted to take liberal arts classes, which I loved."[43] Her father had several sisters who were well-educated, but he felt they had wasted their education. The matter became moot when she couldn't find a job that would pay for her classes.

In 1966, she moved to Sacramento where her older brother, Frank, had a medical practice. She lived with him and worked in his office but then found a job with a local mortgage banking company and moved into her own apartment. It was located in the same apartment complex that hosted the "meet and greet" singles party on that

Friday night in March 1967. It was there that she noticed the stranger wearing the suit and tie.

—

Doc proposed in May. Not long afterward, he had an opportunity to introduce Claire to his parents when they were visiting Reno. Doc and Claire walked into the casino and spotted Flossie at a slot machine. "Mom, I'd like you to meet Claire," Doc announced. Flossie said, "Hi," without breaking her concentration. "She didn't totally ignore me," Claire recalled later with a laugh. "That was just what she did . . . she was *focused!*"[44]

Discussions may have begun during that meeting in Reno and progressed during subsequent telephone calls, but it was decided that Doc would join the company business as a salaried employee with his future prospects to be based on his performance. In September, Doc resigned from Multi-Clean and moved back to Pasco to find an apartment. He and Claire were married in Sacramento on December 16, 1967.

For their honeymoon, the couple drove to San Francisco for a night, then down the coast to Carmel, and back to Sacramento. They loaded everything they owned into Doc's 1964 four-door Chevrolet Nomad station wagon and travelled up the coast to Portland and then to Seattle, where Roger was living. They arrived back in Pasco on Christmas Eve 1967.

CHAPTER THREE

"Intrigued by Politics"

★

DOC AND CLAIRE SPENT CHRISTMAS DAY of 1967 with his family in Pasco before moving their meager belongings into their newly rented apartment. As soon as the holidays were over, Doc began the job he thought would carry him to the end of his career.

Columbia Basin Paper and Supply Company had been primarily a paper-supply business, providing cups, towels, and other paper products to restaurants and institutional customers. The advent of big-box stores and large restaurant chains like McDonald's signaled the end of that business for small local suppliers. They simply couldn't compete. With Doc's experience at Multi-Clean, he intended to build up the janitorial supply part of the business.

—

Doc had returned at an opportune time. The Tri-Cities was finally recovering from a local economic crisis that had been caused by a little-known political deal made 3,500 miles away. In the closing days of 1963, President Lyndon Johnson was looking for ways to reduce the budget in order to satisfy southern conservatives like Harry Byrd, the veteran senator from Virginia and chairman of the Senate Finance Committee, who were concerned about increasing the size of the national debt.

Johnson's advisors believed they had found quite a bit of unnecessary government spending at a remote site in Washington State where the Atomic Energy Commission operated eight plutonium production reactors at full capacity. Because of the huge existing stockpiles of plutonium, they wanted to shut down all the reactors, but Washington's powerful Democratic senators, Warren Magnuson and Henry M. "Scoop" Jackson, convinced the president to phase out the closures over a period of years.

Johnson made the announcement during his 1964 State of the Union message. Within a week, the AEC announced that three of Hanford's oldest reactors would shut down by 1965, cutting about two thousand jobs, or roughly 25 percent of Hanford's workforce. Ten days later, Jackson tried to mitigate the impact of the decision by announcing that a new post office mail processing plant would be built in Pasco, but it was hardly enough.[1] Magnuson had already done his part by declaring that an $8.2 million federal building and courthouse would be built in Richland.

The decision's impact on the Tri-City economy—where roughly 80 percent of all local jobs depended on Hanford—was sharp and immediate. Businesses closed. People left town. Richland business owner Sam Volpentest, along with Robert F. "Bob" Philip and Glenn T. Lee, the president and publisher, respectively, of the *Tri-City Herald*, had tried to prepare the community for the future reactor closures by creating the Tri-City Nuclear Industrial Council (TCNIC) in 1963. Of the announcement, Volpentest later told a reporter, "Hell, it wasn't a crisis, it was an out and out catastrophe."[2] Unlike Hanford workers who could leave town and look for work elsewhere, most business owners had everything invested in their businesses. They had to ride it out. The road to recovery lasted the rest of the decade.

—

Ivan Hastings was fifty-five at the time Doc joined the company. Doc's older brother, Roger, had graduated from Washington State University in 1963, had married, and was living in Tacoma selling pharmaceutical supplies to veterinarians. Roger had once considered working for the family business and did so again in 1969 when the brokerage business he had joined experienced problems. "I thought about it a lot, but when I talked to my dad, he never seemed to have a plan. I couldn't get any specifics out of him. Maybe it was a father-son thing."[3] By 1969,

Doc was there, and Roger went on to found a highly successful pension management company in the Tri-Cities.

Claire was not particularly impressed with her new community. She didn't know anyone there, but Doc certainly did. They socialized with his friends, like Clair Foley, who had married and returned to Pasco. Claire worked part-time for several local doctors until she found out she was pregnant. Kirsten René Hastings was born on May 27, 1969. Another daughter, Petrina Marie, was born on September 1, 1970, and a son named Colin Richard would be born on November 9, 1975.

—

Ivan Hastings had been very active in the Jaycees in Spokane. It was assumed that Doc would follow in his father's footsteps. The opportunity came during one of Ivan's famous late afternoon "happy hours" for visiting salesmen and friends in the back of the store. A member of the local accounting firm that handled the company's work stopped by with a friend who belonged to the local Jaycee group. As they chatted, the topic of discussion turned to the Jaycees.

"Doc, you ought to join the Jaycees," Ivan said. "Hell, I was committed then," Doc remembered.[4]

Doc attended a meeting or two as a guest and then joined the Pasco Jaycees. He and Claire met Bob and Sharlyn Berger through the club, and the two couples became close friends. "We were all young families with little kids," Sharlyn said. "We had no money to speak of, but we had lots of fun."[5] The club's annual community project was decorating downtown Pasco for Christmas. Doc became active in the group, and before long, he was its president.

Over the years, the club had accumulated a lot of decorations and needed a place to store them. They rented a building from the Port of Pasco that was left over from the days when the naval air station occupied the Pasco airport. They called it the "chicken coop," and the club met and stored their decorations there. Doc wanted to make the old building more habitable and approached the port with his ideas. The port happily gave its blessing. Before long, and with a lot of sweat equity, the group had a building with interior walls, a meeting room with a small bar, and a storeroom for the Christmas decorations. Jaycees enjoy visiting other Jaycee clubs, and the word soon got out that the Pasco club was a pretty sociable place to visit.

Like many similar organizations, the Jaycees have an organizational structure that leads from the presidency of a local chapter, up the chain of command to district or regional director, and eventually to state or even international president. Before long, Doc had been elected as a district director and then a regional director in charge of twelve or fifteen clubs in southeastern Washington. It was his responsibility to visit the other clubs in his region and help them with planning, programming, officer training, and membership recruitment. Claire became involved in the Jaycee's auxiliary and would occasionally travel with him on his visits to other clubs.

Over the course of Doc's visits, he met many of the leaders of the other clubs in his area. Like him, they tended to be actively involved in their communities and fellow Republicans. They formed a potential nucleus of support, and he began to think that maybe he could be elected state president.

In 1971, the Jaycees held their national convention in Portland. Doc attended and was fascinated to watch the political maneuvering as candidates organized their supporters and campaigned against each other. "It intrigued me to watch and see how it all played out," Doc explained.[6] The following year he decided to run for state president.

A major potential stumbling block to his plan was Claire. When Doc was gone visiting another club, she was left at home with two small children. It became a long-simmering issue between them, and if he was going to run for state president, it needed to be resolved. She knew he wanted to run, and he knew that she was concerned. The impasse was broken one day when Claire told him that he could go ahead and run. It was a decision that had major, if then unknown, consequences. "It was a defining moment," Doc recalled. "If Claire had not allowed me to do it, I couldn't have done it, then or later. When she told me I could run, I did."[7]

Campaigning for state Jaycee president was a lot like campaigning for public office. There were campaign signs to be made, visits to other clubs asking for their votes, and campaign rallies in different places. Claire and Sharlyn Berger became Doc's campaign workers—positions they continued to hold throughout his legislative and congressional careers.

The race for state Jaycee president in 1972 was hotly contested, and Doc was not the favored candidate. Most of the eastern Washington chapters supported him, but that would not be enough to win. Mike Murphy, a charismatic political operative from Elma who would go on to be elected as a Grays Harbor county commissioner, was one candidate. Another candidate was from the Seattle area. He and Doc joined forces to try to knock Murphy out of the race. "I learned a hard lesson," Doc admitted. "Two isn't necessarily greater than one. Murphy won on the first ballot. It was a long ride home."[8]

But his experience with the Jaycees awakened in Doc some inner attraction to the art and excitement of politics. Doc remembered thinking to himself, "Now that my Jaycee career is over with, what am I going to do?"[9]

THE WASHINGTON STATE REPUBLICAN PARTY held its state convention in Richland in 1972. Doc decided to attend as an observer. By his own admission, he had become "intrigued" by the process of politics.[10] He decided to run for Republican precinct committeeman in Franklin County. No one opposed him. "It wasn't very hard to get elected," he remembered.[11] The job of the precinct committeeman was to survey the residents of his neighborhood to find out who the Republicans were, provide that information to the county party, and encourage them to vote on Election Day. "I did that. I later discovered that I was the only precinct committeeman who did."[12]

Before long, he was being encouraged to run for chairman of the Franklin County Republican Party. But 1974 was a bad year for Republicans—incumbent president Richard Nixon had easily defeated

Democrat George McGovern in 1972 but was by then mired in the Watergate controversy. Doc was elected county chairman. Again, no one ran against him.

As the Republican Party chairman in a county that had traditionally voted Democratic, Doc had no contacts at the state party level and no experience in running a county organization. He received a little help from Jack Metcalf, a state legislator from Marysville, who had run twice unsuccessfully against Warren Magnuson for the US Senate in 1968 and 1974. During the 1968 campaign, Metcalf had campaigned in the Tri-Cities and ended up sleeping for a night on Doc's living room couch.

Doc came to know his counterparts in the other counties, including Dennis Dunn, the powerful chairman of the King County Republican Party, and the other party leaders within his legislative district, like Jeannette Hayner, a Walla Walla Republican who had been elected to the state legislature in 1972 from the Sixteenth District, which then included Franklin County.

As the county's Republican chairman, Doc was expected to host the annual Lincoln Day Dinner. He invited conservative Republican Ken Eikenberry, then a state legislator but later a state party chairman, attorney general, and candidate for governor Only about twenty-five party stalwarts showed up for the event.

Doc had better luck in 1978 when he co-hosted a joint Lincoln Day Dinner with the Benton County Republicans. Several hundred showed up at the Hanford House in Richland to hear Senator Paul Laxalt of Nevada. Doc favorably remembered Laxalt as the chairman of Ronald Reagan's failed 1976 presidential bid and as Nevada's governor during the time when he sold Multi-Clean products in the Reno area.

He sent the senator a list of potential activities to do while he was in town. It included having breakfast at Doc's house on the morning following the dinner. When the senator surprisingly accepted, Claire flew into a panic. Her dishes were not nice enough to entertain a senator! A new set of dishes was quickly purchased and is still packed away at the Hastings home, labeled "Senator's dishes."[13] Years later, when Doc was serving in his final term in Congress, a mutual friend arranged for Doc and the former senator, who was living in Washington, to reconnect. The two had not seen each other since 1978. Doc arranged to take Laxalt and his wife, Carol, to lunch at the member's dining room at the capitol. The subject of his Tri-Cities visit and the story of Claire's dishes came up, and everyone enjoyed a good laugh.

—

Doc was an enthusiastic admirer of Ronald Reagan, the former actor and union lobbyist who had joined the Republican Party in 1962 and become a leading spokesman for Senator Barry Goldwater's presidential bid in 1964. Two years later, Reagan was elected governor of California on a conservative platform that included welfare reform, "cleaning up the mess in Berkeley" (by which he meant the radical, anti-war protesters at the University of California), placing a freeze on government hiring, and instituting a series of tax hikes needed to balance the California budget. Reagan ran briefly against Richard Nixon and Nelson Rockefeller for the Republican presidential nomination in 1968 and then was reelected as governor in 1970, in spite of a recall campaign being waged against him.

Doc had followed Reagan's career with interest and approval since the time he had lived and worked in California. Reagan had become the voice of American conservatism with his speeches, his daily radio commentaries, and his twice-a-week newspaper column, but he yearned to be more than the voice of the movement.

Dennis Dunn, the well-connected King County party chairman, told Doc that Reagan was considering another presidential bid in 1976. In those days, Washington voters expressed their preference for their presidential candidates by voting at their party's county caucuses, rather than in a primary election. If his supporters turned out in force at the county caucuses, they could control the state convention and the selection of the state's delegates to the party's national convention.

By 1975, a small group of insurgents, including Doc, Dennis Dunn, and Dunn's wife, Jennifer, were plotting a coup that would organize Washington's precinct caucuses in support of Reagan for president, rather than President Gerald Ford, who had assumed the presidency after Richard Nixon's resignation. Jennifer Dunn and Doc became close friends. She would later become state party chairperson and be elected to Congress from Washington's Eighth Congressional District.[14]

The state's Republican establishment, including Governor Dan Evan, Attorney General Slade Gorton, Secretary of State Lud Kramer, and the state's only Republican congressman, Joel Pritchard, all supported Ford, but they didn't control the grassroots of the state's Republican Party, particularly in King County.

The Reagan insurgents went to work, poring over lists from previous campaigns to identify possible supporters. "'Who do you know that supports Reagan? Where do they live? Will they attend their precinct caucus?' It was hard work. I wasn't at all sure we could do it," Doc remembered.[15] Franklin County was then in the Fifth Congressional District, and Doc assumed responsibility for organizing Reagan's supporters throughout much of the district. When Reagan announced his candidacy in 1975, their efforts paid off. Reagan carried six of Washington's eight congressional districts in the March caucuses the following year, providing him with the majority of delegates at the state convention.

The Republican state convention was held in May 1976 in Spokane. Reagan flew in and gave a rousing speech. Doc was elected as a delegate to the Republican National Convention, but none of the statewide Republican officeholders was there—not even Governor Dan Evans, who would normally have led the delegation—a move that incited the ire of many of the state's Republican moderates. Doc remembered that the incident taught him one of his first political lessons: "Keeping a sitting governor of your own party from leading your delegation was pretty tough, but that's politics."[16]

Slade Gorton later admitted that he couldn't imagine wanting to go to the national convention in the first place and wouldn't normally have gone.[17] The hard feelings were not permanent, and Doc was able to work effectively with the moderates in later years. Indeed, Slade Gorton, by then a US senator, became one of Doc's most influential mentors after he was elected to Congress.

—

The Republican National Convention was held at the Kemper Arena in Kansas City from August 16 through August 19, 1976. President Gerald Ford beat off a strong challenge from Reagan to be elected as his party's nominee. Kansas senator Bob Dole was elected as his running mate. Reagan had been defeated by a political culture of party insiders who didn't much like him, and he knew it.

When it came time for the nominee's acceptance speech at the convention, the Reagan supporters organized a spontaneous demonstration demanding that their candidate be allowed to speak. Ford, furious at the delay and the showing of a twenty-minute biographical film before he spoke, yelled at Dick Cheney, his chief of staff, to get control of the situation. Finally, around ten p.m., the nominee addressed the convention. When he finished, he invited Reagan to come on stage and make some impromptu remarks in an effort to heal the divisive split in the party.

Referring to a letter he had been asked to write for a time capsule in California, Reagan closed his short remarks by asking his audience if the people who would open that time capsule in one hundred years would "thank God for those people in 1976" who kept us free. He continued:

> This is our challenge and this is why we're here in this hall tonight. Better than we've ever done before, we've got to quit talking to each other and about each other and go out and communicate to the world that we may be fewer in numbers than we've ever been but we carry the message they're waiting for. We must go forth from here united, determined and what a great general said a few years ago is true: "There is no substitute for victory."[18]

Jack Germond, one of the most astute political commentators of his day, believed that at that moment on, Ronald Reagan became the heir-apparent of the Republican Party. Reagan confirmed it the next morning when he spoke to his campaign workers for forty-five minutes: "The cause, the cause goes on," he said.[19]

—

Reagan's final speech at the Republican National Convention speech had not united the party, nor had Reagan intended it to. Although the GOP had controlled the White House for sixteen of the past twenty-four years, only thirteen state governors were Republicans, and the party controlled only four state legislatures—Idaho, Vermont, Kansas, and North Dakota.[20] Conservatives chaffed over the real or imagined slights they had suffered at the hands of the moderate "eastern elites" over the years.

Democratic governor Jimmy Carter of Georgia ran as an outsider untainted by Washington's political scandals, and he defeated Ford in a contest in which many moderate Republicans held bitter memories of Reagan's insurgency. However, Ford's actions in pardoning Richard Nixon and a misstatement during the second presidential debate in which Ford claimed that "there is no Soviet domination of Eastern Europe" probably cost him the election. Carter, once far ahead, saw Ford narrow the gap between them at the end, but he held on to win a narrow victory. In his 2007 book, *Write It When I'm Gone*, reporter Thomas DeFrank, who had many off-the-record interviews with Ford, claimed that Ford blamed Reagan for his 1976 loss to Jimmy Carter to his dying day.[21]

—

Doc and Claire had driven to the convention in Kansas City. When it was over, they drove to Omaha to spend a few days with one of Claire's brothers, an executive with the Mutual of Omaha insurance company. Their daughters, Kirsten and Petrina—seven and six at the time—made their first airplane flight to join them. Their baby son, Colin, was too young to make the trip. Trying to appear very worldly as her parents met her at the Omaha airport, Petrina looked around knowingly and said very matter-of-factly, "Oh, so this is Kansas City."[22]

The Hastings girls spent their early childhood in Doc and Claire's first house, a small bungalow located alongside Highway 395 at 1807 West Jay Street in Pasco. The small-town flavor of the community was such that the girls walked by themselves for nine blocks, crossing busy Court Street, to their school at St. Patrick's Parish school.

The family tradition of bestowing nicknames continued. Claire was "Red," and the girls each received nicknames based on variations of their names. Kristen became "Reense," a take-off on her middle name, Rene, and Petrina became "Pete."

The family moved to an attractive split-level house on a large lot at 5505 West Sylvester Street in 1977, two years after Colin was born. All the Hastings children have fond memories of growing up there. Kirsten took piano lessons for five years and recalled that the piano and the television were in the same room. Her dad loved to watch baseball or basketball games and would often be doing that when she needed to practice. "He would turn down the TV and just listen to me practice."[23]

Petrina remembered her dad mowing the lawn in plaid shorts and his old army combat boots. One summer night the girls slept outside in a tent, and their dad joined them for a while to point out the satellites passing overhead and various constellations. "I think he tended to raise us like boys, as that was his own life experience from having only brothers," Petrina said.[24] Colin remembered learning how to play baseball and fishing off the levees along the Columbia River near their house in the hope of catching a fish large enough to mount.[25]

The children felt that Doc and Claire were pretty laid back as parents, but they were certainly not coddled. Claire was generally the disciplinarian, but Doc always backed her decision, even if he didn't necessarily agree with it. "Dad was always levelheaded about everything. He would come through as the voice of reason, ending the conflict immediately. The proper path always seemed so obvious after he said it," Petrina said.[26] Kirsten added, "You knew something was *really* wrong if dad got mad!"[27] Doc and Claire had decided early in their marriage not to argue in front of the children and to present a united front, but walls have ears. The girls' bedroom was next to their parents. Kirsten remembered, "I could always hear them talking in there after Petrina and I had gone to bed, particularly if they were sorting something out."[28]

THE CITY OF PASCO AND FRANKLIN COUNTY may have been economically tied to the Tri-Cities, but politically they were pulled toward Walla Walla. They were included in Washington's Sixteenth Legislative District, which consisted of Walla Walla County, Franklin County, and a small part of Columbia County. Only 35 percent of the district's voters lived in Franklin County.

The Sixteenth District was represented by Jeannette Hayner from Walla Walla, who had served as the district's state senator in 1977. Representative Gene Struthers, also a Republican, was a Walla Walla businessman who had replaced Hayner when she went to the Senate. The other state representative was Democrat Charles D. "Charlie" Kilbury of Pasco, who had represented the district since 1970.

Hayner and other local Republicans were looking for someone to run against Kilbury, and they thought Doc Hastings, then president of the Pasco Chamber of Commerce, might be just the person for the job. After the excitement of the 1976 Republican National Convention, Doc didn't need much encouragement to run, but Claire was again reluctant, knowing he would be away from the family much of the year. Finally, she conceded. Doc announced his candidacy for the state legislature in the spring of 1978.

Charlie Kilbury, a former railroader and a strong union man with an engaging but rough personality, enjoyed almost universal name recognition in Franklin County. Much of that was the result of his making sure he was seen, particularly when he was running for office, at local events and living up to his reputation as a formidable "doorbeller." He sustained his name familiarity in Olympia by sponsoring a constant flow of new legislation, most of which never passed. Kilbury, chairman of the House Agriculture Committee, was favored to win reelection in 1978 because he had always done so in the past.

Doc received help in his campaign from Ken Eikenberry, now the state's Republican Party chairman and, through him, from campaign consultants provided to the state party by the Republican National Committee. One of them, Tom Gildemeister, helped Doc organize his campaign. At the time, Proposition 13, a measure to limit property taxation, was on the ballot in California, and Doc supported a similar measure in Washington as one of the planks of his campaign platform.

Jack Williams, the owner of Insurance and Financial Consultants in Pasco and a friend of Doc's folks, agreed to serve as finance chairman. One day he asked, "How much money are we going to need to raise?" Doc answered, "About fifteen thousand dollars." "Wow, how are we ever going to raise that?" he responded. They ultimately raised about thirty thousand dollars—all of it needed—because it was the most expensive campaign for a House seat in the state that year.[29]

Doc organized a core group of fifteen to twenty volunteers who put up yard signs, prepared food for gatherings, and put on fundraisers. "We were just common people," Sharlyn Berger recalled. "We weren't particularly politically motivated. We liked Doc, and we liked to have a good time."[30]

To counteract Kilbury's "doorbelling" efforts, Doc decided to duplicate them. After work each night and on weekends, Doc visited houses throughout the district, particularly in Walla Walla County, while Claire and their two young daughters did the same in Franklin County. Sometimes it would be the girls and a few of their friends, "doorbelling" a neighborhood with the promise of a pizza party afterward. He used Kilbury's campaign against him, running newspaper ads featuring a fist knocking on a door, "Knock Knock! Here Comes Charlie Kilbury," followed by a list of four or five negative things he'd done as a state legislator.[31] Doc hammered at Kilbury's voting record and pledged to vote against any new taxes.

Other advertising materials featured a photograph of the attractive young family and, as a novelty, two sets of side-by-side billboards, one in each county, with Doc's message—"listening to, and working for you"—stretched across the double width. On election night, November 7, 1978, Doc defeated Kilbury in what most considered a major upset with 62 percent of the vote. He was one of twelve new GOP members elected to the legislature by mid-Columbia voters.

His victory apparently didn't surprise Doc. "I think the issues were on our side, and we were well-organized. We worked our election plan to a T."[32]

CHAPTER FOUR

Legislative Years

★

THE WASHINGTON STATE LEGISLATURE had a long and well-deserved reputation for disruptive politics. It had been a hotbed of Populism at the turn of the century and was deeply embroiled in the Progressive Movement during the Theodore Roosevelt era. Twenty years later, TR's fifth cousin, Franklin Roosevelt, and his New Deal created a Democratic majority there that lasted for forty years.

By the time Doc ran for the legislature in 1978, it was still controlled by the Democrats, but expanding political fault lines separated the state, east from the west, urban from rural, and business from labor. The two previous legislative sessions had been badly fractured over a number of national and state issues. The national Democratic Party had veered to the left during the Civil Rights Movement, the Vietnam War, and the rise of the environmental movement. The Democrats in the Washington legislature struggled with leadership issues, long-standing differences between their conservative and liberal wings, budget shortfalls, proposed tax increases, and continuing demands from their constituent groups.

The Republican minority mirrored the Democrats with its own growing split that had come to a head at the 1976 Republican National Convention. It consisted of a small group of establishment moderates, a large majority of pro-business, no-tax conservatives that were split between the powerful King County delegation and the rural delegations from the rest of the state, and a small group of very conservative no-tax, anti-government Republicans that might equate to today's Freedom Caucus.

Republican governor Dan Evans, the leader of the moderates, had called the 1975-1977 legislative session the worst in twenty-five years. The 1977-1979 session was not much better. The Democratic majority was so badly fractured that it had to rely on a small group of Republicans in order to pass legislation.

Washington's new Democratic governor, Dixy Lee Ray, a former controversial chairman of the Atomic Energy Commission, was elected in 1976 and quickly proved herself to be a quirky political outsider who almost immediately developed a combative relationship with just about everyone. She named pigs on her Fox Island farm after reporters she disliked and continually dismayed members of the legislature with her personal eccentricities.

The longest legislative session in the state's history ended on June 22, 1977, narrowly passing a state budget that was universally unpopular. John Bagnariol, the Democratic Speaker of the House, was so infuriated by the obstructionist tactics of the House Republicans that he decided there would be no session in the second year of the biennium, as planned, and the governor happily agreed.[1]

—

Doc Hastings was thirty-seven years old on January 8, 1979, when Supreme Court justice Robert Utter swore him in as the newly elected representative from Washington's Sixteenth Legislative District. Claire missed the event because their youngest daughter, Petrina, had come down with a stomach virus the night before. Their oldest daughter, Kirsten, attended along with Doc's proud parents.

For the first time, Doc experienced the excitement of sitting in one of the padded, brown-leather chairs behind a pair of matching oak desks—one of which had his name on it—in the House chamber. He marveled at the warm-hued marble walls and graceful arches above the crowded visitors' gallery while the people's business went on around him.

Doc and Claire remembered visiting Olympia to attend the orientation for new members that was held during the first week of December after the election. "They went over everything briefly. It wasn't much, but it was all brand new to me." Doc remembered that Claire went to a luncheon honoring the wives of the members. She was asked if the family was moving to Olympia. When she replied no, some of the other wives were visibly surprised. "You know what *goes on* over here?" one asked. Claire replied, "I've been married to him for eleven years. If I can't trust him by this time, I'll never be able to."[2]

—

Doc joined the legislature during one of the most difficult periods in its history. Not only had there been no session in 1978, but the historic "one person, one vote" ruling of the United States Supreme Court reduced the number of members of the House from the traditional ninety-nine to an even ninety-eight. The House now faced the unprecedented situation of being evenly split between the Democrats and the Republicans with forty-nine seats apiece. No one knew how to resolve the situation.

The situation was resolved when the Democrats chose John Bagnariol of Renton and the Republicans selected Duane Berentson of Skagit County to be co-Speakers, presiding on alternate days. Fortunately, they had served in the House together for twelve years and were good friends, so the solution worked. Doc was assigned to the Revenue, the Agriculture, and the Constitution and Elections Committees. He had a cubby-hole office on the third floor of the old House Office Building, squeezed in between Bob Eberle from Vashon Island and Helen Fancher from Tonasket.

Doc rented a small apartment in Tumwater and furnished it with a small, black-and-white TV set he had purchased in California. He didn't spend much time there, however. There was a sponsored reception every night during the session, and Doc made the circuit. Other nights, legislators went out for dinner together. It was a good way to network. Doc ate most of his other meals at the inexpensive House lunchroom.

He spent as many weekends as possible at home. Doc would return to Olympia on Sunday night after the kids went to bed or get up in time to leave home by 6:00 a.m. on Monday morning to arrive in Olympia before the session convened at 10:00 a.m. Committee meetings started about 8:00 a.m. Tuesday through Friday. The House would come into session on Friday afternoon as needed and usually adjourn between noon and 2:00 p.m., when Doc would make the long drive back across the state to return home again. Richland Republican Shirley Hankins, who joined Doc in the House in 1980, remembered, "He always went home on the weekends. I always appreciated that about him. He was always very, very close to his family."[3] However, Doc's absence during the legislative session put a strain on the family business. Ivan was now in his sixties, and although he had an employee who could pick up some the slack, Doc's absence was "definitely a sacrifice."[4]

Doc developed his own style of serving in the legislature. He replicated much of what he saw and liked in fellow district legislators, Jeannette Hayner and Gene Struthers. His conservative, pro-business, political philosophy was closely tied to Ronald Reagan's and, like Reagan, he believed that you could disagree politically with someone without being disagreeable. He was personable and was liked by legislators on both sides of the aisle.

His closest associates were the other newly elected conservative Republican members like Dan McDonald, who would become a state senator and run for governor; Bill Polk, who would become Speaker of the House; Bob Eberle, Doc's neighbor in the House Office Building; and Gene Struthers, Doc's seatmate from the Sixteenth District. Polk would later recall that "Doc was one of my favorite new members. He would come up to me and ask, 'Why are we doing this?' and I'd tell him, and he'd look at me and say somewhat skeptically, 'OK, as long as there is a reason.'"[5]

—

Doc had been elected to replace Democrat Charlie Kilbury, who was known as a prolific bill dropper. Doc thought that sponsoring legislation was generally a waste of time and cost taxpayers a lot of money. "I made up my mind that I was just not going to introduce a bunch of bills," he said. "I would co-sponsor them, but I wasn't going to be the lead guy. It was just not my style."[6]

One day, Irv Newhouse, a state representative from Mabton, approached Doc with a bill he had written to allow the transfer of funds between irrigation districts. "Here, Doc, this bill's going to pass. Why don't you introduce it, and you'll have your first bill to your credit." Doc asked him what it was and agreed to introduce it:

> That was almost certainly the first time I stood up and spoke on the floor of the House. You stand up at your desk and address your comments to the Speaker. I remember that I was very, very, nervous. I always admired people who could stand up and speak extemporaneously. I tried to stay as far away from that sort of thing as I could.
>
> If you just listened to people whose views you respected and then ran their ideas through your own values filter, you could learn a great deal.[7]

David Ammons, the longtime political reporter for the Associated Press in Olympia, remembered Doc as "pragmatic in much the same way as his mentor, Jeannette Hayner, was pragmatic. He would work across the aisle. He didn't have sharp elbows, and people enjoyed being around him." Doc's low-key approach was often misinterpreted as ineffectiveness, but that was just his manner. "He was confident of his abilities and the strength of his ideals but not pushy about it," Ammons recalled. "He wasn't a superstar, but he was solid."[8]

Doc generally got along well with the working press. Larry Ganders, the Western Washington Bureau Chief for the *Tri-City Herald*, remembered Doc as "easy to work with and very accessible."[9] Later, when Doc was in leadership positions, he would go over to the press desk and spin his caucus's position on some issue. Reporters found it hard to remember anything Doc did in the legislature. "It was hard to write about him because he never introduced any bills," Ganders said. "Reporters have to have something to write about, and Doc was never news."[10]

Standing at his desk or behind a microphone, Doc looked very much like the small-town businessman he actually was. Not given to rhetorical flourishes or wild gestures, he would say what he wanted to say, occasionally with wry humor, and sit down. Democrat Wayne Ehlers, who replaced Bill Polk as Speaker of the House, remembered that when Doc rose to speak, it was usually in his capacity as the assistant majority leader or caucus chairman. "He wasn't much of an orator, but when he spoke, people listened."[11]

What he said rarely made news, but Doc made an impression on the working press nevertheless. Behind his back, the senior AP reporter at the time, John White, called him "the cobra." It was not pejorative. With his expressive face and engaging smile, Doc in mid-age was a handsome man. But when he spoke intently, his male pattern baldness and the dark circles under his narrow eyes gave the impression of a serpent ready to strike.

—

Doc's conservative political philosophy soon collided with the state's deepening financial crisis. For decades, the state's finances had been buffeted by the conflict between its progressive social agenda and its regressive revenue system. The nation's economy was in a deep recession that was only getting worse. For a state like Washington, whose economy was tied closely to international trade, the global nature of the recession was particularly damaging. The state government remained gridlocked in a test of will between Governor Ray and the legislature.

In the 1979 regular session, the governor demanded that the legislature complete its business in sixty days—something that hadn't happened in twenty years. With the dual control of the House, little got done beyond passing a joint resolution that called for annual sessions of at least 105 days during the first year of the biennium and sixty days during the second. The measure was touted as a way to limit the time the legislature spent in Olympia. It had just the opposite effect.

Ray then reluctantly called a special session, which she tried to limit to twenty days. It lasted two and a half months with the House unalterably divided over the state budget. With no conference committee available to negotiate a compromise solution because of the tie in the House, conflicting versions of bills bounced back and forth between the two bodies like Ping-Pong balls. With no resolution in sight, the Senate went into a rolling recess and went home.[12] The governor threatened to sue the House over its failure to pass a budget. Finally, on June 1, Duane Berentson, the Republican co-Speaker, provided the fiftieth vote to pass the budget and let the legislators go home. Doc kept a framed copy of a poem that the wife of fellow legislator Bob Eberle had written to commemorate that occasion. It was called "Baggy at the Bat," and its last stanza read:

> Baggy's face turned strangely purple, or so the people say,
> When a voice was heard from out in the field where the
> freshmen usually play,
> Doc Hastings, in triumphant tones, was clearly heard to call,
> "Hey Baggy baby—That's 2 fingered hard ball.[13]

That experience taught Doc his next lesson in the art of politics. "You have to cooperate if you're going to pass anything."[14]

The legislators returned to Olympia on January 14, 1980, for the first of their newly approved sixty-day annual sessions. It was best described as a "non-event."[15] The Democrats continued their domination of the Senate, 30-19, and the House remained evenly split. The session ended on March 13.

—

The Tri-Cities that Doc returned to at the end of the session was in the midst of unwanted change. In spite of the growing statewide sentiment against nuclear energy, local community leaders were still fixated by their vision of Hanford as the home of a massive nuclear energy park. The anti-nuclear movement in the state was led by Democratic activists and their supporters in the environmental movement. They were pushing legislation that would allow voters to veto the location of nuclear power plants in their counties. Doc and other Tri-Cities legislators were determined to keep such legislation from passing. "What they are really saying [in a vote against locating the plants] is that they don't want additional power," Doc said. "If it's a risk to build them, why should they get the power from them?"[16]

The problems at Washington Public Power Supply System (WPPSS), the massive public utility that was trying to build five nuclear reactors at the same time, only served as a poster child for the critic's cause. Costs of the design-build construction program for the new reactors climbed to three or four times its original estimate in a period of already high inflation. Labor strikes and stoppages at the construction sites became so severe that the international unions had to intervene. On May 18, 1980, Mt. St. Helens exploded, causing further delays. To make things worse, the Pacific Northwest's sluggish economy was reducing the demand for power just when its cost was increasing.

—

In the national election of 1980, voters faced a stark contrast between President Jimmy Carter, burdened by his problems with high energy prices, a slowing economy, and the Iran hostage crisis, and his ebullient challenger, Ronald Reagan, who saw "Americans awed by what has gone before, proud of what for them is still . . . a shining city on a hill." Reagan won by a landslide in a three-way race.[17] Doc was not involved. He had his own reelection to worry about. He easily defeated Democrat Dot Miller of Connell with 70 percent of the vote. Some local wags called it the Doc versus Dot election.

The major electoral contest in Washington State that year was between Republican challenger Slade Gorton and the state's aging senior senator, Warren Magnuson. "Maggie," as he was universally known, had been a fixture in the nation's capital since 1937, first as a congressman and then as the state's senior senator since 1944. But by 1980, he was slowing down, and the state's population had changed since he had last run six years before. Gorton won the election by promoting himself as "Washington's Next Great Senator." He was the first Republican elected to the US Senate from Washington since Harry Cain in 1946.[18] The controversial Dixy Lee Ray lost to Jim McDermott in the Democratic primary for governor. McDermott was then defeated by Republican King County executive John Spellman in the general election, whose victory ushered in an amiable, if strained, relationship between the Republican governor and his Republican-controlled legislature.

—

When the regular session began on January 12, 1981, the Republicans held a majority of 56 to 42 in the House. They elected Bill Polk from Mercer Island as their Speaker and Gary Nelson of Edmonds as their majority leader. Doc Hastings was elected as assistant majority leader, and his seatmate, Gene Struthers from Walla Walla, became the Republican whip. Doc served as his deputy. He also joined the important Rules Committee, which scheduled the bills that would be acted upon on the floor of the House.

Doc may have seemed an unusual choice to be selected for his party's leadership team after only one term in the legislature, but his upset victory over a strong opponent, his conservative principles, and his easy-going nature helped. Associated Press reporter David Ammons remembered that "he was seen as a sensible mainstream business guy who could represent business issues to the full caucus, some of whom had never signed a paycheck or had any real understanding of the marketplace."[19] Speaker Bill Polk remembered that "Doc was an integral part of the leadership team that set the agenda for the caucus. Because he brought the Eastern Washington viewpoint to each meeting, I would say that he was quite influential."[20] The Democrats continued to control the Senate by one vote, 25-24.

That changed dramatically, however, on the evening of Friday, February 13, 1981, when Doc was tipped off that Peter von Reichbauer, a Democratic senator from Vashon Island, was going to switch parties, throwing control of the Senate to the Republicans. Doc and some colleagues watched from the wings of the Senate chamber as Senator Irving Newhouse of Mabton, introduced a motion to vacate the office of sergeant of arms, a position controlled by the Democrats.

They would know whether the von Reichbauer rumor was true by how he voted on the motion. He voted aye and immediately left the Senate chamber to announce that he was changing parties. Former legislator and historian Don Brazier described the scene in his *History of the Washington Legislature 1965-1982*: "Near pandemonium ensued. Democrats were outraged. Republicans were gleeful. Most lobbyists and interested parties simply disappeared from the Capitol for a day or two."[21]

The new Republican majority quickly passed a supplemental budget that contained deep cuts in social programs. Jeannette Hayner of Walla Walla became the Senate's first female majority leader in her second term in the Senate. Democratic senator Ray Moore of Seattle called Hayner "the Margaret Thatcher" of the state of Washington. "She was the toughest leader on their side of the aisle in my memory," he said, while admitting that she "managed to do it with style and grace."[22] Increased bonding authority for WPPSS was narrowly approved. The Republicans passed a redistricting plan that, strangely, would help lead to their defeat in the next election. They would remain in the minority for the next twelve years.

The Republicans—many of whom had been elected on a pledge of "no new taxes"—next addressed the dire condition of the state's finances. On November 9, Governor Spellman called a special session to deal with the situation. Substantial cuts in state spending were put in place across the board, but that was not enough. Over the objections of three Republican senators who would vote for no new tax under any circumstance, a temporary sales tax increase drew enough votes to pass by the narrowest of margins. Doc's vote was one of them in a rare example of his pragmatism winning out over his political philosophy.

—

When the regular session of the forty-seventh legislature began on January 10, 1982, the body was again consumed by the state's budgetary crisis. Washington's statewide unemployment rate was above 10 percent. Inflation raged, and interest rates were at historic highs. Republicans held a substantial majority in the House and a razor-thin one in the Senate as a result of von Reichbauer's defection. The financial problems created friction between Governor Spellman and a group of twenty-four "no-tax" House Republicans—including Doc—whom the governor called "troglodytes." The popular director of the state's Department of Revenue suggested that it was time—once again—to look at a state income tax. He was promptly fired.

Senator Ray Moore remembered that Doc served with him on the Tax Advisory Council, which was composed of one member from each caucus and eleven selected by Governor Spellman:

> After much research, staff time, and the council's meetings, we finally voted on a revenue-neutral tax plan to cut the B&O tax, the sales tax, the property tax and to institute an income tax. The council voted thirteen to two for the plan. As I recall, Doc Hastings and George Sellar voted no.
>
> At least those two indicated that they liked the present regressive system, which unduly taxes those with lower incomes! Doc is certainly not mean-spirited. He just happened to vote that way both in Olympia and now as a Congressman.[23]

Wayne Ehlers recalled that as the Republican assistant majority leader, Doc:

> had to bridge the gap between the Republicans who were conservative [like himself] and those who were *extremely* conservative. Some of these folks were farther to the right than the Tea Party.
>
> It wasn't too long before John Spellman found out that his pledge of "no new taxes" wouldn't stand up during a period in which [the] economy turned from bad to worse to impossible. He cut and cut and cut to the point where the moderates in that caucus told him that they couldn't vote for any more cuts and that they were ready to vote for some moderate tax increases.
>
> Bill Polk, then the Speaker, wanted to solve the problem within their caucus and he tried, but he wasn't very successful. The troglodytes were saying "no way," and Polk and I started to discuss how we could bail them

out. I don't remember Doc having much of a role in those negotiations. Doc really believed in limited government, but he [was] also a pragmatist who understood the needs of the Tri-City area he represented.[24]

As assistant majority leader, Doc was asked on occasion to preside over the House chamber. It was generally during routine consent items, but it was something that Doc enjoyed immensely. He learned parliamentary procedure and gained a reputation for treating other members with fairness. Allen Hayward, the Republican's senior counsel, said that he loved working with Doc Hastings at the rostrum. "He was very smooth and could really move the calendar along at a fast clip."[25]

—

John Spellman called the legislature into yet another special session in March. Both branches of the legislature promptly ran out of money and had to appropriate funds to finance the session. An unpopular compromise agreement was reached on the final day by cutting state spending by an additional $142 million and raising taxes by $272 million. It soon became evident that even that draconian fix would not be enough. Democrats made it clear that the cost of their support in solving the state's financial crisis depended on extending unemployment benefits, and the session closed without finding a solution to the problem.

Spellman called a second special session on June 26, 1982. He threatened to enforce an across-the-board spending cut of 8.2 percent. The legislature cut another one hundred million dollars from the budget, imposed a 3 percent surcharge on all taxes, and to the delight of many, approved a long sought-after state lottery. House Speaker Bill Polk remembered that "the tax hikes killed us."[26] Doc recounted the difficult position the lottery put him in: "Gene Struthers was the primary sponsor of the lottery bill. He was my seatmate. Our senator, Jeannette Hayner, was absolutely opposed to the lottery. They were both my friends, but this was one of those situations where you couldn't keep everyone happy. The smarter course was to keep Jeannette happy, so I voted no with Jeannette."[27]

—

The Tri-Cities economy was on life support in 1982. The loss of 5,300 jobs at WPPSS between May and September came on top of a stream of bad news for Hanford. BWIP, the Basalt Waste Isolation Project, which had explored Hanford as an underground nuclear waste depository and would have created many jobs, was cancelled. The future of the dual-purpose N Reactor was highly questionable. Unemployment rates in Benton and Franklin Counties averaged 14.6 percent. The population of the Tri-Cities dropped by 10 percent within ninety days after the announcement of the WPPSS layoffs. Housing values dropped by 25 to 30 percent.

Small business owners like Ivan Hastings, now seventy, really suffered. On weekends, Doc stopped by the store to see how things were going. He could tell by the sales receipts that it was not going well.

Doc also faced the challenges of raising two teenage daughters and a young son as an absentee father for large portions of the year. The family considered his election to the state legislature a mixed blessing. "I was nine and in the fourth grade when he was elected to the legislature," Kirsten remembered. "I wore my GOP sweatshirt to school, and from that day forward, I was always 'Doc's girl.' It wasn't too bad; it was just something that he did. I was always proud of him."[28] Petrina agreed. "The fact that he was a politician seemed quite normal to me, but there came a point where I realized that other people didn't necessarily like him. My reaction was a combination of pride and guardedness."[29]

All three Hastings children served as pages in Olympia. Kirsten and Petrina paged for their father when they were fourteen and twelve, respectively. Colin paged for Senator Hayner when he was sixteen. Kirsten most remembered the beautiful marble in the Legislative Building as she followed her father through his daily rounds.

Petrina's most vivid memory was of an end-of-the-week party for the pages at a local pizza parlor. Doc dropped her off at the restaurant and drove away. The fact that the restaurant was closed was not obvious from the street, and the twelve-year-old was stranded in a strange city in the dark. She had confidence that he would return, and he did—two hours later—something she has never let him forget.[30]

Republican Shirley Hankins, Eighth District representative, sat near Doc on the House floor and remembered his sense of humor. "He would slip me little notes," she remembered. "'Do you want to have some fun?' he'd ask. He'd want me to introduce some motion that he suggested, and I said, 'Why would I do that?' His response was that 'it would be interesting.'"[31] On another occasion, he was talking with Hankins and several other female members on the floor when he inadvertently called one of the other women Shirley and then, soon after, called a third woman by the same name. That afternoon, one of them went shopping and purchased a supply of pins with the word "Shirley" on them. For the next several days, about a dozen female members walked around the House chamber wearing "Shirley" pins.[32]

———

Doc and his legislative colleagues went home to face angry voters in November 1982. Ronald Reagan's economic policies were being widely blamed for the national recession. Nationally, the Democrats picked up twenty-six seats in the House of Representatives and one seat in the Senate. Statewide, the Democrats picked up eleven seats in the House and two in the Senate. Luckily, Doc was in a fairly safe district and defeated Sandy Dodd of Kennewick by 55 to 45 percent.

———

The legislators returned to Olympia for the opening of the forty-eighth session of the Washington legislature on January 10, 1983. The front page of the *Seattle Times* screamed, "New Taxes Loom as Legislators Convene."[33] Governor Spellman welcomed them by saying that $145 million were needed immediately in order to pay the state's bills, "and the budget can't be funded by gimmicks," he added.[34]

With the Democrats back in control of the legislature by margins of ten in the House, 54-44, and three in the Senate, 26-23, Wayne Ehlers of Parkland was elected Speaker of the House. The Republicans elected Gary Nelson of Edmonds as their minority leader, and Doc became the caucus chairman. Losing the majority was yet another lesson in Doc's political education. He may have recalled former Speaker John O'Brien's famous quote: "I like being in the majority. Being in the minority isn't all that pleasant."[35]

It helped that he and Ehlers shared a common interest in the Chicago White Sox. Doc became a fan back in the 1950s when each of the kids on his block supported a different major league team. The two men occasionally exchanged White Sox stories or mementoes. It was one way of reaching across the aisle.[36]

As caucus chairman, Doc regularly presided during the frequent meetings of the Republican caucus. In those meetings, he helped mold the party's position on issues, strategized with a committee's ranking member about legislation, and participated in negotiations with his counterparts in the Senate.

Wayne Ehlers summed up Doc's service in the Washington legislature—and indeed his entire future congressional career—best when he said:

> Doc was always more interested in working the inside game than engaging in the daily grind that was the norm for most legislators and congressmen. It enabled him to be selected by his caucus to be the go-to guy on the insider jobs that needed to be done and that most others really didn't want to do. The Ethics Committee is only one example. His leadership knew they could trust him, and his fellow members knew that he would be fair.[37]

On September 1, the other half of Washington State's vaunted senatorial team, Henry M. "Scoop" Jackson died suddenly at his Everett home of a heart attack. He had served in the US Senate since 1952. The legislature was called back on September 10 to approve a special election to be held later that year. In the meantime, John Spellman set off a firestorm among the Democrats in the legislature by appointing former Republican governor Dan Evans to Jackson's seat. The Democrats felt the appointment should have gone to a Democrat. "I agreed with Spellman's decision. That was an easy pick," Doc remembered.[38]

Back in the Tri-Cities, the dream of a nuclear energy park at Hanford finally died when, on July 25, WPPSS defaulted on $2.25 billion of its bonds, the largest municipal bond default in United States history.

—

As dire as the state's economic problems were, there was always time in Olympia for a little fun. Former Speaker and co-Speaker John Bagnariol loved to play pool. Each year, he hosted a fundraiser at the Brotherhood Tavern where maybe fifty lawmakers and lobbyists gathered for a pool tournament. Doc smiled as he remembered:

> The Republicans were not invited to Baggy's pool tournament. When we got into that 49-49 tie, some of us decided to show up. Well, I could play some pool; I was never real good at it, but I could play.
>
> I worked my way up in the tournament, and when there's four or five guys left, Baggy arrives and wants play the winners. It happened that he got paired with me.
>
> He had it set up where he could run the table and beat me if he made this shot. Just as he was lining up his shot, I said, 'Hey, Baggy, do you breathe in or out when you shoot?'
>
> He stopped, looked up at me, and I'll never forget the look on his face. He missed the shot, and I ran the table and I won.[39]

When the Republicans gained majority in the next session, Doc decided that the tournament should continue. He started the Doc Hastings World Championship Pool Shootoff. Shirley Hankins remembered that she and Doc each received a blue-and-white jacket with the Brotherhood Tavern's name displayed on the back, along with a note naming them as "the most fun representatives of the Republican caucus from the Democrats who had attended the tournament."[40] On another occasion, Doc and the Democratic caucus chairman thought it would be entertaining to call each other's caucuses to order. "I walked into the majority caucus conference room, and everyone there was looking at me and saying, 'What are you doing in here?'"[41]

—

Lobbying and lobbyists were a way of life in Olympia. Doc would occasionally go out to dinner with them, but not frequently. Not surprisingly, the lobbyists who represented organized labor generally left him alone, understanding they weren't going to get his vote. However, most lobbyists were well-informed and persuasive, and some facilitated friendships that crossed party lines and made compromise possible.[42]

Doc's approach to lobbyists was similar to his relationship with the salesmen who tried to sell him their products at his family's company. "You don't become friends with lobbyists. Their job is to befriend you. They would come in and make their best pitch—which was often very good indeed. I would weigh that against my own views and then make up my mind." On contentious issues, Doc tried to reach a decision as quickly as possible. "I thought it was in my best interest to try to know the issue well and to let others know that I had made up my mind. Others waited till the last moment to announce their decisions and then asked for favors for their vote."[43]

—

Lawmakers returned again to Olympia for the second year of the forty-eighth Washington legislature on January 9, 1984, with the Democrats still remaining in firm control. With the Reagan tax cuts starting to have an effect, the state's economy finally started to improve. For the first time since 1957, legislators completed their work on time, passing a $54.3 million supplemental budget, half of which was set aside for various public assistance programs favored by the Democrats. "It was not a great session any way you look at it," said an exasperated John Spellman.[44]

—

Doc was up for reelection in 1984. In the middle of the campaign, he got a call from the vice-chairman of the state Republican Party. The various factions of the party were squabbling over who would represent

the state on the Platform Committee at the Republican National Convention in Dallas, Texas. Doc agreed to go. The House minority whip,
Trent Lott of Mississippi, chaired the whole committee, while Senator
Bob Kasten of Wisconsin chaired the tax subcommittee on which Doc
served. A spirited debate ensued over the inclusion of the comma in
the phrase, "We therefore oppose any attempts to increase taxes, which
would harm the recovery and reverse the trend to restoring control of
the economy to individual Americans." Those favoring the inclusion,
including Doc, believing that the phrase without the comma opened
the door to new taxes.[45] Doc smiled as he remembered that the "Battle of the Comma" attracted the attention of the pugnacious political
columnist, Robert Novak, who wrote about the "young guns" on the
Platform Committee. "He singled out two people, Clark Durant from
Michigan and me."[46]

—

The presidency of Ronald Reagan redefined the national Republican Party in several fundamental ways. The Civil Rights Movement of the
1960s changed the political balance of power in the South. By the time
Reagan was elected in 1980, most Southern Democrats had switched to
the Republican Party, and the GOP carried every southern state except
Georgia. Reagan's social conservatism and his economic policies that
cut taxes and reduced inflation appealed to many former working-class,
blue-collar Democrats in the rest of the country. His upbeat campaign
slogan was "It's morning in America again."

The convention easily re-nominated Ronald Reagan and George H.
W. Bush. In spite of their edgy personal relationship, they easily defeated Walter Mondale, the former vice president, and his running mate,
Geraldine Ferraro of New York, in a landslide victory in which Reagan
carried forty-nine of fifty states. Reagan ran on a platform that touted the
nation's strong economic recovery from the 1981-82 recession, as well as
the widespread perception that his presidency had revived the nation's
confidence and prestige. The only bright spot for the national Democrats
in the 1984 election was picking up two seats in the Senate, but Reagan's

grassroots popularity helped elect sixteen new Republicans to the House of Representatives.

Democrat Booth Gardner, the adopted stepson of Weyerhaeuser timber magnate Norton Clapp, unseated Republican John Spellman as Washington's governor. Spellman was probably glad to leave. Dealing with the legislature "was a lot worse than I thought it would be," he later told a television interviewer."[47]

—

Doc was elected to a fourth term in 1984, but it was his most difficult race to date. He faced the well-known Bill Grant from Prescott in Walla Walla County, whose family had farmed the area for generations. Most of the vote in the Sixteenth District still came from Walla Walla County, and Doc won the narrowest victory of his legislative career—52 to 48 percent.

On January 14, 1985, the state's lawmakers were welcomed to Olympia by an air force band. Democrats had a five-vote advantage in the Senate and an eight-vote majority in the House. Wayne Ehlers was again elected Speaker. Lawmakers were asked to celebrate the upcoming Washington Centennial Celebration by passing a $152 million bond issue to fund projects associated with the event.[48]

Washington's upcoming centennial did nothing to brighten the spirits of the House Republicans. The troops were not happy and looked for new leadership. Doc, who had served as caucus chairman, was asked to run for minority leader. His opponent was Sim Wilson, a newspaper publisher from Marysville. When the votes were counted, Wilson had won a narrow victory.

The new governor, Booth Gardner, had served briefly as a state senator and as Pierce County executive. Ray Moore, the acerbic but insightful long-serving senator from Seattle, liked to say that Gardner's great regret was that there were only twenty-four hours in a day to be adored. "Gardner was a very nice guy and loved to banter with people," he added, "but what the hard-core Democrats wanted after Ray and Spellman was a combination of FDR, Truman, and Kennedy with a dash of Johnson."[49]

Agreement to end the 105-day regular session was deadlocked over how to fund $510 million to clean up Puget Sound and other state waterways and approving the state's budget. Doc called the deadlock "a battle of egos," as each house clung to its version of the budget, which bounced back and forth between the two houses like a ball in a tennis match.[50]

—

After the session ended, Doc and Claire had the opportunity for a pleasant diversion. They planned to attend the West Point graduation ceremony for the son of Clair Foley, one of Doc's close childhood friends, who had passed away. Doc and Claire stopped in Washington, DC, and Jennifer Dunn, who was the state Republican Party chairman at the time, arranged for a number of Washingtonians to attend a reception at the Naval Observatory, the home of Vice President George H. W. Bush. Doc and Claire were invited to meet the future president for the first time.

—

Governor Gardner called a special session for June 10 and 11, in which the majority Democrats passed a $9.13 billion budget in six hours and forty minutes—something they had failed to do in the 105-day regular session. Not one Republican voted for it.

—

Doc returned home to find a contentious consolidation issue facing voters on the November ballot. The matter had been brewing since 1972. The effort was led by Richland attorney Tom Heye, but there were proponents of consolidation in all three cities. The strongest opposition was led by city councilmember, Ed Hendler. Ed represented a strong faction in Pasco that had distrusted Richland since the beginning of the Manhattan Project during World War II. Richland voted to merge 4,875 to 3,943. Kennewick approved 4,619 to 3,064. Pasco overwhelmingly voted no, and the measure failed. Doc avoided taking a public position on the matter but voted no in the election. He felt that the difficulties of consolidating the two counties were too great to overcome. The issue came up for a vote again in 1988 with Pasco left out of the mix, but this time Richland voted yes and Kennewick voted no, and the measure failed again.[51]

—

Doc returned to Olympia for his final session of the state legislature on January 13, 1986. The Democrats held the same majorities they had enjoyed in previous regular and special sessions, and they faced many of the same issues. Over Doc's objections, the House Ways and Means Committee passed an eight-cent increase in the cigarette tax to fund the cleanup of state waterways, while the Senate Ways and Means Committee finally approved a negotiated settlement between the state and its public employee unions over comparable worth. The measure passed in spite of Senator Jeanette Hayner's strong objections. She quickly pointed out that she was for "equal pay for equal work" but not for increasing the pay for 75 percent of the state's workers while lowering the pay for none.[52] Doc joined Jeannette Hayner in his strong opposition to the measure.

The session adjourned a day early for the first time since 1925. Gardner got his sales tax deferral program to help attract new industries, but Eastern Washington senators defeated his proposal to give him authority to hire and fire the directors of the state departments of transportation, game, and parks.

—

At home, Doc was facing some hard choices. He had considered stepping down from the legislature for several years. He had wanted to do so in 1984, but his seatmate, Gene Struthers, had announced his retirement that year, and Doc promised Jeannette Hayner that he would not leave two seats open in the Sixteenth District at the same time. But the next two years were difficult. The family business was suffering because of the Tri-Cities economy. Doc had bought out his father's interest in the company and brought in someone to help with managing the company while Doc was in Olympia, but that wasn't working out very well.

The other problem was the children. Kirsten and Petrina were seventeen and sixteen, respectively, and Colin was eleven. A few years before, Colin had asked his mother after Doc left for Olympia, "Why does Daddy leave home after we go to bed?" His son's innocent question weighed on him.[54]

After talking it over with his family, Doc decided he would not run for reelection in 1986. Had he won the election for minority leader, he might have stayed on. "I would have felt I had an obligation to stay on," he explained, "and who knows? Lightning might [have struck], and I could have become Speaker. But that didn't happen, and it was time to go."[55]

On April 23, Doc called a press conference at the Pasco Red Lion to announce that he would not seek reelection. His surprise announcement sent ripples through both political parties. Doc's 1978 victory over Charlie Kilbury had ended the Democratic control of Franklin County, and Democrats were unsuccessful in finding a candidate to run against him in the fall. Republicans began lining up to run for his seat. "It's interesting to think that at this point in time I'm politically stronger than I've ever been," Doc said.[56]

A reporter asked him what his crowning achievement in office had been. His answer was typical Doc. He told a long story about how he had equalized the state B&O tax for beef processors.

In response to a question about whether he had any future plans in politics, Doc responded, "Well, one thing I've learned in politics is to never rule out anything like that. I certainly will not rule out running for elective office in the future. When that will be or which position that will be I can't tell you at this point, but I will not rule it out."[58]

Doc adamantly denied ever thinking about running for higher office while he was in the legislature, but others were not so sure. The *Tri-City Herald*'s Larry Ganders always thought Doc had a strange fixation with national Republican politics. Others, like fellow Tri-Cities legislator Shirley Hankins, believed that Doc was looking ahead at a run for Congress.

—

But Doc's career in the Washington legislature was not quite over. On August 1, 1986, Governor Gardner called a one-day special session to vote on a bill that would place a measure on the November ballot challenging the federal government's inclusion of Hanford as the site of a possible national underground repository for nuclear waste. The bill had broad, bipartisan support and only the three representatives who lived in the Tri-Cities argued against it.

Speaker Wayne Ehlers stood at the rostrum, gavel in hand, looking like a man who had the votes he needed and was in a hurry to go home. Doc repeatedly tried to argue against the measure, only to be gaveled down by the Speaker. Finally, Ehlers had had enough. He banged his gavel so hard that the handle separated from the head. "Too bad. Your time is up. Your three minutes has expired." It was Doc's last floor speech in the Washington legislature.[59]

It took only ninety-three minutes for the Democrat-controlled House to vote 91-3 to approve the measure—and a further ninety-five minutes for the Senate to pass the referendum by a vote of 44-3. The matter would become moot when Congress chose a location in Nevada instead.

—

Not long after he first arrived in Olympia in 1979, someone asked Doc what his future plans were, assuming that, like so many others, his legislative service was but a stop on a longer political journey. Doc had responded, "I don't have a plan other than to serve."[60] He had done just that, quietly and without fanfare for the most part, a consistent conservative who represented the majority views of his agricultural constituency. He lent an Eastern Washington viewpoint, serving as assistant majority leader when Republicans held the majority and as caucus chairman when they did not.

In his eight years in the legislature, he had been the prime sponsor of fewer than twenty-five bills. He estimated that fewer than ten of those were ever signed into law. "That's just not what I was about."[61]

> In light of my philosophy of government, I didn't go over there [to Olympia] just to pass a whole lot of bills that meant more government. Sometimes, you can be more effective by stopping things from happening.
>
> During the tied session and the two years when we were in the majority, we were successful in curbing the growth of government, but when the recession of 1981 and 1982 came into play, I learned then that you have

to govern, regardless of the circumstances and your personal wishes.

And he learned that you can't always forecast what will happen in the future:

> I voted for the tax increases that were supposed to be temporary, but then became permanent, but by that time, we were in the minority and couldn't change the outcome.
>
> From a personal standpoint, the time I served certainly opened my eyes to government and how it works. I learned about the legislative process, and that really served me well when I got to Congress.
>
> It reaffirmed my belief in the importance of having basic philosophy to guide you when issues come before you. [62]

His constituents in the Sixteenth District must have approved of his service on their behalf. They had elected him and reelected him four times, generally by wide margins. Commenting on his announced retirement, the *Tri-City Herald* seemed worried more about losing a Tri-Cities seat in the legislature than losing Doc, but the paper's editorial writers were more complimentary on this occasion than they would be later in his career. They wrote that he had been an "excellent legislator: thoughtful, principled, and respected in both parties. . . . Mr. Hastings was not the kind of lawmaker who measures success by how many bills he passed or by how much bacon he brought home to his constituents. Instead, he tirelessly sought to hold the line on taxes and curtail the growth of state spending."[63]

"So much for that!" Doc thought. He was sure he would never serve in elected office again.

CHAPTER FIVE

Two Campaigns and a Contract

★

By 1991, Washington's political landscape had changed percepti-
bly since 1986. In the presidential election of 1988, George H. W. Bush
pulled off a Republican landslide, defeating Democrat Michael Dukakis
in Washington and all but ten other states and the District of Columbia. Bush benefitted from a good economy and President Reagan's continuing popularity, but also from the Democratic Party's left-leaning tilt
during the 1980s

While the national Democratic Party became more liberal during
the 1980s, the national Republican Party tilted in the opposite direction,
often riding to victory on social wedge issues like abortion, gun control,
race, and gender. But another indisputable factor was that many voters
were simply tired of—or upset by—the Democrats who had controlled
Congress since 1954.

The trends were even more evident in swing states like Washington. Since 1986, when Doc Hastings retired, more members of the religious right had been elected to the state legislature. The conservative
commentator Pat Buchanan challenged President Bush in 1992, and a
sizable number of voters in the Fourth Congressional District voted for
him. The Mormon Church was also growing in influence and supported
many of the same social issues as the evangelicals.

When the state Republican Party convened in Yakima in June 1992,
the Christian activists were in firm control, adopting a party platform
that declared that "Western cultural values" were superior to all others.
The platform called for a constitutional ban on abortion, even in cases

of incest and rape, denounced the United Nations, and condemned the "deviant lifestyle" of homosexuals. "This doesn't sound like the party of Abraham Lincoln to me," declared Congressman Sid Morrison, the Fourth District's popular Republican Congressman for Life.[1] On November 4, 1991, Morrison had announced he would run for governor to replace the Democratic incumbent, Booth Gardner, who was not seeking a third term in 1992.

———

Morrison's decision to run against Gardner put his congressional district seat up for grabs. Doc Hastings reviewed the list of potential candidates and decided, "Hey, I think I can do this." By this time, his children were in or had graduated from high school, the family's business had recovered from the 1980s recession, and his discussion with Claire about entering the race had gone well.

Kirsten had recently graduated from Gonzaga University with a degree in political science and a minor in psychology. She hadn't decided whether to attend law school yet. When Doc announced his candidacy, she was working for McCaw Cellular in Seattle. She came home to join the campaign. Petrina was pursuing a degree in international economics at Eastern Washington University in Cheney, so she was unavailable. Politics did not attract her as it did Kirsten. Doc understood. He advised his daughters to major in something they enjoyed and not worry about what they were going to do for the rest of their lives. Colin, sixteen, was still at home and attending Pasco High School.

Doc was reasonably familiar with the large Fourth Congressional District and knew a number of potentially important contacts through his business connections and his past service in the legislature. On Thursday, November 21, 1991, he called a press conference to announce he was forming an exploratory committee to look at the possibility of becoming a candidate.[3] He hired Brett Bader, a young political consultant recommended to him by Jennifer Dunn, to advise the campaign.

Bader was a political whiz kid who had been active in Republican politics at the University of Washington. Doc received more than a little shock to his ego when Bader's initial polling indicated that Doc's name familiarity across the district was at something like 10 percent. He was only slightly encouraged by the fact that some of the other candidates had scored even lower than he had. Doc remembered that at that point he realized the truth of the adage, "Out of sight, out of mind."[4]

Not dissuaded by his polling numbers, Doc assembled a campaign team. He selected Darryl Howard, a young political activist from Richland, as his campaign manager and his brother Roger as finance chairman. Sharlyn Berger volunteered again to fill out financial disclosure forms. Family members, particularly Claire and Kirsten, and the longtime friends and volunteers who had supported Doc during his legislative years came on board.

Doc met with prominent local Republicans to gauge their support. His parents wrote the first check to his campaign, and others stepped forward with one-thousand-dollar checks. The campaign raised about thirty thousand dollars from 140 donors in little more than a month. Doc estimated it would take another $170,000 to knock off the three other Republicans in the primary.

—

With his campaign team in place, Doc formally announced his candidacy at 8:45 a.m. on February 13, 1992, to a packed audience of reporters and supporters at the Pasco Red Lion Hotel. He looked and sounded as if it hadn't been six years since his last political press conference. "For someone running for Congress, timing is everything, and I think the timing is right for me now," Doc told the crowd. His campaign would focus on crime, free trade, and agriculture. "It's important to keep the district in the Republican column," he said.[4]

Seven other candidates entered the race. The Republicans included Jeff Sullivan, the Yakima County prosecuting attorney; Bill Almon, a successful commercial realtor from Yakima; Alex McLean, a state legislator from Chelan County; and Doc. The Democrats included Jim Jesernig, a handsome former WSU track star and current state senator from Kennewick; Joe Walkenhauer, a Yakima businessman; and Jay Inslee, a state representative and Selah attorney.

Under the state's then-current election laws, the top Republican vote getter and the top Democratic vote getter in the September primary would square off in the November general election.

Although Doc was better known in the Tri-Cities than any of the other Republicans, he was relatively unknown throughout the rest of the district, a fact shown by his early polling results. His team devised an aggressive strategy based on holding coffee hours throughout the district to introduce Doc to as many grassroots Republicans as possible. Sharlyn Berger remembered, "The election was hectic. The district was so huge. The issue was how to get him out into it."[5]

With no party registration in Washington State, it was impossible to identify Republican voters, so the campaign relied on voter records to locate so-called perfect voters—those who had voted in each of the past four elections—who lived in predominantly Republican precincts. They asked someone in each of those precincts to host a coffee hour at his or her home where Doc would speak. Then they sent out postcards to the frequent voters in that precinct, inviting them to attend the event. Sometimes only one or two came.

Kirsten drove Doc to the events and made sure every attendee signed in. The following day, they sent postcards to those who had missed the event and listed Doc's key points from his presentation. In that way, they effectively communicated with voters, identified Doc, and told potential voters what he stood for. The campaign also participated in Lincoln Day Dinners, parades, and local debates. "I don't think we turned any of them down,"[6] Doc remembered. "Maybe not," Sharlyn Berger said with a smile, "but he hated the parades."[7]

—

Among the Democrats, the contest was between two young, articulate, and photogenic candidates: Jim Jesernig of Kennewick and Jay Inslee of Selah. Inslee gave up his seat in the state legislature to run, although he thought twice about it, taking the highly unusual move of calling a press conference in four different cities in January to announce that he was not running and then announcing his candidacy four months later. Inslee was one of the most liberal legislators from Eastern Washington and a strong supporter of abortion rights. Jesernig styled himself as a conservative Democrat in the Henry M. Jackson mode. "I didn't know much about politics back in 1986 when I was first running," Jesernig remembered. "I liked Scoop Jackson, and he was a Democrat, so I guessed that I was one too."[8] Inslee entered the race because, in his words, "the issues facing my community were the same as the ones we were struggling with on a national level, and I thought I could make the most change and a real difference."[9]

The Republican candidates were led by Doc, who described himself as a Reagan Republican who was fond of repeating that government was most often the problem, not the solution to the problem. Five days before the primary, one of his opponents criticized him on Yakima public television for his failure to sponsor legislation in the state legislature. Doc responded that there were enough laws on the books already.[10] He promoted a balanced budget, a presidential line-item veto, and a major rewrite of the Endangered Species Act to reduce the economic impact of the northern spotted owl decision.[11] He was also strongly pro-life on the issue of abortion.

The articulate, silver-haired Jeff Sullivan, the Yakima County prosecutor, ran on a law-and-order platform. Bill Almon, also from Yakima, ran largely against Sullivan. Alex McLean boasted that he was the only farmer in the race. He complained that there were already 183 attorneys in the House of Representatives, a dig at Sullivan, Inslee, and Jesernig.[12]

Led by its publisher, Kelso Gillenwater, who liked Jesernig, the *Tri-City Herald* enthusiastically wrote, "In November we expect to endorse Jesernig, so we are doing it now." They expected Doc to carry the Republican nomination, "but that will happen, we think, because the field is so large and Hastings' views appeal to a core group of deeply conservative individuals."[13] The *Yakima Herald-Republic* at the time did not endorse candidates for office.

Doc's strategy was to do well in the Tri-Cities, win Grant County, hope that Sullivan and Almon split the vote in populous Yakima County, and come in second in the Chelan, Douglas, and Okanagan Counties. That was exactly what happened.

When the results of the primary came in on the night of September 15, Doc was the top vote getter with 23.86 percent of the vote. Inslee was second with 22.61 percent on the basis of a late surge in ballots from Yakima County, and Jesernig came in third with 21.69 percent.

In the run-up to the general election, both candidates painted the other as an extremist. Inslee claimed Doc's opposition to abortion put him in the right-wing camp of televangelists Pat Robertson and Jerry Falwell. Doc pointed to Inslee's liberal voting record and asserted he was out of step with Eastern Washington values. Inslee had also been endorsed by an anti-war group that opposed the nuclear site at Hanford. But the sharpest difference between the two men was their stance on abortion, an issue that was almost a litmus test in 1992 separating conservative and liberal.

The campaign was not without its lighter moments. In a parade in Moses Lake, Doc was standing on a flatbed truck, waving to the crowd along the parade route, when Inslee decided to hop on the truck and stood behind Doc, imitating his arm-waving motions without Doc noticing he was there. "The crowd was wild with laughter, and Doc thought that they were going wild for him," Inslee recalled with a smile.[14]

The *Tri-City Herald* supported Inslee. In its general election endorsement, the paper's editorial board expressed its concern that "the election of Doc Hastings of Pasco, a conservative Republican, could jeopardize vital Tri-City projects and interests." Referring to the Democratic control of Congress, they claimed that whereas "Inslee will find a welcome, Hastings will find a wall."[15] Again, the *Yakima Herald-Republic* did not endorse, opting to write a story comparing the two candidates and letting voters decide for themselves.

When the polls closed on the evening of November 3, 1992, Inslee narrowly prevailed, helped along, Doc thought, by the national news media's reporting that Bill Clinton was winning the national election even before polls closed in Washington State. The gathering of Doc's supporters at Kennewick's Clover Island Inn was a muted affair. Inslee received 50.84 percent of the vote, while Doc received 49.16 percent, a difference of only 1.68 percent. Inslee agreed the Clinton victory probably played a role in his victory but felt his personal connection to the community was the most important factor.[16]

It took Doc a month or so to decompress and allow the disappointment of his loss to sink in. Claire took the defeat harder than he did. Looking back, Doc remembered, "Having lost the election, it's amazing how little interest people have in you.[17] He consoled himself with one of his favorite Teddy Roosevelt quotations:

It is not the critic who counts; not the man who points out how the strong man stumbles, or where the doer of deeds could have done them better. The credit belongs to the man who is actually in the arena, whose face is marred by dust and sweat and blood; who strives valiantly; who errs, who comes short again and again, because there is no effort without error and shortcoming; but who does actually strive to do the deeds; who knows great enthusiasms, the great devotions; who spends himself in a worthy cause.[18]

WHILE DOC HASTINGS WAS CONSOLING HIMSELF in Pasco, Bill Clinton was rejoicing in what had once been thought to be an unlikely victory over Ronald Reagan's successor, George H. W. Bush. The patrician Bush—probably the most qualified man ever to be elected president of the United States—had enjoyed approval ratings of 80 percent only a year and a half earlier during the First Gulf War, but he encountered unexpected problems in his bid for reelection. Foremost was the fact that the Cold War was over, negating his overwhelming advantage in foreign policy experience. The country was demobilizing and focusing its attention on domestic policy and balancing the budget. The Clinton campaign staff in Little Rock understood this. Its main campaign theme was scrawled on a prominent whiteboard at its headquarters, "It's the economy, stupid!"[19]

During the 1988 campaign, George Bush had promised, "No new taxes, read my lips!"[20] Now, four years later, the national economy was in recession, and the economic stimulus package that Bush was promoting included some tax increases. Bush had also reneged on his campaign promise not to raise taxes when he tried to compromise with Congress on lowering the federal deficit. That alienated many of the conservative congressional Republicans led by Newt Gingrich of Georgia, as well as others across the heartland, even though conditions then had been much different than they were in 1992. Bush bridled under the criticism and confided to his diary, "Newt is out there, part of the leadership, saying he wasn't elected to support the President . . . and those right-wingers love it. . . . It just makes me furious."[21]

Bush also faced opposition from Christian conservatives and a third-party bid from fellow Texan Ross Perot, who many felt had entered the race only to spoil Bush's reelection bid. In the end, Clinton rallied his divided party and attracted large numbers of African American and younger voters to win with 43 percent of the vote. But the effect of having Perot in the race meant that in many congressional districts Clinton's margins of victory were often lower than those of the congressional Democrats who were elected at the same time. Although losing nine seats in the House, the Democrats retained control of both the House and the Senate continuing the political monopoly they had enjoyed since 1954.

—

In 1992, William Jefferson Clinton was forty-six, the third youngest man and the first baby boomer to assume the presidency. The former Arkansas governor had defied political convention by picking another southerner and moderate, Senator Al Gore of Tennessee, as his running mate. They billed themselves as "New Democrats" and persuaded many former Reagan Democrats to return to the fold to vote for them.

Almost immediately, Bill Clinton began to send mixed messages about just what kind of Democrat he would be. He signed the Family and Medical Leave Act, which had passed with broad bipartisan support, but then, two days later, he reversed restrictions on family planning programs promoted by Reagan and Bush. In his first State of the Union address—a speech that political cartoonist David Horsey wrote in an op-ed in the *Seattle Post Intelligencer* could have been written by the House Republicans—he announced a plan to raise taxes and reduce the federal deficit in order to spur the growth of the economy.[22] In August, he doubled down on these themes by signing the Deficit Reduction Act, which cut spending and raised taxes on the wealthiest taxpayers. House Republicans wanted deeper cuts to entitlements, but the Democratic majority passed it without a single Republican vote.[23]

Clinton and the Democratic Congress appeared to be on a roll, but the American people soon balked at the pace of change that was being driven by the White House. In September 1993, the president proposed a major healthcare reform plan, developed by a task force led by his wife, Hillary. "Hillarycare," as it was derisively called, was probably doomed from the start. Conservatives in both parties saw it as governmental overreach, and special interest groups whose incomes were threatened, as well as many of the public who were bombarded by negative media messages funded by the proposal's opponents, criticized it.

After much consideration and emotional discussion, the president pushed the North American Free Trade Agreement (NAFTA) through both houses of Congress in November 1993, and signed it into law on December 8, alienating many protectionist Democrats from important Midwestern states in the process. Constitutional conservatives and gun owners from both parties were outraged when an assault weapons ban passed as a part of a broader crime bill in September 1994. Clinton signed it the same day. He dismayed social conservatives and some high-ranking military leaders when he supported an unsuccessful policy to allow gays to serve openly in the military.

DOC CLOSELY FOLLOWED THE EVENTS in the nation's capital, where now Congressman Inslee voted with the Democratic majority on many of these controversial issues. Doc began to ask himself the question, "Am I interested in running again?'" He decided he was.

However, if he were going to run again, he would have to clear the field of other potential Republican candidates, eliminating a divisive primary. He assumed that most of his potential opponents were serving in the legislature, so he travelled to Olympia to talk with each of them to ascertain their interest in running, while telling them of his. The two candidates that Doc thought were most likely to run, House Speaker Clyde Ballard from Wenatchee and Barb Lisk from Zillah, told him they were not interested. Lisk would later become Doc's district director.

The only Republican who expressed an interest in the race was Kraig Naasz, a Yakima native who had served as the communications and legislative director for several members of the Washington congressional delegation, including Sid Morrison. Naasz informed Doc that he was seriously considering entering the race, forcing Doc to move up his formal announcement to December 1993. Naasz ultimately decided not to run and later became a very successful trade association executive in Washington, DC.

—

For his 1994 campaign, Doc pulled together the same core team that had supported him in 1992. Darryl Howard was again the campaign manager. Brett Bader served as his political consultant. Ralph Holbrook and Skip Schoff proved helpful in Yakima County. But the real test of Doc's campaign was how much money he could raise. To attract funding from the National Republican Campaign Committee (NRCC), he had to raise at least one hundred thousand dollars by June 1, 1994. An early fundraising letter netted positive results. "Fortunately, there were enough people who had faith in me and contributed early on."[24] Ultimately, the campaign was able to raise approximately four hundred thousand dollars.[25]

The issues that defined the second Inslee-Hastings race were similar to those in 1992, but the overall political metrics had changed for Inslee and the Democrats. The party in power normally loses seats in a midterm election, and Bill Clinton's activist policies weren't winning over many voters in Eastern Washington. Inslee represented one of the most government-dependent districts in Washington State but found that a close working relationship with the government was not necessarily a strong selling point in a year of growing discontent with big government.

Doc kept Inslee on the defensive because of his support for Clinton's proposed healthcare reform program. The issue never made it into bill form, but the many questions about it were exploited to the maximum by the Republicans, who played on the voters' fears of the unknown and concerns about the size of government. Inslee had a well-deserved reputation as an environmentalist but found himself having to defend the 1973 Endangered Species Act, which was highly unpopular with many Eastern Washington farmers.

Inslee tried to get Doc into a debate on women's issues—a reprise of the 1992 campaign—but Doc declined. Darryl Howard called Inslee's challenge "a standard ploy by a desperate incumbent whose polling must show he's weak with women."[26] Inslee also challenged Doc over his votes to increase taxes during his time in the legislature. Doc responded that those votes had been for temporary measures addressing the state's dire fiscal situation.

A continuing issue in the district involved the shortage of agricultural workers. Local farmers had relied on illegal farmworkers from Mexico and Central America for years. The Simpson-Mazzoli Act, which made it illegal to knowingly hire undocumented immigrants, had been signed by President Reagan in 1986, but its provisions were still being implemented. Doc sympathized with the plight of the farmers. "You can't ask the farmers to be a policeman," he said, but he opposed any form of amnesty.[27]

Gun control was an even bigger issue in 1994 than it had been in 1992 because of the Democrats' proposed federal assault weapons ban. Inslee held town hall forums in the district and asked for feedback from his constituents. Ultimately, he had voted for the ban. The way Inslee saw the issue, it came down to his job or the life of a child. The night before the vote, he told his wife, Trudi, "Tomorrow the assault weapons ban [vote] is probably going to cost me my job."

She responded, "So be it."[28]

Inslee, like other incumbents, was also subject to the vagaries of the congressional schedule, which was famously flexible under Democratic leadership. Members never knew when they would be able to come home and campaign. Doc's campaign organizers took advantage of the situation, scheduling debates and other joint meetings for a Thursday or Friday when they knew Inslee would be tired from flying on a red-eye from Washington, DC.

That strategy worked on at least two occasions. In one debate in Yakima, Inslee noted how hard his job was because of having to fly across the country, and at another radio debate in the Tri-Cities, Doc caught the incumbent unprepared by asking him what a series of obscure governmental acronyms stood for. Inslee didn't know. It was payback for a previous debate in Yakima when Inslee had made political hay out of the fact that Doc couldn't remember what LIGO—the Laser Interferometer Gravitational-Wave Observatory at Hanford—stood for. Doc had responded, "LIGO has to do with—I can't pronounce the *I*—intergrav something. It's laser . . . I can't tell you. It's inferom something. The *I* is . . ."[29] Doc had been embarrassed, but he wasn't the first to get tripped up by LIGO's name . Sam Volpentest, the legendary Tri-Cities lobbyist and go-to guy for Hanford funding, used to sit in his office at TRIDEC for hours at a time, repeating the name—Laser Interferometer Gravitational-Wave Observatory—over and over so he could say it flawlessly when he was lobbying Congress for funding in the early 1990s.[30]

Doc's campaign hired Terry Cooper, a political operative in Washington, DC, to do opposition research on Inslee. Cooper found out that Inslee had not been attending some of the meetings of the Agriculture Committee on which he served. Roll was not taken at the meetings, but a committee member's absence was noted. Doc's campaign sent out a press release to the agricultural areas of the district, noting that Inslee hadn't been attending all the meetings. Inslee shot back with a release that argued it was not worthwhile to attend meetings that dealt with matters that were unimportant to his Central Washington constituency, like the tsetse fly. Hastings had Cooper check the agendas of the meetings Inslee had missed, but the tsetse fly hadn't been on any of them. That called for another press release from the Hastings camp.

On September 20, the voters went to the polls in the 1994 primary. Doc received 49.5 percent of the votes and carried eight of the ten counties in the district. Inslee, who had a Democratic primary opponent—strangely enough, the president of the Kennewick chapter of the John Birch Society—received only 41.2 percent. Doc responded to the lopsided victory with more caution than he probably felt. "I've never been one that banks on the primary vote. They can show trends, but that's all they do."[31] Doc was counting on the fact that the voter turnout in the general election would be significantly higher than it had been in the primary—and would mean even more Republican votes.[32]

Because of Jennifer Dunn's influence in Washington with the congressional Republican leadership (she had been elected to Congress in 1992) and the demographics of the district, the Fourth Congressional District was firmly in the crosshairs of Republican strategists in 1994. John Boehner of Ohio remembered that "it was a seat we thought we could pick up. The National Republican Campaign Committee had a list of seats we thought we could win, but each of us ran our own political operation and our own due diligence. Jay Inslee just wasn't a good fit for that district. Doc, having been an experienced legislator and having run his own business, looked like a winner to me."[33]

The rock stars of the Republican congressional conference came out to Washington to campaign for Doc. Newt Gingrich of Georgia, Bob Walker of Pennsylvania, Tom DeLay and Dick Armey of Texas, Duncan Hunter of California, Bill McCullum of Florida, and Boehner all campaigned for Doc in the district. Senator Bob Dole of Kansas, who would be his party's presidential standard-bearer in two years, also campaigned for Doc. "You better start packing," he said, turning toward Doc at a rally attended by four hundred people at the Tri-Cities Airport. "Your opponent better start packing, too."[34] When Gingrich came to the Tri-Cities, Doc had asked Joe Gaylord, one of Gingrich's staff members, if he thought they would win back the majority. "We're going to win, and *you* are a part of that."[35]

Of course, it helped that Doc's district abutted House Speaker Tom Foley's. The Republicans saw Foley as vulnerable, and his district was one of their prime targets. Foley had long opposed efforts to impose term limits on Washington State's elected officials. In 1992, Washington's voters approved a term limit ban and Foley sued, ultimately winning the case in federal court and obtaining a ruling that said the states did not have authority to impose term limits on their elected officials. The decision resulted in the Republicans adding a provision in the Contract with America calling for a constitutional amendment to impose term limits nationally and painting Foley as a poster child for the Democrats' insatiable desire to remain in office. Term limits were a major campaign issue in the 1994 election and would continue to remain an issue for as long as Doc served in Congress.

Four days before the general election, Doc created a last-minute stir when he pledged during a television debate that he would not accept a congressional pension. "I don't believe a public servant should get rich off the congressional retirement system. Only nineteen members of Congress have had the courage to say no to this pension. I'll be one more." He claimed that his pensions from his business and his eight years in the legislature would tide him over. He said his decision was in keeping with the Contract with America. "I don't consider myself a professional politician," he said. "I think this is the way our Founding Fathers wanted our country to be run."[36]

Unimpressed, the *Tri-City Herald* again endorsed Inslee, arguing that "even were control of the House to switch to the Republicans, we need someone who can talk to the [Clinton] administration, which in the two years it has remaining could wreak havoc on the Tri-Cities economy .... Hastings calls that political blackmail. It is political reality."[37] The *Yakima Herald-Republic*, now with a new publisher and a new policy, also endorsed Inslee.[38]

Inslee got under Doc's skin with a last-minute series of radio and TV ads showing an image of Bugs Bunny asking, "What's up, Doc?" and listing a series of tax increases Hastings had voted for in the state legislature. Doc complained about a copyright violation to no avail, but the ads succeeded in drawing him off message for a week or so.[39] As the two campaigns traded charges and counter-charges, Sid Morrison, who had earlier endorsed Hastings, suggested the race was now Inslee's to lose because of the district's history of supporting the incumbent.

Mark Walker, the political writer for the *Herald-Republic*, perhaps expressed the exasperation of many of his readers at the end of the bitter and highly partisan campaign when he wrote, "Whoever wins Tuesday's election, one thing is certain: These guys are no Sid Morrison, who in twelve years in Congress became known for his easy manner and political savvy."[40] What Walker had no way of knowing was that the tone of the election was but a hint of the national political climate to come.

The general election was held on November 8, 1994. Doc and his supporters gathered at the Pasco Red Lion Hotel believing they would win. It was a completely different atmosphere from 1992, and it felt good. Before the polls closed in Washington, anchors for the national TV networks were calling one congressional race after another in the East and the Midwest for the Republicans. Local TV and print media reporters were on hand, asking for comment and analysis.

By the end of the evening, Republicans had picked up more congressional seats in Washington State—including Tom Foley's, the first sitting Speaker of the House to be defeated since 1862—than in any other state in the nation. Doc Hastings won with a surprising 53.3 percent to Inslee's 46.6 percent. In an evening where humor must have been in short supply, the defeated congressman called Doc to concede the election—collect. "I thought it was a chance to bring humor into a difficult situation," Inslee said, "and it was a mark of honor that Doc Hastings took the charges."[41]

Inslee might have been out of touch with the changing mood of the voters in this district, but he got caught up in a national wave election. He did an accurate job of analyzing his defeat when he told a *Tri-City Herald* reporter: "I did everything I could. I worked as hard as I could; I used every fiber of my body. I don't think anyone could have done more for Hanford. But this was just part of a national trend. I could have cured cancer and the common cold, and I don't think it would have changed this election."[42]

"He made mistakes, and we took advantage of them," Doc said."[43] Behind the scenes, others questioned whether Inslee had really been prepared for his reelection campaign.

The year 1994 was a wave election of historic proportions. Republicans picked up fifty-four seats in the House of Representatives and became the new majority. They picked up nine seats in the Senate—not enough to gain a majority but enough to make things more difficult for the ruling Democrats. The front page of the *Washington Post* featured a wide-eyed Newt Gingrich under the headline, "A Historic Republican Triumph: GOP Captures Congress."[44]

BEHIND THAT DRAMATIC HEADLINE was a brilliant and visionary concept called the Contract with America. The Contract, as it became known, was the result of many people's efforts, but it would always be indelibly linked to one man, then the House minority whip, Newt Gingrich of Georgia. He and Dick Armey of Texas unveiled the idea during a snowy February weekend in 1994 at a meeting of the Republican House conference leadership when they met in the historic seaport town of Salisbury, Maryland.

Gingrich and Armey began by showing polling results that clearly demonstrated there was a wide divide between the American people and their elected officials across racial, income, geographic, and cultural lines. They argued that in 1992 the Republican Party had been largely defined by the Clinton campaign as the party of the rich and was out of touch with the average voter. Could they create a simple document that would clearly and concisely spell out a vision of the Republicans' platform and show how they would change the direction of government if they won the next election?

Utilizing input from a variety of Republican think tanks, first, they formulated a basic philosophy based on individual liberty, economic opportunity, limited government, personal responsibility, and national security.[45] Second, Gingrich proposed a creative strategy that called on all Republicans running for the House in 1994—both incumbents and new candidates—to sign the Contract with America. If the Republican philosophy could be successfully communicated to the public through the language of the Contract and voters were sufficiently weary of the Democrats after forty years in power, the Republicans would gain control of the House in the upcoming midterm election.

Gingrich and his team drafted eight specific reforms that a new Republican House would pass on its first day in office. Over the following months, eleven working groups drafted specific bills that would implement their philosophy and promised to bring them to a vote within the first one hundred days of the new session. They included a balanced budget, a limitation on taxes, and a line-item veto amendment to the Constitution, a strong anti-crime package, prohibiting welfare to minor mothers and denying aid for additional children born while on welfare, a five-hundred-dollar-per-child tax credit, repealing the marriage tax penalty, creating savings accounts for middle-class families, a prohibition of US troops serving under UN command and a restoration of national security funding, raising the Social Security earnings limit, approval of a series of business incentives, tort reform, and a constitutional amendment to enforce term limits on elected officials. Only proposals that polled higher than 60 percent in nationwide opinion polls were included. The authors avoided divisive social issues like abortion, school prayer, or Second Amendment Rights that many conservatives would have liked to include.[46]

Major Garrett, a congressional reporter for the conservative *Washington Times* before he went on to a television career at CNN, Fox News, and CBS, had interviewed a senior Republican congressional aide at the time the Contract was being compiled. He was told that the Contract was meant to be a political document, not a governing document. "We don't care if the Senate passes any of the items in the Contract," the aide said. "It would be preferable, but it's not necessary. If the freshmen [Republicans] do everything the Contract says, they'll be in excellent shape for 1996, and we can add to our majority in Congress. But if we compromise the Contract in order to pass laws, we will lose support."[47]

—

The Contract challenged the idea that all politics are local. For the first time, a clear description of the Republican philosophy influenced congressional races throughout the nation. On a fundraising trip back to Washington, DC, in the summer of 1994, Gingrich had said to Doc, "You have to come back in September and sign the Contract." Doc put the date down in his calendar.[48]

On a warm, sunny afternoon on September 27, 1994, 367 Republican congressional candidates stood on the west front of the US Capitol to have their picture taken behind Newt Gingrich. Afterward, they filed off in small groups to sign the document. "It nationalized an election in a way that had never been done before," Doc said. "It set a common tone for all Republican candidates and informed the voters about what we would do if we were elected."[49]

CHAPTER SIX

"It Was All So New to Me"

★

THE EUPHORIA OF HIS ELECTION VICTORY gave way to reality as Doc and his family considered the impending changes in their lives. They needed a break from the frenzy of the campaign trail, and Hawaii, their favorite holiday destination, provided it. Within days, Doc and Claire were in Maui. With so much on their minds, their vacation wasn't as relaxing as it could have been, and five days was all the time that could be spared. "I'm not going back to Hawaii again if it's only for five days," Claire declared.[1]

The children, too, were turning new pages in their lives. Kirsten had met her future husband during the campaign. They married the following year. Doc's youngest daughter, Petrina, was living in Seattle and working two jobs to make ends meet after graduating from Eastern Washington University. She had just completed a three-month unpaid internship for an English member of the European Parliament in Brussels. Colin was a freshman at Seattle University.

The two weeks following Doc and Claire's return from Hawaii were filled with telephone calls to Jennifer Dunn and others about potential committee assignments and countless other details. The experience was overwhelming. "It was all so new to me. I didn't know a thing," Doc said.[2] He arranged the sale of the family business to his brother, Regan, and resigned from the board of the Yakima Federal Savings and Loan Association.

Then Doc and Claire flew back to Washington, DC, for the congressional orientation and organizational meetings that were held between

Thanksgiving and Christmas. He was joined there by 230 returning and newly elected Republicans who had won election in what would come to be called the "Republican Revolution." For the first time in forty years, the Republicans controlled the House of Representatives, having gained the largest number of seats since 1946. Doc recalled: "Those were really intense, long days. We met in a conference room of the Cannon House Office Building, and they went over everything you could possibly imagine. They were nothing like the rather perfunctory orientation briefings I had received in the Washington legislature."[3]

—

Doc and Claire somehow found time to interview and hire a staff. "We were given a stack of applications for potential staff members about a foot high," he remembered. "Generally, these were people who had worked in some capacity for a member who had resigned or been defeated and wanted to continue to work on the Hill. I wanted some people who had ties to the Northwest, which I thought would be important."[4] Doc was advised that his first hire should be his chief of staff—preferably someone who had already served in that capacity for another House member. Doc narrowed the selection to Ed Cassidy and Doug Riggs.

Cassidy, forty-one, was a 1975 graduate of the Jesuit-affiliated Fairfield University in Connecticut and had received a master's degree in public administration from American University in Washington, DC. He had worked on the staffs of four Republican congressmen, including a stint as chief of staff for Martin Hoke, a congressman from Ohio. He'd been a deputy chief of staff and deputy assistant secretary in the Department of Interior, a staffer for the National Republican Campaign Committee, and finally, a member of the campaign staff for George H. W. Bush during his 1992 campaign.[5] Cassidy was feisty, opinionated, and stubborn but also politically smart, loyal, and a talented administrator. He would work for Doc in various capacities for the next twelve years.[6]

Doug Riggs was just twenty-nine, a 1987 graduate of Lewis and Clark College in Portland with a degree in political science and a resume that included legislative positions on the staffs of three California congressmen. Doc initially offered the chief of staff position to Riggs but changed his mind after interviewing Cassidy and learning of his far greater experience. Doc and Cassidy called Riggs and offered him the legislative director's job. Riggs accepted immediately. "It was probably best for me," Riggs admitted, "and best for Doc because Ed was more of a thirty-thousand-foot, administrative, big-picture guy and I was more of a ten-to-fifteen-foot, in-the-weeds guy, so it was a good combination."[7] Riggs also assumed responsibility for the important Hanford portfolio.

Doc and Cassidy hired the remaining staff positions. Todd Ungerecht, a thirty-year-old Pasco native and graduate of Gonzaga Law School, served as their legislative assistant in charge of hot-button social issues. He had worked on Doc's 1992 and 1994 campaigns and would manage his 1996 campaign. Darryl Howard, who had been Doc's campaign manager in 1992 and 1994, became his district director. Doc also hired Sharlyn Berger, who had been with him in every campaign since he had run for president of the Jaycees. She would remain with him for the entire twenty years he served in Congress.

"Ed Cassidy was a tough manager," Ungerecht remembered. "He expected his staff to work hard and expected a lot out of them. He would occasionally yell at you, but he would reward you as well. Doc didn't get involved in the details of personnel issues. Ed took care of that."[8]

—

The next step was finding an office. A *Washington Post* staff writer once wrote that if Capitol Hill were a prison, office suites would be its cigarettes.[9] Offices with a convenient location and a good view were rare. At exactly 9:00 a.m. on the Friday of orientation week, the new members or their designees met in the Rayburn House Office Building to draw small numbered metal disks out of a box. The number determined their draft order in the traditional House office lottery. New members and their staffs then had four hours to scout out the available offices based on their knowledge of the layouts of the various office buildings or a map. Location mattered. A conveniently located office might save a member eighty or ninety hours a year spent walking to and from the Capitol to vote.

Doc's low number allowed him to select Suite 1229 in the Longworth House Building. A visitor entered the building from Independence Avenue, climbed a flight of stairs, and walked down the right side of the corridor to reach it. The immediate view consisted of looking out over a small park on top of the Rayburn Building's parking garage. Above it was a wide view of Arlington, Virginia, in the distance beyond the city. There were three rooms—a reception area with desks for the chief of staff and scheduler, Doc's office, and a room called the "bullpen" that housed everyone else. A small space originally designed for storage and referred to as the "broom closet" was later claimed by Ed Cassidy.

Members could paint the walls of their offices one of six bland wall colors approved by the architect of the Capitol or another color if the member bought the paint. The previous occupant's furniture remained in place, but a new member could supplement or replace it from the piles of surplus funiture left in the corridors by departing members. The exception was the member's desk. New members were entitled to a new desk, which they could take with them when they left—as long as they paid for the original cost of the desk and the cost of shipping it to a new location.[10]

—

Another important task during orientation was the selection of committee assignments. A member might know which committees he or she wanted to serve on, but the trick was convincing the leadership to appoint you to them. Each member could serve on two of the House's twenty standing committees. Almost from the hour of their election, all new members began lobbying whomever they thought could help them land their choice of committee assignments. Most were disappointed and didn't receive their top choices in their first term.

Doc knew what he wanted: "There were two issues I knew we had to address. Hanford cleanup needed to go forward, but in a way that was cost effective. We also had to resolve the Yakima River water storage problem. If you get a drought, the junior districts don't get water. There hadn't been any new water storage developed there since the 1930s."[11]

Many wondered why Doc didn't seek an appointment to the Agriculture Committee. His reasoning was that most of the farmers in his district didn't receive federal subsidies for their crops. "We didn't have to worry about price supports except for wheat. Potato farmers don't want subsidies. Besides, Natural Resources had jurisdiction over the Bonneville Power Administration that provided power throughout the Pacific Northwest."[12]

The committee assignments were made by the Republican Steering Committee. Chaired by the Speaker, it included the entire party leadership, the chairs of the six most powerful committees, fourteen regional representatives, and three members from Doc's large freshman class. Votes were heavily weighted toward the leadership's desired outcomes.

"Doc was older than a lot of other people in his class," remembered John Boehner of Ohio, who would become the new Republican conference chair.[13] "Not a lot older, but he was older. He had the experience of serving in the legislature and—let's put it this way—he was a mature adult. He knew how to be a team player. Those are the kinds of things that the leadership and the members value."[14]

To his relief, Doc received appointments to both Natural Resources and Armed Services, the two committee assignments he had sought. Doug Riggs remembered: "There is always more demand for seats on [the Armed Services Committee] than there is a supply of seats, so we weren't initially certain that we'd get such a prime assignment, but Doc, Ed, and I all made contacts with the Speaker's office and leadership. Doc lobbied his colleagues, and as I recall, Slade Gorton and his staff were also helpful."[15]

———

During orientation week, another newly elected congressman, Sam Brownback of Kansas, approached Doc to see if he would be interested in running for the position of representative of the freshman class to the House Leadership, which consisted of the Speaker, majority leader, majority whip, and conference chairman. That member sits in on all leadership meetings and provides two-way communication between the leadership and the members of the freshman class. The position had both real and implied clout, not only because it opened an avenue of access between the member and the leadership team but also because it offered inside knowledge and a chance to express personal views at the leadership meetings.

Doc agreed to run, realizing that "if you're at the table, and issues come up, at some point you're going to develop an opinion about what's going on and then you can make your observations known."[16] Doc was defeated by Sue Myrick of North Carolina for the position, but that race continued a pattern of how he approached public service that would continue for the rest of his congressional career.

The Republican conference (the Democrats called their counterpart entity a caucus) organized during orientation week as well. The top two positions were foregone conclusions. Newt Gingrich of Georgia was going to be Speaker, and Dick Armey of Texas was going to be majority leader. The third leadership position was the party whip, which was contested between Tom DeLay of Texas, Bob Walker of Pennsylvania, and Bill McCollum of Florida. Doc supported Walker, but he made sure he went to both DeLay and McCollum in advance to tell them he was supporting Walker. There was a similar situation in the race for conference chairman, where John Boehner was running against Duncan Hunter of California.

Boehner had arrived in the House in 1991 from his suburban Cincinnati, Ohio, district. Almost immediately, the newcomer had established a reputation as a reformer by exposing the operations of the House Bank and Post Office, leading to indictment of the powerful Democratic chairman of the House Ways and Means Committee, Dan Rostenkowski of Illinois. Doc recalled: "Both of them had come out and campaigned for me. I went to John Boehner and told him that I was going to support him. Then I had to go to Duncan Hunter and tell him that I was supporting Boehner. But that's the way I've always done things. I have to assume that it impressed upon them the fact that I was a straight shooter."[17]

Rounding out the leadership team were two unelected positions. Dennis Hastert of Illinois, a protégé of DeLay's, was appointed chief deputy whip, and Bill Paxton from Western New York, served as a member of leadership because of his job as chairman of the National Republican Congressional Committee.

—

Doc and Claire needed to find somewhere to live temporarily, and Jennifer Dunn came to the rescue. She had just moved into a new condominium and had three months remaining on her leased apartment near the Pentagon City Mall in Arlington, and Doc was able assume the lease.

After the intense days of orientation and organization, Doc and Claire flew back to Pasco just in time to pack up and enjoy a last round of farewells with friends and neighbors and then fly back to the nation's capital. They arrived there dead tired and without their luggage on New Year's Eve. Undeterred, they celebrated at the nearby Ritz Carlton Hotel, still wearing the same jeans they'd travelled in. The next morning, they checked to see that everything had been moved into Doc's office and spent the next two days with their children, who had driven their parents' car back to Washington, DC, and treated themselves to a little sightseeing.

—

Then it was Tuesday, January 3, 1995, the day of the swearing-in of the 104th Congress. After a reception at the Capitol, the clerk of the previous Congress called the House to order and asked all members in attendance to acknowledge their presence by inserting their voting cards into the electronic voting machines located throughout the chamber. After a quorum had been established, the two party conference chairmen nominated their candidates for Speaker of the House. John Boehner of Ohio nominated Newt Gingrich of Georgia. Vic Fazio of California nominated Richard Gephardt of Missouri, the majority leader in the former Congress and now the highest-ranking Democrat after the defeat of the previous Speaker, Tom Foley, for House minority leader. After the nominations were closed, it was time to vote. The clerk called the roll of the House members in alphabetical order.

"Ms. Harmon."

The California Democrat responded, "Mr. Gephardt."

"Mr. Hastert."

The future Republican Speaker from Illinois, declared, "Mr. Gingrich."

"Mr. Hastings of Florida."

Democrat Alcee Hastings said, "Mr. Gephardt."

"Mr. Hastings of Washington."

Doc responded, "Mr. Gingrich."

As a result of the Republican landslide, the result of the vote was a foregone conclusion. Newt Gingrich was the newly elected Speaker of the House. The senior member of the Congress, John Dingell of Michigan, rose from his accustomed seat in the second row and went to the well to swear in the new Speaker.

At the Speaker's rostrum, Gephardt and Gingrich stood side by side. Grasping the gavel, Gephardt spoke: "So with partnership but with purpose, I pass this great gavel of our government. With resignation but resolve, I hereby end forty years of Democratic rule of this House."[18]

Gingrich then asked the newly elected members to stand, raise their right hand, and affirm the oath of office, which he read aloud:

> I do solemnly swear that I will support and defend the Constitution of the United States against all enemies, foreign and domestic; that I will bear true faith and allegiance to the same; that I take this obligation freely, without any mental reservation or purpose of evasion, and that I will well and faithfully discharge the duties of the office on which I am about to enter. So help me God.[19]

Richard "Doc" Hastings, the newly elected representative to Congress from Washington's Fourth Congressional District, responded, "I do."[20]

As Doc took in the magnificent scene around him, he looked up at the Speaker's rostrum and set a personal goal. Someday he would sit there and preside over the Congress as Speaker pro tempore, just as he had done when he had served in the Washington State legislature.[21] As he observed the other members around him and their friends and families in the packed gallery, he thought, "There are 265 million people in the United States, and only 435 of them are elected to serve in Congress at any one time. I'm one of them. Not too bad for a kid from Pasco."[22]

—

In a highly unusual step, that first session ran long into the night, passing after debate four or five provisions of the Contract with America that had been introduced six weeks before the election. The session ran so long that when Doc drove away from the Capitol for the first time in the early hours of the morning, he took the wrong turn on the freeway and ended up way out in Virginia before making his way back to the apartment in Pentagon City.

The early pace of the new Congress was just as hectic as the orientation week had been. There were endless long and late-night sessions as the new leadership pushed the Contract with America reforms through the House. A few of the new freshman members had served in public or appointed office, but no one could be prepared for the thousands—indeed the tens of thousands—of issues, variations on issues, bills, amendments, and potential votes that awaited them in Congress. Doug Riggs likened it to drinking through a fire hose.

—

Newt Gingrich encouraged members not to live in Washington but to go home each weekend and campaign for reelection. After three months of apartment living, however, Doc and Claire decided they needed a place to call home. "I gave Claire a number, and she started looking for a place to buy," Doc remembered. "After about two weeks, she came back and told me, 'This isn't going to work.'"[23] Then, quite by coincidence, she found a condominium located almost across the street from their apartment in Pentagon City.

The red brick Southampton Condominiums were located less than a mile from the Pentagon and looked more like a neighborhood of row houses than a condominium development. Built in 1979, the buildings featured a tall mansard roof that extended below the third-floor windows. An outside stairway led to the upper unit, while the lower unit's entrance was at ground level and included a basement. Their unit had three bedrooms on the top floor, two and a half baths, and a full-sized kitchen. Doc bought it on favorable terms at the bottom of a bad real estate market, helped out by a loan from the Yakima Federal Savings and

Loan Association, which made an exception for its former board member by financing a property in Virginia.

Claire remained in Washington for the first month. During Doc's first term and much of his second, they commuted to and from Pasco. Doc might be returning home for some event in the district while Claire travelled to Washington, DC. She remembered, "After a while, I figured out that I wasn't seeing that much of him anyway, so I said, 'You know, if I'm going to be alone, I'd rather be alone at home,'" [24] Still, she joined the Republican Congressional Spouses Club and the bipartisan Congressional Club, but it was hard to get acquainted because many of the most active members lived in nearby states and were rarely in the capital.

The condominium became an important refuge. They called it their Northern Virginia vacation home. Doc remembered:

> Later on, after a long evening session, [it was important] to be able to go to some place that was mine where I could relax, rather than being in a hotel room. We'd be in session until 7:30 or 8:00 at night, and [it was great] to be able to come back and have a glass of wine and watch a ball game. More than anything else, it was a place I could call home.
>
> After Claire left, the only time I ever cooked in the condo was on weekends. If we were in session on a Friday and a Monday, I'd just stay in DC, and if I'd stay, I'd often go up to Baltimore and see [my old friend from Pasco] Ron Grey because I knew we could have a cocktail and a wonderful dinner there.[25]

A CONGRESSIONAL OFFICE IS VERY MUCH like a small independent business. The office tends to assume the character of its elected member and operates with very little outside supervision. The staff are normally intensely loyal, agreeing with their member's politics and admiring him or her personally. Most importantly, the staff's future careers are often closely tied to their member's future success. If their member resigns or is defeated, they need to look for another job. In Doc's case, he and Ed Cassidy had chosen the staff well, and it was not long before other members, lobbyists, and knowledgeable observers concluded that they were among the best of Washington's House delegation. Most of them remained with him for long periods—always a mark of a happy staff in the high-stress, contentious work environment of Capitol Hill where many staffers put in eighty-hour weeks. When his staff did leave, they almost always went on to more responsible positions.

Doc and Claire did what they could to keep the staff happy. At first, office parties consisted of cake or cookies for a staff member's birthday in Doc's office. Since Doc wasn't big on sweets, the later fare was more likely to be fried chicken or takeout from one of a handful of favorite local restaurants while the conversation turned from work-related topics to NASCAR or other sports, the weather, or weekend plans. Ilene Clauson, Doc's longtime scheduler, reminisced:

> The food was always good—especially since the food in our cafeteria wasn't the greatest, but it became more about the camaraderie amongst our team. It, for certain, was a welcome way to keep office morale high.
>
> As co-workers, we all spent a lot of time together in a not very large space, and so it was nice to actually like the people we spent all of our time with and nice to have a boss who also liked to participate whenever his schedule permitted.[26]

Holidays were always special occasions. Claire would make homemade Almond Roca for everyone, accompanied by a small gift card, sent to the office with Doc, or she would bring it herself. Doc would always buy the staff lunch for the holidays, either out at a local restaurant or barbecue in the office. "For many years Doc and Claire hosted the staff holiday party at their condo, but maybe it was the combination of the red wine with their white carpet that made them rethink things," Clauson recalled.[27]

Sharlyn Berger, the mainstay of Doc's Pasco office, would host visiting members of the Washington, DC, staff at backyard parties at her home in Pasco when they visited the district during recess or one of the reelects.

—

Some newly elected members come to Congress with a predetermined personal or political agenda and a mind closed to anything else. They don't want to be challenged or hear anything other than what they believe to be true. Doc was different. He arrived in Washington, DC, with strong, well-defined political views, but he also had a curiosity that made him willing to be briefed about all the issues, so he could weigh them against his personal values and political philosophy. He wanted input, and he wanted to know what the options were.

He was curious about why and how things happened. When he served in the Washington legislature, he would often show up at Speaker Bill Polk's office at the close of the day's session. "Why did you do that, Speak?" he would ask. "I'd explain my reasoning, and Doc would invariably respond, 'As long as there's a reason,'" Polk recalled. "He was interested in the *art* of politics, not just the issues. His question was always, 'How do we *advance* those issues?'"[28]

Doc approached his staff the same way. He was deferential to them and to Ed's management style. He knew that many of them knew more about the day-to-day operations of Congress than he did, but he made sure they knew what his policies and priorities were. "You want to make sure that your staff understands where you're coming from on key policy issues because you're playing in a brand-new ball game with a very short period of time in which to get up to speed, and working with people that you really don't know."[29]

Ed Cassidy organized the office staff in a way that supplied Doc with the information he needed. Regularly scheduled staff meetings lasting an hour and a half or two hours were held three times a week. Participants included Ed, Doug, the three legislative assistants, and sometimes the legislative correspondent in charge of handling the constituent mail. Doug Riggs remembered the meetings well:

> There were very wide-ranging, free-flowing discussions. There were debates and disagreements at times over philosophy, tactics, and strategy—all of the above.
>
> There was an agenda: here's what's coming up on the floor; here's what the leadership is telling us; here are the bills that we're working on, including the latest updates; here's an update of what's in the mail and what people are calling in about. Doc encouraged it all and asked a lot of questions.[30]

Similar staff meetings were held whenever Doc returned from an extended recess during which he visited the district or traveled overseas. Doc would carefully go over his schedule and fill the staff in on what he had seen and heard, particularly if it was a complimentary constituent comment about the work done by a staff member.[31]

—

Like all congressional offices, Doc's was a busy place. His staff had to cope with the amazing volume of correspondence and telephone calls that flowed into his DC and district offices in the era before email. Riggs estimated that the DC office received twelve thousand to fourteen thousand pieces of mail a year. It arrived in huge plastic bins. The district office received its own large volume of mail, stuffed inside canvas bags. Each letter had to be read, its contents summarized on a special form, and a response prepared. Doc insisted that he see a representative sampling of the mail each week.

The telephone constantly rang. Doug Riggs recalled that when he arrived at the office, often before 7:00 a.m., several of the phones would already be ringing. He'd answer one, and it would be some farmer in Ephrata calling at 4:00 a.m. his time—before he went out to his tractor—wanting to let Doc know about the impact of some tariff that Japan wanted to impose on his crop. A contact form had to be filled out for each call and a response letter prepared. Sometimes the staff member could use a couple of standard paragraphs, but each letter had to be personalized. Often, when Doc heard about the call, he recognized the farmer as someone he'd met during a campaign swing around the district.

Doc told his staff that anyone who had taken the trouble to come to Washington, DC, to see him should be able to do so. "The problem was that at first we didn't know if fifteen minutes or a half hour or five or ten minutes would work," Doc said. "Very shortly, we figured out that we needed to limit the time slots to fifteen minutes."[32] He rarely had time to eat with a visiting constituent because he had no idea what the House schedule was going to be.

—

Many of the Democrats who had survived the 1994 election onslaught were bitter, and some of the departing members' staff trashed their offices before leaving. "There were some very, very hard feelings by some of the senior Democrats, particularly because they had been beat by Newt," explained Norm Dicks, one of only two Washington State Democrats to escape defeat in 1994. "I don't think any Democrat thought they were going to lose the majority."[33] At the same time, the new Republican majority—full of disdain for the past and faith in its vision of the future—was hardly in a mood to reach out to the remaining Democrats. Doc remembered: "There was almost no personal interaction between members of the opposing parties. You were either a Republican or a Democrat, and the divisions between the two were pretty deep."

The four-day workweek included sessions that lasted long into the night. Doc remembered: "Sometimes Tom DeLay or Dick Armey would order out BBQ or sandwiches. When the schedule permitted, we'd go out to dinner with other members, or if we had to remain in session, the cloakroom had a concession stand that offered hot dogs or sandwiches. "

Doc recalled that the stand was run by an elderly African American woman who had inherited the business from her father many years before. "You had to be really senior before Helen knew your name."[34]

—

Doc's freshman class included fifty-four new Republicans. A newly elected congressman from Minnesota, Gil Gutknecht, suggested that a high-quality, gold, class ring be created as a remembrance of their recent victory. Twenty members, including Doc, ordered the handsome rings. They had the Great Seal of the United States on top with "Contract with America" and the American flag on one side of the ring and the Capitol dome and "104th," signifying the current Congress, on the other. The member's name and district were engraved on the inside.

The members of Doc's class remained close, even after many of them left Congress. Ilene Clauson remembered that Doc's close friends included Bob Ehrlich of Maryland, a future governor; Roger Wicker of Mississippi and Lindsey Graham of South Carolina, both future US senators; and Ray LaHood of Illinois, a future secretary of transportation. "They had all served in their state legislatures, and that gave them a common bond."[35] Other friends included veteran congressmen: Hal Rogers of Kentucky, Jimmy Duncan of Tennessee, and Charlie Norwood from Georgia, who once arranged for Doc to play a round of golf at Augusta National Golf Course, the home of the Masters Tournament.

Golf outings between members, often sponsored by lobbyists, were common until new House ethics rules eliminated them in the late 1990s. John Boehner and Lindsey Graham were frequent golf partners. Doc remembered, "The southerners were fun to hang out with."[36]

Graham remembered Doc as an avid golfer, but frugal. "He's not wasting any of the taxpayer's money on the golf course, I can tell you. He was excruciatingly honest when it came to his score. If you played golf with Doc you better know the rules."[37]

—

Six of the nine members of the Washington House delegation were also brand new. The exceptions were Democrats Norm Dicks, elected in 1976, and Jim McDermott, elected in 1988, and Republican Jennifer Dunn, elected in 1992. Senator Patty Murray had been elected that same year, and it became known as the "Year of the Woman" in Washington State political circles. As the chair of the Washington State Republican Party from 1981 to 1992, Dunn had helped many new members, including Doc, win their victories and was instrumental in connecting them with the new House leadership.

George Nethercutt's status was a little different. He had defeated the sitting Speaker of the House, Tom Foley, and as a result became one of the stars of the new Republican freshman class. Others class standouts included football stars like Seattle Seahawks wide receiver Steve Largent and J. C. Watts of Oklahoma, the star quarterback of the Oklahoma Sooners, and entertainment personality Sonny Bono from California. Doc and George Nethercutt had a special relationship. "He was on Appropriations so we didn't interact all that much, but his dad and my mom had gone to high school together in Spokane, so we had a lot in common," Doc recalled.[38]

Given the residual bitterness among many of the remaining Democrats, there could easily have been more discord within the ranks of the Washington delegation. One reason there wasn't was the political professionalism of Norm Dicks. He had once been a staff aide and then chief of staff to Warren Magnuson, the legendary Washington senator, and he learned how Magnuson kept the delegation working together for thirty-six years. "Norm was an exception. He was a real pro. He and his staff were always willing to work with me," Doc said.[39]

Another reason was Doc's personality. He believed in the old adage that you can disagree without being disagreeable. Gary Petersen, vice president of government programs for TRIDEC, the Tri-Cities economic development agency, commented: "Doc avoided conflict whenever possible. He didn't like it. He would keep quiet and not openly take on the Democrats. Sometimes it takes a really big person NOT to pick a fight. He was the right guy, with the right attitude, at the right time."[40]

Republican Senator Slade Gorton and his staff were a great help during Doc's transition. Magnuson had established a tradition of holding delegation-wide breakfasts once a month, and Gorton continued the practice when he became the senior senator after Senator Henry M. Jackson's death in 1983. The meetings provided an opportunity to discuss state affairs and coordinate policy on those issues they could agree on. Gorton's rule was not to bring up contentious issues. Doc recalled: "Normally, [the issues] impacted Western Washington and didn't have much to do with my district with the exception of Hanford. It was a good opportunity to see where everyone was coming from. It was also a big help in getting acclimated after all of the new members were elected in 1994."[41]

—

While Doc Hastings was getting to know his new colleagues, he was also thinking of ways to be noticed by the new Republican leadership. Doc would run into them at various events and on the floor of the House and stop to chat. With his competent staff and his legislative experience, he never had to be reminded how to do his job. He was soon seen as someone who was trustworthy and whose views were valuable.

Like other freshmen members, Doc routinely presided over the mundane business of the House in order to learn the proper procedure and experience the flow of business. That often entailed being asked to preside over what is known as the Special Orders—the hour-long period at the end of the day when members could come down to the floor and talk about anything they wanted to. Some members, like New Gingrich, Michelle Bachman of Minnesota, or Joe Scarborough of Florida, first achieved their notoriety that way. But, "sitting there for hours and listening to someone pontificate could be very painful," Doc recalled.[42]

But later, when he was asked by Speaker Hastert to preside over the debate on substantive issues, he became known as a stickler when it came to respecting the rules and traditions of the House. "I believe that the courtesies of the institution are important—like talking in the third person. You don't want to direct your comments to other members, just to the Speaker."[43] Republican Cathy McMorris Rogers, first elected from Washington's Fifth Congressional District in 2004 and later chairman of the House Republican Conference, was in a position to see Doc in action: "No one knows the rules better than Doc Hastings, having served on the Rules Committee, and he was never afraid to give me little tips when I was not quite doing the rules right for the [Republican] conference. It is like, 'Cathy, you need to brush up here, study up, gotta do this right.'"[44]

It was something Doc appreciated doing and enjoyed, just as he had when he had presided over the Washington House. "I think that raised my credibility with members because I really tried to be even-handed. Even [future Speaker] Nancy Pelosi of California told me I was fair."[45]

—

Doc found ways to reach out to other members. He observed that the Texans always sat together when Congress was in session. Many of the southerners sat in the front of the chamber, and often the really conservative members would sit in the back. Doc would intentionally move around and sit next to different groups and members in order to become acquainted.

He was selective about joining various regional, ideological, and single-issue member organizations referred to as caucuses, coalitions, study groups, or task forces. Newt Gingrich created the Conservative Opportunity Society, which Doc would have joined but for the fact that they required substantial dues. He joined the Western Caucus but re-signed after it, too, instituted dues.

—

One way for Doc to gain the confidence of the Republican leader-ship was by showing some leadership of his own. Obviously, Hanford cleanup was a major issue for him. He had campaigned on it. After he arrived in the capital, he discovered three of the other four major clean-up sites were represented by first-term Republicans. Lindsey Graham represented the area around the Savannah River site in South Carolina. Charlie Norwood represented the district in Georgia across the Savan-nah River. Zach Wamp represented Oak Ridge. Wamp was also one of the three freshman members who had been appointed to the Steering Committee, and Doc had talked with him about serving on the Armed Services Committee. Mike Crapo from Idaho, who represented the Ida-ho site, had been elected two years earlier. Doc remembered, "We all believed that these cleanup missions should go forward; the government was responsible for them. But we didn't want to waste any money. We had all run opposing governmental waste."[46]

Very early in February, Doug Riggs arranged for the group to meet with Newt Gingrich and his legislative director in the Speaker's office in the Capitol. Riggs remembered it well. "It was my very first time in that office after spending eight years on the Hill. For forty years, it had been in Democratic hands."[47] Lindsey Graham remembered what happened next:

> Doc started out by making the argument to the Speaker that the Republicans have to be seen as caring about the environment and being responsible and putting the federal government's feet to the fire here.
>
> Newt was really a big thinker, and Doc tapped into his intellectual curiosity. We've got a Cold War problem. How can we bring technology to bear to fix it?
>
> We convinced the Speaker that there was a lot of innovation out there and we needed to turn waste into an asset.[48]

The group discussed various approaches but finally decided to create a task force vested with the Speaker's full authority. Gingrich named Doc Hastings as its chairman.

Almost immediately, the task force began holding interviews with DOE administrators from the various sites, along with their contractors, officials from DOE headquarters, and others that would be helpful in developing the Hanford budget. The meetings might attract as many as fifty attendees, including committee staff from both the House and the Senate, lobbyists, and other interested parties. The creation of the Nuclear Cleanup Caucus, as it became known, was probably Doc's most significant accomplishment during his first term.

—

Doc became acquainted with work of the two committees to which he had been assigned. House committees vary widely in size. The large House Armed Services Committee had a membership of more than sixty members in 1995. Its new chairman was Floyd Spence of South Carolina, who assumed the chairmanship from Ron Dellums of California, who now became the committee's ranking member.

The major purpose of the committee is to authorize and provide oversight over the Department of Defense and the US Armed Forces, as well as substantial portions of the Department of Energy. They did this annually by passing the National Defense Authorization Act (NDAA). Nuclear cleanup represented a very small part of the committee's budget, but it was very important from a policy standpoint and even more important to the members who represented those areas. Doc would later become skilled at including his pet projects in the annual NDAA.

The Natural Resources Committee consisted of more than forty members and had jurisdiction over issues such as water resources, energy production, mineral lands and mining, fisheries and wildlife, and public lands. The new chairman was Don Young of Alaska, who replaced Democrat George Miller of California, who became the ranking member.

—

Doc's first term established the pattern of practice and priorities that he followed for the next twenty years. Doc already had a well-defined political philosophy closely patterned after Ronald Reagan's. Jon DeVaney, one of Doc's legislative assistants and now a trade association executive, remembered:

> One of the most important things to understand about Doc is the role that Ronald Reagan played in his political career and how much in common he has with Reagan. I believe he was both drawn to Reagan because of the similarities in their approach to politics, and that was reinforced by Reagan's compelling model of political success.
>
> Like Reagan, Doc had also thought deeply about his political philosophy. He knew what he wanted to accomplish, where he stood on issues, and why.[49]

In those rare instances when Doc deviated from his political philosophy—as when he voted for Bush's No Child Left Behind legislation—he often regretted his decision.

Doc was a partisan Republican and made no apologies for it. He was known to repeat Peter Finley Dunne's adage that "politics ain't beanbag," referring to the rough side of political campaigns.[50] Bill Polk remembered that even back in the 1970s, "He didn't care what other people thought. He was comfortable in his own skin and if he felt he was right, that was good enough. How many can say that?"[51] Lindsey Graham agreed:

> The word I would use to describe Doc is reliable. He's just a reliable conservative. He's really easygoing—a team player.
>
> Let me tell you, there's a lot of fight in Doc, but he's a consensus builder.
>
> He was there for the right reasons. He wasn't there for Doc. It wasn't about making him look good; it was about his district and trying to change the government in a way he thought it needed to be changed.[52]

Doc believed in party loyalty. "You have to be loyal to your party because you accrue whatever position you gain over time through party loyalty," he said.[53] That party loyalty was, perhaps, most evident later in his career when he would always accept the jobs—like sitting on the Rules or Ethics Committees—that few others sought or wanted.

Inevitably, later in his career, the question would be asked if he ever contemplated becoming Speaker of the House. "No, I never thought about getting in line to do that. If you asked me if I thought I could do the job, yes, I thought I could do the job, but I never had it in mind. For one thing, I was fifty-four when I was first elected, and you have to be there for a while to gain enough stature to become Speaker."[54]

—

Doc always preferred to work behind the scenes rather than in the public spotlight. That made the job of communicating his positions on issues a challenge to his staff. "We had to push him to make floor speeches," Todd Ungerecht recalled. [55] While he spoke frequently to the press when he was at home in his district, Doc didn't hold a press conference in Washington, DC, until he was in his fifth term. He would speak to the press only if they sought him out. Todd Young, a communications director who would become the chief of staff remembered, "We used to turn out reams of press releases and meaty policy position papers that would rarely be reported in the hometown papers. Doc didn't seem to mind, but it drove *us* crazy!"[56]

Doc became much more visible after he became a committee chairman. It was unavoidable, given the challenges he later had to deal with as chairman of the Ethics Committee, but Doc never craved the limelight. Republican Cathy McMorris Rogers remembered, "You know, there are some that like to get up every week and speak at our weekly meetings of Republicans. That's not Doc. But, I can tell you, when Doc speaks, people listen. And you know that when Doc grabs the microphone, that it is something worth listening to."[57]

He learned to navigate his way through the Republican conference, which was sometimes a challenge, as a succession of later Republican Speakers would discover. In spite of those challenges, Doc always tried to follow Ronald Reagan's Eleventh Commandment: "Never speak ill of a fellow Republican."[58]

> The dynamics of that are that you have well over two hundred strong personalities who each think that they can run the world, but who basically share the same political philosophy, and that is the philosophy of less government.
>
> Then you add personal and parochial differences into the mix, and it sometimes becomes very difficult. I approached it from the standpoint that they were *all* on my side, and it was just a matter of degree.
>
> The real differences politically were with the Democrats.[59]

But whether it was presiding over a debate on the House floor or considering a piece of legislation in committee, Doc learned that while each member is unique, all have one thing in common: "Each of them got elected by convincing a majority of the voters in their districts that he or she shared their views. Each of them had to work hard to earn those votes, or they wouldn't be in Congress."[60]

The second thing Doc learned was that relationships between members—Democrats or Republicans—were largely transactional: "These are colleagues with whom you work. Business is conducted between individuals who each has something he or she wants to accomplish. Only very rarely are they friends in the same way as the friends you grew up with, a fraternity brother, a close teammate, or a friend you went to high school with."[61]

Doc *did* make many lasting friends while he served in Congress, but he remembered and liked to repeat what Harry Truman said about friendship: "If you want a friend, get a dog." Personal relationships were hard to establish because of the public nature of the job. "You live in a fishbowl," Doc explained. "For example, one day four of us were on one of the member's elevators, and another person got on board. Someone shared a confidence that perhaps he shouldn't have, and the next morning it was in *Roll Call*. Everyone was wondering, 'Where did that come from?'"[62] He noted that members were more like independent contractors who belonged to the same association than employees of the same organization. Their districts and local issues were incredibly diverse, as were their local politics, and he had to learn about each of them in order to make informed decisions. Doc explained how he accomplished that:

It is just a fact to say that there are complex issues that impact other parts of the country that you know very little about.

You learn to rely on the judgment of members from those parts of the country because you have learned to trust them. I believe that as long as their proposed solution is consistent with my principles that is the art of legislating.[63]

For Doc, "consistent with my principles" was the operative phrase, but he was also pragmatic. Jon DeVaney remembered: "The fact that Doc had thought about what he wanted to accomplish, and knew what he could and couldn't accept meant that he was open to working with anyone and everyone on areas of common interest. It meant that he could strike principled compromises because he knew what was negotiable and what was for him a matter of principle."[64]

Doug Riggs agreed:

> He wanted to get things done. If he could get 70 or 80 percent of what he wanted as opposed to getting zero, he would go for it. He would never let the perfect be the enemy of the good.
>
> His pragmatism was best illustrated by the issues he chose to spend his time on. There were big debates on social issues, on national policy issues, and on the Clinton impeachment, but you didn't see Doc on the floor of the House railing about them.
>
> He spent his time working behind the scenes on the issues he was focused on, like Hanford, agriculture, and the environment.[65]

And that, perhaps, was the most important point to make about Doc's twenty years in Congress. He believed that being a Republican was important but his first responsibility was to his constituents back home.

CHAPTER SEVEN

"He Wanted to Get Things Done"

★

A CLASSIC BATTLE OF WILLS ENSUED between the Democratic president, Bill Clinton, and his administration on one side and the Republican House Speaker, Newt Gingrich, and his allies in Congress on the other. Clinton had won election as a "New Democrat," a moderate who would be willing to compromise with Republicans when it served his purposes. Instead, his administration pursued an aggressively liberal agenda.

Newton Leroy "Newt" Gingrich was a big-picture thinker with seemingly boundless energy and an ability to organize and inspire most of his Republican colleagues. His chief deputy whip and future House Speaker Denny Hastert wrote that "he always thought he would eventually win. One question he never asked was 'What's the exit strategy?'"[1]

As promised, the House leadership brought all ten provisions of the Contract with America to the floor for a vote during the first one hundred days of the new session, dividing each provision into one or more bills. Thirty-one of the resulting thirty-two measures passed the House. Doc voted for each of them.

Lindsey Graham remembered those days vividly:

> We got sworn in, and everybody's full of piss and vinegar. We were going to burn down the place. We'd signed that Contract—and by God, we were going to fulfill it in the first hundred days—so we started in on the institutional reforms.

Normally you get sworn in and you go home. But Newt keeps us in session until about three in the morning.

Either the first day or the second day—I can't remember which—and after the twenty-fifth walk from my office in Longworth over to the Capitol and back, my shins were killing me. I was getting shin splints. I had on hard-soled shoes and, literally, walking back and forth was killing me!

I went out and bought new shoes that were more comfortable.[2]

Fifty days following the start of the new session, on the morning of February 22, 1995, Doc Hastings and seventy-three of his Republican colleagues gathered in the Cannon Building Caucus Room for a full-blown pep rally. As they waved small American flags, Dick Armey assured the assembled press, "We are on schedule. We will enact the Contract in 100 days."[3] Gloria Borger wrote in *U.S. News and World Report*, "The early agenda was mostly about process. The second half will revolve around real life issues—like welfare, regulatory and legal reform and, of course, budget and tax reform."[4]

Considered by many of his colleagues to be pushy and presumptuous, Dick Armey was a college economics professor from Texas who had once worked on a construction crew in North Dakota. "He lined up the bills like an assembly line," Hastert remembered.[5] While Gingrich was the conceptualizer and the public face of the Contract, Armey was the field general or, more often, the enforcer. "Newt has the Contract, I have the schedule," he said.[6]

Only one of the provisions—the proposal to institute congressional term limits—failed because it could not muster the necessary two-thirds majority to pass.[7] The subject had been an important issue in Doc's 1994 election when, unlike many other congressional candidates in the state, he had refused to take a term-limit pledge. "I got beat up on that a lot. I voted for the provision in the Contract with America because it was across the board and affected everyone," he explained. "But I don't believe in unilateral disarmament and didn't want to limit my constituents to what benefits seniority might bring."[8]

To celebrate the end of the first one hundred days, Doc hosted his entire staff for dinner at a nearby restaurant. Todd Ungerecht remembered how amazed they were when Speaker Gingrich stopped by their table to greet Doc and each of the staff members. "It was a tribute to Doc's ability to get acclimated to the workings of the House and leadership so early on."[9]

The Senate Republicans generally supported the policies included in the Contract but decided to slow Newt down a little. Unbound by the promises to revamp America in the first one hundred days, they were far less eager to pass sweeping reforms. When the balanced budget amendment to the Constitution came before them, they fell one vote short of the two-thirds needed to pass it on a bipartisan basis. Doc believed the nation had missed an excellent opportunity. Years later, Doc recalled, "My God, if we had passed a balanced budget amendment, assuming it would have been ratified, just think of how much better financial shape the country would be in right now!"[10]

—

As the end of 1995 approached, the battle of wills between the president and the Speaker reached a climax of sorts over the timetable for balancing the federal budget. John Kasich of Ohio, the chair of the House Budget Committee, represented the House in the negotiations. Hastert remembered, "He kept goading Newt into being tough. 'Don't give in,' he said. There wasn't any compromise [on our part], and the White House got its back up."[11] The matter came to a head in an Oval Office meeting between the president and the Republican leadership on November 1.

When Gingrich refused to agree to another continuing resolution to keep the government open, Clinton lost his temper. "I've accepted all of your principles—a balanced budget, welfare reform . . . and you haven't accepted any of ours. Do you think you're the only ones who have principles? . . . I worry that hidden behind your Contract . . . you want to destroy the federal government." Gesturing to the chair behind his desk, he said he would rather let Bob Dole sit in it than capitulate.

Gingrich replied, "You know, the problem here is that you've got a gun to my head. It's called the veto. But . . . I've got a gun to your head, and I'm going to use it. I'm going to shut the government down![12]

And he did. Twice.

On November 14, significant parts of the government were shut down, creating considerable chaos. Only essential government workers remained on the job, but without pay. Government-funded programs like Meals on Wheels that provided food for six hundred thousand elderly citizens, were suspended. Government mortgages for housing sales went unprocessed, and tens of thousands of tourists were stranded in the nation's capital, unable to visit the Smithsonian and other government landmarks.

To end the shutdown, Clinton agreed to accept a balanced budget that included modest spending cuts and tax increases. Gingrich still wasn't satisfied. He demanded a new budget that slashed Medicare—Republicans called it reform—and included more tax cuts. Clinton vetoed the new budget on December 6, and the government shut down again over the holidays until January 6, 1996.

Senate majority leader Bob Dole finally ended the impasse, parting ways with his fellow Republicans who wanted to continue the shutdown until Clinton agreed to all their demands. Gingrich and Dole were potential rivals for the 1996 presidential nomination and had a tense working relationship.[13] By January 4, the House Republicans were also ready to move on, voting to end the shutdown by a vote of 401 to 17. Doc reluctantly voted with the majority, believing that his party had caved in to public pressure. "The whole process ha[d] not run its course, but because part of the government was shut down, then the focus was on the government being shut down rather than on getting to a balanced budget," he said. "We thought the president would want to sit down and negotiate in good faith. That was not the case."[14]

The experience taught Doc a lesson he never forgot. "In the future, whenever there was talk about a government shutdown, I argued against it. It is bad policy. [In those situations,] politics trumps policy every time."[15]

—

Most Americans blamed Newt Gingrich for the government shutdown, an event that many believed began his eventual political fall from grace. In a 1995 ABC news poll, 46 percent blamed Gingrich for the first shutdown while 27 percent blamed Clinton.[16]

Gingrich had misunderstood the country's mood. Americans might dislike their government, but they demanded and needed its services. As much as some conservatives might agree with the Republicans' policy objectives, other Republicans felt disempowered by Gingrich's imperial style, and the majority of the nation believed the Republicans had gone too far.

The personal styles of the two men also played a role in the public's perception. Gingrich's approval ratings fell to about 35 percent while Bill Clinton used the event to frame his 1996 reelection campaign, pointing to the fact he had balanced the budget and calling it a "threshold issue." "Swing voters care," he said.[17] In a nationally televised speech on June 13, 1996, he announced his plan to balance the budget in ten years, co-opting one of the Republicans' most effective talking points. The government shutdowns raised serious questions about the ability of America's elected leaders to manage the day-to-day affairs of their government and further increased the levels of political polarization in both the Congress and the nation.

—

Following the test of wills that resulted in the government shutdowns, it was time to get back to the business of running the country. The Line Item Veto Act, part of the Contract with America, allowed the president to utilize the line-item veto for the first time. The House approved the measure quickly and sent it to the Senate, where it took a year to pass. However, after Clinton signed it into law on April 9, 1996, a group of senators challenged it in federal court. When the case reached the Supreme Court, the court declined to hear it, saying the senators lacked standing in the matter. Clinton exercised his new line-item veto authority twice and then was sued by the city of New York. When that case reached the Supreme Court, they found the line-item veto was unconstitutional in a 6-3 ruling. Doc had voted for the legislation.

"I supported it because Washington State has the line-item veto, and I thought it was a good idea," he explained.[18]

On August 21, 1996, Clinton signed the Health Insurance Portability and Accountability Act, mercifully shortened to HIPAA. The act protected health insurance coverage for workers that changed or lost their jobs and required national standards for electronic healthcare transactions.

The following day, Clinton signed the Personal Responsibility and Work Opportunity Act—better known as welfare reform. Perhaps nothing illuminated Clinton's mastery as a politician more than his ability to take credit for "ending welfare as we know it," the phrase he uttered as he signed the legislation.[19] Like many pieces of landmark legislation, the bill was the result of many previous bills and countless amendments. Indeed, the first piece of legislation that Doc sponsored was HR1146, introduced on March 7, 1995, that would have replaced a range of federal welfare programs with block grants to the states. "It was one of those ideas we brainstormed in our staff meetings," Doc remembered. "Not everyone agreed with it."[20]

Bill and Hillary Clinton had supported welfare reform since 1980, but the president vetoed the Personal Responsibility Act, part of the Contract with America, deeming it too severe. Congress passed a similar bill with only minimal changes, and Clinton vetoed it again. A third bill, the result of an intense series of triangulation negotiations, was "something he could live with, we could live with, and the Democrats could live with, and it was signed it into law," Doc said. "If there is one program that has had some positive benefits over what we had before, it is this."[21]

WHILE THE EFFORT TO PASS the Contract with America was important, Doc understood his first responsibility was to his district. Many of the issues there had been growing in complexity and importance for years. Foremost among them was the Hanford Nuclear Site. Doc's conservative, budget-cutting mentality found it hard to justify the vast federal spending at Hanford, but he also believed it was the government's responsibility to clean it up. "If it hadn't been for the Second World War and the Cold War, we wouldn't be in this situation," he reasoned, "so I have no problem at all justifying the federal money that is being spent."[22]

The Hanford Federal Facility Agreement and Consent Order—more commonly known as the Tri-Party Agreement—had been signed on May 15, 1989, between the US Department of Energy (DOE), the Environmental Protection Agency, and the state of Washington. Washington's attorney general, Christine Gregoire, distrusted the internal politics of DOE so much that she required Mike Lawrence, DOE's local manager of Richland Operations, to obtain written permission from DOE's abrasive secretary, Admiral James Watkins, to sign the agreement on behalf of the agency. The agreement had two parts. The first was a series of binding legal agreements. The second was an action plan governing the cleanup of the site.[23]

The cleanup of the site had proceeded slowly and with great difficulty as managers and workers struggled to cope with the technical and emotional transition from producing plutonium to cleaning of the site. New projects and missions, such as the Environmental Molecular Sciences Laboratory (EMSL), the Laser Interferometer Gravitational-Wave Observatory (LIGO), and the Hazardous Materials Management and Emergency Response Federal Training Center (HAMMER) were being promoted as ways to compensate for the loss of the production reactors, while others, like the Fast Flux Test Facility (FFTF), were operating on life support.

Doc had tried to familiarize himself with these highly technical projects and issues when he ran for Congress in 1994. However, the situation worsened during the final months of the campaign when Hanford's prime contractor, Westinghouse, installed a new management team on site in a last-ditch effort to save their contract, laying off almost five thousand workers in the process.

Soon after the election of 1994, Doc met with DOE officials, local contractors, and the leadership of TRIDEC, the area's economic development organization. While TRIDEC as an organization did not take positions on individual candidates, two important members of its board, Bob Ferguson and Jim Watts did. They had endorsed Jay Inslee in the final days of the 1994 campaign. All that changed with Doc's victory. As soon as he returned home from orientation week, he recalled, "TRI-DEC wanted to meet with me, and Ferguson took me under his wing. He told me that there were rumors of pending layoffs at Hanford, and sure enough, around Thanksgiving in 1994 they were announced. They were heavy on my mind when I went back to Congress."

The community wanted immediate answers, and Doc didn't have them. He recalled, "Jack Briggs [publisher of the *Tri-City Herald*] wanted to have the TRIDEC meeting open to the public. TRIDEC refused, but Jack wanted to know what I was going to do about Hanford. I told him, 'Jack, for God's sake, I haven't even been sworn in yet.'"[24]

—

The most important component of the Hanford cleanup was the proposed construction of the massive Hanford Waste Treatment Plant (WTP)—often called the "vit" or "vitrification plant"—that would transform the fifty-three million gallons of nuclear waste being stored in single- and double-shelled underground tanks into glass logs under intense heat. These would then be stored in an underground nuclear waste repository for perpetuity. Some of the storage tanks dated back to the Manhattan Project during the Second World War. The technology was untried and was reminiscent of building the first full-scale plutonium reactor at Hanford in the 1940s without the benefit of blueprints or computers.

By the time the new Clinton administration came to office in 1993, it was clear that the technical problems associated with the vit plant and the waste storage tanks were bigger, costlier, and more long-term than anyone had anticipated. Thomas P. Grumbly, DOE's new assistant secretary for environmental management, estimated that the eventual cleanup of the Hanford site might cost as much as fifty billion dollars and that about a third of the estimated $7.4 billion already spent on the project had been wasted.[25]

Another issue delaying Hanford cleanup was the maze of more than fifty-five federal environmental laws, nearly a dozen state laws, and roughly 1,300 additional orders from DOE, some of which were duplicative or contradictory.[26] Still another problem had to do with funding. The fiscal 1996 environmental cleanup budget was $1.35 billion, 8.3 percent less than the Clinton administration had asked for but enough to limit the job losses at Hanford to the 4,800 already announced.[27]

On July 25, 1995—very early in his first term—Doc sponsored legislation that would have made the state of Washington the sole regulator of the Hanford Site and given more authority to local DOE officials. It had been partially written by Slade Gorton's staff, and both Senator Patty Murray and Congressman Norm Dicks endorsed it.

Another Hanford funding priority related to cleanup was the construction of the HAMMER education and training facility. Local fire districts originally proposed it as a place to train first responders and Hanford workers to deal with hazardous materials. It was the last and favorite project of ninety-one-year-old Sam Volpentest, the legendary community activist and lobbyist who had been the go-to guy since the 1950s for funding local projects. Norm Dicks and Patty Murray had already secured a pledge of $29.9 million for the project before Doc was elected. He supported what was already a *fait accompli*, but the project was also the source of a little Tri-Cities folklore.

Volpentest was a lifelong Democrat and no supporter of Doc's, but because Doc had been helpful to HAMMER after he was elected, TRIDEC's Gary Petersen convinced Sam to contribute to Doc's 1996 re-election campaign in the hope that it would improve Sam's opinion of his new congressman. Sam reluctantly sent a check to Doc's campaign. However, the amount was so small that Doc returned it to him with a note that read, "Sam, I'm returning your check to you. From the size of your contribution, it is clear to me that you need the money more than I do. Doc." After that, the two men got along better.[28]

Yet another Hanford funding problem Doc faced was the unresolved future of the special sodium-cooled Fast Flux Test Facility reactor, which became operational for the first time in 1982 after incurring massive construction cost overruns. It had operated more or less flawlessly until April 1992 when George H. W. Bush's energy secretary, Admiral James Watkins, decided to deactivate it, throwing approximately a thousand Hanford workers out of their jobs. Prior to Doc's election, Washington's Democratic governor, Booth Gardner, TRIDEC, and other local supporters frantically scrambled to find a long-term use for the reactor. Two potential options were producing isotopes for medical research or tritium for fusion research. Doc hoped that one of the proposed solutions would bear fruit because of the large numbers of jobs associated with the reactor.

—

Another issue that would dog Doc for the remainder of his time in Congress was the illusive issue of water storage for the Yakima Basin. During the 1994 election, Doc campaigned for office citing the need to update the existing Yakima River Basin Storage Plan, but the issue wasn't prominent during his first term in office. Former congressman Sid Morrison had promoted a bill dealing with the issue, but it hadn't gained much traction in Congress. Jay Inslee had passed a more limited version of it during his term of office. Doc felt the bill still didn't adequately address the problem but had little interest in tinkering with a piece of legislation that had just been passed.

—

Yet another issue Doc had campaigned on was the impact of the 1973 Endangered Species Act (ESA) on his district. In Doc's view, the ESA was an example of legislation that had been passed with every good intention but had ended up becoming a regulatory nightmare. While environmentalists claimed the act had been successful in protecting endangered species from extinction, opponents said it was an economic sledgehammer used to destroy local economic development and resource-dependent activities.

In 1990, the northern spotted owl was listed as a threatened species under the ESA. The owls nested on old-growth stands of timber, causing the Clinton administration to set aside 690,000 acres of national forest. In 1991, US District Judge William Dwyer ordered a halt to timber sales and logging on twenty-one million acres in seventeen national forests, including the Wenatchee National Forest in Doc's district. A federal judge agreed with environmentalists that government agencies supposed to be protecting the owls had engaged in "a remarkable series of violations" of environmental laws. More than three hundred local lumber mills closed, some in Doc's district. This action led to significantly reduced timber harvests and increased unemployment in several of Doc's counties by the time he was elected.

Beginning in 1992, twenty-six species of salmon and steelhead in the four western states were also listed as either endangered or threatened under the ESA, including thirteen of them native to the Snake and Columbia Rivers. Efforts to save the fish soon collided with the operations of the various hydroelectric dams located on the two rivers, many of which were located in Doc's district. In the late 1930s, the great hydroelectric dams—first Bonneville and then Grand Coulee—had been built along the Columbia River to provide electricity to the growing Pacific Northwest. The aluminum industry and Hanford nuclear reactors relied on the power they produced to win the Second World War. After the war, more dams were built to irrigate the vast Columbia Basin Project in Eastern Washington.

The Sierra Club Legal Defense Fund, representing a group of commercial fishermen and environmentalists, filed the first lawsuit in federal court in 1992, seeking to prohibit the Bonneville Power Administration (BPA) from entering into any new sales contracts with Northwest utilities and aluminum producers. The issue would remain in the courts for as long as Doc served in Congress. The dams became involved in the issue when environmentalists called for drawing down water levels in the dam reservoirs and demanded studies of breaching one or more of them in order to protect or mitigate the fish runs. When the public utilities, ports, and agricultural interests realized the potential impacts on irrigation, navigation, and power generation, they filed their own lawsuits challenging federal management of the fishery.

Doc Hastings and Senator Slade Gorton particularly objected to a National Marine Fisheries Service (NMFS) plan to increase river flows to help save endangered fish. The cost in lost hydropower alone was estimated to be $120 million, but the head of the BPA estimated it to be as high as $175 to $180 million. Gorton claimed that "each saved Chinook would cost its weight in gold."[29]

Irrigation districts relied on contracts to provide river water to local farmers. As irrigation methods improved, the farmers used their excess water to irrigate more farmland, which aided, in particular, to the economy of Grant County. Ports located along the Snake and Columbia Rivers relied on barge traffic to deliver millions of tons of grain to Portland and Vancouver. Public utility districts relied on the power generated by the dams to expand the Columbia Basin Project and provide power to their current customers.

Doc believed the ESA was being administered in ways that far exceeded its intended purpose. He joined forces with Slade Gorton to pass legislation that would update the Endangered Species Act, fighting with environmentalists and battling over birds, fish, and dams during the rest of the 1990s. Hastings and Gorton often introduced companion legislation in the House and the Senate, and their staffs worked closely together, routinely facing opposition from the Sierra Club, the Audubon Society, native tribes, and other environmental groups.

The League of Conservation Voters, a congressional rating service for twenty-seven national environmental groups, gave Gorton its lowest possible rating—zero. Doc and George Nethercutt from the neighboring Fifth District each received a grade of thirteen, the lowest ranking among Washington's congressional members. "With these votes, Slade has completed his metamorphosis from a moderate Republican to an anti-environmental zealot," said Bill Arthur, Northwest representative for the Sierra Club, one of the rating groups.[30] Doc, who had never pretended to be a moderate Republican, took pleasure in his low ranking by the group. "I must have been doing *something* right!" he said.[31]

—

Yet another increasingly contentious environmental issue involved the future of the Hanford Reach, the last free-flowing section of the Columbia River in Eastern Washington located just north of Richland. The first recorded reference to it was by Captain William Clark of the Lewis and Clark expedition. Clark noted a "reach" of river in his journal after visiting the confluence of the Yakima and Columbia Rivers on October 17, 1805.[32]

When the federal government began building the great dams on the Columbia and Snake in 1937, administrators didn't consider the future of the millions of salmon who used the rivers to spawn.[33] Their focus was on providing cheap hydroelectric power and irrigation water for the Columbia Basin. In the 1960s, the Corps of Engineers explored a plan to building a large hydro dam along the Hanford Reach, dredging a channel that would open the river to barge traffic all the way to Wenatchee. That dam's reservoir would have flooded 11,500 acres of wildlife habitat and was opposed by environmentalists, tribal officials, sports and commercial fishermen, but most importantly, the Atomic Energy Commission, which was still producing plutonium at the Hanford Site.

In 1981, the corps released a report that ruled out the dam, but the corps still had dreams of opening the river to commercial traffic.[34] That became evident one day in December of 1986 or 1987 when Rich Steele, a local agent for the Internal Revenue Service and an avid fly fisherman, and Eric Gerber, a senior engineering manager for Westinghouse Hanford Group, were fishing for steelhead in the upper Hanford Reach. They noticed survey stakes along the banks of the river. After returning to the site on several occasions, Steele met a surveyor who said he was working on the corps' river-dredging project. The corps was proposing a $180 million plan that called for dredging part of the river and building giant lifts over three dams to extend barge traffic from Richland to Wenatchee.[35] Alarmed, Steele and Gerber alerted Jack DeYoung, a fellow fishing enthusiast and a former Kennewick city councilmember who also happened to be on the *Seattle P-I*'s editorial board. The paper printed an extensive report that helped generate opposition from the same phalanx of opponents that had earlier opposed the dam, including DOE.[36]

Steele, Gerber, and others, including Rick Leaumont, a leader of the local Audubon Society, formed a broad-based, local grassroots "Save the Reach" organization. They appealed to Congressman Sid Morrison for help. In 1988, Morrison successfully passed legislation that precluded dredging or other similar activities for eight years and authorized a study of the Hanford Reach as a potential National Wild and Scenic River.[37] "The leaders of the 'Save the Reach' effort favored the Wild and Scenic River effort. It is less restrictive and it has a lot more flexibility," Gerber remembered. "You have to have a management plan, and it's tailored to that specific river."[38]

In September 1995, Doc introduced legislation making the prohibition against damming the river permanent, but he excluded Morrison's language prohibiting development for eight years and authorizing the study. "We wanted to protect the free-flowing part of the river, but we wanted local control," Doc said.[39] Three months later, Senators Patty Murray and Ron Wyden of Oregon cosponsored legislation to designate the Hanford Reach as a Wild and Scenic River. Both bills were introduced in response to the upcoming expiration of the eight-year study period in Morrison's legislation.[40] Both sides wanted to protect the Reach, but Murray took the position that the Reach should remain under federal control. "We simply can't afford to take chances with the one part of the river that works well," she said.[41] She was supported in the House by Norm Dicks and by local environmental groups, fishermen, tribes, and others who wanted to protect the river and its adjacent lands. Resolution of the issue was postponed when neither of their competing bills could get out of committee during the 104th Congress.

—

The Hanford Reach, while important, was not the only issue on Doc's plate. Immigration was not yet the national hot-button issue it would become, but problems with obtaining enough legal farmworkers to bring in the district's bounteous crops generated many contacts to Doc's office and more than a few complaints from unhappy constituents. The Immigration Reform and Control Act (IRCA), better known as Simpson-Mazzoli, had been enacted in 1986. It required employers to attest to their employees' immigration status and prohibited knowingly hiring or recruiting illegal immigrants.

In March 1996, Doc voted for amendments to an immigration bill that assisted smaller farmers and orchardists with labor-intensive crops who were often unable to meet the strict guest-worker provisions under

Simpson-Mazzoli. They would be left with huge losses when the US Border Patrol rounded up their illegal pickers during periodic sweeps. "A lot of guys will tell you frankly that the guys they hire are illegal, but they couldn't bring in their crop without them," Doc said. "You can't ask the farmers to be policemen."[42]

—

Another piece of legislation Doc introduced in March exemplified how politics could interfere with a seemingly non-controversial issue. It dealt with the taxation of workers, many of them union electricians, who helped build federal dams along the Columbia River. These workers lived in Washington (which has no income tax), but because the dams spanned the river to Oregon (which has an income tax), the state of Oregon asserted it could tax their entire income. Doc sympathized with the worker's plight and introduced a bill to solve the problem. It was seen as a non-controversial measure and was scheduled to be considered on the floor with limited debate. However, the Democrats sensed a chance to deny Doc an accomplishment leading up to his first reelection campaign. The bill failed to receive the necessary two-thirds of the votes required for passage because of a straight party-line vote. He reintroduced the bill in his next term after he had been reelected, and it eventually became law.

—

That summer, an unanticipated discovery led to an intense new debate that would not be resolved for twenty years. The annual Water Follies hydroplane races on the Columbia River were, and continue to be, a summertime staple in the Tri-Cities. On July 28, 1996, two college students walking along the Kennewick bank of the river upstream from the event found a portion of a partially submerged human skeleton. Archeologists ultimately examined more than 350 bones, determining through radiocarbon testing that the skeleton was over nine thousand years old.

Once the discovery of "Kennewick Man" became public, local tribes demanded that the skeleton be released to them under the provisions of the federal Native American Graves Protection and Repatriation Act (NAGPRA). The statute had been designed to ensure that human remains and cultural artifacts would be returned to the family members and native communities to which they were related. The native community was assumed to be whatever tribe had occupied the area when it signed a treaty with the government. The statute presumed that the patterns of settlement hadn't changed before the arrival of the first white settlers. Nor would it be possible to prove otherwise if all archeological evidence were transferred and buried without study.

The scientists who studied the bones claimed the man was not related to today's Native Americans and was thus exempt from NAGPRA. Doc had no problem with the law, passed to protect native burial sites, but he felt something that old, even if it proved to be a Native American, needed to be studied. He and Senator Slade Gorton introduced legislation to limit the authority of NAGPRA in such cases, but it failed to gain traction in Congress.

ANOTHER SURPRISE CAME IN SEPTEMBER 1995 when, after serving only nine months in office, Doc found himself running against an opponent for his seat in Congress. He had known, of course, that he would have to defend his seat. "You may have gotten there, but you have to get reelected—the first reelect is always the hardest—but to have your first opponent announce for your seat only nine months into your term, that was unanticipated."[43]

His opponent was thirty-four-year-old Glenn Phipps, a program specialist with the Kittitas-Yakima Economic Development District. On October 5, 1995, Phipps formally announced his candidacy. His only political experience was a one-year internship in the office of Democrat George Miller of California, but he made up for his inexperience with overblown rhetoric, comparing Gingrich to Adolph Hitler and claiming that Doc had voted with Newt Gingrich "100 percent of the time." Doc responded, "I am accused of supporting what I campaigned on. I stand convicted."[44] It took only two days for the editorial board of the *Tri-City Herald* to write of Phipps, "This campaign is a real loser."[45]

In February, filings with the Federal Elections Commission showed that Doc had raised $234,049 for his reelection bid in 1995. Almost 60 percent of it came from individual contributions in his district. About 40 percent came from political action committees. Doc estimated that he spent an average of two to three hours a week on the telephone fundraising.

Local Democrats looked for a more disciplined candidate to oppose Doc. In March, Joe Walkenhauer, who had run in the Democratic primary in 1992, entered the race, but union leaders sought a stronger candidate.

Their hopes increasingly focused on Richland's Rick Locke, a chemist and entrepreneur who was on entrepreneurial leave from the Pacific Northwest National Laboratory after licensing a technology that turned organic chemicals into methane. Locke had a master's degree in public policy from Harvard's Kennedy School of Government. After months of indecision, Locke announced his candidacy in early May and quickly won the endorsements of the Washington State Labor Council and several Hanford unions.

The field of candidates running for Doc's seat expanded in June when Kennewick's Craig Williams, the local chair of the John Birch Society, announced he was entering the race as an Independent because he didn't consider Doc Hastings's voting record to be conservative enough.

With Congress adjourned for the summer and Doc returned home, the campaign settled down for the final run-up to the primary. Todd Ungerecht moved to Doc's district to manage the campaign on a daily basis. Ed Cassidy periodically changed hats and employers to travel out to the district to oversee the campaign. Even Doc's son, Colin, took a semester off from Seattle University to help.

Colin remembered, "You could tell that Ed was very fond of my dad—almost protective. But Ed had a policy. Campaigns and family don't mix. When my sister or I would drive my dad around during the campaign, Ed was hard on you if you screwed something up." He related:

A case in point occurred one day when Ed and I were watching my dad give a speech in Kennewick's Columbia Park. Ed expressed his critique to me, telling me what my dad could have said better.

Later, I was driving my dad somewhere, and he asked me what I thought of the speech. I just basically regurgitated what Ed had said. It got back to Ed, and that really set him off. He called me into his office, "That's MY job to talk to the candidate. It's not YOUR job. You're the driver." I think he called me in three times to yell at me before he was through.[46]

As Doc's campaign geared up, his team opened an office in Kennewick, and soon dozens of volunteers worked there and in every county in the district. In late July, they fended off a flurry of thirty-second television ads funded by the national labor unions, accusing Doc and other Republicans of voting with Gingrich to "destroy Medicare." When the Democratic Congressional Campaign Committee sent out a press release noting that Doc had voted with the Republican leadership 97.6 percent of the time, he sent a tongue-in-cheek letter to Martin Frost of Texas, chair of the DCCC, thanking him for keeping his constituents up to date on his voting record. "As we say, promises made, promises kept. Again, Martin, keep up the good work."[47]

A certain level of pointed sarcasm was a staple of Doc in campaign mode, and it was not lost on either his opponents or the press. Ken Robertson, the managing editor of the *Tri-City Herald* at the time, remembered that Doc was always cordial and pleasant in person, but when he put on his political hat, "There was always kind of this edge about him. And Doc's chief of staff, Ed Cassidy, was a horse's patoot!"[48]

Charges that Doc opposed plans for preserving two hundred thousand acres around the perimeter of the Hanford Site as a natural habitat or that he routinely opposed environmentalist issues didn't bother Doc. They were true. Other claims that he hadn't vocally opposed a Dole-backed proposal to cut funding for the nation's national laboratories and that he accepted large campaign donations from the tobacco industry were at least partially true. The most difficult accusation to counter, leveled during a time of massive layoffs, was that he hadn't done enough to block the loss of 4,800 jobs at Hanford. The *Tri-City Herald* prominently featured this last charge in its election coverage.

This negative press prompted a five-page, single-spaced rebuttal that listed what the campaign called "Doc Hastings' Extensive Record on Hanford Issues." The campaign was furious when the local newspapers neglected to print the rebuttal, an indicative exchange of the tense relationship between it and the local papers.

When voters went to the polls on primary election day, September 17, 1996, Doc received 53.95 percent of the votes to Locke's 29.40 percent. Walkenhauer and Phipps split the remainder. Doc had received the highest percentage of any of Washington's new GOP freshmen.

The race between Locke and Hastings heated up. Knowing that he was at an organizational and funding disadvantage, Locke turned up the rhetoric. Doc defended his voting record: Like it or not, he had voted in the way he had promised he would. John Boehner did a golf event with Doc in Yakima. "Doc was one of those members who wasn't there for himself," Boehner asserted. "He wasn't there to bring home the bacon. He was there to do a job *and* on behalf of his constituents and the rest of the country."[49] Claire did her part by holding "Coffees with Claire" throughout the district. By September, Doc had raised $520,349 to Locke's $242,134. Doc's concern that Locke's personal wealth might be brought to bear failed to materialize.

The *Seattle Times* and the *Yakima Herald-Republic* endorsed Locke, a fact that Doc's staff would not let the Yakima paper and its editorial page editor, Bill Lee, soon forget. The *Tri-City Herald* provided a lukewarm endorsement of Doc, agreeing that he had done what he had said he would do.[50]

In the general election on November 5, Doc Hastings again received approximately 53 percent of the vote to Rick Locke's 47 percent, even though his party lost both the presidential and gubernatorial elections. "It's been a very unusual election year, but I believe very strongly that this election reaffirms what we started in 1994," Doc said on the night of the election.[51] It would be the last really competitive race that Doc would face.

—

Doc was not alone in winning his reelection handily. Bill Clinton won a surprisingly easy victory over Republican Senator Bob Dole, Reform Party candidate Ross Perot, and by extension, the House Republicans. National polls showed that potential voters saw Clinton as acting presidential rather than partisan in the face of foreign and domestic crises, while the congressional Republicans were seen as having been willing to shut down the government.[52] Dole had not displayed strong gifts as a campaigner in three previous runs for national office, and 1996 was no different.

Clinton would become the first Democratic president since Franklin Roosevelt to serve two full terms, but his political coattails were barely noticeable. The Democrats picked up two seats in the House and lost two in the Senate, ensuring that Congress would stay in Republican hands. In his victory speech, Clinton claimed that "the vital American center is alive and well," but increasingly, the forces driving divisiveness and political partisanship were growing stronger.

The day after the election, when the newly elected president walked the rope line at the White House and accepted the well wishes of his staff, he embraced a young woman in a black beret.

CHAPTER EIGHT

"Suddenly, You're a Go-To-Guy

★

DOC'S SECOND TERM IN CONGRESS WAS DOMINATED by a series of national crises that further widened the political divide among the American people. In 1997, the Algerian civil war, which had raged since 1991, began to wind down but signaled the future turmoil in Libya and North Africa. Long-suppressed ethnic divisions in the Balkans intensified as Bosnia and Herzegovina tried to separate themselves from the former Yugoslavia. That conflict would lead to US and NATO airstrikes against Serbia in 1999 and then to the deployment of US peacekeepers. In February 1998, Iraq's dictator, Saddam Hussein, allowed to remain in power after the first Gulf War, was forced to negotiate an agreement with the UN allowing weapons inspectors back into Iraq amid rumors that he had stockpiled weapons of mass destruction. In May, India and Pakistan announced they possessed nuclear weapons, and in August, Islamic terrorists bombed the US embassies in Kenya and Tanzania, killing 224 and injuring more than 4,500. The attacks would soon be tied to a little-known Saudi citizen named Osama bin Laden, the leader of al-Qaeda.

—

Meanwhile, at home, the attentions of the national news media and the American public were increasingly fixated on the futures of their two most prominent politicians, President Bill Clinton and House Speaker Newt Gingrich. Both men were like moths flying too close to the candle of controversy.

Bill and Hillary Clinton had been controversial figures since he served as governor of Arkansas. Rumors about an obscure Arkansas real estate development called Whitewater and Bill's extra-marital affairs followed them onto the national stage in 1992. Gingrich and other Republicans had long railed against what they saw as the ethical lapses and administrative abuses of the Democrats, so the seemingly endless allegations regarding the Clintons played into an existing narrative the Republicans wanted to believe. So, too, did the sudden death of the Clintons' close, longtime friend and White House counsel, Vince Foster, and a minor scandal involving the White House Travel Office. The Republicans seized on every allegation to try to discredit the popular president.

Back in January 1994, attorney general Janet Reno appointed a special prosecutor to investigate the allegations. In May of that year, a former Arkansas state employee, Paula Jones, filed an unrelated sexual harassment charge against the president. The special prosecutor's draft report absolved Clinton of any wrongdoing, but in August, a three-judge panel appointed by Chief Justice William Rehnquist named Kenneth Starr, a former federal judge and Republican solicitor general in the Reagan administration, to replace him. Then, in the midterm election of 1994, Newt Gingrich and his Republican Revolution gained control of Congress for the first time in forty years.

The Republican victory reenergized Clinton's detractors. For the first time, it dawned on them that the long-simmering scandal might turn into an issue they would have to address in their congressional capacity, rather than as interested bystanders. Congressional investigations of the Clinton scandals increased markedly. Clinton hardly helped his cause in 1995 when he became involved with Monica Lewinsky, a White House intern and the young woman in the black beret on the White House rope line. In May 1997, the Supreme Court ruled that Jones could pursue her lawsuit against Clinton while he was in office. Testifying under oath in that investigation, Clinton denied having an affair with Lewinsky.

On January 27, 1998, Tom Brokaw anchored the *NBC Nightly News* prior to the network's coverage of Clinton's State of the Union message. His lead story announced that Kenneth Starr had opened a grand jury investigation into the Lewinsky matter, followed by coverage of Hillary Clinton's contention that the couple was the target of a "vast right-wing conspiracy." The next story reported on Pentagon plans to bomb Baghdad.[1]

The chain of events reinforced a narrative that had been widely promoted by right-wing commentators and believed by millions of Americans who hated the Clintons with a visceral intensity that went far beyond any disagreement with their politics. Historian William E. Leuchtenburg wrote, "To many, the Clintons symbolized the 1960s with its civil rights movement, feminism, sexual tolerance, and abortion. For a lot of people, that's when America went wrong." But perhaps by promising to create "an administration that looks like America" and by following through on his pledge by appointing women and minorities throughout the government, Clinton threatened the traditional hierarchy of white America even more in ways that went far beyond the 1960s and resonated to the current day."[2]

Clinton's personal actions essentially squandered the last three years of his presidency. The scandal limited the wounded president's ability to put his policy proposals into place. Opportunities to reform Social Security and Medicare were missed because he now lacked the necessary clout to forge bipartisan coalitions. He also had less time and energy to devote to foreign affairs. An exception would be his personal involvement in promoting peace between the rival factions in Northern Ireland.

A constant drip of leaks and legitimate news stories about the Clintons continued for the rest of the year. Clinton's supporters claimed the investigations were politically motivated; Clinton's detractors believed that Starr was only doing his job. On September 9, Starr submitted a 445-page report to Congress outlining a list of impeachable offenses against the president. The following day, the House Rules Committee convened in their intimate and tightly packed hearing room to refer the Starr Report to Henry Hyde and John Conyers, the chair and ranking member, respectively, of the House Judiciary Committee. Each member of Congress, including Doc—who had recently been appointed to the Rules Committee—received a copy of Starr's report in a black, plastic-covered three-ring binder, approximately an inch and a half thick.[3] When Doc's turn to comment at the Rules Committee hearing came, he disagreed with the contention that the nation faced a constitutional crisis. Instead, he declared, "We have a potential crisis in governance and crisis in the confidence of the people who sent us here."[4] A day later, Clinton told a Washington, DC, prayer breakfast, "I don't think there is a fancy way to say that I have sinned," and expressed regret to Lewinsky and her family.[5]

Given the highly charged nature of American politics at the time, most Republicans and Democrats saw the unfolding events from starkly differing perspectives. Their dramatic rhetoric raged for the rest of the year in what *New York Times* columnist Frank Rich called a *mediathon*, a "hybrid of media circus, soap opera, and tabloid journalism."[6]

The Republicans believed the Clinton scandal spelled victory for them in the upcoming elections. "You're in a game where partisanship cannot be ignored," Doc stated. "I don't think I did much to engage in that, but there were people attacking him and people defending him. That's free speech and part of an open society." He added, "It just kind of repelled me that the whole thing was going on."[7]

On October 5, 1998, by a 21-16 vote, the House Judiciary Committee recommended a full impeachment inquiry. The full House agreed on October 8, authorizing an open-ended inquiry by a vote of 258-176. Thirty-one Democrats voted yes along with the Republicans.

—

Across town, House Speaker Newt Gingrich found himself in the middle of a different kind of controversy. He had been blamed for the Republicans' loss of three House seats in the 1996 election, widely seen as political payback for his actions in precipitating the partial government shutdown during the 1995-1996 holidays. Some questioned whether Gingrich could survive as Speaker when the new Congress convened in January 1997. However, he remained unapologetic and in 1998 stated, "Everybody in Washington thinks [the shutdown] was a big mistake. They are exactly wrong . . . our base thought we were serious. And they thought we were serious because when it came to a show-down, we didn't flinch."[8]

Years earlier, Gingrich had helped bring ethics charges against the popular Democratic Speaker of the House, Jim Wright of Texas, forcing him to resign in 1988. The Democrats did not forget. Eventually, they filed eighty-four charges against Gingrich with the House Ethics Committee. In what some thought was a form of plea-bargain agreement in order to retain his speakership in the next session of Congress, Gingrich acknowledged that his responses to the Ethics Committee had contained misleading information. He eventually became the first Speaker in history to be reprimanded by the House Ethics Committee and fined three hundred thousand dollars, but he saved his job.[9] On January 7, 1997, the Republican majority reelected Gingrich as Speaker by a vote of 215 to 205, a vote that Denny Hastert wrote, "Was much closer than it appeared."[10]

With 228 Republican members in the House, Gingrich found it difficult to keep everyone happy. In July 1997, members of Gingrich's leadership team, including Dick Armey, Tom DeLay, John Boehner, and Bill Paxton, met for dinner to discuss a revolt that was brewing among a group of younger, more conservative members. Former Seattle Seahawks wide receiver Steve Largent and Tom Coburn, both of Oklahoma, and Lindsey Graham of South Carolina wanted to replace Gingrich as Speaker. They claimed his public image and leadership style were a liability.

The *New York Times* got word of it and reported that Boehner and Paxton tried to convince Armey and Delay to present Gingrich with an ultimatum: resign or be voted out. Armey warned Gingrich, who refused to step down, and the plot fell apart.[11] Boehner denied that he was ever part of a coup: "It may or may not have happened. All I know is that I did not go to Gingrich with an ultimatum. At one point, I had lunch with Armey, DeLay, and Paxton to talk about the turmoil in the caucus and what to do about it. When we finished voting for the day, I went home and went to bed, only to learn in the morning that I had been involved in some sort of a coup."[12]

Armey, too, backed away from the story, sending out a two-page letter to the Republican conference, apologizing for having met with the dissidents when they engaged in what he called "what if" scenarios.[13]

Denny Hastert remembered what happened next. "Toward the end of July, there was a nearly three-hour meeting of the whole Republican conference in a cramped room in the basement of the Capitol. All our members were asking, 'What in the world is the leadership doing? Can't they get along?' It was a kind of a 'Come to Jesus' meeting."[14]

Doc was not party to the revolt. He supported Gingrich, but he never forgot the impassioned plea that Sonny Bono of California made during the meeting of the Republican conference, calling for unity and reconciliation. Although Doc personally liked Boehner, Paxton, and Graham, he understood that Gingrich was the Speaker. "Once you elect your leaders to make decisions for the whole body, it's your responsibility to follow them." His concerns with Gingrich had more to do with his management style than his politics:

> He was not as good at [administering the House] as he needed to be. He would have discussions in leadership, and they would make a decision on something. Newt would hear about some different approach and go off and adopt it without telling anyone. He was often influenced by the last person that talked with him. Perhaps it was his intellectual curiosity, but that was his biggest work-related shortcoming.[15]

—

Doc returned to Washington, DC, in early December 1996 for the organization of the 105th Congress. Readers of the daily newspapers in his district were surprised to learn he was giving up his seats on the Armed Services and Natural Resources Committees in order to accept a seat on the House Rules Committee. Most of them had no idea at all of what the function of the Rules Committee was, and Doc's explanation to Les Blumenthal, the *Tri-City Herald*'s Washington, DC, bureau chief, did little to inform them. "Rules deals with members, one-on-one. I would put it in the same status as Appropriations or Ways and Means."[16] He explained that the House Committee on Rules is what is called a "leadership committee" because the Speaker of the House personally chooses each of its members. The other three leadership committees are the House Administration, Ethics, and Intelligence Committees.

A small committee, Rules consists of nine members of the majority party and four members of the minority party. At the beginning of Doc's second term, the committee's chairman was Gerry Solomon of New York, an outspoken former Democrat. Joe Moakley of Massachusetts served as the Democrats' ranking member.

The chairman of the Rules Committee is one of the most powerful men in the House. The committee serves a vital function in the administration of the House because all legislation to be debated on the House floor must first come before the committee. The members of the committee determine the rule on each piece of legislation—how to conduct the debate, how many amendments to allow, how long the debate will be, and the order in which any amendments will be offered. Almost any legislation that requires a rule is, by definition, contentious. If it is not, it is placed on what is known as the "suspension calendar" and voted on with limited debate.

Normally, both the chair and ranking member of the committee proposing legislation appear before the Rules Committee to explain their bill. Then, other members who wish to amend the legislation describe their proposed changes. During the discussion period of a bill, members of the committee can ask questions without time limit, providing a unique opportunity to influence the bills before the committee. Doc reflected, "Suddenly, you're a go-to guy. You are interacting with members all the time. When you interact with members, you build relationships, and I felt that was a good way to get to know people. It also has the added value of learning about issues that impact other parts of the country in a detailed way."[17]

Jeff Markey, Doc's deputy chief of staff from 1999 to 2003, worked with Cassidy on the committee staff. He described the rationale for going on the committee in slightly more practical terms: "We used our position on Rules to influence any bill that we cared about. We would talk with the senior leadership of the committee bringing legislation [before the committee] and let them know what we needed to make us comfortable so that their bill could go to the floor. If you don't use your influence on Rules to support your district, you shouldn't be on it in the first place."[18]

Doc had lobbied hard to get on the committee. He had served on a similar committee in the Washington legislature and understood its function and the benefits that could accrue to a member serving on it. Prior to the meeting of the House Republican conference, he learned of two openings on the committee and expressed his interest in getting one of them to Solomon. Then he approached Speaker Gingrich, who would make the appointment, and each member of the Republican leadership, hoping they would influence Gingrich on his behalf. "I wanted to be on there because I liked the process part of it," he stated. "If I wanted to speak for twenty minutes in order to try to influence the outcome of something, I could do it."[19]

The Republican House leadership saw the benefits of including Doc on the committee. Dick Armey talked of Doc's "low-key style of leadership." Lindsey Graham—not a member of the leadership team but close to many of them—described what the leadership was looking for in new committee members:

> You put people on the Rules Committee that you feel you can rely upon to deal with the tough stuff, because the Democrats would try to amend our policy provisions. You have a majority but you need people who can be tough.
>
> [The leadership] saw in Doc somebody who would fight for our reforms. You never put someone on the Rules Committee who is worried about getting re-elected because you had to take some tough votes for the team. You've got to have people you can count on to do the heavy lifting.[21]

That argument didn't much impress community leaders like Sam Volpentest or the editors of the *Tri-City Herald*, who were incredulous that Hastings would give up his seat on committees they considered vital to the district's economy to serve on one of questionable value. After all, the Armed Services Committee had jurisdiction over Hanford funding, and Gingrich had made room there for Doc. The Natural Resources Committee had jurisdiction over the nation's public lands and water issues, including one of Doc's pet projects, the rewriting of the Endangered Species Act. He would have to give up both committees to serve on the Rules Committee, although he would be able to retain seniority on Natural Resources.

—

It was not long before Doc found an opportunity to use his membership on the Rules Committee to influence an issue of importance to his district. The Department of Energy was spending more than a billion dollars a year on the Hanford cleanup effort, yet little progress was apparently being made.

Fifty-three million gallons of highly toxic nuclear waste were stored in aging underground tanks, some of which were nearing the end of their effective life cycle.[22] Experts feared the older tanks would leak, or worse, were already leaking. No system to transfer the tank waste to the vit plant existed and planning for the project was hopelessly stalled. It was even unclear whether the planned Yucca Mountain facility in Nevada would be available to serve as the depository for the vitrified waste.

In addition, DOE's projected budget kept it from meeting all its legal obligations under the 1987 Tri-Party Agreement. The states, environmentalists, DOE, and local community groups were equally frustrated by the lack of progress. DOE's centralized decision-making process stymied local administrators. Everyone realized there was a problem, but opinions differed as to the solution. Doc believed what was required was "a new and coherent policy."[24]

Doug Riggs remembered that after they established the Nuclear Cleanup Caucus, they quickly realized they needed a new approach. "We needed an organization that focused just on the waste," he pointed out. "In April, a possible solution presented itself when the task force was briefed by the DOE folks in Ohio where responsibility for the cleanup at the Mound and Fernald nuclear sites had successfully been separated. We thought that the same principle could be applied to Hanford."[25]

For the next two months, Doc and his staff discussed the idea with other members of the Washington delegation and community leaders in the Tri-Cities. "It was a lot of work, and there were a lot of skeptics," Riggs said. "Folks wanted to keep doing things the way things had always been done. Change is hard. We had to convince the staff on the Armed Services Committee first, and that took some time. But its members respected Doc, respected that it was his district, and deferred to his judgment."[26]

In June 3, 1997, Doc introduced legislation proposing the creation of a new Office of River Protection (ORP) at Hanford. When the Armed Services Committee brought the annual National Defense Authorization Bill to the Rules Committee in July, Doc's bill already enjoyed broad, bipartisan support. Therefore, it was not difficult to use his position on the committee to propose an amendment to the authorization bill that would create ORP, whose focus would be on cleaning up the nuclear tank waste. The amendment also established the Pacific Northwest Site Office within DOE to oversee the Pacific Northwest National Laboratory, and it increased Hanford funding by three hundred million dollars.

ORP became a reality in December 1998 and was the most significant achievement of Doc's second term. "It would likely not have happened had I not been on Rules in my second term," Doc asserted. "We had been working on ORP for some time, and we thought that it was a perfect time to offer it as an amendment to the National Defense Authorization Bill. Because I was on Rules Committee, that amendment was made in order, and it was accepted in the bill on the floor without any debate at all."[27]

—

Early in the new session, on January 9, 1997, Doc introduced HR 412—the Oroville-Tonasket Claims Settlement and Conveyance Act. In terms of lasting significance, perhaps it wasn't on a par with the creation of ORP, but it helped resolve a longstanding problem and represented the kind of help that constituents expected from their congressman.

The legislation approved a negotiated settlement going back to the 1950s between the Oroville-Tonasket Irrigation District in Okanogan County and the US Bureau of Reclamation. Doc had inherited the issue. He recalled, "It was a small amount of money, but it was very important to those irrigation districts up there to have this issue settled."[28]

Its passage should have been a simple matter but was not. The bill was referred to the Natural Resources Committee where Doc had served. It affected no other member and would normally have sailed through the committee and on to the suspension calendar. However, George Miller of California, the former chairman and current ranking Democrat on the committee, objected to Doc's bill, forcing him to take it to the Rules Committee. "I don't know what his motive was, but I believe he was just trying to get back at me and embarrass me because I had defeated his friend, Jay Inslee. However, that's politics, and I understand it."[29] The bill sailed out of the Rules Committee on March 12, and the House approved it on a voice vote on March 18. President Clinton signed it the same day. It was the first piece of legislation Doc introduced that was signed into law by the president.

But what goes around, comes around. On the last day Doc presided over Congress in 2014, the last item on the agenda was some esoteric bill that Miller supported from his district. "I considered asking, 'George, do you remember the Oroville-Tonasket Settlement Act?' But I let it go."[30]

—

Doc had been interested in auto racing since grade school. As a small boy, he had carved miniature cars out of balsa wood, less than a half-inch long, and each painted a different color. He played with them by himself for hours, rolling dice to advance them along a track he had built. He would faithfully listen to Sid Collins announce the Indianapolis 500 on Memorial Day. He knew the names and car numbers of all of the drivers. In high school, he would drive to Spokane and attend the stock car races. But he had never been a NASCAR fan.

The NASCAR's Winston Cup Series began on February 16, 1997, early in Doc's second term, with the Daytona 500. Driver Jeff Gordon won the race and then followed up with a second victory at the Goodwrench

Service 400 at the North Carolina Motor Speedway in Rockingham. No one had ever won the first three NASCAR races of the year. Doc and Claire decided to attend the third race of the season at nearby Richmond.

His office staff obtained tickets, and on Sunday, March 2, Doc and Claire drove the ninety miles to Richmond to attend the Pontiac Excitement 400. By the time they fought the traffic, made it through the line at the will call window, and found their seats, the race had already begun. "You couldn't hear yourself think. Claire couldn't make heads or tails out of what was going on, so she started following the No. 2 car driven by Rusty Wallace, who eventually won the race."[31] From that point on, they were hooked on NASCAR.

At one time or another, Doc attended one or more races at every track in the East, often with Claire or their son, Colin; sometimes with members of his staff or other members of Congress; and sometimes with old friends like Ron Grey. His enthusiasm and the excitement of the sport was contagious, and he often turned his guests into race fans, including future governor and vice president Mike Pence who, along with his son, Michael, attended a race at Richmond with Doc. In 2005, when Doc was Speaker Dennis Hastert's controversial pick to head the House Ethics Committee, Republican Mike Simpson of Idaho was once asked by a reporter about his colleague. He mentioned several favorable qualities but then branded Doc as a NASCAR nut: "If you really want to get him going, ask him about NASCAR. He knows every driver, every number, and the color of every car. He's a nut. We've always known he was crazy. Why else would he be on the ethics committee?"[32]

Before leaving Congress, Doc would sponsor a fundraiser in a suite at Richmond. On another occasion, Robin Hayes, a congressman from North Carolina, sponsored a fundraiser that Doc attended at a driving school in North Carolina, and Doc and Claire had a chance to drive around the track at Rockingham in a racecar. Doc collected scores of model racecars, each an exact replica of an original car. He was fond of telling friends, "A sport that does not discourage tobacco or beer and promotes everything you can possibly sell under the sun is not a bad sport to be in."[33]

WHILE THE TWIN DRAMAS SWIRLING AROUND the president and the Speaker played out in Washington, the ongoing issues in Doc's congressional district demanded his attention.

Kennewick Man, the nine-thousand-year-old skeleton found on the banks of the Columbia River in 1996, became news once again in late March 1998 when the Corps of Engineers acceded to the desires of the tribes and sealed the site on the Columbia River with tons of riprap rock dropped by helicopter. The disposition of the remains was already the subject of a three-way nine-year court battle between the corps, scientists who wanted to examine the remains, and the tribes.

Doc and Slade Gorton introduced legislation to prohibit the corps from closing the site. Doc also appealed to Bruce Babbitt, President Clinton's interior secretary and a former governor of Arizona, and asked him not to proceed. However, within weeks of Doc's request, Babbitt ordered the site sealed, "without," Doc recalled, "even giving me the curtesy of a call."[34]

In 2004, the federal court ruled that the ancestry of the skeleton, which had resided at the Burke Museum at the University of Washington since 1998, could not be determined because of its age and allowed scientific study of the remains to continue. In 2015, after Doc left office, additional DNA research determined the skeleton was indeed that of a Native American, and the House voted to return the bones to the tribes. Doc, now out office, remained unconvinced. "If I were on the committee, [the legislation] probably wouldn't have gotten out of committee."[35] The issue was finally resolved on December 19, 2016—more than twenty years after the skeleton had been found—when President Barack Obama, in one his last official acts, signed a directive instructing the Corps of Engineers to turn over the remains to a coalition of five Columbia Plateau tribes. On Saturday, February 19, 2017, more than three hundred gathered to bury Kennewick Man in an undisclosed location.[36]

—

Meanwhile, two groups with very different visions of the future sparred over how to protect the Hanford Reach. One group was led by Doc, supported by Senator Slade Gorton and a coalition of local governments, developers, and irrigators. The other was led by Senator Patty Murray, supported by a coalition of eco-friendly congressmen, environmentalists, and fishermen. For Murray, the issue was personal. Her grandfather had farmed along the banks of the Reach. She remembered spending her summers there as a young girl. Her father had fought in the Second World War, and she was deeply cognizant of the role that Hanford had played in winning the war. By June, both sides had reintroduced their competing legislation. Doc's approach was more philosophical and rooted in his basic distrust of big government: "We need not lock up the entire area to save what everyone agrees must be saved."[37] Agricultural interests that had supported Doc's election were already lobbying him to develop the Wahluke Slope portion of the Reach for farming.

Both sides collided on June 21, 1997, at a field hearing sponsored by the Senate Energy and Natural Resources Committee. Senator Slade Gorton moderated the hearing, which was held in a high school gymnasium in the small town of Mattawa. Patty Murray, Doc Hastings, Sixth District congressman Norm Dicks, and a crowd estimated at more than a thousand people attended. Some wore prison garb to suggest they were prisoners of the federal government. Few, if any, minds were changed, including President Clinton's. On October 10, he announced he would veto Doc's bill if it ever reached his desk and suggested that administrative action might be necessary to preserve the Hanford Reach. Negotiations between the two positions continued into Doc's next term.

On April 6, 1998, American Rivers, a national river conservation group, named the Columbia as America's "most endangered river." While their designation was broader than the Reach itself, Doc felt their announcement was purely political. "Anytime American Rivers names a river, it's always targeted toward a Republican member somewhere. It's a political tool."[38]

While the original focus of the battle was on the future of the Hanford Reach corridor, the battle increasingly expanded to include nearly two hundred thousand acres of unique shrub-steppe habitat included within the Hanford Site but never utilized for plutonium production. Because of Hanford, the lands had been virtually undisturbed for thirty years. These included the Saddle Mountain National Wildlife Preserve and the Wahluke Slope Wildlife Refuge, both located north and east of the Columbia River from the plutonium reactors, and the large Fitzner-Eberhardt Arid Lands Ecology Reserve (ALE), to the west of the main Hanford Site and a large part of Rattlesnake Mountain.

Another disputed stretch of the Hanford Reach was the fragile, chalk-like cliffs along the eastern side of the river in Franklin County, called the White Bluffs. Experts worried that intensive agricultural development above them might cause them to slide into the river, destroying the intricate salmon spawning grounds along the backwaters and inside shoals. This process had already begun in the lower portion of the Reach where irrigated farming was nearer to the river. The two sides continued to support their parallel but competing solutions for protecting the Reach without coming to an agreement until President Clinton resolved the issue two years later.

Doc hosted several high-profile visitors to his district in the late spring and summer of 1998. Majority whip Tom DeLay had come out to campaign for Doc in 1994. In May 1998, he visited the district again and held a fundraiser and a standup press conference with Doc at Yakima's Apple Tree Golf Course. The Clinton impeachment controversy was just heating up after the president's settlement with Paula Jones and the new revelations about the president's relationship with Monica Lewinsky had been revealed. Not surprisingly, that's what DeLay wanted to talk about. "All of this could be over tomorrow if the president would just come forward and tell the truth."[39]

DeLay's visit was followed in August 1998, during Doc's reelection campaign, by a visit from Newt Gingrich. The Speaker and several other members were on an annual tour to acquaint them with western land and water issues. Followed by several boats full of press, Doc took them on a tour of his district, which culminated with a jet boat tour of the Hanford Reach. Facing potential revolt and probably happy to escape the nation's capital, Gingrich refused to comment on the future of the Reach, but his presence allowed Doc ample opportunity to lobby for his proposed solution.

Doc was elated to host Gingrich in Pasco for a one-hundred-dollar-a-plate fundraiser. More than 750 supporters and 150 protestors showed up for the event at the Pasco Red Lion. The Speaker took time to watch the new blockbuster movie, *Saving Private Ryan*, at Kennewick's Columbia Center Mall before heading to Seattle for another fundraiser. Gingrich's visit was great publicity for Doc. The Speaker was the highest-ranking federal official to visit places like Lake Chelan, Ellensburg, and Wenatchee in many years, but he was probably the only sitting Speaker of the House to ever visit Stehekin and Manson.

—

The Hanford Reach was far from the only battle Doc fought with environmentalists and their supporters in Congress. He continued to oppose what he considered the disastrous impacts of the Endangered Species Act on his district's economy. First, it had been the northern spotted owl. Now it was how to protect the salmon and steelhead in the Columbia and Snake Rivers. He opposed legislation sponsored by Democrat Jim McDermott of Washington's Seventh Congressional District and others who wanted to breach the four lower Snake River dams to improve water flow and protect endangered salmon species.

In 1998, Senator Slade Gorton introduced legislation that required Congress to approve any plan to alter the hydropower dams on the Columbia-Snake system, even if a federal judge ruled such action was mandated by the ESA. Clinton's secretary of the interior, Bruce Babbitt, claimed that Gorton was using the dams to create a wholesale exception in the nation's environmental laws and ordered the National Marine Fisheries Service (NMFS) and the US Army Corps of Engineers to study the best way to rebuild the runs of endangered Columbia and Snake Rivers salmon species. One option was removing the four lower Snake River dams. Gorton countered by saying that what was best for salmon was an important question, but an even more important question was how society valued the various uses of the river—power, irrigation, flood control, transportation, and, yes, fish.[40]

On September 2, Doc secured a congressional field hearing of the Natural Resources Committee in Pasco to assess the effectiveness of the

NMFS water policies intended to save endangered fish and to show that dam removal was not the only way to restore salmon runs. The hearing was a response to vocal criticism from Washington House Speaker Clyde Ballard of East Wenatchee, who said the NMFS was "treating us as though we are their prisoners, and that's wrong."[41] An agency of the Department of Commerce, NMFS was responsible for administering the ESA as it related to endangered fish species. Ballard supported the transfer of responsibility for administering the ESA from NMFS to the Department of the Interior. More than four hundred people showed up at the hearing to blast the NMFS. The hearing achieved two objectives. It allowed Doc to promote his policy positions and demonstrated the power associated with his incumbency prior to an upcoming election.

THE 1998 MIDTERM ELECTIONS WERE HELD AMID the combined spectacle of the president's personal problems and fast-moving international events. The Clintons, Gingrich, and Kenneth Starr were all polarizing figures, but for better or worse, Gingrich was the face of the Republican Party. In many districts, the election was more about him than the local Republican candidate. His pollsters optimistically forecast that the Lewinsky scandal would gain Republicans between six and thirty seats in the next Congress, but other polls suggested that most voters opposed impeaching Clinton in the middle of a booming economy and in the face of growing international threats.[42]

When votes were counted on November 3, Republicans lost five more seats in the House—the worst midterm performance in sixty-four years by a party not holding the presidency—although they still retained a twelve-seat majority in the next Congress.

The members of the Republican conference blamed Gingrich for their midterm losses, and the revolt against him as Speaker flared up anew. Again, Doc was not part of it. "I'm not so sure that he would have lost if he had run again," Doc said. "You never know until the votes are counted. However, he knew if he was reelected, his leadership would be tenuous, at best, and he would always have to be looking over his shoulder. He just felt, 'Who needs this?' Personally, I would have voted to reelect him."[43]

An intense series of meetings and conference calls between members of the Republican leadership led Gingrich to announce on November 6, 1998, that he was stepping down as Speaker effective immediately and would resign from the House when it convened in January. He was, he said, "not willing to preside over people who are cannibals."[44] Dick Armey was the obvious choice to replace him, but Bob Livingston, whom Gingrich had chosen as chair of the House Appropriations Committee, decided to run for the position.

Denny Hastert remembered, "Armey's situation was precarious. He had two real challengers in Steve Largent and Jennifer Dunn. It was also unprecedented that a sitting majority leader be challenged for his job." People asked Hastert to run for majority leader, but he had already pledged himself to Armey.[45]

In the wake of Gingrich's announcement, the Republican conference met on November 17 in the large Cannon Building conference room. Amid intense internal divisions that were largely hidden from the public, the members attempted to select a new leadership team. The conference still contained a few members who were viewed as centrists, but they were a rapidly vanishing breed. Most members who were referred to as "moderates" were actually the conservative followers of Ronald Reagan. The new conservative faction was mostly younger and even farther to the right. Then there was a small group with a variety of hard-right views on fiscal and social issues, the role of government, and individual liberties. Doc recalled: "There were also divisions between the members that had more to do with how the conference would be run under a new Speaker than matters of political philosophy. Others dealt with competing strategies to be pursued against the Democrats in order to win back the seats that had just been lost."[46]

Armey and DeLay decided they could not win the speakership but felt secure in their current positions. The conference elected Bob Livingston as Speaker-designee without opposition. He had a reputation as a consensus builder who worked well with Republicans as well as

Democrats. Livingston also chaired a committee, which none of the other members of the Republican leadership had done. With the Republicans still holding a majority, Livingston was all but assured of becoming the next Speaker.

Both Jennifer Dunn and Steve Largent contested Dick Armey as majority leader. Denny Hastert was also nominated, but Armey would not release him from his pledge of support. Dunn represented the moderate faction of the conference, and Largent the more conservative one. Doc supported Dunn and unofficially managed her campaign to unseat Armey. Lindsey Graham did the same for Largent. The two good friends, now supporting different candidates, met for dinner in Arlington, Virginia, where each hoped to convince the other to switch candidates after the first ballot.

Even before dinner began, Doc had what he called an "awkward" moment when he realized that Largent had more votes than Dunn. Doc and Dunn then decided to support Armey, who won on the third ballot.

DeLay ran unopposed for whip and won what he jokingly told reporters was a "tough-fought race." J. C. Watts of Oklahoma, the only African American in the 223-member Republican conference, defeated John Boehner for conference chair. Some believed that Boehner's loss was payback for his perceived involvement in the coup against Gingrich. On November 18, they all appeared before a massive press conference to introduce Livingston, their new Speaker-designate, spinning their recent disagreements and putting a united face on their majority status. Doc stood on the podium with them, right beside Dunn. [47]

But there were still more surprises to come. Larry Flynt, the publisher of *Hustler* magazine and a strong Clinton supporter, offered one million dollars for stories about the sexual indiscretions of Republican members of Congress. One such story about Livingston surfaced. Another surfaced about Henry Hyde, the chair of the House Judiciary Committee who would manage the House impeachment presentation to the Senate. Hyde admitted to a five-year affair with a married woman in the 1960s but said, "The statute of limitations has long since passed on my youthful indiscretions."[48]

Only two days after the House Republicans had selected their new leadership, the House Judiciary Committee began hearings for the Clinton impeachment with independent counsel Kenneth Starr presenting his case first and the president's lawyers following. Three days later, the Republican-dominated committee agreed on four articles of impeachment against the president. Two articles alleged that he lied in the Paula Jones sexual harassment case and in his testimony before Starr's grand jury. The other two alleged that he abused the powers of his office and obstructed justice in the Monica Lewinsky matter. Two days later, the committee approved the first three articles of impeachment.

Doc remembered that Saturday, December 19, 1998, was one of the most historic day he experienced as a member of Congress. It was an unusual Saturday session. In the early morning came the news that US warplanes had begun the long-threatened bombing of Iraq in an effort to remove Saddam Hussein from power.

Then, the House met to vote on the charges of impeachment against the president of the United States. During the debate, Henry Hyde, the impeachment floor manager, recognized Livingston for two minutes. Hastert was sitting in his usual place by the back exit of the House chamber on the Republican side and described what happened next:

> Livingston began in a rambling, roundabout way by discussing Saddam Hussein's Iraq, then regretting the "enmity and hostility" that "has been bred in the Halls of Congress for the last months and years." He then abruptly changed the tone of his comments to address Clinton directly as if he were in the chamber. "Sir, you have done great damage to the nation over this past year. You have the power to terminate that damage and heal the wounds that you have created. You, sir, may resign your post."[49]

Maxine Waters, the fiery member from South-Central Los Angeles, rose, her supporters beside her yelling, "No, no, no. You resign."

Livingston raised his hand and continued, "And I can only challenge you in such fashion if I am willing to heed my own words . . . I will not stand for Speaker of the House."[50] Hastert remembered, "You could have heard a pin drop on the floor of the House. Even before Livingston finished his remarks, one of our floor assistants came out to find me and said, 'The Speaker wants to talk with you. He's on the phone in the cloakroom now.' First, it was Newt. Then it was everybody saying, 'You've got to be Speaker.'"[51]

"Denny just came out of nowhere," Doc remembered. "He had never been a committee chairman, but he was a guy we all knew, and we came to the conclusion that he was the guy that should take over."[52]

Don Manzullo, a colleague from Illinois, approached Hastert on the floor. "You're the next Speaker," he said. "Can you withstand the scrutiny?"

Hastert told him he could.[53]

The House approved the charge of perjury before a grand jury by a vote of 228 to 206. The charge of obstruction of justice passed 221 to 212. The other charges failed by votes of 205 to 229 and 148 to 285. Doc voted in favor of all four articles.

Doc had always been interested in history, and now, he said, he had seen it made three times in one day.

Doc had faced a tough race against Rick Locke in 1996, and it was rumored that Locke was considering another run in 1998. Ed Cassidy hired Todd Young, a young political science major from American University who had worked for Senator Slade Gorton, to run the campaign. Doc recalled, "It was our first experience with Todd, and he was very good." However, the 1998 election was not, perhaps, the most challenging test of Young's abilities.

Fourth District Democrats were struggling. It had been difficult to recruit a viable candidate in 1996, and after Locke looked at a Democratic poll taken in the spring, he decided to pass on a second race. Locke told a *Seattle Times* reporter, "I don't know what the Democrats did to these people, but it sure must have been bad."[54] For decades, state Democratic leaders, like Senator Brock Adams and Governor Mike Lowry, had routinely beaten up on Hanford, the largest source of jobs in the district, and local residents remembered. Tim Peckinpaugh, a Kennewick native and Washington, DC, lobbyist, suggested those former divisions were changing now that Hanford's mission had moved from plutonium production to cleanup. "The delegation now all supports Hanford cleanup," he said.[55]

Into the void stepped three unknown candidates. Ron Routson and Peggy McKerlie belonged to Ross Perot's Reform Party. Gordon Allen Pross, a forty-three-year-old unemployed son of an Ellensburg farmer, ran as a Democrat without the party's endorsement. Rouston quickly dropped out of the race after the primary, but McKerlie conducted an impassioned campaign based broadly on reforming the political system, although hardly referencing issues involving the Fourth District.[56] Pross rambled disjointedly about "democracy" but still garnered a quarter of the votes in the primary, against almost 70 percent for Hastings, and a 5 percent split between the Reform Party candidates.

The *Tri-City Herald* endorsed Doc again—a little more enthusiastically this time—saying he had "become a strong, effective legislator for his district." They credited him for stopping the Hanford budget from being slashed and for creating the Office of River Protection.[57] The *Yakima Herald-Republic* endorsed him for the first time. Noting that it had supported his opponent in 1996, the paper explained, "We're not changing our position because Hastings has changed his, but because the caliber of opposition makes the incumbent the viable candidate in this election." However, it did recognize Doc's work to obtain federal funding for the Yakima River Basin, acquire funding for the Prosser Research Center, and get the Office of River Protection included in the federal budget.[58]

The results of the general election on November 3 were nearly a mirror image of the primary. Doc won with 69 percent of the vote—the highest percentage of the vote in his congressional career—while Pross received almost 25 percent and McKerlie just under 7 percent. "From that point forward, we figured the total percentage of the vote received by the two of them—approximately 30 percent—represented what we called the 'yellow dog vote,'" Doc said wryly.[590]

Doc believed the good economy was largely responsible for the results. "When it's good, there's not much need to change your guy in office." After the election, Todd Young returned to Slade Gorton's staff until Doc hired him again in 2001 as his new communications director.[60]

MOST AMERICANS WERE CONFLICTED by Clinton's impeachment. No single issue had so captured their attention since the Nixon impeachment proceedings in 1974. Polls conducted at the time showed that only one-third of Americans agreed with the House decision to impeach the president. After a year of intense coverage and analysis both in the mainstream media and on cable television, the percentage of people who believed that Clinton should have been impeached had climbed to 50 percent, but an even greater majority—57 percent—agreed with the Senate's decision to acquit him. Two-thirds said the process had been harmful to the country.[61]

Most people blamed Newt Gingrich for leading the effort to impeach the president. Had he misjudged the American public's mood again? The effort he led spoke volumes about the venomous state of politics in the nation's capital. Many believed the impeachment had been used as just another tool in the partisan political wars. The whole episode left bitter and acrimonious feelings on the part of many of the participants that would not soon be forgotten.

We now know that at the same time Gingrich was pushing the impeachment of the president, he was carrying on an affair with a congressional staffer. We now also know that in late 1997 Gingrich and Clinton came close to creating a centrist political coalition to fix the long-term problems facing Social Security and Medicare. The outline of the agreement was to have been announced in Clinton's 1998 State of the Union address. And then the story broke about Clinton's relationship with Monica Lewinsky, and the deal evaporated and, with it, an opportunity to prove to the American public that the kinds of centrist solutions they kept demanding in the polls were actually possible.[62]

CHAPTER NINE

Dams, Fish and a Reach

★

THE NEW CONGRESS BEGAN in much the same way as the old one had ended—awash in political turmoil and uncertainty. The resignations of Newt Gingrich and Bob Livingston became effective on January 5, 1999, the first day of the new Congress. Dennis Hastert was elected as the new Speaker of the House. He broke with tradition by handing the Speaker's gavel to minority leader Dick Gephardt and delivering his remarks from the floor of the House.

Hastert acknowledged the internal controversies that had racked his party in recent months. "In the turbulent days behind us, debate on the merits often gave way to personal attacks. Some have felt slighted, insulted, or ignored. That is wrong, and that will change. Solutions to problems cannot be found in a pool of bitterness." He said the country faced four great and immediate challenges: Social Security and Medicare reform, slowing the growth of government, economic security, and national security. "These are not Democratic or Republican issues. They are American issues. We should be able to reach agreement quickly on the goals." As Doc listened to his words with hope and optimism, he thought, "Now, let's move forward and see if we can try to get something done together."[1]

Two days later, on January 8, the Senate opened its trial of the only elected president ever to be impeached.[2] William Rehnquist, the chief justice of the Supreme Court, presided over the proceedings. Henry Hyde, the chairman of the House Judiciary Committee, led a team of thirteen House managers—in essence, prosecutors—who presented the evidence against the president for two days between January 14 and 16. Doc walked over to the Senate to watch history being made. "I was sitting in the back of the Senate Chamber in a place they had set aside for us," he recalled. "The general consensus was that they would not get the sixty-seven votes needed to impeach, but you never know until the votes are counted." They didn't get the votes, and Clinton was acquitted. Doc believed that the case against Clinton justified his impeachment by the House and that the vote in the Senate was more about politics than it was about the law. Doc understood their decision, even if he disagreed with it. "There is a reason why we have divided government. The House is the *only* body that has *always* been elected directly by the people. The Senate is different. Politics is the price of self-government," he said.[3]

On January 19, 1999, Clinton delivered his annual State of the Union to a joint session of Congress without mentioning the impeachment proceedings. Sally Bedell Smith, Hillary Clinton's biographer, wrote that Bill Clinton had been livid when he entered the House chamber that night, the place where he had been impeached only a month earlier. Clinton had told her, "I realized I had to just purge myself of any thought of anger at them."[4] Doc was thinking along the same lines but he had a different perspective. "I never expected him to mention it. However, I couldn't stop thinking that we had impeached this man just one month ago and here we were, inviting him to come down and speak to us."[5]

The country moved on, but the emotional and political fallout of the impeachment lingered on. Although his poll numbers remained high, Bill Clinton was a wounded president from that point on, his family under tremendous strain, and his personal ambitions separated from those of his wife and vice president, Al Gore, as each plotted his or her future paths. Smith wrote, "The president used his bully pulpit . . . to exhort the Congress, announce initiatives, tout achievements, and promote studies, but no major legislation reflecting any of his top priorities ever reached his desk."[6] Hillary Clinton was being recruited to run for the US Senate from New York. Al Gore, the heir apparent and likely Democratic candidate for president in 2000, took steps to distance himself from the president.

Most people were happy to have the politically divisive and polarizing political crisis behind them and to focus on their own lives. Because of the bipartisan compromise on the budget and tax cuts that had been worked out earlier, the nation's economy was expanding. In March, the Dow Jones Industrial average soared above 10,000 for the first time. In May, it rose above 11,000.

One of Bill Clinton's biographers called him the ultimate survivor.[7] He completed his term with favorable poll numbers and an extended period of economic prosperity but also with a sense of lost opportunity and unfulfilled promise. The episode so poisoned the political environment that neither branch of government would successfully move its policy agenda forward during the rest of his term. He had failed to rebuild the Democratic center, and the party would become increasingly fragmented. George Bush would win the next presidential election, at least in part, because he appeared to offer a moral and ethical alternative to Bill Clinton.

—

The sense that all was well again was shattered on April 20, 1999, when two eighteen-year-old boys murdered a teacher and twelve of their classmates, wounded twenty-one others, and then committed suicide at Columbine High School, south of Denver, Colorado. Not surprisingly, the event reignited the debate about gun control in America. While Doc felt great personal empathy for the victims and their families, he didn't change his views on gun control: "If anything, it made me think that no-gun zones are not as safe as areas where people are allowed to carry guns."[8]

The twin issues of gun violence and gun control were another of those wedge issues that were increasingly used by political operatives of both parties to exploit cultural or societal differences to their advantage. While this had long been true, modern technology and mass communications have made the practice much easier.

Twenty years of polling by the Pew Research Center showed that support for gun rights among Republicans increased by almost 30 percent between 1993 and 2014, while support for gun control among

Democrats, already high, grew to almost 70 percent. Both sides saw the issue in starkly different terms, with Republicans supporting guns on constitutional grounds and as a personal freedom issue, while Democrats saw it as a public safety issue in which they were willing to accept more government regulation for what they perceived to be more safety.[9] Doc essentially had a pass on this issue. His rural district was reliably pro-gun, and he felt the Democrat's anti-gun stance in the 1970s and 1980s had helped to turn his district into a Republican stronghold.

—

The term "whip" in politics is said to derive from British fox-hunts where a "whipper-in" directs the dogs toward the fox. Politicians in Parliament co-opted the term to describe the person who makes sure party members attend meetings and vote the way their party wants them to.[10] To do the job effectively, a whip has to know each member and how he or she plans to vote on each new piece of legislation. Sometimes the leadership employs a carrot or stick to obtain the desired result.

Tom DeLay had been elected as the Republican whip in 1995. He rewarded Denny Hastert for running his campaign for the office by appointing him as his chief deputy. DeLay had campaigned hard for the job and helped many of the new members, including Doc, get elected. After getting the job, DeLay reinvented it with innovations like organizing whip teams to track a member's views of new legislation when it was introduced, rather than waiting until it was about to be voted on. DeLay was known as "The Hammer"—a term he was said to enjoy—for his strict enforcement of party discipline on close votes and his reputation as an intense partisan who exacted political vengeance on his opponents. DeLay also took credit for the new Republican strategy of framing every policy initiative from as far to the political right as possible. In his memoir, he shared:

> If there was a spending bill under consideration we would propose spending that was drastically low, because we were committed to cutting spending, and thus cutting the size of government. Clinton would naturally

pull toward the left, and the Senate would always pull toward the middle. So the lower the numbers we used to start the discussion, the lower the compromise number would be. This strategy gave us a much greater success rate than we had ever known.[11]

In January, as the Clinton impeachment trial was going on, Tom DeLay was building his whip team, and Doc wanted to be a member of it. He had served in a similar capacity in the Washington legislature and enjoyed the work. DeLay agreed, and Doc's appointment as an assistant majority whip was announced in the local newspapers on January 27. Asked why Doc had been selected, one of DeLay's top aides, Mike Scanlon, replied, "Doc is a very well-liked guy inside the conference. He's basically our eyes and ears for the Pacific Northwest."[12]

Each of the approximately forty-five members of the whip team was responsible for three or four other members of the House whenever there was a vote count. Doc said that he enjoyed the work because the whip meetings gave him access to the House leadership and allowed him to learn more about bills coming to the floor.

—

At the same time, there were also some changes on Doc's Washington, DC, staff. Doug Riggs, the legislative director since 1995, left to marry and move back to Oregon. Craig Kennedy replaced him for one year, and then, in August 1999, the position fell to Jeff Markey, who had served as legislative director for Jack Metcalf, another Washington congressman. Markey staffed the nuclear cleanup caucus, managed the Hanford portfolio, and would later become Doc's deputy chief of staff under Ed Cassidy until he left in early 2003.

DOC CONTINUED TO WORK on the many ongoing issues facing his district. First among them was the vexing problem of how to dispose of the fifty-three million gallons of radioactive waste stored in aging underground tanks. In September 1995, Hazel O'Leary, then President

Clinton's secretary of energy, decided to privatize the construction of the Hanford Waste Treatment Plant, essentially admitting that DOE didn't know how to proceed with vitrifying the nuclear tank waste. It took until August 1998 for DOE to select British Nuclear Fuels, Ltd. (BNFL) as the contractor that would build the new plant. The estimated cost of the project was $6.9 billion in 1997 dollars. However, it took until August 2000 for DOE to negotiate a contract with BNFL. When the company finally submitted its construction bid in April, the price tag came in at a shocking $15.2 billion.

Doc supported the BNFL bid because he felt there was no other alternative. "Unless DOE started treating the waste by 2007," he wrote to Bill Richardson, Clinton's new energy secretary, "additional underground storage tanks would have to be built because some of the existing tanks were leaking. This will be an unacceptable alternative. While it appears that the proposed privatization package as structured will not work, we must ensure that the construction of facilities to treat waste begins next year."[13] It was not to be. Richardson cancelled the contract with BNFL based on its high bid in May.

In late July 2000, while Doc was in Philadelphia for the Republican National Convention, news broke that Richardson had fired Dick French, the hard-charging first and only manager of the Office of River Protection at Hanford. Since the office was created in 1998, French had increasingly found himself at odds with DOE headquarters. When BNFL had submitted its $15.2 billion bid to build the plant, French had terminated the contract, and DOE found itself liable for hundreds of millions of dollars in claims from BNFL for past work.[14] Richardson provided Doc with a heads-up before the official announcement. Doc was concerned but realized the decision was Richardson's to make. DOE rebid the project in August 2000 and awarded a $4.4 billion contract to Bechtel National and a consortium of other contractors in December.

Doc and the Nuclear Caucus worked through the summer to ensure adequate funding for other Hanford projects in the giant 2001 Energy and Water Development Appropriations bill. When the House-Senate conference report was passed on September 28, 2000, it included almost

$1.5 billion for Hanford, with $800 million for the new Office of River Protection. The bill also accommodated funding to maintain the Fast Flux Test Facility on standby status, money for the K-Basin removal project, and money for a future museum for the B Reactor. Doc's language made sure that none of the funds could be diverted from cleanup to be used for the newly designated Hanford Reach National Monument. The bill was passed over President Clinton's veto on October 11, 2000.[15]

—

Another unresolved issue was the seemingly endless controversy over removing the Snake River dams. Many environmentalists, Indian tribes, fishermen, and Democrats supported breaching the dams, but the majority of congressional members from the Pacific Northwest opposed it. A study prepared by the National Marine Fisheries Service recommended applying more of the same solutions it was already employing— more water flow, more barging of fish, more spilled water, and no doubt more unhappy stakeholders. Doc wondered why no one was studying the effects of El Niño or the impacts of natural predators or the practices of commercial fishermen. "They're making these suggestions, and they're not looking at all the facts," he said.[16]

Already controversial, the issue now became even more so. Tom Flint, a Grant County farmer and future public utility commissioner, used the brand-new internet to form a non-profit Save Our Dams coalition. On the evening of February 18, 1999, more than three thousand Save Our Dams supporters from the Mid-Columbia braved the winds and rain to rally at the Cable Bridge between Pasco and Kennewick. The state legislature had adjourned for the day so they could attend, along with farmers, utility district employees, dam workers, trade unionists, port employees, and citizens who had been encouraged to attend by the *Tri-City Herald*.

One after another, elected officials, including Slade Gorton, Doc Hastings, and Fifth District congressman George Nethercutt, bashed the Clinton administration—and, in particular, Bruce Babbitt, his interior secretary and an advocate of breaching the dams. Doc told the group, "If rallies like this don't make Bruce Babbitt and his friends think twice about tearing down dams, nothing will. I can tell you that as a member of Congress, he will not get it approved on my watch."[17]

A month later, Doc introduced a "sense of Congress" resolution with ten co-sponsors—all Republicans from western states—that recommended that the Columbia River and Snake River dams be retained, that federal fish protection plans not rely on removing the dams, that efforts to maintain fish populations address all factors, and that all fish recovery plans be based on sound data and consider economic and social costs.

On May 27, 1999, a hearing on the legislation was held in Washington, DC, and in July, it was passed out of the Natural Resources Committee. Doc saw it as a means of educating Congress on all aspects of the salmon recovery issue, not just those put forward by environmentalists. In June, Slade Gorton inserted an amendment in the Senate Energy and Water Appropriations bill that prevented the Bonneville Power Administration from using any funds to breach or remove the dams. The measure passed the Senate by voice vote.

Around this time, a consortium of national environmental groups and supporters ran full-page ads in the *New York Times* calling to remove the four lower Snake dams. This would become an issue in Slade Gorton's 2000 reelection campaign and even in the 2000 presidential campaign.

Doc was able to secure another field hearing of the House Natural Resources Committee in Pasco on April 27, 2000. Chaired by Republican Helen Chenoweth of Idaho, it included Doc, George Nethercutt, and Mike Simpson of Idaho. For five hours, they heard testimony from scientists about ocean conditions, seals, terns, and other salmon predators and grilled representatives of the US Army Corps of Engineers. "We shouldn't miss the opportunity to make real progress toward salmon recovery now while we wait for the outcome of the debate on the dams. Nor is it clear that we should trust the recommendations of our federal agencies on the dams once it is made," Doc said.[18]

In July, the chairman of the President's Council on Environmental Quality announced that the Snake River dams would be kept for another ten years. Gorton stated that no legislation approving the removal of the Snake River dams would pass Congress "if this senator has anything to say about it." He would be unable to keep that pledge. In November, he was defeated by Maria Cantwell by fewer than two thousand votes, and the Snake River dam controversy remained unresolved.

—

One local issue that did get resolved—although not to Doc's liking—was the future of the Hanford Reach. At the beginning of the new Congress in 1999, both sides reintroduced their legislation to protect the Reach. Doc hoped his proposal would lead to a compromise that would allow more local control, but he was not prepared to compromise if it meant the federal government was going to control the Reach. "Their [the Democrats'] legislation was never going to go anywhere. We had the majority in both the House and the Senate, and I was not going to allow it to go anywhere in the House. They were just rallying the troops."[20] But Doc's legislation also failed to go anywhere. "It died in committee. I never thought that the Reach would become a national monument. I thought we would eventually come to some sort of an understanding."[21]

Meanwhile, the Save the Reach group continued to mobilize its efforts to support a federal solution for protecting the Reach. Rich Steele and Eric Gerber expanded the number of tours of the Reach they conducted each year. "Sometimes, it might be one boat for one official," Gerber said, "but often there would be convoys of ten or more boats, stopping at specific locations on shore for presentations by highly qualified experts on subjects like geology, fish biology, history, birds, and other wildlife. There would also be picnic lunches, local beers, and Washington wines available."[22] Soon the tours became must-do stops on the itineraries of visiting state and federal officials. On November 6, Gerber and Steele conducted a special tour for Senator Murray, President Clinton's environmental policy advisor, Kathleen McGinty, and Washington's governor, Gary Locke. McGinty was impressed with what she saw and heard, but it would take seven more months for the future of the Reach to be decided.

Eric Gerber remembered: "When it became clear that this [compromise] was not moving, there was growing pressure to seek a presidential mandate to create a [Hanford Reach] national monument, which he had the power to do without congressional approval. It was kept relatively quiet in that it was discussed among a small number of people, including Senator Murray and members of the volunteer movement."[23]

On May 16, 2000, Bruce Babbitt, President Clinton's interior secretary, visited the Tri-Cities and toured the Reach.[24] Afterward, he announced he was recommending to the president that the Reach and almost two hundred thousand acres of adjacent shrub-steppe be designated a national monument, although he promised to "make every provision I reasonably can" to give locals a say in managing the monument.

Reaction to the announcement was predictable and immediate. "I am overwhelmed," said a joyous Senator Patty Murray, who had been urging the Clinton administration to act after Gorton and Doc continued to block her Wild and Scenic River legislation. Sixth District congressman Norm Dicks told the *Tri-City Herald*, "We did everything possible to work out a compromise, but it was essential that we do this."[25] Idaho congresswoman Helen Chenoweth called it the "biggest land grab since the invasion of Poland."[26]

The Republicans were livid. Doc, or one of his staff members, focused his anger on Murray, releasing a statement that read in part, "It is an insult to the people of Central Washington. Either Senator Murray doesn't know what the residents of Central Washington want—or she doesn't care."[27] In a later interview, the target of Doc's wrath shifted from Murray to President Clinton, but his view of the decision remained the same. "The Antiquities Act of 1906 gave the president authority to do it. I think the act should be changed. A monument is one thing, but something as big as the Reach is an abuse of the act. I felt that federal control of that land was just not good policy. Period."[28]

Ten days later, Al Gore—vice president and the presumptive Democratic candidate for president in 2000—toured the lower Hanford Reach with Patty Murray and Gary Locke in a flotilla of jet boats led once again by Save the Reach advocates Rich Steele and Eric Gerber. After the tour, Gore, accompanied by Murray, Locke, and Rick Leaumont, another Save the Reach advocate and president of the local chapter of the Audubon Society, drove to WSU's north Richland campus to make the formal announcement to a crowd of about three hundred. "We act today so that years from now, Americans will be able to paddle free-flowing waters and hike pristine peaks, enjoying these extraordinary stretches of our national heritage," Gore said.[29]

Doc Hastings was in full campaign mode when he stopped on the steps of the Capitol by a reporter for the *Tri-City Herald* and responded to a question by saying, "At least the Gore campaign is paying for this announcement today, since the people of Central Washington will be stuck paying the price for the decision for generations to come." [30]

—

Only twenty days after Gore announced the creation of the Hanford Reach National Monument, a large part of it went up in flames. At approximately one o'clock on the afternoon of June 27, 2000, a car and a tractor-trailer rig collided on SR 24 near the Hanford Site, killing the driver of the car and jack-knifing the tractor-trailer rig. Vegetation ignited on both sides of the highway.

The weather was over 100 degrees, and the hot winds blew at a sustained speed of twenty miles an hour. It was estimated that during one ninety-minute period, the fire traveled twenty miles across the Arid Land Ecology Reserve (ALE) and was consuming an average of two thousand acres of shrub-steppe an hour.[31]

Energy secretary Bill Richardson and Doc flew to the Tri-Cities on Thursday, June 29, to view the situation firsthand. By the time they arrived, the fire had burned over 190,000 acres and three radioactive waste sites. At least twenty homes in Benton City and West Richland had been destroyed, and seven thousand houses had been evacuated. Governor Locke issued a state of emergency, and nine hundred firefighters using aerial tankers fought the blaze.

On Friday, Richardson announced that the fire had been contained. "There does not appear to be any contamination whatsoever," Richardson said. He hedged slightly when asked if he was absolutely certain about that. "I never say 'absolutely' anymore. We are satisfied at this time there was no radiation release."[32]

Meanwhile, controversy erupted over how the fire had spread so quickly and who was to blame. A man hauling a backhoe was one of the first to come upon the accident after the Hanford Patrol arrived. He offered to use his equipment to control the size of the fire but was refused because of jurisdictional concerns over the ability to use the equipment on the ALE reserve. Hanford watchdog Gerald Pollet, director of the anti-nuclear organization, Heart of America, claimed that the Hanford Fire Department's initial response had been "totally inadequate, and others claimed that the Fish and Wildlife Service was slow to respond when the fire was handed over to them." A state trooper, the first to arrive on the scene, said that the fire "just basically took off."[33] Subsequent investigations by the US Department of Energy and the US Fish and Wildlife Service found no wrongdoing but recommended additional training and firebreaks in the ALE Reserve.

—

Another troublesome and controversial issue had to do with apples. In November 1999, Doc had held a press conference in Yakima where he had been asked about apples. Six out of every ten apples grown in the United States were grown in Washington—most of them in Doc's district. However, some varieties, like the mainstay red delicious, were losing popularity in the face of competition from newer varieties. Growers produced more apples than they could sell, and sales to Asia—one of their prime markets—had declined due to the economic recession there. Other markets were closed to them because of protectionist trade policies. Apple growers lost an estimated $760 million in three years, according to an industry trade group.[34]

There were several ways to deal with the apple glut. One of them was to open up new markets, and Doc talked about his recent meetings with Charlene Barshefsky, the US trade representative, about opening up new markets for Washington State agricultural products. The other way was to provide various forms of government financial support to help the growers. Doc responded that Congress had done what it could, but he recognized that it might not have been enough to help everyone.[35]

Few realized it at the time, but his response demonstrated Doc's growing influence on the Rules Committee and was an example of why he had wanted to serve on the committee in the first place.

In the previous Congress, a member from New York who represented an apple-growing district there had attempted to amend the annual agriculture appropriations bill while it was still being considered by the Appropriations Committee to authorize spending one hundred million dollars in new, low-interest loans for the nation's apple growers over a multi-year period. Under the rules of the House, an amendment that proposes authorizing a new spending program could be included only if the Rules Committee protected it from being removed by a point of order during debate on the House floor.

Apples are not a program crop like cotton or rice that are eligible for annual subsidies, so when the Appropriations Committee brought the bill to the Rules Committee with the new spending program for apples attached to it, they were asking the committee to protect the price support language from being removed during floor debate. Doc had both a political and a philosophical problem with that. If he didn't support his apple growers, he would be held accountable in the next election. But he believed that approving the bill if it included the price support language for apples was bad policy.

The issue escalated, and the Republican leadership became involved. The Rules Committee agreed with Doc and Tom Reynolds of New York, whose district included many apple growers, that the price support language should not have been included in the appropriations bill and told the chairman of the Agriculture Committee that if he wanted to subsidize apples, he and the rest of the committee would have to take the money from the other subsidized crop programs. They could not add net new spending, and any program that was approved would be limited to two years. Doc remembered: "The easiest thing to do would have been to go along with it. The sponsors didn't like it, but we told them that the Appropriations Committee had screwed up by putting the language in the appropriations bill in the first place." Doc was adamant in his objection. "It was bad policy, and it would have created another subsidized crop. I was pretty blunt. I wasn't going to go along with it. I could do that because I had the backing of the chairman of the Rules Committee and the other member of the committee whose district was affected."[36]

Doc's solution was to provide crop insurance that reduced the need for future bailout programs and allowed the apple growers in his district to obtain low-interest loans without creating a new government spending program. Unfortunately, approving the money for the apple growers didn't equate to the growers actually receiving it in a timely manner.

BY THE SUMMER OF 2000, the nation's attention was firmly focused on the upcoming election. There was little suspense on the Democratic side. Vice President Al Gore was his party's presumptive nominee. Gore was a determined campaigner and a skilled debater, but with his stiff demeanor and preachy tone, he was not the natural campaigner that Bill Clinton had been.

The Clintons were deeply engaged in Hillary Clinton's campaign for the Senate in New York, which limited the opportunities for White House events that could be used to highlight Gore's achievements. Their competing personal agendas and the Gore team's concerns about the president's personal liabilities kept the two men from campaigning together.

George W. Bush, governor of Texas and son of the former president, led in the Republican polls but faced opposition from Senator John McCain of Arizona, and thirteen others. Bush ran as a "compassionate conservative," a phrase he co-opted from a book that Marvin Olasky wrote while Bush was governor.[37]

An early Bush supporter, Doc encouraged the candidate to visit Washington State during its Republican preference primary. When Bush accepted the invitation, Doc took the opportunity to lobby him to take a position against breaching the dams. Doc was not disappointed. Bush hit the issue repeatedly during his remarks on February 28, 2000, at Columbia Basin College in Pasco. "We are not going to breach the dams," he told his cheering audience.[38] Bush won the Washington presidential preference primary in February with 58 percent to McCain's 39 percent. "[Bush] said that he believed that he won the primary on the basis of his taking that position on the dams."[39]

Gore ran a campaign that recognized the gains made by the Clinton administration during the 1990s but said it was time to move on and "write a new chapter" with a decidedly more populist theme. In his acceptance speech to the Democratic National Convention, he told the delegates, "I stand here tonight as my own man. . . . I will work for you every day, and I will never let you down."[40]

When the votes were counted on the night of November 7, Gore seemed poised for victory—he was winning the popular vote by more than half a million votes. It all came down to Florida, which the networks first called for Gore and then changed their predictions to "undecided" before calling the state for Bush.

Gore called Bush to concede the election. When it became clear that his deficit was only 537 votes, triggering an automatic recount, he called Bush again to withdraw his retraction. After six weeks, the outcome of the election ended up in the Supreme Court, and George Bush became the president of the United States. *Bush v. Gore* embittered millions of Americans who questioned whether the 2000 election had been fairly decided, and it intensified the degree of political polarization that had already been created in the American public. That polarization would only increase in the years ahead.

Sixteen years later, in the aftermath of another presidential election, pollster Frank Luntz told CBS's *60 Minutes*: "In those six weeks we went from being Ds and Rs to being outraged and believing that the other side was trying to steal the election. The election was over. There was no coming together. There was no honeymoon. And from that point on, the goal has been to delegitimize, not to respect, but to *delegitimize* the opposition."[41]

—

In Washington State, forty-two-year-old Maria Cantwell was still smarting after her 1994 reelection loss after serving only one term in the House of Representatives. The Seattle Democrat had adjusted to her private sector career by making a fortune in the dot.com boom, but she missed serving in Congress. And she believed she could beat Slade Gorton.

Gorton had served in the US Senate with one brief absence since he knocked off Warren Magnuson in 1980. He was a brilliant lawyer and one of the brightest minds in the US Senate, but he was also the primary target of environmentalists, Indian tribes, and the National Sierra Club. The *Seattle Times* abandoned Gorton and endorsed Cantwell after she entered the race, praising her "expansive view of the future."[42]

When election night came, the results of the Washington Senate race mirrored what was happening in Florida. About the same time that Al Gore retracted his concession call to George Bush, Gorton was ahead by about 3,000 votes, with about half a million absentee ballots, mostly in King County, still to be counted. Twenty-four days later Cantwell defeated Gorton by 2,229 votes out of 2.5 million votes cast. Gorton won thirty-four of the state's thirty-nine counties, but he didn't win them by enough to offset Cantwell's plurality of 155,000 votes in Seattle and the rest of King County.[43] Doc was shocked. "That was really tough. He had been my mentor, my close associate on many issues we worked on together, and my guide to what was going on in the Senate. His loss was devastating to us."[44]

Cantwell remembered it took some time to determine the outcome of the race. She had flown back to Washington as soon as it had been determined:

> I went to [Senate majority leader] Trent Lott's office almost as soon as I arrived to discuss my committee assignments. As soon as I got there, they handed me a phone, and I thought, "Who even knows I'm here?"
>
> It was [Washington Sixth District congressman] Norm Dicks on the line. "Maria, you need to get on the Energy Committee! Sam Volpentest would kill you and me both if you don't get on the Energy Committee!"[19]

—

Doc had his own reelection campaign to worry about. In early 1999, the conjecture began over who would run against him in 2000. Rick Locke looked at another run but decided to pass. In June, John Lawson, a fifty-three-year-old Bechtel Hanford waste management supervisor and former Kennewick police officer, announced he was running against Doc as a Democrat. His campaign ended three months later when he died from an apparent heart attack.

Without a significant Democratic opponent, Doc bided his time. He welcomed Speaker Dennis Hastert to Yakima for a fundraiser and a press conference in August 1999, and presidential candidate George W. Bush stopped there in October during a campaign swing through the West.

Doc's Democratic opponent became known on October 8, 1999. He was Jim Davis, a fourth-generation wheat farmer from Coulee City, who declared that he "wanted to bring bipartisan solutions to problems facing the district."[45]

Davis's family had close ties to former House Speaker Tom Foley and the state Democratic Party. A self-described "Blue Dog" conservative Democrat, Davis held a degree in education from Eastern Washington University, was active in various statewide boards and commissions, and had served as a commissioner of the Douglas County Public Utility District since 1987. A former Seattle stockbroker, Davis knew how to raise money and set out to do so, attracting Doc's attention in the process. When the DCCC suggested that he raise twenty-five thousand dollars by the end of 1999, he raised one hundred thousand dollars. Still, it declined to support him in the face of polling that showed the Fourth District would remain Republican. "It became obvious that I was going to have to do this on my own," Davis said.[46] In spite of his disadvantages, he waged an unexpectedly aggressive campaign.

With Congress in session, Doc could only visit the district during weekends, relying on his campaign war chest and a well-organized ground game to produce slick radio and television ads. He hosted majority leader Dick Armey for a fundraiser in Yakima on April 8, 2000, before formally announcing his reelection bid on June 25. Brett Bader again served as Doc's campaign consultant. Doc had the advantage of six years of incumbency, an experienced campaign team, and a substantial war chest of $255,000 in cash on hand that offset the fact that Davis out-raised Doc in the first six months of the campaign.

Whereas Doc was often seen as partisan and confrontational—even by supporters—Davis adopted a more conciliatory position. "My mom's family were all Democrats, and my dad's family were all Republicans," he told a Young Democrats rally in Richland's Howard Amon Park in July.[47] That month, Doc attended the Republican National Convention, where he helped frame the conservation, agriculture, and natural resources section of the party platform, including a plank that opposed dam breaching.

When the results of the September primary election were counted on September 20, Doc had received nearly 60 percent of the vote, while Davis, who did not have a challenger, received slightly more than 30 percent. Gordon Allen Pross, the Democrat-turned-Republican who had run a marginal campaign in 1998, and Libertarian Fred Krauss each received less than 4 percent. "By that time, the cake was already baked," Davis said. "There were things we could improve on, but we couldn't change the demographics of the district."[48]

Doc campaigned with Republican vice presidential candidate Dick Cheney when he visited the district on October 9, and he could claim credit for thirty-five million dollars for emergency payments to apple growers when the House passed the Farm bill on October 18.

Originally scheduled to adjourn on October 5, Congress remained in session in Washington, DC, to pass a budget agreement. Back in August, Doc's and Davis's campaign staffs had agreed to a series of weekly debates once Doc returned to the district. An October 18 debate in Pasco had already been scrubbed by the time the two were scheduled to meet on Yakima public television on October 30. Doc called to cancel hours before airtime. "Doc is back here doing the job he was elected to do," said Ed Cassidy, Doc's chief of staff. Each new cancellation frustrated the Davis camp even more. "He can't complain that he didn't have the opportunity," Davis said. "He's been back in the district campaigning every weekend."[49]

Doc strongly disputed the claim but wasn't going to be rushed into a debate. He remembered how in 1994 the pressure to hold debates had forced Jay Inslee to leave Washington after a late session and fly out to the district on the red-eye—tired and perhaps underprepared—for a debate, and Doc was determined the same thing would not happen to him.

In the last weeks of the campaign, Davis released a blizzard of press releases and advertising, including one in which a grandmotherly actress who had recently appeared in a national marketing campaign promoting Granny Smith apples asked, "Why is a guy named Doc so bad on the issue of healthcare?" Davis claimed the ad was based on an actual grandmother who had asked the same question in Wenatchee.

Doc's limited availability in the district became an issue with the *Yakima Herald-Republic*. When Doc declined to be interviewed on the date they had specified, the paper proceeded to interview Davis only, leading to a testy exchange of emails. The two candidates were finally able to appear together for an extensive interview with the editorial board of the *Tri-City Herald* on October 24.

The *Seattle Times* and the *Yakima Herald-Republic* endorsed Davis, the latter praising him for his approach to the campaign. "It's about bringing people together," Davis told their editorial board.[50] The *Tri-City Herald* endorsed Doc but called Davis "the most impressive candidate yet to try to unseat Hastings."[51] Doc agreed with them. "He was a quality candidate, but he had a difficult road to hoe. I had been there for six years. The biggest issue that separated us was when we would be able to schedule a debate."[52]

The campaign finished with a flourish, with Davis bringing Clinton's agriculture secretary, Dan Glickman, to Yakima on November 1. The long-awaited public debates were finally held in Yakima and the Tri-Cities only days before voters went to the polls. Libertarian Fred Krauss showed up at the Yakima debate to join Davis in taking on Doc, even though he had endorsed him three days earlier. The debates were surprisingly civil and generated little news. "By the time we could hold the debates, I had accepted other appearances and arrived at the debates with my tongue hanging down," Davis remembered. "He was orchestrating the whole thing just like he planned."[53]

Doc's campaign ended with an election-eve visit from Republican vice-presidential candidate Dick Cheney, who spoke to hundreds of supporters in a hangar at the Tri-Cities Airport before heading back to Wyoming. The outcome of the race was never in doubt. Doc received 61 percent of the vote to Davis's 37 percent.

It had been another difficult and polarizing year in American politics. It began with half the country believing their president should be impeached. It ended with the other half believing the election had been stolen from them.

CHAPTER TEN

Never the Same Again

★

ALONG WITH GEORGE W. BUSH'S CONTROVERSIAL victory in the 2000 presidential election, the Republicans retained control of the House of Representatives, in spite of losing two seats to the Democrats. The Senate remained tied 50-50, requiring Al Gore, still vice president, to serve as the tiebreaker during the lame duck session. That changed on January 20, 2001, when George Bush was sworn in as president and his new vice president, Dick Cheney, became the tiebreaker.

With control of both houses of Congress and a young, supportive president in the White House, Doc believed his party was on the verge of achieving its long-held policy goals of smaller government, reduced taxes, tax cuts, and deficit reduction. "With Bush in office," Doc told his listeners at a Lincoln Day Dinner at Yakima's Double Tree Hotel, "I am looking forward to this session as I have not looked forward to any other."[1] But it was not to be. The Democrats regained control of the Senate once again in June when James Jeffords of Vermont switched from Republican to Independent and caucused with the Democrats.

In his speech accepting his party's nomination, George Bush sounded a conciliatory note: "I was not elected to serve one party but to serve one nation. The president the United States is the president of every American, of every race and every background. Whether you voted for me or not, I will do my best to serve your interests, and I will work to earn your respect."[2] Once again, a new president said he intended to bring the nation together.

The normal transition period from one administration to another—from election to inauguration—is normally about seventy-five days. But by the time the Supreme Court decided *Bush v. Gore*, that period had shrunk to only thirty-eight days. Inauguration day dawned cold and rainy. Doc sat with Bob Ehrlich of Maryland and Sue Kelly of New York, who was counting down the remaining minutes of the Clinton presidency with obvious pleasure. Doc and Claire attended one of the eight inaugural balls at the Washington Armory that evening, but the rain turned to snow, and the temperature plummeted. Their children were in town, so Doc and Claire ducked out of the ball early to enjoy a glass of wine with them in the comfort of their warm condo.[3]

Doc attended every presidential address to a joint session of Congress—first addresses are not billed as State of the Union speeches—and Bush's first message, delivered on February 27, 2001, was no exception. The speech served as the new president's budget proposal. Bush proposed more money for education, Medicare, and debt reduction. To pay for it, he proposed lowering tax rates for low-income Americans and capping the rate for the wealthiest Americans at 33 percent.

—

Denny Hastert was reelected as Speaker of the House. His easy, collegial manner of listening to members' concerns made him a more effective administrator than Newt Gingrich had been. Dick Armey and Tom DeLay remained majority leader and majority whip, respectively.

With his small but workable majority, Hastert tried to soften the unflattering image the GOP had gained during the preceding years—an image political columnist Stuart Rothenberg characterized as one of "partisanship, political confrontation, and uncompromising ideology."[4] Hastert agreed with the president's priorities, and by the end of the first hundred days of the Bush administration, the *Washington Post* could report that the new president had a 63 percent approval rating and that the approval rate for Congress, at 51 percent, was the highest it had been in more than a decade.[5]

—

Three days after being sworn in, George Bush proposed a sweeping package of education reform. The No Child Left Behind Act enjoyed bipartisan support and was coauthored in the House by Republican John Boehner of Ohio and Democrat George Miller of California and in the Senate by Democrat Edward Kennedy of Massachusetts and Republican Judd Gregg of New Hampshire. Probably the most far-reaching piece of federal education reform in history, it promoted standards-based education and measurable goals, aiming to improve individual student achievement. Boehner's role in drafting the legislation helped revive his leadership position in the House. It certainly helped define his role as a centrist among the conservatives, but it also cemented his reputation as an effective dealmaker. Roy Blunt of Missouri, the Republican chief deputy whip, said "To some members that probably defined him a more moderate than they would like but, to others, it defined him as a guy with capacity to get hard things done."[6]

The act required the states to develop assessments measuring basic skills in order to receive federal school funding. It didn't set the state standards, but the act expanded the federal role in public education by requiring annual testing and higher teacher qualifications. The House passed the bill on May 23 by a vote of 384-45, and the Senate followed on June 14 by a vote of 91-8.[7]

Doc voted for the legislation but later had second thoughts:

> I had always been a strong proponent of local control of education. In 1976, the Washington State Supreme Court ruled that local property taxes were not sufficiently funding basic education. As a result, the state legislature increased the amount it was spending and assumed added responsibility for funding education.
>
> I felt uncomfortable with that then, and I feel uncomfortable with the federal government taking control over the states and local communities now.

I only voted for it because there was no mandate for national student testing. In retrospect, it hasn't worked all that well.[8]

The House and Senate also voted to approve a $1.35 trillion tax cut that President Bush signed in June, commenting that "the surplus is the people's money. And we ought to trust them with their own money."[8] The tax cut was followed by an energy bill that achieved most of the president's goals, including oil and gas drilling in Alaska. Doc voted for both measures.

—

Soon after the start of the new session, Doc was asked by his congressional colleagues to assume two new jobs. The chairman of the House Rules Committee, David Dreier of California, appointed Doc to represent the committee on the House Budget Committee, and Speaker Hastert asked him to serve on the House Ethics Committee.

The Committee on the Budget was responsible for developing what Doc liked to refer to as the "federal budget blueprint." Its primary responsibility is to adopt a concurrent budget resolution between the House and Senate that establishes aggregate levels of government spending and revenue for the fiscal year.

House rules required that the committee include five members each from the Ways and Means and Appropriations Committees, one member from the Rules Committee, and one member designated by the majority and minority party leadership. Since Doc was already a member of the Rules Committee and was being appointed to the Ethics Committee, he was granted a waiver from the rule prohibiting members from serving on more than two committees. He recalled that "I was appointed to the Budget Committee, perhaps because of my seniority but also because they thought I could do the job."[10]

The committee crafted its budget proposal in line with the new administration's priorities. As Doc listened to the testimony from the newly appointed heads of the government agencies, he reaffirmed his belief that the growth in Medicare entitlements was a major problem:

We had passed a Medicare fix in 1996, but all that did was kick the can down the road for four more years. Now, we were really going to try to tackle the problem.

We were in the process of developing some real reforms when 9/11 happened. Then everything was off the table. We had to focus on how we were going to protect the homeland. The economy went downhill, and federal revenues evaporated."[11]

The House passed its version of the 2002 federal budget in March 2001 and reached agreement with the Senate just before Vermont senator Jim Jeffords left the Republican Party—largely because of his opposition to the size of the proposed tax cuts.[12] Doc felt no such reservations. He believed that "every time we have cut taxes it has had a positive effect on the economy."[13]

—

Doc was quick to use his new clout as a member of the House Budget Committee to protect Hanford funding. "Every new OMB [Office of Management and Budget] director comes in wanting to cut federal spending, and you have to educate them about Hanford," Doc said.[14] Mitch Daniels, George Bush's new OMB director, was no exception, but Doc was shocked when the president's proposed budget was announced and Hanford funding was four hundred million dollars less than officials had requested.

Doc and Jeff Markey, his deputy chief of staff, met with Daniels in March. "The federal government created the problems at Hanford. It needs to accept responsibility for cleaning it up," Doc explained to Daniels. "Hanford wouldn't be there and there would be no problem if it weren't for the need to win the Second World War." Daniels listened and agreed. "So when it came time for him to testify before the Budget Committee," Doc recalled, "I asked him a question about Hanford cleanup, knowing what the answer would be because we had already obtained his support in our private meetings."[15]

But Bush's new energy secretary, former Michigan senator Spencer Abraham, refused to endorse additional spending for DOE. "In my judgement, a billion more dollars isn't going to do much more because most of the [DOE cleanup] sites don't have a short-term game plan," he said.[16]

However, during the summer and the fall of 2001, Doc was able to restore Hanford's funding level to $1.8 billion for 2002. Markey remembered:

> We got language built into the House budget resolution which said that a certain amount of money shall be included to support environmental management work.
>
> We used our position on the Budget Committee to include that language, and we used our position on the Rules Committee to make it stick when it came to the appropriations process. We had to educate each new administration, and we had to educate the committee too. That's one of the primary reasons that the Nuclear Caucus, which Doc chaired, was created.[17]

On the other hand, an invitation to join the House Ethics Committee came as a complete surprise. When one of Denny Hastert's aides told Doc that the Speaker would like him to serve on the Ethics Committee, Doc asked for several days to think about it. Nobody ever seeks to serve on the Ethics Committee. Doc remembered, "On the negative side, the Ethics Committee can be very difficult because you're passing judgment on people you're serving with. On the positive side, it meant that the leadership had enough confidence in me to make the right decision. After thinking about it in this way, I agreed to serve."[18]

The Ethics Committee was another of the so-called leadership committees. It includes five members of the majority party and five members of the minority party. The committee is authorized to enforce the standards of conduct for members, officers, and employees of the House and to investigate alleged violations of any law, rule, or regulation. The committee investigates potential ethics violations and recommends specific action, if necessary, to the House. Allegations against a member can be made only by another member or as the result of a news story published by a reputable news organization. In either case, the motivations of those making the allegations are often unclear.

Most issues resolve themselves without the Ethics Committee ever having to take any action. Others are settled with a simple formal advisory opinion agreed to by both the member and the committee. If necessary, a member of the leadership might tell someone to change his or her behavior, or even advise the individual to resign. If all else fails, an investigative subcommittee is appointed to look into the matter.

After serving for a year on the committee, Doc received his first assignment: investigate the flamboyant Ohio congressman, James Traficant. A populist Democrat from Youngstown, Ohio, Traficant had been elected to the House in 1984. His constituents loved him. As the sheriff of his local county, Traficant once refused to execute foreclosure orders on several unemployed steelworkers. In 1983, he was charged with racketeering and accepting bribes. Traficant claimed he had accepted the bribes as part of his investigation into corruption, and a local court acquitted him of all charges.

In the House, he was colorful and eccentric, always taking full advantage of "one minutes," the one-minute blocks of time that allowed members to speak on any subject they chose. Traficant often concluded his rambling dissertations with the phrase "beam me up" from the television series, Star Trek.

After the Republicans gained the majority in 1995, Traficant often voted with them. When he voted for Hastert for Speaker in 2001, the Democrats stripped him of his seniority and refused to give him any committee assignments. The Republicans wouldn't assign him to committees either, and he became the first member in more than a century not to have a single committee assignment.

In February 2002, Traficant was indicted on federal corruption charges for using campaign funds for his personal use. After a two-month federal trial, he was convicted of ten counts of bribery, racketeering, and tax evasion. The matter was referred to the Ethics Committee, and Doc was chosen to chair the subcommittee that was formed to investigate the charges. They reviewed the full transcript of the trial in federal court and reported there was reason to believe Traficant had violated House rules. An adjudicatory subcommittee then reviewed the evidence presented by Doc and his subcommittee and confirmed their findings.

On July 19, 2002, the full Ethics Committee held a hearing to consider the recommendations of its subcommittees. Traficant was allowed to defend himself. Dressed in a white, western-cut coat, Traficant chided the committee for already having decided to throw him out of the House, but he had kind words for Doc. "I have just read the subcommittee report, and I just wanted to say that Doc Hastings is a very fair man," he said.[19] That didn't keep Doc from voting with the rest of the committee to expel Traficant from the House.

"He could have short-circuited the whole thing by simply resigning," Doc remembered, "but he wanted to go through the whole thing."[20]

—

George Bush's presidential honeymoon could not be expected to last indefinitely, and it didn't. Some members questioned the younger Bush's preparation and readiness for the job. Others were bothered by what appeared to be deficits in his attention span and curiosity, but as the historian David Halberstam wrote, they were "reassured by their friends that if he was not exactly a big boy himself, he was surrounded by all the big boys from his father's administration."[21] The former White House chief of staff to President Ford, Dick Cheney, was vice president. Colin Powell was secretary of state; Donald Rumsfeld was secretary of defense. James Baker never seemed far away.

The president's national security advisors were well aware of the Saudi-born Osama bin Laden and his militant Sunni Islamist terrorist organization, al-Qaeda ("the base" or "the foundation" in Arabic). The group fought alongside the CIA to oust the Russians from Afghanistan in the 1980s. Bin Laden remained in Afghanistan as the guest of the Taliban government, financing a continuing campaign of terror against the

United States and its allies, believing that their support of Israel was an effort to destroy Islam.

Al-Qaeda claimed responsibility for bombing the US embassies in Tanzania and Kenya in 1998 and for attacking the navy destroyer USS *Cole* in Yemen in 2000. While US intelligence agencies tried to track bin Laden down, efforts to bring him to justice were complicated by the complex relationship between the US and Saudi Arabia, where some wealthy families provided funding for al-Qaeda. And, although Osama bin Laden and al-Qaeda caused serious concerns, America's intelligence community believed the greatest threat came from Iraq, where Saddam Hussein was suspected of developing weapons of mass destruction. The necessity of forcing Saddam to accept United Nations weapons inspectors had led the Clinton administration to bomb them periodically in the 1990s.

—

While the president's national security team worried about Saddam Hussein and Osama bin Laden, Denny Hastert was worrying more about the nation's faltering economy. On Monday, September 10, 2001, the Speaker flew back to Washington from his Illinois district early to meet with the president about an economic stimulus package he had been developing.

Doc and Claire Hastings were at their Arlington condominium on Sunday, the day before, just having returned from a driving trip through New England. They planned to attend the annual White House picnic—billed by the Bush team as a "congressional barbeque"—on Tuesday evening.

On the morning of Tuesday, September 11, Doc drove to the White House for an early breakfast with fellow members Rob Portman of Ohio, Jim DeMint of South Carolina, Bob Ehrlich of Maryland, and others for a meeting with members of the Bush economic team that Portman had organized. It wasn't hard to get onto the White House grounds in those days, and Doc parked between the White House and the Old Executive Office Building, exchanging pleasantries with the vice president, Dick

Cheney, as he entered the ground floor entrance to the West Wing and walked down the stairs to the White House Mess.

At 8:46 a.m., while they were finishing their breakfast meeting, five hijackers flew American Airlines Flight 11 into the North Tower of New York's World Trade Center complex. Nineteen minutes later, the TV networks switched from their morning programming to live coverage of the events in New York just in time to watch another five hijackers crash United Airlines Flight 175 into the World Trade Center's South Tower.

As Doc and the others were leaving the Mess, someone came up to Portman to say that a plane had crashed into the World Trade towers. Everyone rushed back their offices. DeMint and Ehrlich drove back from the White House up Pennsylvania Avenue to the Capitol with Doc, listening to WTOP on the car radio.[22]

Claire had turned on the TV to watch a morning news program just in time to see the second tower being hit. She thought it was "strange that they were showing a movie thriller that early in the morning." She called Ilene Clauson, Doc's scheduler and office manager, to tell her what she was seeing on television. Clauson remembered, "I didn't really understand the magnitude of it at that point and immediately turned on the office TV set."[23] She was quickly joined by Jeff Markey, Doc's deputy chief of staff, and Todd Young, his communications director, around the small TV.

Doc was scheduled to hold a 10:00 a.m. press conference on the Endangered Species Act with other members at the House Triangle on the Capitol grounds, about a block away from Longworth House Office Building where Doc's offices were located. Markey and Young left the office for the press conference, anxious to alert Doc to what they had just witnessed on television. At 9:37 a.m., American Airlines Flight 77, under the control of five more hijackers, slammed into the West Front of the Pentagon in Arlington, Virginia.

Almost immediately after Claire hung up from talking to Ilene Clauson, she heard what she thought was a sonic boom. Sirens wailed from first responders, including from the fire station across the street. Claire went into the street with dozens of her neighbors. "Everyone was on their cell phones," she recalled. "Of course, Doc only had a pager." At the corner of the street, she could see smoke billowing up from the Pentagon.[24]

Doc began to speak at the press conference before his staff could reach him with the news of the attack. From his location on Capitol Hill, Markey spotted smoke rising in the distance from what looked to be Virginia. He used his Blackberry to call Liz Fortunato, one of Doc's legislative assistants, at work at Doc's office and asked her to look out of the window to see if the smoke was coming from the Pentagon. She said she thought it was.

At 10:03 a.m., four more hijackers gained control of United Airlines Flight 93 and headed toward Washington, DC, where they planned to crash into the Capitol or the White House. When passengers fought to regain control of the aircraft, it crashed outside Shanksville, Pennsylvania, near Pittsburgh.

Markey grabbed Doc, told him the news, and said, "We've got to get out of here." "Just then," Todd Young remembered, "a Capitol police officer came running over toward us, waving his arms, and telling everyone to get away from the Capitol building," as members and their staffs hastily evacuated the Capitol, streaming down the stairs and onto the grounds. Markey saw a large plane circling in the sky. "I was quite sure we were going to die," he recalled.[25]

The three ran down Independence Avenue to Second Street Southeast, where Doc suggested they duck behind the massive James Madison Building of the Library of Congress in case a plane hit the Capitol. Markey, a Roman Catholic, proposed they seek shelter at the nearby St. Peter's Catholic Church, located just ahead on the corner of Second and C Streets. They banged on the rectory door and identified themselves to the monsignor and his staff.

Doc used the church telephone to call his father in Pasco to let him know he was all right. His second call was to Claire at their condominium in Arlington, less than a mile from the Pentagon. Jeff tried to call the office without success.[26]

In the meantime, Markey and Young desperately tried to locate their fellow staff members. They finally got through to Jessica Gleason at her apartment on Capitol Hill. The rest of the staff had huddled there, watching TV after being told to evacuate Longworth. Doc, Jeff, and Todd walked across Capitol Hill to join them.

After about an hour, Doc, Todd, and Ilene walked to the Capitol grounds to pick up Doc's car and drive to Doc's condominium in Pentagon City. Ilene remembered, "Claire made tuna fish sandwiches. I was a pretty young staffer at the time and appreciated Doc's gesture in making sure that I was able to get to my home about two blocks away."[27] As they crossed the Potomac River on the Fourteenth Street Bridge, they saw the Pentagon burning.

At some level, each of them realized America would never be the same again.

—

President Bush was in Sarasota, Florida, at a local grade school when he was alerted and driven to the airfield to board Air Force One at approximately 9:45 a.m. With much difficulty, he called Dick Cheney in Washington. "We're at war, Dick," he said, according to Ari Fleischer, the president's press secretary, who took verbatim notes. He told the others in the aircraft, "When we find out who did this, they're not going to like me as president. Somebody's going to pay."[28] The plane flew to Louisiana and then Nebraska before the president overcame his staff's objections and ordered a return to the White House where he arrived that evening. At 8:30 p.m., he addressed the nation. In what would later be known as the Bush Doctrine, he declared, "We will make no distinction between the terrorists who committed these acts and those who harbored them."[29]

Contacted by the *Yakima Herald-Republic* in his DC office on September 12, Doc said that he had passed the still-smoldering Pentagon on the way to work and that Congress would provide the president whatever he needed to fight terrorism. "What it boils down to is whatever President Bush concludes he needs, we will deliver," Doc said.[30] That was true for the victims of the attacks as well, as Congress considered emergency appropriations bills.

—

In the aftermath of the attack on 9/11, no one knew for sure if, or how many, other al-Qaeda operatives were in the country or whether there would be more attacks. Unbelievably, it seemed as if the second wave of attacks might occur in the form of biological warfare when various news outlets and Capitol Hill postal workers opened the mail on September 18 to discover what turned out to be deadly anthrax bacteria spores in a white powder, along with notes that read, in part:

DEATH TO AMERICA.
DEATH TO ISRAEL,
ALLAH IS GREAT.

Most of the disruption occurred in Senate office buildings, which were closed for three months, but some of the letters arrived at the Longworth House Office Building. It was shut down for several weeks. Doc and Todd Young went out to the district, while the rest of the staff operated in shifts at a temporary office in the Government Accountability Office building, corresponding by Blackberries and email. They were still not receiving daily postal mail as late as December.

Todd Ungerecht remembered that when they finally returned to their buildings, "Everything sat eerily on our desks just as we had left it when we ran out of the building: calendars, pencils, coffee cups."[31] Ultimately, seventeen people were infected and five died. Nine years later, the Justice Department concluded that a disaffected government scientist who committed suicide in 2008 had been the source of the letters.[32]

On September 20, with the Capitol still in the grip of the anthrax scare, President Bush spoke to a Joint Session of Congress. British Prime Minister Tony Blair was present to show the support of America's strongest ally. Doc kept an embossed printed copy of Bush's speech as a keepsake. "I've heard a lot of speeches, but I've never heard a speech that elicited as much unity. You could feel it," Doc remembered. Bush spoke for about forty minutes, demanding that the Taliban deliver Osama bin Laden and his network to the United States or face military attack. On October 7, 2001, Operation

Enduring Freedom—the War in Afghanistan—began. It would last as long as Doc Hastings served in Congress.

—

On January 29, 2002, George Bush addressed the Congress in his second State of the Union address. In a forty-eight-minute speech that was interrupted by applause more than seventy times, he addressed an audience more unified behind their president than any since Franklin D. Roosevelt. More than 80 percent of the public approved of his performance in the five months since 9/11. In the most memorable line from his speech, Bush referred to North Korea, Iraq, and Iran as an "axis of evil."[33]

He also used the speech to address the effects of the deepening recession that had started months before 9/11 but had certainly become worse as a result of it. Following the attack, Speaker Hastert and his team quickly fashioned a one-hundred-million-dollar economic stimulus bill that the House passed in late October 2001. Bush pushed for its passage in his speech as a stimulus to aid relief efforts. "My economic security plan can be summed up in one word: jobs," he said and argued that the most effective means of creating jobs was by speeding up tax relief in order to speed up investment in factories and equipment.[34]

Doc voted for the bill but with deep reluctance, knowing there was no other alternative at the moment. Unfortunately, the Senate refused to act on the plan, and nothing was done.

—

In February 2002, the House and Senate formed a joint inquiry into the performance of the various US intelligence agencies. Their report, released in December 2002, detailed repeated failures of the FBI and CIA to use information that had been available to them. An independent, bipartisan presidential commission, which included former senator Slade Gorton of Washington, spent two years preparing another detailed account of the circumstances leading up to the attacks and listed recommendations designed to guard against future attacks.

The two reports resulted in massive changes in how the government protected the homeland. The USA PATRIOT Act eliminated many obstacles that had been keeping law enforcement and the intelligence services from sharing information with each other. It passed Congress with votes of 357-66 in the House and 98-1 in the Senate and was signed by the president on October 26, 2001.

More than a year later, in December 2002, a new cabinet-level Department of Homeland Security (DHS) was created. It combined the functions of twenty-two formerly separate government agencies. Perhaps, most importantly, the National Security Administration (NSA) launched a Terrorist Surveillance Program to monitor the communications of citizens who were suspected of having ties to terrorists.

Bush authorized the program without congressional approval because of fears that debate on the subject would expose their methods of obtaining information. "He believed that he had the authority and that he was following the law," Doc said. "He held regular classified briefings with the leadership of both parties to brief them on the progress of the program."[35] His actions would be questioned later on. Doc remembered:

> We had two problems. We had cut back on our foreign intelligence after the fall of the Soviet Union. Now we had to rebuild them, and that takes a long time. The other problem was that we had to find a way to monitor communications, and there's no question that it crosses the line of civil liberties.
>
> There was always a question as to whether we should listen in on conversations between Americans, but I had no problem with us listening in on conversations between Americans and others.[36]

—

All of it, somehow, had to be paid for. Denny Hastert remembered that Don Nickles of Oklahoma, the Senate minority whip, came to him saying, "Geez, this thing may be five billion dollars." Hastert replied that it would be more like forty billion dollars.[37] In 2011, the New York Times put the cost of the physical damage, the economic impact, homeland security and related costs, war funding, and future veterans' benefits at $3.3 trillion.[38]

Doc tried not to think about the cost. "At least with the military budget, there were experts who could tell you how they arrived at the estimates. With things like rebuilding lower Manhattan, you were forced to just throw money at the problem. One of the dangers of going to war is that you give too much power to the executive branch."[39]

Doc's misgivings were minor compared to the issues facing the president. In addition to concerns about the budget, he was dealing with where to hold captured enemy fighters, how to determine their legal status, and what methods to employ to interrogate them.[40]

—

In spite of the demands created by 9/11 and its aftermath, Congress found time to pass some non-related but otherwise important pieces of legislation. Both Houses passed the economic stimulus bill the president had been seeking to help prop up the faltering economy, which he signed on March 9, 2002. He also got some of the tax cuts he had been advocating. The Job Creation and Worker Assistance Act provided companies with an additional 30 percent, first-year tax break on business equipment and added three years to the period that business losses could be carried forward. "We were in a recession, and we wanted to stimulate the economy. That's one way to do it . . . cut taxes," Doc remembered.[41]

On March 27, Bush signed the Bipartisan Campaign Reform Act, generally referred to as "McCain-Feingold" after Senators John McCain of Arizona and Russ Feingold of Wisconsin, although it was the House version of the bill that the president ended up signing. The controversial law decreased the role of soft money in political campaigns by placing limits on the contributions by interest groups and national political parties. Sections of the law were later struck down by the Supreme Court, allowing corporations, labor unions, and very wealthy individuals to contribute large sums of money to political campaigns. "I voted against McCain-Feingold on the basis of prior Supreme Court decisions that decided that political contributions were part of free speech," Doc explained. "When you take action to limit free speech, I have a problem with that."[42]

—

A major farm bill was passed over White House objections and reluctantly signed by the president into law on May 13, 2002. It directed that approximately $16.5 billion in agricultural subsidies be spent each year and included the $100 million in apple relief. The size and timing of the bill made its passage highly contentious. Sweeping amendments in the House and Senate delayed the bill's passage after the 1996 farm bill had expired in 2001.

On August 6, the president signed the Trade Act of 2002, providing him the authority to negotiate fast track trade agreements with other countries. Congress retained the authority to approve or disapprove the agreement but not to amend it. The issue had been controversial since the founding of the republic, but particularly since the passage of the North American Free Trade Agreement in 1994. Economic fault lines transcended political parties to divide states like Washington that benefited from foreign trade from states like those in the industrial Midwest that had lost jobs because of it. The last fast track authority had expired in 1994, and George Bush was anxious to get it back. Doc favored it too. Both campaign finance reform and free trade would remain contentious issues for the rest of Doc's time in Congress.

—

And then there was the issue of what to do about Iraq. At a meeting of the National Security Council at Camp David on September 15, Bush's secretary of defense, Donald Rumsfeld, suggested using the 9/11 attack as a pretext to take out Saddam Hussein. Secretary of State Colin Powell disagreed, arguing that the coalition supporting the US against Afghanistan would view it as a "bait and switch."[43] No one, he argued, could look at Iraq and say it was responsible for September 11. The next day, Bush told his national security adviser, Condoleezza Rice, that while the US was going to focus on attacking Afghanistan first, he also wanted to do something about Saddam Hussein. "We won't do Iraq now. But it is a question we're gonna have to return to."[44]

It took more than a year, but Bush finally decided to deal with Iraq. On October 4, 2002, Doc and other members attended a classified briefing by Rice and officials from the CIA describing the intelligence they had about Saddam's efforts to hide his weapons of mass destruction. Doc told a reporter for the *Yakima Herald-Republic*, "We need to be ready for conflict." Asked if he was satisfied with the documentation that had been presented authorizing a military strike, Doc responded, "I've been briefed. There is ample reason why we have to do it. If Saddam isn't stopped, it's going to happen somewhere else. And, if we don't do it, who will?"[45]

By October 11, both houses had passed a joint resolution authorizing the president to use military force against Iraq in any way he deemed necessary, provided it would not hinder the efforts against al-Qaeda in Afghanistan. However, they failed to confront the critical questions surrounding how they would win the peace. Neither the House nor Senate Armed Services Committee pursued questions of force size, post-invasion plans, or the roles of the reserves and the National Guard.

Hastings saw the war with Iraq as an extension of the current war on terror and downplayed any similarities between the Iraq situation and Vietnam. "The United States will pursue victory more aggressively with a clear-cut goal of setting up a democracy in Iraq. This will not be a quagmire like Vietnam," he maintained.[46] The House voted 296-133, and the Senate voted 77-23 for the war authorization against Iraq, which Bush signed on October 16, 2002.

—

One of the unquestioned perquisites of being a member of Congress is congressional travel. CODELs, or congressional delegations in government parlance, are a time-honored tradition going back many decades, although the practice expanded greatly after the onset of air travel. Some are sponsored and paid for by interest groups like the Heritage Foundation or AIPAC, the American Israel Public Affairs Committee. Most are financed by the taxpayers. The stated intent of going on a CODEL is to inform and educate the members so they can better understand positions espoused by the sponsoring organization or issues related to their committee assignments. First-class travel arrangements for a member and spouse can easily cost five figures apiece, not including accompanying military or State Department coordinators. In 1996, Doc went on a decidedly no-frills trip to Kosovo during the Balkans War, and in 1997, he and Claire participated in a trip to Hong Kong and Shanghai, sponsored by the Heritage Foundation.

In April 2001, Doc and Claire joined a CODEL to Japan, Okinawa, and Hong Kong led by David Dreier, the chairman of the Rules Committee. They had been scheduled to go to Beijing, but were rerouted to Okinawa after a navy signals intelligence plane was forced to land on an island in the South China Sea after a mid-air collision with a Chinese military fighter jet just six days before the start of the trip. In August 2002, Doc and Claire took a leisurely trip to Europe and Russia led by Henry Hyde, the chairman of the House Foreign Relations Committee, where they had a chance to meet and compare notes with many legislative leaders.

WITH DRAMATIC EVENTS PLAYING OUT in the nation's capital and around the world, 2001 began for Doc's constituents with the most severe drought in recorded history. Farmers and orchardists living in the three counties with junior water rights from the Yakima River learned they could expect only 28 percent of their normal water supply. Crops and fruit withered in the summer heat.

At the same time, market manipulations, illegal shutdowns of pipelines owned by the collapsing energy consortium, Enron, and capped retail electricity prices created an energy crisis in California. Multiple large-scale blackouts and the collapse of Pacific Gas and Electric, one of the state's largest energy companies, resulted. Federal regulators asked and then ordered Washington's power producers to sell power to California, which depleted water supplies in the region's reservoirs.

The historic drought greatly exacerbated the problems of the region's apple growers. The US Department of Agriculture estimated that overproduction, reliance on less competitive apple varieties, trade barriers, and global competition had cost the industry more than $1.5 billion over the past five years. Doc had been instrumental in obtaining $100 million in aid for losses that had occurred in 1998 and 1999 and simultaneously took action to keep apples from becoming another subsidized crop. Growers needed the money in January to begin pruning and other spring work, but bureaucratic wrangling and the transition from the Clinton to the Bush administration kept the aid from reaching them. Frustrated growers complained to Doc and his staff, who blamed the outgoing Clinton administration for the delay. "We appropriated this money last October, but for some reason they failed for three months to approve the regulations required to issue checks to eligible growers," Doc said.[47]

In June, Doc teamed up with Senator Patty Murray to support an additional $250 million in aid, although the growers hadn't yet received their checks from the first round of help. Their prospects did not improve when the House Appropriations Committee cut the request from $250 million to $150 million, and the Senate zeroed it out entirely. In November 2001, a House-Senate conference committee ultimately approved $75 million and diverted half the money to fund a family nutrition program. "I'm really disappointed and frustrated," said Murray. "Apple growers shouldn't have been put into competition with women and infants." Doc blamed the Senate more than the family nutrition program. "You are starting from a tough position when the other chamber is at zero," he said.[48]

The apple-aid saga didn't end there. Doc and Senator Murray obtained $100 million more in apple relief in a 2003 farm bill, which passed in May 2002, "to make them whole," Doc said.[49] In the end, the nation's apple growers received about 40 percent of the money they had requested over a three-year period.[50]

In April 2001, before the full impact of the drought was known, Doc was already pushing for drought relief money, but he also wanted water and power consumers to pitch in. "The issue of the energy and the drought will have a huge impact on Central Washington. Above all, we need to conserve. It is a situation no one anticipated." As one solution, Hastings called for the completion of a partially built nuclear plant at Hanford, but he realized this was unrealistic as a response to a periodic drought.[51]

—

Monday, July 9, was another typical midsummer day in Central Washington. When weekend campers in the Okanogan National Forest failed to extinguish their campfire and left the scene, they started what, at first, seemed like an easily controllable fire. The twenty-one firefighters assigned to the fire estimated they would have it out by nightfall. But, during the course of the next day, as temperatures rose and the winds picked up in the afternoon, the fire spread from ten acres to 2,500 acres that night. The firefighters called for help, including a water-toting helicopter. However—not unlike the Hanford fire—bureaucratic red tape allowed the fire to spread. In this case, there was a question about the legality of letting the helicopter dip water from a protected river in a special Forest Service study area. Four firefighters died, and fourteen others survived only by crawling into their fireproof survival shelters.[52]

The *Yakima Herald-Republic* conducted a seven-week investigation and found a series of safety violations and bad management decisions that combined to lead to the deaths. The Forest Service initially claimed that the four who died had disregarded orders to evacuate but later concluded that the orders may not have been clear. The victims' families and the paper came to the conclusion that the culture of the Forest Service played a role in the tragedy. Todd Young remembered, "A lot of issues converged."[53] As a result of the paper's reporting and meetings with members of the firefighters' families, Doc and Senator Maria Cantwell became involved in the issue. Cantwell, a member of the Public Lands and Forests Subcommittee of the Senate Interior Committee, agreed to hold a hearing on the matter in October.[54]

Unfortunately, the hearing fell victim to the anthrax scare that closed down the Senate office buildings. Cantwell scheduled another hearing and called officials of the Forest Service, family members of the victims, and Doc to testify. As result of the hearing, Cantwell introduced an amendment to the Senate version of the farm bill that required the inspector general of the Agriculture Department to investigate future firefighter deaths.

In March 2002, Doc introduced legislation in the House that mirrored Cantwell's bill but wasn't tied to the future fortunes of the farm bill.

That difference proved prescient because on April 29, Cantwell's amendment fell prey to a political disagreement between the Democratic-controlled Senate and the Republican-controlled House over timber thinning practices and aid to apple growers.[55] Doc was able to bring his bill, HR 3971, to the floor on the suspension calendar with limited debate. It passed the House by a voice vote and the Senate by unanimous consent. Two weeks later, it was signed by the president into law—slightly more than a year after the fire.

Some in the firefighting community saw the legislation as a knee-jerk reaction to the tragedy. They claimed the Office of Inspector General in the Agriculture Department had no experience or training investigating wildfires and required those involved in such incidents to "lawyer up" to defend themselves.[56]

—

The effects of the drought were made even worse by the lack of enough water storage in the Yakima River Basin. No reservoirs had been constructed in the Yakima Valley since 1933.

While Doc pushed conservation and new power plant construction, Benton County commissioners explored constructing a new reservoir in the Black Rock Valley that would more than double the water storage capacity in the basin. In April 2002, they asked Doc for federal help in adding $300,000 to the Bureau of Reclamation budget to study the project. Cost estimates put construction at $1.8 billion, but the reservoir would hold 1.7 million acre-feet of water, which would be pumped into the reservoir from the Columbia River.[57]

By September, Benton County joined Yakima and Kittitas Counties in calling for two million dollars in federal aid to help cover the cost of the environmental impact statement on the Black Rock reservoir. "We had to change the legislation to include Black Rock in the study because it was physically located outside of the Yakima Basin," Doc explained. "It was a last-minute deal. I got a provision including Black Rock in an appropriations bill and got the point of order waived so that it could be approved on the House floor."[58] Doc felt the state of Washington should also help pay for the study. "All projects of this size have been a partnership between the state and federal government."[59] By then, the 2002 election cycle began, and further discussion was postponed until the next session of the 107th Congress.

—

And, as always, there were Hanford issues to attend to. Some, like the Fast Flux Test Facility (FFTF), seemed to have developed lives of their own. Back at the end of the Clinton administration, the outgoing energy secretary, Bill Richardson, had ordered the permanent closure of FFTF. But before that action could be implemented, Doc had been able to convince the new energy secretary, Spencer Abraham, to hold off while DOE looked at potential new missions one last time. A local proposal to produce medical isotopes surfaced, provided DOE would keep the reactor in standby mode while the program geared up over three years, but DOE decided the proposal failed to adequately identify specific markets for the isotopes, and on December 19, 2001, Abraham ordered the facility be shut down.[60]

It was a difficult blow to the Tri-Cities community. Many in the community felt Doc had not done enough to save the reactor. A few, led by Benton County commissioner, Claude Oliver, continued to blame Doc and used FFTF as part of the rationale to oppose him when he ran for reelection in 2006. Doc felt that two energy secretaries in two different administrations had decided there was no mission for FFTF, so he was willing to agree to pull the plug. There was not much else he could do once two different administrations had decided to shut down the facility.

Another continuing saga was the on-again, off-again efforts to construct the Hanford Waste Treatment Plant. On July 9, 2002, DOE finally gave permission to Bechtel National to proceed with the pouring of structural concrete into the five-foot-thick, steel-reinforced basement foundation wall of the first waste processing building. Bechtel National was now estimating that 10 percent of the tank waste could be vitrified by 2018 and all of it by 2028 at a cost of $4.4 billion.[61]

THE 2002 MIDTERM ELECTIONS were held on November 5 against a backdrop of the war on terror, a war in Afghanistan, an impending war in Iraq, and a growing national recession. The Republicans gained eight seats in the House and two in the Senate. It was only the third time since the Civil War that the party in office gained seats in a midterm election and the first time that the Republicans had done so.

—

Back in Doc's congressional district, Jim Davis announced in January 2002 that he would not challenge Doc again. "I would need to see that the district has changed substantially for it to make sense to run again," Davis said. Yakima County Democratic Party chairman Erik Noel Nelson admitted the party had been virtually swept from the playing field in recent years and was trying to rebuild. "It's easier to lose your reputation than to build it," he acknowledged.[62] During his annual round of meetings with Fourth District state legislators in Olympia, Doc announced he would run again.[63]

When the filing period ended on July 26, it appeared Doc might not face a plausible Democratic opponent. Perennial candidate Democrat-turned-Republican Gordon Pross had filed, as had Democrat Thor Amundson, who attracted a mere 243 votes in Yakima County when he ran against Patty Murray in 1998. On the following Monday, however, first-time Democratic candidate Craig Mason's name was added to the ballot after failing to be listed originally because of a technical blip.

Mason, a forty-four-year-old sociology professor at Columbia Basin College, formally announced his candidacy on August 2. A libertarian and self-identified "twenty-first-century New Deal Democrat," he held conservative views on gun control and religious issues but favored a Hanford cleanup effort similar to the post-Depression public works programs that built the hydroelectric dams. "If the Senate was full of Doc Hastings, there wouldn't be any cleanup," Mason claimed. He blamed Doc and the Republicans for the recent corporate scandals, like Enron, that had rocked the financial world, saying that "Hastings and the other Republicans in Congress . . . allowed big business to get away with it. They simply came to power to try to help the rich."[64]

Mason had virtually no funding, while Doc entered the race with $225,000 cash on hand. To run his 2002 campaign, Doc hired Ellen Murray Howe, an Ohio native who had worked for John Boehner and now lived in Ellensburg. The campaign was also assisted, at least indirectly, by Karl Rove, President Bush's political operative, whose consulting firm had written the book on how to tailor direct mail to known voter preferences.

Doc and Mason didn't debate each other during the primary. The news was dominated by peripheral events in which Doc played a role, like the lively spectacle of James Traficant's defense against the ethics charges that had been brought against him, the arrival of the most recent aid to the region's apple growers, and Bechtel National's unwelcome announcement that the cost of the Hanford Waste Treatment Plant had risen to $5.6 billon.

In the primary, Doc received 75,745 votes, just under 70 percent, to Mason's 18,726. Mason hoped to become a much more active campaigner in the general election in order to gain name familiarity. He aimed to win 40 percent of the vote to improve his chances when he ran again in 2004. "Realistically, that's how most challengers have to do it—run twice," he said. "You really have to spend a year fundraising."[65]

In the Washington Voter's Guide statement, Mason claimed that political action committees had contributed more than one million dollars to Doc's campaign, including "large PAC contributions from Enron," the failed energy company. Doc adamantly denied the charges, and the Federal Election Commission's records backed him up, showing that Enron's PAC had not contributed to Doc's campaign, although individual Enron executives and employees had contributed to other PACs that supported Doc. The candidates faced off in a joint interview with the editorial board of the *Yakima Herald-Republic* newspaper, which had maintained a frosty relationship with Doc. They reported that Doc had received $131,400 in PAC money in 2002, which accounted for about half the money raised for his campaign. Mason claimed Doc had received more than one million dollars from PACs since 1994. Todd Young, Doc's spokesman, said that Mason hadn't demonstrated anything. "He's just making things up as he goes along because he can't prove Doc took one dime from Enron."[66]

The Yakima paper called the race "a cakewalk" and offered a lukewarm endorsement of Doc. The *Tri-City Herald* also endorsed Doc, writing that he "has an unnecessarily rigid loyalty to his political party, but . . . has grown into the job enough to take initiative on many issues that might not adhere strictly to the GOP agenda but are vital to his district."[67]

Jon DeVaney, one of Doc's legislative assistants, thought he understood the source of Doc's tensions with the local newspapers. Like his political hero, Ronald Reagan, Doc had thought deeply about his political philosophy and knew where he stood on issues. According to DeVaney, the newspapers didn't understand Doc's mind-set: "His more intellectual and ideological approach to politics put off the newspaper editors who viewed his clarity of thought as doctrinal rigidity. They felt that this made Doc too conservative for a district that had elected Democrats prior to Sid Morrison in 1980 and again with Jay Inslee from 1992-1994."[68]

The two candidates appeared together on a Halloween-night TV call-in show in Yakima, which was later rebroadcast in the Tri-Cities. In a "spirited but collegial discussion," Doc said that less government was better. He supported partial privatization of Social Security. Mason, an unapologetic liberal, asserted that the federal government should fund Medicaid reimbursement of drugs, and opposed any changes in Social Security.[69]

Doc handily won the general election with almost 67 percent of the vote. In an email statement released on election evening, Mason said he had run "to stop the vicious class warfare that the Bush legislative agenda had launched against the working class." He had undertaken a nearly insurmountable hurdle in his run against Doc, raising only eight thousand dollars and not launching his campaign until the first week of August.[70] "Craig was an interesting guy," Doc remembered. "He was pretty liberal but, like [senator] Bernie Sanders, pro-gun. He was just not a match for the district he was running in."[71]

CHAPTER ELEVEN

A Nation at War

★

DOC HASTINGS BEGAN HIS FIFTH TERM in the House of Representatives on January 7, 2003, when Speaker Denny Hastert swore in the members of the 108th Congress. The Republicans under George W. Bush had gained eight House seats in the midterm elections, when almost all previous presidents had lost them. Bush had personalized the contest, asking voters to elect a team of Republicans who would help him succeed, and many observers felt his plea had made the difference in the election.

The Republican conference voted to promote Tom DeLay from majority whip to majority leader after Dick Armey stepped down. Roy Blunt of Missouri moved up to become majority whip, Eric Cantor of Virginia became his chief deputy, and Deborah Pryce of Ohio was elected as the conference chair to round out the Republicans' leadership team. The Democrats elected new leaders as well, consisting of Nancy Pelosi of California as House minority leader and Steny Hoyer of Maryland as minority whip.

—

In his first inaugural address, President George W. Bush had acknowledged the deep divisions that separated the country he was about to lead:

> And sometimes our differences run so deep, it seems
> we share a continent, but not a country.
> We do not accept this, and we will not allow it. Our
> unity, our union, is the serious work of leaders and citizens

in every generation. And this is my solemn pledge: I will work to build a single nation of justice and opportunity.[1]

Now, three years into his presidency, those differences—which had been muted after the country came together following 9/11—were growing louder again. The nation's economy was entering a recession. The country was already at war in Afghanistan, and now there was increasing talk of going to war in Iraq, leaving many, particularly among the Democrats, questioning both the justification for war and the president's motives. Doc believed the growing the partisan divide was unavoidable. "Some people worried about the money we were spending. Others worried about civil liberties. Some just said, 'Let Bush own this.' The farther away you get from an event like 9/11, the more second-guessing is going to happen. It's just predictable."[2]

Doc was in the House chamber for the president's second State of the Union message on January 29, 2003. Bush recognized reality as he began with the words, "Our nation is at war, our economy is in recession, and the civilized world faces unprecedented dangers. Yet the state of our union has never been stronger." He again called Iraq, Iran, and North Korea an "axis of evil," and noted that evidence found in Afghanistan confirmed that "far from ending there, our war against terror is only beginning."[3] While he made no specific threats, his comments were clearly intended to build public support for future action.

On February 5, the secretary of state, Colin Powell, addressed the United Nations Security Council and accused Iraq of hiding weapons of mass destruction. Doc told the *Tri-City Herald*'s Washington bureau chief, Les Blumenthal, that he found Powell's presentation persuasive.[4]

On March 17, Bush issued an ultimatum to Saddam Hussein: leave Iraq or face military conflict. Saddam refused, and the United States and its allies attacked Iraq two days later. Three weeks later, Saddam had fled, and American troops entered central Baghdad.

Powell had once cautioned Bush about the consequences of military action in Iraq, citing what he liked to call "the Pottery Barn rule: 'You break it, you own it.' You are going to be the proud owner of twenty-five million people. You will own all their hopes, aspirations, and problems. You'll own it all."[5]

As Powell had feared, the Allied occupation of Iraq did not go well. Almost immediately, the Americans found they had inadequate troops on the ground to prevent the wide-scale looting in the cities that followed Saddam's collapse. The American decision-makers also failed to understand the strength and nature of the religious divides and cultural traditions of the country. In its short history as a nation, Iraq had become dependent on the well-entrenched, Sunni-dominated dictatorship of Saddam Hussein who maintained order with a large and very efficient internal security force. Once that had been destroyed by the allied invasion, the majority Shia and large Kurdish populations faced an uncertain future and, almost immediately, began to exert their long-suppressed influence.

Instead of leaving Saddam's army and government intact but under coalition control, Paul Bremer, President Bush's appointed head of the Provisional Authority in Iraq—and a man with no experience in the Middle East—decided to purge thirty thousand to fifty thousand of Saddam's party members down to the level of teachers and minor functionaries in the government. To make matters worse, in the ten months following the invasion, the Bush administration decided to cut troop levels in Iraq from 192,000 to 109,000 because of increasing political pressure at home. Further, a detailed search of the country failed to find the weapons of mass destruction that had been predicted by just about every reliable intelligence source, further weakening the president's credibility for ordering the invasion in the first place.

By early summer, Iraq had become a magnet for extremists of all kinds—the armed remnants of Saddam's army, tribal militias, al-Qaeda terrorists, and later, Shia, Kurdish, and Iranian militias. A full-scale insurgency was soon underway throughout the country. By the time the administration decided that military occupation was the wrong policy, it was too late. Congressional critics and more and more American citizens blamed the Bush administration not just for its handling of the occupation but also for getting the country into the war in the first place.

Following the passage of the Iraqi War Resolution in 2002, Congress had played only an episodic and many felt, inadequate, role in overseeing the planning for and the conduct of the war. As conditions deteriorated, more Democrats who had voted for the war began to question their decision and the administration's policies in Iraq.

—

On March 19, 2004, the first anniversary of the Iraqi invasion, Doc and five other members participated in a CODEL to Jordan and Iraq led by Joe Knollenberg of Michigan, the chairman of the Defense Appropriations Subcommittee. "I had never been to a war zone, but I voted for the war and wanted to go over there," Doc explained. By coincidence, the pilot of the US Air Force C-130 that ferried them from Jordan to Iraq was from Finley, a rural community located southeast of Kennewick. Doc had nominated him to attend the US Air Force Academy.

The delegation met with troops, Paul Bremer, and members of the Iraqi Governing Council, which days before had adopted a provisional constitution. After his meetings, Doc was "confident" that Bremer "had a handle on everything" and that democracy could be established" in the war-torn country.[6]

The heaviest fighting of the war came toward the end of the year as coalition forces tried to clear insurgents out of the Sunni strongholds of Samarra and Fallujah. By this time, local polling found that 92 percent of the Iraqi people considered the United States and its allies to be occupiers rather than liberators. Coalition forces played into al-Qaeda's hands by occasionally abusing the civilian population and their treatment of Iraqi prisoners held at the infamous Abu Ghraib prison.[7] Jessica Gleason, Doc's communications director at the time, remembers him coming out of a meeting where members had been shown a video and pictures taken at the prison. "He came out of that room in deep thought, I can tell you."[8]

—

Back in January when the Republican conference was organizing for the new session, Doc had been encouraged by Jennifer Dunn and others to run for an open position on the twenty-three-member House

Republican Steering Committee as the representative of his fellow Republicans from the ten western states. The Steering Committee, which Doc called the "committee on committees," made the final decisions about who would receive the chairmanships and committee assignments in the new Republican-controlled Congress. Unlike his other committee assignments, this one operated entirely within the confines of the Republican conference and allowed him to exercise a level of partisan power and influence unlike any other job he had held.

Doc campaigned hard for the job by writing letters and talking to fellow members from the western states. As it turned out, he was the only one nominated for the position. Later, he tried to explain his new role to a reporter by saying, "Anytime you have an opportunity to interact with colleagues on a different level, it ultimately helps your constituents."[9]

In reality, his new position turned out to be one of significant importance because of the timing of when he had been elected to Congress. In 1994, one of the reforms implemented by the new Republican majority had been to institute six-year term limits for new committee chairmen. Those chairmen had stepped down following their three terms at the end of the session in 2000, and the competition to replace them was often fierce. Seniority played a role, but so did everything else about the candidates: "their personalities, their politics, everything. Discussions about them were *very* candid. Sometimes there was considerable tension when a chairmanship was involved, but 95 percent of the rest of [the committee] appointments just fall into place," Doc recalled.[10]

—

Doc's activities on the Rules, Budget, and Ethics Committees continued as before. He used his positions on the Rules and Budget Committees to influence legislation and policy that were important to his district. For example, "every year, there would be a series of Hanford or environmental issues that would arise, and I was almost always able to shape them to our satisfaction through the committee process," Doc said.[11]

Jim Nussle, a fiscal conservative from Iowa who would later become director of the Office of Management and Budget, wanted to address

entitlement reform. Doc recalled that a meeting of the Budget Committee to look into the issue had been scheduled to start right after his
eventful morning press conference on September 11, 2001. "Nine-eleven
changed all that. After that, it was all about funding Homeland Security,
the TSA, and finding more money for the military."[12]

In addition, the defection of Vermont Republican Jim Jeffords in
2001 meant the Democrats now controlled the Senate. When the Republican-controlled House passed its budget for 2003, it couldn't reconcile
its differences with the Senate. The impasse meant the two bodies had
to pass a series of what are known as "continuing resolutions" to fund
the government for short periods—almost always amid great controversy and a highly polarized political environment. Doc believed he knew
where the problem lay: "The congressional process is broken. There are
not common rules between the House and the Senate. Efficiency is very
hard to obtain. The budget process is just one example." He continued:
"The last major reform was the 1974 Budget Reform Act. They came up
with a process by which the House and Senate would both pass a budget
and there would be spending limits imposed on the various appropriations bills. So if you don't pass a budget in the first place, it's hard to pass
anything else."[13]

—

Even with his new committee assignments and the fact that he had
been elected and reelected five times by margins that approached 70 percent, Doc Hastings was still virtually unknown outside of Congress and
his home district. An extensive backgrounder about him that appeared
in the *Seattle Times* on October 23, 2003, noted that he had never held a
Capitol Hill press conference.[14]

The article also mentioned the fact that Doc was one of a half-dozen
members that Speaker Denny Hastert relied on to preside over the House
during debate on important issues, not just because he was a loyal partisan—which he was—but also because the Democrats knew they would
get a fair shake with Doc in the Speaker's chair. "He is someone who
quietly moves the ball forward without bringing attention to himself,"

said John Feehery, Hastert's spokesman. "The Speaker appreciates that. The Speaker trusts him."[15]

Doc's staff would contact the Speaker's office to see when he was scheduled to preside and then call Claire and the district office so they could watch him live on C-SPAN. Jeff Markey, Doc's deputy chief of staff in those years, remembered, "He played an important role in the institution, not because he was always in the public eye but because he wasn't. Perhaps because he had the good fortune to represent a safe district, he willingly agreed to take on the hard jobs that no one else wanted to do, with fairness and generally without controversy."[16]

—

All that was about to change. In the early morning hours of Sunday, November 23, 2003, Doc Hastings was a key participant in what many congressional observers felt was one of the most egregious examples of congressional dysfunction in many years. So much so that Thomas Mann and Norman Ornstein—veteran Congress watchers, one a Republican and one a Democrat—chose to use the event to open the first chapter in their 2006 book, *The Broken Branch*.[17]

In a rare Saturday session, Congress considered HR 1, the Medicare Modernization Act, a top legislative priority of President Bush and the Republican leadership. Six years in the making, it represented the largest overhaul of Medicare in its thirty-eight-year history by expanding the role of private health plans, providing billions in federal subsidies and tax incentives, and adding a prescription drug benefit. The *New York Times* described the upcoming vote on the measure as "fiercely polarized." Democrats feared the legislation would undermine and ultimately privatize Medicare with subsidized plans, allowing private health insurers to select only the recipients they wanted.

To ensure the vote ran smoothly, Speaker Hastert asked Doc to preside over the debate. The Republican leadership knew they were a few votes short but believed most of the fence-sitters would change their mind after intensive lobbying by the whip team.

At 11:36 p.m., Hastings announced the start of two hours of debate on the measure. Saturday night had already become Sunday morning when, at 3:00 a.m., Doc announced the time for debate had expired and members had fifteen minutes to vote. At 3:15 a.m., the measure was failing with twenty-two conservative Republicans, concerned with the cost of the program, voting against their leadership. Doc kept the vote open beyond the announced fifteen minutes, a relatively common tactic used by both parties when necessary. "It's part of the art of getting the votes," a spokesman for majority leader Tom DeLay told a reporter. "The pressure of the vote, the reality of the bill actually being on the floor pushes people from the undecided column into the yes column."[18]

At 3:30 a.m., the Republicans still needed two votes. It was clear that some of the Democrats were abstaining until they saw which way the vote would go. Doc remembered vividly that David Wu, a Democrat from Oregon, was one of those who hadn't voted. "Other Democrats hung around his desk waiting for him to vote. I swear that he stared at me for three hours. I would stand up or sit down, and Wu was still staring at me." Charlie Johnson, the House parliamentarian, was sitting on Doc's right. At one point he stepped up to the dais and said, "I've never seen anything like this before."[19]

Ten minutes later, the Republicans picked up a vote as Dana Rohrabacher of California was convinced to change his vote. But by 3:48 a.m., the vote was 215 for the measure and 218 against. The Democratic opposition now had the votes to defeat the measure if only they controlled the Speaker's chair. But they didn't. At 4:00 a.m., another Republican changed his vote from present to no.

Increasingly frantic, members of the Republican leadership were engaged in animated private conversations in small groups in the corners of the chamber and in the Republican cloakroom where some members were receiving telephone calls from President Bush flying on Air Force One on his way home from England. By 4:20 a.m., the Republican leaders were focused on just a few recalcitrant members, including Nick Smith of Michigan who was set to retire in 2004 but whose son was already running to take his place. At 5:53 a.m., a smiling Tom DeLay emerged from the cloakroom, having convinced "Butch" Otter of Idaho and Trent Franks of Arizona to change their votes from no to yes. With enough votes now in hand to pass the measure, DeLay quickly signaled to Doc to close the vote. At that point, the remaining Democratic hold-outs voted for the bill and provided a final majority of 220 to 215.

Democrats were infuriated by the maneuver. It was one thing to hold the vote open while members were in the well waiting to vote. It was another to hold it open indefinitely—in this case for two hours and fifty-three minutes, during which the Democrats had enough votes to defeat the measure—until the Republicans convinced enough of their members to change their votes. "The extended vote was an outrage. We won it fair and square, so they stole it by hook or crook," minority leader Nancy Pelosi cried. Hastert responded with typical understatement, "Our job was to get our people on board. It took some time."[20]

Doc voted for the bill. "I had a problem with expanding Medicare, but I thought the Part D benefit was good policy. It provided choices to seniors on prescription drugs, and as a result of those choices, the projected expenditures of Part D came in something like forty million dollars under budget five years later. I was also a big fan of the provision to expand medical savings accounts."[21]

Doc questioned what all the fuss was about: "The vote was in complete compliance with the Rules of the House that say that the minimum time for a vote is fifteen minutes. There is no maximum. The time rule is exceeded all the time. Admittedly, it was the longest vote on record, but I also hold the record for the shortest vote on record by one second."[22] He accused the Democrats of prolonging the vote: "The vote went long because some of the Democrats wouldn't vote while they tried to figure out what we were going to do. Some of our members changed their votes. Once we crossed the threshold of 218, then the Democrats who had been holding out voted for it. It could have passed very easily if the Democrats who voted for it hadn't waited until the end."[23]

—

The vote in the House that night represented a turning point in several careers. Hastert's desire to secure a domestic win for his president and give the congressional Republicans an issue to run on in the next election changed the way others perceived him. Until then, he had been widely seen as an amiable, almost invisible sidekick to Tom DeLay, the House majority leader. Now he was seen as a strong leader in his own right. DeLay's actions in pressuring Nick Smith to change his vote led to an admonishment from the House Ethics Committee. Doc's role in keeping the vote open became an issue in his own 2004 reelection campaign.

As a member of the Ethics Committee, Doc couldn't escape the controversy that followed the Medicare vote. Within a week of the vote, Nick Smith wrote a newspaper article claiming unnamed House leaders had promised to provide one hundred thousand dollars for his son's campaign to succeed him. On January 20, 2004, minority leader Steny Hoyer called for an ethics investigation into Smith's accusations of bribery, threatening the unofficial truce the two parties had observed since the 1990s when ethics complaints were commonly used as political weapons against members of the other party. [24]

A six-month investigation by the Ethics Committee concluded DeLay had told Smith he would endorse his son's election bid if he voted for the Medicare bill. Doc recalled: "[Chairman Joel] Hefley [of Colorado] and [ranking member Alan] Mollohan [of West Virginia] came out and presented [their decision] to us. I objected to the fact that we were just seeing this for the first time and thought that we should have had more time to consider it. However, I also thought that the committee's decision should be unanimous."[25]

On September 30, the committee voted to admonish DeLay, the lowest level of punishment available, and took no further action. Doc voted with the rest of the committee to admonish DeLay.[26] "Alan Mollohan was really after DeLay and wanted more," Doc recalled. "They couldn't get the votes to reprimand him, so they admonished him."[27]

And then, only six days after the first admonishment on September 30, the committee admonished him again for asking federal aviation officials to track an airplane involved in a Texas political spat and for conduct that suggested political donations might influence legislative action.[28]

While Doc hadn't initially voted for DeLay for majority whip in 1995, he had always gotten along with him, and DeLay had made him a member of the whip team in his third term. "There were issues with DeLay going way back," Doc said. "He was trying to elect Republicans, and he was winning. Of course, the Democrats were going to go after him."[29]

IN SPITE OF THE INCREASING LEVELS of political polarization, Doc and his staff still had to deal with the everyday issues that mattered to his constituents back home. In addition to the ongoing issues like Hanford cleanup, new events demanded Doc's attention, such as a financial crisis at a Pasco hospital, citizenship for immigrant members of the military, an impending visit by the president, an outbreak of mad cow disease, and the creation of a historic trail and monument.

Only five days after the start of the new Congress, Doc and the other members of the Nuclear Cleanup Caucus sent a letter to the Office of Management and Budget, reminding it of their agreement to include three hundred million dollars in a special cleanup account in DOE's 2004 budget. In the previous Congress, the House and Senate Appropriations Committees had voted to allocate $7.5 and $7.3 billion, respectively, for cleanup, but they hadn't reached a compromise before they adjourned. "Now we have to make sure [in the 108th Congress] the appropriations process follows that, including the commitment that OMB made for adequate funding. We are asking the executive branch to live up to that," Doc wrote.[32]

—

On February 4, 2003, news broke that Lourdes Health Network, based in Pasco, had lost $1.2 million in the last six months of 2002 and would have to cut 10 percent of its staff. The hospital's chief executive blamed lower patient volumes and significant increases in the cost of liability insurance and electric rates that were not reimbursed by Medicare, Medicaid, or the insurance companies. The next day, Kennewick General Hospital announced it was cutting a quarter of its management staff for many of the same reasons. The hospitals turned to Doc for help.

Doc and his staff soon discovered the problems were not limited to the Benton-Franklin Counties, where at least one of four persons— about twenty-three thousand people—was uninsured. Many small and rural hospitals faced the same problems nationwide. Doc quickly signed on to legislation providing more funding for community health centers and lobbied the Appropriations Committee to increase the 2004 budget. He also met with the director of the Centers for Medicaid and Medicare Services, which managed the Medicare program, and found an administrative fix that solved many of Lourdes's reimbursement problems.

Later, in August, Doc voted against his party leadership and the pharmaceutical industry in a rare vote of independence to support a bill that allowed Americans to buy drugs in Canada and other countries where they are less expensive. "I don't care if there turns out to be a political price to pay for opposing the drug companies. I just think this is the right decision," he said.[33] However, that issue and the problems with the smaller hospitals only reinforced his strong view that Medicare had to be that reformed.

———

On February 12, 2003, it was reported that the US Forest Service had taken action against eleven employees after the tragic deaths of four Central Washington firefighters almost two years before. Citing privacy laws, the agency refused to release the details of their disciplinary actions, even to the families of the young firefighters who had been killed. Ken Weaver, the father of one of the firefighters and a business owner in Moxee, was outraged. "Why didn't they guard my son's right to life as zealously as they guard the privacy of their employees?" he asked.[34] Doc's and Senator Maria Cantwell's staff worked to get the full report released later that year.

———

On February 13, Doc voted to approve the $397.4 billion appropriations bill that included $1 million to study the construction of the proposed $1.8 billion Black Rock Dam, as well as other alternatives. Doc added the money as a member of the Rules Committee and got the point of order waived so it could be approved when the legislation reached the House floor. While less than the amount they had been seeking, Doc was happy to take what he could get. "When we began this process several months ago, it was extremely doubtful we would get any funding at all." By July 2004, the study had received $6.5 million in state and federal funds.[35]

—

In March 2003, Hanford's regulators, the state of Washington, and the US Environmental Protection Agency claimed that DOE's plan for eliminating Hanford's tank wastes—released only in January—was already "in disarray."[36] In May, a federal district judge issued a restraining order prohibiting DOE from sending transuranic waste to Hanford from other nuclear sites. Those events and stop-work orders issued by the Washington Department of Ecology prompted DOE to halt all major cleanup activities.[37] An ongoing test of wills over how much authority the state had to regulate cleanup activity continued as the parties spent most of the rest of the year in and out of the federal courts.

In June, a coalition of anti-nuclear activists in Washington launched a successful initiative drive that banned future waste shipments to Hanford. The campaign collected almost two hundred thousand signatures for what would become Initiative 297, far more than enough to put it on the November ballot where it was approved by almost 70 percent of the voters.

In July, the government's General Accounting Office (GAO) released a report saying that after spending eighteen billion dollars on nuclear cleanup nationally over two decades, the program was far behind schedule and was badly in need of an overhaul. The GAO report challenged DOE's decision to build a facility to separate the wastes stored in underground tanks without first testing the technology. Jessie Roberson, DOE's assistant secretary for environmental management, defended the decision before a House committee, contending that full-scale testing would lead to lengthy delays.[38]

Not surprisingly, DOE's request was opposed by four states, environmental groups, and Indian tribes. Doc was slow to speak up against the idea, drawing a negative editorial from the *Tri-City Herald*, which said his response was troubling. "Not only has the issue been brewing for more than a year, but the outcome is critical to the future of the mid-Columbia as well." Doc clarified his position two days later when he voted in favor of a motion by Congressman Jay Inslee to leave the current definition of high-level waste alone.[39]

Doc and others continued to press the litigants to resolve their dispute. In November, DOE and its regulators released a joint announcement that they had largely settled their dispute over the classification of wastes and related timetables. "My constant message to DOE was that 'you have to come up with a *plan.*' I always tended to side with the state because of my belief in local control, but I kept telling them not to push it so hard that you end up in court."

In 2004, Congress directed the US Army Corps of Engineers to review the escalating costs for constructing the Hanford Waste Treatment Plant. The estimated cost of construction had been $4.35 billion when the contract had been awarded in 2000. The current estimate had grown to $5.7 billion—a 30 percent increase, but still slightly under the amount that had been allocated by Congress. However, the study concluded there was a considerable risk that the cost of the WTP would significantly increase and not enough money had been set aside for construction contingencies or problems that might arise.[41]

—

During his previous two terms, Doc had worked tirelessly to obtain federal aid for apple growers. Now the region's asparagus growers were in trouble due to cheaper imported products and high labor costs. Tariffs on Peruvian asparagus had been dropped to encourage the farmers there to grow asparagus instead of opium poppies and cocoa leaves. The Washington asparagus industry was worth $44.9 million in 2002, and Yakima and Franklin Counties accounted for at least 60 percent of it. Doc had been instrumental in convincing the Agriculture Department to buy more asparagus for federal nutritional programs, but after Seneca Foods, the last asparagus packing plant in the state, announced it would close its Dayton facility in 2005, there was not much more he could do beyond obtaining funding for Washington State University so it could study the development of a mechanical harvester that would lower labor costs.[42]

—

Not long after the beginning of the war in Iraq, Doc learned of the deaths of soldiers from his district who were not US citizens. Some of them had been in the process of becoming citizens but had been unable to attend a ceremony due to their deployment or their unfortunate death in combat. In March 2003, after learning from the Department of Defense that approximately thirty-seven thousand legal immigrants currently served in the armed forces, Doc introduced legislation that would grant such legal immigrants immediate US citizenship if they met the other existing criteria. Doc's legislation passed out of the House Judiciary Committee in May and passed the full House in June.

When Doc's legislation was incorporated into a larger bill, the Senate objected to granting immediate citizenship and proposed a one-year waiting period instead. That still cut two years off the previously required time for obtaining citizenship. The act easily passed both the House and the Senate and was signed into law by President Bush on November 24, 2003. Doc was disappointed but went along with compromise. "By the time that they had completed their extensive training before being deployed, many if not most had passed the one year threshold required for citizenship. You have to compromise sometimes, and I could live with that."[43] That didn't keep Doc from listing it on his website as one of his proudest accomplishments after the legislation had been signed.

—

Another problem reared its head in July 2003. Since its creation in the last years of the Great Depression, the Bonneville Power Administration (BPA) had marketed the power generated by the system of dams on the Columbia and Snake Rivers, developed a massive Northwest power grid, and tried to help fund the ill-fated Washington Public Power Supply System (WPPSS). Over the years, it had developed a contentious relationship with the public and private utilities that purchased its power and with its government watchdog, the GAO. The GAO announced the BPA was at risk of defaulting on its debt to the federal government. Ratepayers who bought power from the agency complained about its high cost and wasteful management practices.

Without exception, all the parties would come to Doc and other members from the Northwest to complain about the other parties. "My constant message to BPA and the utilities was, *"You guys figure this stuff out!* I'm not going to get involved. If you let Congress get involved with this, you're going to come out with answers that *none* of you are going to like."[44] By November, the parties had come to an agreement to lower rates and spending, but it would not be the last time they would seek Doc's help.

—

On August 15, 2003, the White House announced that President Bush would visit Washington State for the first time since the 2000 election. Bush was scheduled to make a speech on salmon recovery in Seattle on Friday, the twenty-second, but the threat of large anti-war demonstrations there led his staff to move the event to Ice Harbor Dam on the Snake River. "He liked it here and wanted to come back," Doc recalled. In 2000, Bush had won the Washington primary by taking a strong position on saving the dams.

Bush was the sixth president to visit the Tri-Cities in the past one hundred years. Even most local historians had forgotten that President William McKinley had visited Pasco in 1896 on a campaign swing through the Pacific Northwest or that Theodore Roosevelt visited the city in 1903 to discuss the promise of irrigation. Harry Truman had dedicated the Pasco Elks Lodge in 1950 and told twenty-five thousand people jamming Lewis Street that plutonium would be man's "greatest benefactor if turned to peaceful purposes." President John Kennedy had been welcomed by thirty-seven thousand people standing in the desert in the hot September sun when he dedicated the Hanford Generating Plant in 1963. Fifteen thousand attended the dedication of the first building on the Battelle campus (now Pacific Northwest National Laboratory) when President Richard Nixon visited in 1971.[45]

President Bush had first visited the area just before Washington's 2000 presidential primary, and Doc was delighted to see him return for a second visit. Doc happened to casually mention that his oldest daughter, Kirsten, had delivered his sixth grandchild the night before.

The public who wanted to see the president were largely disappointed. For security reasons, neither Bush's itinerary nor his route was released. Perhaps only a thousand onlookers glimpsed him at the airport or along the route to the dam. The actual event at the dam was an invitation-only affair with invitees vetted by Doc's office staff. "Security was really tight. They had people across the river, along the travel route, everywhere," remembered Todd Young.[46]

Speaking for about twenty minutes, Bush appeared to enjoy being back in the Tri-Cities and pleased Doc by remembering to mention that Doc's daughter had just delivered a new grandchild. Bush also scored points by repeatedly hitting themes he knew would be popular with his audience. "This facility is a crucial part of the past, and I'm here to tell you it's a crucial part of the future as well. . . . We've got an energy problem in this country, and we don't need to be breaching any dams."[47] He also noted that new fish passage technologies had boosted salmon runs. The president mingled with the invited guests for about fifteen minutes, and then it was back to the Tri-City Airport along a closed highway to board Air Force One, which had been flown into Pasco for the trip to Seattle and a two-thousand-dollar-a-plate fundraiser that night in Bellevue, which was expected to raise $1.4 million. Doc flew to Seattle with the president. It was his one and only flight aboard Air Force One.[48]

—

The president's comments re-ignited the controversy over breaching the Snake River dams. Republicans and Democrats alike were soon energized by a Portland federal judge's ruling in May 2004 that rejected the government's new salmon plan, which had determined that the dams could be operated without jeopardizing the survival of endangered fish. "Here we go again," Doc thought. "It's always the dams."[49] Todd Young recalled that the Portland judge was very biased in favor of removing the dams. "He was injecting his personal opinions in his decisions and substituting them for the scientific and engineering conclusions of the federal government. No judge can order the dams removed. Only Congress can do that."[50] The issue of the dams never seemed to go away, but at least the battle lines were predictable.

—

As 2003 came to an end, a new issue surfaced that was anything but predictable. In December, a dairy cow in the Yakima County town of Mabton was diagnosed with bovine spongiform encephalopathy (BSE), commonly known as mad cow disease. The disease can be fatal to humans who eat food contaminated with blood or tissue from an infected animal. The disease was first discovered in England in 1986 and spread to Canada in 1993. It's generally transmitted when the remains of infected cattle are unintentionally included in concentrated food supplements fed to dairy herds. The cow from Mabton was one of eighty-one cows that had originated in Canada. Others were traced to farms in Quincy and Mattawa.

More than thirty countries immediately banned beef products from the United States, threatening a major industry in Doc's district and initiating a frantic search to locate each of the other eighty-one cows. Restaurants took beef off their menus, and more than five thousand dollars' worth of french fries produced in the mid-Columbia were unable to be exported because they had been pre-fried with beef tallow. In some cases, entire herds were euthanized because authorities couldn't determine whether they had been infected. At the same time, vivid television pictures of infected animals created panic about the safety of the beef supply.[51]

Doc struggled to calm the fears of his worried constituents. He attended a rally of 2,600 in Mabton at a support-the-beef-industry rally, eating hamburgers and soothing fears. Talking to a town hall attended by 250 in Richland, he said, "Our beef industry is still very, very sound. It's just our international trade partners we have a problem with."

By mid-summer of 2004, the Agriculture Department had come up with a National Animal Identification System that allowed better tracking of animals and a new regimen of periodic testing. By December 2004, no new cases of mad cow disease had been found in the United States. Beef consumption, beef prices, and consumer confidence were at pre-mad cow levels, and officials were looking to reopen the border with Canada while negotiating to reopen and renew exports to Japan, Korea, and other countries.

—

Meanwhile, Doc promoted two projects of unique historic value. In July 2004, Doc and Senators Patty Murray and Maria Cantwell introduced legislation in the House and Senate proposing a study leading to the creation of an Ice Age Floods National Historic Trail. The results of the Ice Age floods were evident throughout the mid-Columbia, from its Channeled Scablands and Palouse Falls to creating the channels of the region's major rivers. Ice Age floods enthusiasts envisioned a trail managed by the National Park Service that described the historic significance of the floods, and Doc agreed.

On September 28, the Congress approved and sent to the president's desk Doc's legislation to study the creation of a new national historic park that would include the B Reactor at Hanford and other facilities associated with the Manhattan Project at Oak Ridge, Tennessee, and Los Alamos, New Mexico. That project ultimately became a reality on September 15, 2015.

As GEORGE W. BUSH PREPARED to defend his presidency in 2004, he faced Senator John Kerry of Massachusetts. Kerry, who had served in the Senate since 1985, was a decorated Vietnam veteran who had married into the H. J. Heinz fortune. In February, Kerry defeated former Vermont governor Howard Dean in Washington's Democratic primary, winning nearly 50 percent of the Washington delegates to the Democratic National Convention in Boston. In a convention in which Kerry was assured the nomination, many agreed that the greatest highlight was the keynote address by a young Illinois senator named Barack Obama.

While Kerry was being nominated in Boston, Vice President Dick Cheney visited Kennewick to raise money for Republican gubernatorial candidate Dino Rossi. Doc worked with Cheney's staff to add another stop in Yakima four days later. Speaking to a large crowd of partisans packed into a high school gymnasium, Cheney accused the Democrats of wanting to raise taxes and appease the enemies of the United States. "Terrorist attacks are not caused by the use of strength. Instead they are caused by the perception of weakness."[52]

The 2004 election was really a national referendum on the conduct of the war in Iraq. In another election cliffhanger, Bush's victory was not decided until 4:59 a.m. on November 3, the day following the election after waiting for provisional ballots to be counted in Ohio.[53]

Bush's margin of victory in the popular vote was the smallest ever for a reelected incumbent president. His 286 to 251 victory in the Electoral College clearly showed the political divide as the Democrats won the Northeast, upper Midwest, and Pacific states, while the Republicans carried the rest of the country. Republicans picked up three seats in the House and four in the Senate, ensuring they would remain in the majority in Congress.

—

Washington State had its own partisan divide with voters in the populous western part of the state voting mostly for Kerry and every county in Eastern Washington voting for Bush. The state also produced the nation's closest election contest when Democrat Christine Gregoire was finally declared the winner over Republican Dino Rossi in their race for governor. While both candidates were economic centrists, Rossi, a King County real estate agent, campaigned on economic issues and regulatory relief. Doc was one of his strongest supporters in Eastern Washington. Gregoire, who had roots in Eastern Washington, had helped to negotiate the Tri-Party Agreement that regulated the Hanford Site and challenged tobacco and pharmaceutical companies as the state's attorney general.

The race was too close to call on election night, and it took two weeks to declare Rossi the winner by a margin of 261 votes, triggering an automatic recount. After the recount, Rossi still led by 42 votes out of more than 2.8 million votes cast. Democrats paid $730,000 for a hand recount in King and several other counties, which revealed that some

Doc's parents, Ivan Hastings and Florence "Flossie" Johnson in 1934. They met at Spokane's North Central High School and were married in 1937. *Hastings family*.

Doc's uncle Perry (*back row, left*), grandfather Harold (*center*), and father Ivan (*left*) with Doc and his older brother, Roger, at Harold's home in Spokane, 1943. *Hastings family*.

The 1948 flood left large portions of Pasco, Kennewick, and Richland under water. The approaches to the old Green Bridge on the Pasco side of the Columbia River are still open in this picture taken in early May. *Port of Kennewick*.

Hanford's B Reactor was the first full-scale plutonium reactor. Completed in thirteen months in 1944 without benefit of blueprints or computers, it changed the history of the Mid-Columbia forever. *US Department of Energy*.

Doc (*stocking cap, lower left*), his brother, Roger (*above Doc*), and the neighborhood boys play football in an open field near today's Pasco High School on New Year's Day 1951. The Hastings' house was the neighborhood hangout. *Washington State Library/Tri-City Herald/Ralph Smith.*

Doc's senior picture, Pasco High School, 1959. *Hastings family.*

Doc (*left*), Ron Grey (*right*), and Doc's 1946 Chevrolet coupe. Lifelong friends, the two high school classmates took a three-month road trip throughout the United States in 1961. *Hastings family.*

Claire's father, Arthur Montmorency, and her mother, Jessie Irene (Burke) Montmorency, on their twenty-fifth wedding anniversary in 1947. *Hastings family.*

Ivan Hastings founded Columbia Basin Paper and Supply Co. in downtown Pasco in 1947. The company is owned by one of Doc's brothers today. *Hastings family.*

Newlyweds Doc and Claire. They were married in Sacramento on December 16, 1967. *Hastings family.*

Campaign sign from Doc's unsuccessful effort to become president of the Washington State Jaycees in 1972. *Hastings family.*

President Gerald Ford listens as Ronald Reagan stuns the 1976 Republican National Convention with an impromptu speech after losing the nomination to Ford. Doc became a devoted lifetime fan and philosophical follower of the future president. *National Public Radio.*

Campaign picture taken of Doc and his family for use in his first campaign for the Washington Legislature in 1978. *Hastings family.*

Doc's two daughters, Petrina (*left*) and Kirsten (*right*), served as pages during Doc's eight years in the Washington Legislature. *Hastings family.*

Doc and Republican Speaker of the House Bill Polk. Doc was always curious. "Why did you do that, Speak?" *Hastings family.*

After Doc beat Democratic co-Speaker John Bagnariol during his annual pool tournament at an Olympia tavern, Doc decided to continue the event when the Republicans gained control of the state legislature. *Hastings family.*

Doc and his family attend a reception at the Naval Observatory, home of vice president George H. W. Bush, on May 21, 1985. *Left to right*: daughters Kirsten and Petrina, Doc, Vice President Bush, son Colin, and Claire. *Hastings family.*

Washington governor Jay Inslee and Doc opposed each other twice for Congress. Inslee won in 1992, and Doc won in 1994. *Wikipedia Commons.*

Doc (*second row, third from left*) and the other fifty-three freshman Republican House members in 1994. *Hastings family.*

House Speaker Newt Gingrich administers the oath of office to Doc. *Left to right*: Kirsten, Petrina, Newt Gingrich, Claire, Doc, and Colin. *Hastings family.*

Doc with his DC staff, December 1995. *Left to right*: Ed Cassidy, Chuck Berwick, Linda Bradley, Doug Riggs, Doc, Todd Ungerecht, Caroline Charles, Jennifer Parsons, and Dan Aldrich. *Hastings family.*

Doc pitching the idea of the Nuclear Cleanup Caucus to Speaker Gingrich in February 1995. *Left to right*: Lindsay Graham, South Carolina; Zach Wamp, Tennessee; Newt Gingrich, Georgia; Charlie Norwood, Georgia; and Doc. *Hastings family.*

Unsuccessful White House budget negotiations to try to stave off a government shutdown on December 29, 1995. *Left to right*: Treasury secretary Robert Rubin, Speaker Newt Gingrich, President Clinton, and Senate majority leader Bob Dole of Kansas. *Associated Press/Wilfredo Lee*.

Television coverage of a Corps of Engineers' helicopter dropping rocks on the Columbia River site of the discovery of Kennewick Man in March 1998. *Hastings family*.

Doc comments during the September 10, 1998, Rules Committee hearing on the impeachment of President Bill Clinton. "We have a potential crisis in governance." *Hastings family*.

Doc speaks to three thousand supporters of efforts to protect the Snake River dams at the Save Our Dams rally in Kennewick on the evening of February 18, 1999. *Hastings family*.

Doc and Speaker Gingrich tour the Hanford Reach on November 3, 1998. Doc is setting the groundwork for his contention that this portion of the Columbia River ought to be protected but under the control of local government. *Hastings family*.

Doc (*left*) stands next to Washington congresswoman Jennifer Dunn (*center*) and Dick Armey of Texas (*right*) during a press conference in November 18, 1998, after Armey defeated Dunn to become the House majority leader, *Hastings family.*

The Hastings boys gather to celebrate their mother's eighty-fifth birthday on May 3, 1999. *Left to right*: Robert, Florence, Roger, Ivan, Regan, and Doc. *Hastings family.*

Vice president Al Gore visits Richland to announce the creation of the Hanford Reach National Monument on June 10, 2000. *Hastings family.*

A truck speeds along the Hanford highway on June 29, 2000, as a wildfire sweeps towards it from the west. More than 190,000 acres of the Hanford Site burned. *Tri-City Herald/Scott Butner.*

Doc and vice president Dick Cheney appear together at a Yakima fundraiser for Cheney during the 2000 presidential election, October 9, 2000. *Hastings family.*

Members of the House of Representatives evacuate the House Chamber at 9:47 a.m., September 11, 2001, as Doc holds a press conference on the Endangered Species Act on the Capitol grounds. *YouTube.com/MSNBC*.

President George Bush delivers his "Axis of Evil" State of the Union address on January 29, 2002. *YouTube.com*.

President George Bush is given a tour of the Ice Harbor Dam fish ladder by Scott Sutliffe of the US Army Corps of Engineers, August 22, 2003. *Tri-City Herald/Bob Brawdy*.

Representative James Traficant of Ohio defends himself before the House Ethics Committee on July 15, 2002, before he was expelled from the House. Doc led the investigation, leading Traficant to say, "Doc Hastings is a very fair man." *Associated Press/ Dennis Cook*.

Doc always made a special effort to attend annual Veterans Day events. Here he is in Columbia Park in Kennewick on November 11, 2003. *Hastings family*.

absentee ballots had not yet been counted, and Gregoire was declared the winner by 133 votes.[54]

Years later, Doc still believed that political mischief had played a role in Gregoire's victory. "Dino won two out of three. They kept finding new ballots in King County. Dino accepted the final result, and so did I, but I still suspect that it was just a repeat of what had happened to Slade Gorton in 2000."[55] In the highly polarized state of the national political environment, the race attracted national attention, and its political fallout would still be in the news three years later.

—

Civic leader Sandy Matheson had been the CEO of the Hanford Environmental Health Foundation, a Hanford contractor, between 1993 and 2000. During that time, the organization consistently won excellent and outstanding performance ratings from DOE. She had resigned in November 2000, saying that she was "open to new possibilities."[56] She subsequently started a consulting company, served as board chairman of Kennewick General Hospital, taught business courses at Washington State University Tri-Cities, and become the first female board chairman of TRIDEC, the region's economic development organization.

Matheson announced on February 2004 that she was thinking about running for Congress as a Democrat. She made it clear that she supported individuals and issues based on their merit rather than party. Indeed, Doc had once appointed her to a group advising him on Hanford matters back in 1995. The editorial board of the *Tri-City Herald* was giddy with anticipation, writing that "Mid-Columbia voters got a glimpse of what a congressional race can be when Sandy Matheson announced her tentative interest in running earlier this month."[57] Her visibility in the community increased in March when the local Rotary Clubs named her "Tri-Citian of the Year" on March 15. She formally announced her candidacy ten days later. She remembered: "I was deeply troubled by the increasing congressional partisanship that I believed was creating dysfunction and problems in our lives. When approached to consider running for Congress, I thought it was important to try to help relieve our district in some way from the effects of that deep partisanship."[58]

Many were surprised by her decision to run as a Democrat since it was widely known that she had supported both Democrats and Republicans in the past, including Doc. A hint of the upcoming campaign was evident in the reaction of Brenda Alford, Doc's campaign chairman in Franklin County, who had served with Matheson on the TRIDEC board and knew her well. "My suspicion is there are a small handful of pushy people that have convinced her to do this." Alford said. "She's a big fish—a good fish—in a very small pond."[59] However, those who knew Matheson well, like former *Tri-City Herald* publisher Jack Briggs, understood she was not someone to be pushed to do anything she didn't want to do.[60]

On April 6, Matheson was joined in the race by Craig Mason, a self-described "western conservative," who had run against Doc in 2002. Businessman Richard Wright, a Pasco native who had built his physical therapy practice into a chain of rehabilitation clinics in Washington and Oregon, also announced his candidacy. A political novice, Wright called himself a fiscal conservative who believed that government spending had spiraled out of control and that the presidency had too much power, citing the war in Iraq and the prescription drug program as examples.[61]

Matheson hired a hard-charging campaign strategist from Illinois with a background in intelligence and organizing political campaigns around the world. By September 1, she had raised an impressive $224,548. Mason struggled to raise money, and Wright self-funded his campaign. The Democratic primary turned out to be the most spirited in years, with Mason questioning the others' Democratic credentials.

The *Tri-City Herald* endorsed Matheson in the primary, saying that past bipartisanship made her "a good match for independent-minded voters in Eastern Washington."[62] Perhaps it was telling, however, that she had been unable to attract any funding from the Democratic Congressional Campaign Committee. Meanwhile, Doc had raised $540,411 by September 1. Based on fundraising, the results of the September 14 primary should not have surprised, although they disappointed, Matheson's supporters. Doc received 64 percent of the vote, Matheson received 22.5 percent, and Mason and Wright split 13.5 percent of the vote.

The campaign heated up following the primary as Doc's and Matheson's campaign managers argued over polling data that showed Doc with a commanding lead. Matheson's campaign leveled charges that Doc narrowly adhered to a conservative Republican agenda, citing his role in the Medicare prescription drug vote. Doc defended his increasingly influential positions on the House Rules and Budget Committees as examples of how he could help his constituents.[63] At times, Doc almost seemed like the challenger, running what the *Tri-City Herald* called a "hardball" campaign—pushing for a series of four debates, accusing Matheson's campaign of making up poll numbers to confuse the public, and complaining about media coverage, even to the point of refusing an interview on election night with the *Herald* reporter who had written two offending polling articles.[64] Matheson later said it had all been a mistake. "One of our staff members misread the data, and then shared that information without our knowledge. It was unfortunate and I apologized for it, but mistakes happen."[65]

Doc had indeed been angered by the *Herald*'s story, but his anger wasn't directed at Matheson. It was directed at the paper and its political reporter, Chris Mullick. Doc claimed Mullick had failed to check the authenticity of the polling data he used in his story, accepting it at face value from the Matheson camp.[66]

The high degree of public interest in the election was evident by the 350 people who turned out on October 18 to listen to a debate between the two candidates at Columbia Basin College. The "wide-ranging, substantive, and civil exchange of ideas" was rebroadcast five times on cable television before the election. The two clashed on term limits and hot-button social issues such as abortion and gay rights. Hastings affirmed that he supported a constitutional amendment to ban gay marriage "so that the issue would be put to voters nationwide rather than be decided in the courts by 'activist judges.'"[67]

A much more heated battle was being waged behind the scenes between Doc's staff and the staffs and editorial boards of the two major mid-Columbia newspapers. Doug Riggs, Doc's legislative director between 1995 and 1998 remembered, "When we first got elected the

[*Tri-City*] *Herald* was very condescending toward Doc. They had known him for quite a while, and I would say that they treated him with disrespect. They did not believe he was up to the job, and it showed. We would put out meaty press releases on policy issues or on things we had done almost every day, but hardly any of them would be printed." Doc seemed to take it in stride, but "it drove his staff crazy!" Riggs recalled.[68] Todd Young, Doc's communications director, felt their attitude had not improved much in ten years.

Ken Robertson, the executive editor of the *Herald* from 2000 to his retirement in 2011, said, "We were disappointed in the fact that Doc never seemed willing to venture out beyond his party's line." He particularly remembered Doc's chief of staff, Ed Cassidy as the "most difficult political aide I encountered (and that's putting it diplomatically) in forty-three-plus years of dealing with politicians from small-town school boards on up through a US Senate majority leader."[69] Although the paper had endorsed Doc in four previous races, there was always the sense they had done so because of the weakness of his opponents, rather than for his views or accomplishments.

The *Yakima Herald-Republic* previously had a policy of endorsing candidates only in contested primary elections. That changed after Mike Shepard arrived as the publisher in 2003:

> Doc was a conundrum for us, to be honest. An objective look of the editorial pages of the [*Yakima*] *HR* would have shown us to be pretty objectively moderate to conservative.
>
> There seemed to be this level of distrust and lack of transparency on Doc's part as it related to our editorial board. That's not to say that we were entirely supportive of Doc.
>
> We felt, quite frankly, that he was not a particularly strong representative for our part of the district. And, honestly, our point of view was that Doc was not a particularly innovative member of Congress, nor was

he all that interested in espousing anything beyond the party line.

That may get you reelected, but we didn't think that it made you an effective legislator in what was a very safe seat and one in which he could have taken more political chances.[70]

Doc's campaign correctly perceived that both papers leaned toward Matheson. Bill Lee, the *Herald-Republic*'s editor, remembered: "We used a side-by-side interview format with both candidates and no staff present. I always felt that made [Doc] uncomfortable. He also, I would imagine, saw no value in lending a platform to what were usually very weak candidates, with a couple of exceptions. I might add that his staff also had a reputation of being very protective of him."[71]

The paper endorsed Matheson, as did the *Seattle Times*. The *Tri-City Herald* endorsed Doc but criticized him for his slowness in supporting important issues like benefits for Hanford earlier and criticized Ed Cassidy by name. In the end, the paper credited Matheson for making Doc a better candidate.[72]

In the final analysis, Matheson's excellent resume didn't translate into being an effective candidate. Doc had been ahead from the beginning and won reelection to this sixth term with 62.5 percent of the vote. "The people of this district have made their philosophy known," he said. "This district has made its preference known by political party and that's the Republicans."[73]

CHAPTER TWELVE

A Matter of Ethics

★

WITH THE CLOSE VICTORY over John Kerry behind him, George W. Bush began his second term as president of the United States. With a Republican majority in both houses of Congress, he still hoped to achieve some of his policy objectives, if only he could overcome a unified Democratic opposition and the growing concerns about the war in Iraq.

Doc and Claire were present on January 20, 2005, for the president's second inaugural address. It was referred to as the "liberty speech" because Bush used the words "liberty," "freedom," or "free" a total of forty-nine times in a twenty-one minute speech. Cognizant of the threats to internal security and the struggles to build democratic institutions in Iraq and Afghanistan, he defined his view of America's new role in the world:

> We are led, by events and common sense, to one conclusion: The survival of liberty in our land increasingly depends on the success of liberty in other lands. The best hope for peace in our world is the expansion of freedom in all the world.
>
> So it is the policy of the United States to seek and support the growth of democratic movements and institutions in every nation and culture, with the ultimate goal of ending tyranny in our world.[1]

Doc was in the House chamber to hear the president's fifth State of the Union address on February 2 when Bush previewed his domestic policy agenda. He talked of reforming the Social Security system through the use of personal retirement accounts. He also briefly mentioned another issue that would become an important policy initiative. "It is time for an immigration policy that permits temporary guest workers to fill jobs Americans will not take, that rejects amnesty, that tells us who is entering and leaving our country, and that closes the border to drug dealers and terrorists." There was a phrase in the speech—hardly commented upon at the time—that was prescient. "Because one of the deepest values of our country is compassion, we must never turn away from any citizen who feels isolated from the opportunities of America."[2]

In his memoir, *Decision Points*, Bush wrote that his first legislative priority was modernizing the Social Security system. Immigration reform would follow.[3] He noted that the Republican leadership's reaction to Social Security reform was "lukewarm, at best." One unnamed Republican leader had told him, "Mr. President, this is not a popular issue. Taking on Social Security will cost us seats." Bush had responded, "Failing to tackle this issue will cost us seats." Another leader had said, "If you lead, we'll be behind you, but we'll be *way* behind you."[4]

Doc disagreed. He had long supported Social Security reform and the use of personal savings accounts. "I felt it was a good issue," he said, but he understood that his leadership heard "lots of different things from lots of different people and they may have concluded that the votes just weren't going to be there, so why pursue it? My point of view was the sooner we get to it, the better."[5]

Bush decided to press on in the face of the objections. On April 28, 2005, he called a primetime press conference to lay out his Social Security proposal. It featured progressive indexing—a sliding scale of benefits for the poorest to the wealthiest of Americans—and personal retirement accounts. The Republican response was tepid, while the Democrat's response was predictably more heated, charging that the Republicans were trying to "privatize" Social Security. Without bipartisan support, the proposal evaporated in the aftermath of Hurricane Katrina. "The collapse of Social Security reform is one of the greatest disappointments of my presidency," Bush would write.[6] The failure cost him important political capital and showed he could be defeated on an issue that was personally important to him.

On May 15, 2006, the president delivered the first-ever presidential address on immigration. He laid out a four-point program that doubled the size of the Border Patrol, deployed six thousand National Guard troops to support them, created a temporary guest-worker program, tightened enforcement of businesses that hired illegal immigrants, and required recent immigrants to learn English. The Senate soon passed a bill that met Bush's criteria, but the House focused solely on the issue of border security and was unable to pass a bill that included the other provisions before the midterm elections in November.

—

By then, of course, it was too late. It was another lost opportunity. Doc remembered, "The House *was* focused on securing the border, but some of us—particularly from the West—had been saying for some time that there also needed to be a guest-worker program."[7] In retrospect, Bush realized he had made a tactical error by not pushing for immigration reform ahead of Social Security reform. It would have enjoyed some bipartisan support, but funding it would have competed with Hurricane Katrina and the war in Iraq.[8]

In the early morning hours of August 29, 2005, the Gulf Coast was hit from Florida to Texas by Hurricane Katrina, one of the largest and deadliest hurricanes in American history. While there was extensive damage in each of the states, the hurricane centered on New Orleans where protecting dikes failed and flooded most of the city. State and local governments were incapable of dealing with the situation, as was FEMA—the Federal Emergency Management Agency—in the days and even weeks following the disaster. Between 1,200 and 1,900 died, and property damage exceeded $108 billion.[9]

At first, the public's attention focused on the hurricane itself and the dramatic relief efforts to rescue people trapped on their rooftops or in the crammed New Orleans Superdome, which had been turned into an emergency shelter. But soon after, attention shifted to the long-simmering fissures of race and class in American culture that allowed most of the white residents of the city to leave before the hurricane struck while poor African Americans remained trapped in their flooded homes.

The federal government was too slow to act, raising more questions about the competency of the Bush administration. No one understood this more than the president when he wrote, "Just as Katrina was more than a hurricane, its impact was more than physical destruction. It eroded citizens' trust in their government. It exacerbated divisions in our society and politics. And it cast a cloud over my second term."[10]

The hurricane wiped out much of the nation's oil refinery capacity, hiking oil and gas prices just at the time when the nation's economy was slowing down after the overheated economy that had seen housing prices climb by 50 percent since 1997.[11] Concerned economists cited a number of reasons for the housing bubble, including the effort by the nation's largest financial institutions to get Congress to liberalize the provisions in the Glass-Steagall Act of 1933—a law that had been enacted to prevent a commercial bank from merging or expanding to become an investment bank, insurance company, securities firm, or some combination of the three.

—

The nation's economy had boomed in the 1990s, and Congress had repealed Glass-Steagall with broad, bipartisan support. President Clinton signed the Gramm-Leach-Bliley Act into law on November 12, 1999, and Doc supported it "because the market ought to decide how financial institutions should run. That was a major overhaul, and I think it freed up a heck of a lot of capital that we wouldn't have had otherwise."[12]

It did, but by 2005, the combination of low interest rates, massive credit card debt, relaxed mortgage underwriting standards, and unregulated, speculative trading in derivatives (a financial instrument whose value derives from underlying assets) created nationwide housing and credit markets that were simply unsustainable.[13] The economy was not yet a factor leading up to the 2006 midterms, but it presented a dire warning of what lay ahead.

—

Another growing problem was the seemingly endless war in Iraq. The illusion of progress that Bush had described in his second inaugural address bore little resemblance to the reality on the ground. The freedom that George Bush spoke of in such glowing terms was what the Sunni insurgents believed *they* were fighting for—freedom from the revenge of the Shia majority and powerful Kurds and, most of all, freedom from the coalition occupiers who supported them. On January 30, 2005, large numbers of Iraqis turned out to vote in the first free elections since Saddam had fallen, but the Sunni largely boycotted them.

The war was becoming harder and harder to justify in the face of casualty rates that climbed to include three Americans per day. It was even more difficult to justify the war in the face of a unified Democratic opposition that was winning the war for the hearts and minds of the American people. As their constituents soured on the war, more and more members of Congress began to seriously engage on the issue and challenge the president's decisions. Many wondered with perfect 20/20 hindsight if the war might have turned out differently if Congress had exercised more oversight.

—

Between March 22 and April 2, 2005, Doc and five other congressmen, along with Claire and three other wives, travelled on a CODEL led by David Dreier, the chairman of the Rules Committee, to the region. They visited Egypt, Jordan, Iraq, Israel, Lebanon, Cyprus, and Belgium, meeting with top officials in each country. Again, their visits coincided with important events. The wives remained in Cyprus, as the members flew into Baghdad on a C-130 and then departed for Fallujah, the site of a recent fierce battle, by Marine helicopter. Doc recalled, "We were in a pretty secure area north of the city, but to see what a combat zone looks like for the first time is a real eye-opener." In the afternoon, it was back to Baghdad for meetings with coalition and Iraqi officials and then out before nightfall to the Kurdish city of Kirkuk. When asked about his briefings in Baghdad, Doc remembered:

> When you're in a war, you rely on the military to complete their mission. I went in there knowing that the mission was ongoing. I wasn't going there to be a critic. I just wanted to see how things were going.
>
> I was cognizant of the fact that everyone is going to try to put the best face on things. I expected nothing else. But to read between the lines when you don't know the full scope is pretty difficult.[14]

The next day they were in Israel when the Israeli Knesset voted to disengage from the Gaza Strip, and they later visited Lebanon only months after former Prime Minister Rafic Hariri had been assassinated.

After he returned, Doc was in Yakima facing voters during the summer recess and supporting the war in Iraq in spite of new polling that showed a drop in public support. "I think the commander-in-chief is doing what he thinks is the right thing," Doc told a local reporter.[15] He was unaware that the commander-in-chief was at the same time receiving conflicting advice from his top advisors.

The inability to make progress in Iraq ate at the president, as well as his opponents. The policy of "stay the course" advanced by Rumsfeld and others was clearly not working. General George Casey, commanding in Iraq, and some members of the Joint Chiefs of Staff wanted to reduce the American footprint in Iraq. One of those who argued against it was former secretary of state Henry Kissinger. In 1969, he had written President Nixon what became known as the "salted peanut memo." It read, "Withdrawal of U.S. troops will become like salted peanuts to the American public; the more U.S. troops come home, the more will be demanded."[16]

National security advisor Steven Hadley quietly recommended another alternative. He had been influenced by the writings and opinions of Col. H. R. McMaster, who had written *Dereliction of Duty*, the definitive book on the shortfalls of leadership of the Vietnam War, and of General David Petraeus, who both promoted the counter-insurgency tactic of using large numbers of troops for a limited time to clear an area of insurgents, holding it long enough to build relationships with the local inhabitants. Bush became convinced that a new strategy was necessary and announced it at the start of the next Congress.

—

The Republican leadership of the House remained as before: Dennis Hastert as Speaker, Tom DeLay as majority leader, and Roy Blunt as majority whip. Nancy Pelosi and Steny Hoyer continued to lead the Democrats.

On January 5, 2005, just a day after Hastert gaveled the 109th Congress to order, the Republican leadership pushed through a new set of House rules that required a majority of the members of the Ethics Committee to vote to approve any new investigation before it could be launched. Since membership on the committee was evenly divided, that meant that at least one member of the minority party would have to agree before the committee could begin an inquiry. Previously, a tie vote had allowed an inquiry to begin automatically.

The move was widely seen by the Democrats as a ploy to make it more difficult to investigate majority leader Tom DeLay, who had been admonished three times in the previous Congress and was now under investigation in Texas.[17]

As a member of the committee, Doc had a reputation as a loyal supporter of the Speaker's, but he also wanted to avoid alienating DeLay. He voted for the new rules. So did the chairman of the Ethics Committee, Joel Hefley, but Doc believed the new changes were a mistake because they had been implemented by the Republican leadership without any discussion or consultation with the committee itself. Hefley was term limited from continuing to serve as chairman and told a reporter, "I expect to be booted." Many believed, however, that Hefley's departure had more to do with the Republican leadership's unhappiness with his handling of the DeLay and Nick Smith ethics investigations, which resulted in DeLay being admonished by the Ethics Committee, than anything else.[18]

On February 2, it was announced that Doc would become the new chairman of the Ethics Committee. Within hours of the announcement, Hefley was describing Hastings as "a savvy politician, a peacemaker, an institutionalist, a wit, and, above all, a bit of a car racing nut."[19]

Democrats, saw Doc's appointment in starkly different terms. Minority whip Steny Hoyer issued a statement that said: "Hastings is now under an obligation to prove that he is not simply a partisan loyalist who will use his position on the ethics panel to rebuff attempts to investigate allegations of wrongdoing by Republican members."[20]

Doc responded in the same way he always did in such situations. He said, "I didn't seek this appointment, but I'm honored by it, and will do my best to carry out my duties fairly without regard to friendship, favor, or political party."[21] But as often happens, there was a back story.

—

Doc was the only member of Congress who served on both the Ethics and the Rules Committees. He had been moving up in seniority on the Rules Committee and hoped that when its chairman, David Dreier, became term limited he would be chosen to replace him—something he wanted very much.

However, under the new 2005 Rules of the House, Hastert decided the term limit rule no longer applied to the Rules Committee, allowing Dreier to continue as chairman. "I can't prove it, but I have a feeling that DeLay convinced Hastert not to appoint me as chairman of the Rules Committee after I had voted to admonish him in the Ethics Committee," Doc recalled.[22]

Doc also felt another issue might have been a factor in keeping him from becoming chairman of the Rules Committee. Back in 2003, Doc had encouraged Joel Hefley to run for the chairmanship of the Natural Resources Committee against Richard Pombo of California. Pombo was the favored candidate of Tom DeLay, which put Doc again at odds with DeLay. Pombo won, and Hefley resigned from the committee. Doc said, "You could make a connection between DeLay's support for Pombo and Hefley's later support for admonishing DeLay. I don't know, but one could assume that there was payback there."[23]

Doc knew one of his greatest challenges as chairman would be his inability to describe or defend what he was doing on the committee and that he, not it, would almost certainly come under fire:

> Uniquely, it is the one committee in Congress in which the minority party has more power than the majority. The reason lies in the potential to do political mischief.
>
> The minority can leak that there is some allegation against a member of the majority party, and the press will ask, "Are you looking into that, and if not, why not?" We couldn't respond because we were not allowed to talk about it.[24]

There was plenty of opportunity for mischief in the highly charged and contentious political atmosphere surrounding Congress in general and congressional ethics in particular. At the same time Speaker Hastert appointed Doc to chair the committee, he removed two Republican members of the committee who had objected to replacing Hefley and replaced them with members who were loyal to DeLay and Hastert.[25]

Doc liked Hefley but had long felt that he and Alan Mollohan, the ranking Democrat on the committee, had allowed the committee's professional staff to have too much power. On February 15, 2005, Doc fired John Vargo, the committee's staff director, and Paul Lewis, another senior staffer, without bothering to confer with Mollohan.

Doc's action broke with the tradition that held that all major committee decisions should be made jointly since neither political party held a majority. Mollohan objected, and he and his fellow Democrats cried foul, boycotting the committee meetings and keeping it from obtaining a quorum or being able to organize in order to do business. Ed Cassidy defended the staff firings to reporters on behalf of his boss, saying that, "Anyone suggesting these decisions were made for partisan reasons is flat-out wrong,"[26]

Then Doc allowed an already difficult situation to get worse by appearing to make a decision to replace Vargo with Cassidy. Both the chairman and the ranking member are allowed to have their own staff members on the committee, but they work for the member, not the professional committee staff. The *Tri-City Herald* reported that Cassidy had "quickly emerged" as the committee's chief spokesman soon after Vargo and Lewis were fired.

On March 10, the evenly divided committee met in closed session. None of the five Democrats on the ten-member committee would support a set of committee rules proposed by Doc that would allow the committee to organize or function. "We're still in a position of trying to organize," Doc told *CQ Today*. "There is some question about what we are able to do."[27]

Cassidy's apparent candidacy as staff director sparked a round of leader-to-leader communications between Leader Pelosi and Speaker Hastert, with the minority leader writing in separate letters that she opposed the partisan Cassidy as the committee's staff director. After that, Hastert became personally involved in what he referred to as "this flow chart issue," and Doc soon clarified his intentions with regard to Cassidy. It had all been a big misunderstanding.

On April 28, Cassidy told the *Herald*, "I am not the staff director. I never wanted to be staff director. . . . We are not wedded to it."[28] However, on June 10, the *Herald* was still reporting that Doc's efforts to appoint Cassidy to the staff position had prompted Leader Pelosi to offer a resolution requiring the committee hire a non-partisan staff, which had been tabled on a straight party-line vote.[29]

Doc later contended Ed just wanted to be given the title "chief of staff to the chairman" but he never intended to make Cassidy "chief of staff to the committee." He recalled, "It was an unfortunate use of terms. There was no way I could have done it if I wanted to because I couldn't have gotten the votes in the committee. It would have been tied 5 to 5."[30] Ultimately, Cassidy split his time between the Ethics Committee and the Rules Committee, where Doc also served.

The controversy was finally resolved in January 2006, when Hastings and Mollohan jointly announced that they had chosen a Washington, DC, lawyer, William O'Reilly, as the new staff director. In retrospect, Doc realized he had made a mistake in the way he had handled the situation. "Alan was difficult to deal with, and I suppose he would say the same of me. Everything was supposed to be equally divided.

I screwed up when I fired those staff members without going to him first. It was not a good way to do it. Now, we were without professional staff, and it took a while to replace them. It was not my finest hour. Let's just leave it at that."[31]

—

While the committee struggled internally over staff and other issues, Tom DeLay remained at the heart of the broader ethics controversy. He had been privately rebuked by the Ethics Committee in 1999 for threatening to retaliate against a trade group that had hired a Democrat as its top lobbyist.[32] In 2004, Doc joined the rest of the committee in voting to admonish DeLay three times after the Nick Smith investigation. At the same time, DeLay was in trouble back home in Texas. A Texas grand jury had indicted three of his political associates in a case involving one of his political action committees.

In March 2005, media reports tied DeLay to prominent lobbyist Jack Abramoff who was under federal investigation. It was alleged that Abramoff and his partner, Michael Scanlon, had received at least forty-five million dollars in fees from various Indian tribes to influence state and federal officials to grant or deny casino gambling licenses and that the matter was under investigation by the Senate Indian Affairs Committee. DeLay had once called Abramoff "one of my closest and dearest friends." Whether in response to the media reports or suggestions from the Republican leadership or both, DeLay asked the Ethics Committee to review the allegations that Abramoff or his clients had paid some of DeLay's overseas travel expenses.

On April 20, Doc stepped before a bank of reporters and cameras in an attempt to break the impasse on the Ethics Committee that had paralyzed it since the adoption of the new House rules back in January. Doc offered a compromise. He was willing to begin an investigation of DeLay if the Democrats would allow the committee to convene under the GOP-backed rule changes. Doc said, "Let me emphasize that this is an unusual and extraordinary step for the committee to take. This should remove any doubt about the true intent of these rules. They were designed to treat all members more fairly, not to protect any individual member from any action by the committee."[33]

Democrats were having none of it. Steny Hoyer called the proposal a "charade and an absolute non-starter. The Republican majority has neutered the ethics committee . . . by imposing partisan rules that hamstring a meaningful inquiry."[34]

Six days later, the House voted 406 to 20 to reverse the rule they had approved in January after Speaker Hastert said he was willing to "step back." DeLay responded by saying that he looked "forward to providing the facts to the committee once it is up and running."[35]

—

In Jack Abramoff's 1995 sales pitch to the government of the Northern Marianas to get them to retain his lobbying firm, he bragged of his "excellent relationship" with Doc Hastings and several other members of the Natural Resources Committee. The Northern Marianas subsequently hired Abramoff and paid him millions. The investigation uncovered billings that listed at least three dozen contacts between Abramoff's staff and Doc's office, including two conversations between Abramoff and Hastings. In June 2005, Ed Cassidy told reporters that Doc had never spoken to Abramoff.[36]

In September and October, DeLay was indicted by two separate grand juries in Texas for violating state political fundraising laws and money laundering. Under the new House rules approved in April, DeLay resigned his position as majority leader but remained in Congress. House members gathered within hours of the news and chose Roy Blunt of Missouri to replace him on an acting basis until the Republican conference reorganized itself at the start of the next session in January.[37]

In Yakima, just before DeLay's second indictment in October, Doc repeated DeLay's assertion that he was the victim of a "political vendetta."[38] Those comments were widely published in the *Seattle Times* and other news outlets, along with the facts that the committee had not formally met since May and that Hastings had received $4,500 from DeLay's political action committee.[39] Doc's office felt the need to issue a clarifying statement:

> Anyone suggesting that I have publically defended Rep. Tom DeLay, expressed any personal opinion on the substance of the charges pending against him in Texas, or indicated the slightest reluctance to investigate fully—at the appropriate time and in the appropriate way—any matter properly before the Ethics Committee is utterly mistaken.
>
> I have absolutely no predisposition concerning this case. I can't say it any more plainly than that.[40]

The scandal further intensified in November 2005, when Michael Scanlon pleaded guilty to trying to bribe Republican Bob Ney of Ohio.[41] On January 3, 2006, Abramoff pleaded guilty to federal charges of fraud, tax evasion, and conspiracy to bribe a public official. Other federal officials were implicated and charged during the rest of the year. Four days later, DeLay announced that he would not attempt to regain his position as majority leader. On January 15, Speaker Hastert pressured Ney to resign his chairmanship of the House Administration Committee, but he did not resign from Congress.

Doc was being criticized for the committee's inactivity. On January 14, 2006, he spoke to a Yakima Rotary Club and the member who delivered the invocation included a special request of Doc: "Please, Lord, help him get control of Congress." The same newspaper article also quoted the respected Congress watcher, Norman Ornstein, who asked in an op-ed, "Are we dealing with a committee that's functioning?" Ornstein then answered his own question. "I don't think so. The committee is a farce."

Doc's response to Ornstein's comments hardly engendered confidence. He released a statement saying that his committee had provided "significantly more responses to requests for written opinions from members, congressional staff and outside organizations than ever before."[42]

—

DeLay's announcement that he would not seek to regain the majority leader's position resulted in both Roy Blunt, the current whip, and John

Boehner, the former Republican conference chairman, announcing their candidacy to replace him.[43] That race put Doc in a difficult position when both candidates asked for his support. He was serving on the whip team at the time and liked and respected Blunt. But he was even closer to Boehner, who had been part of the Contract with America. Doc supported Boehner for conference chairman in 1995, and the two men occasionally socialized together. "I went to see Roy and told him that I was going to support Boehner because I thought the conference would be stronger if both of them were in leadership."[44] On February 2, 2006, Boehner was elected the majority leader by a vote of 122 to 109.[45]

On April 4, under pressure from other members, DeLay announced his resignation from Congress after two former aides pleaded guilty to corruption charges.[46] Ney remained in Congress until August when he announced he wouldn't seek reelection. Finally, in November 14, 2006, he formally resigned. In November 2010, DeLay was found guilty of all charges filed against him in his Texas trial. He appealed his conviction to the Texas Court of Appeals where in 2013 he was exonerated of all charges.

—

But if the Abramoff, DeLay, and Ney scandals were not bad enough, Doc and the Ethics Committee faced yet another scandal. In June 2005, reports surfaced in the San Diego newspapers that defense contractors had provided California Republican Randy "Duke" Cunningham with as much as $2.4 million in bribes. Cunningham was a respected member of the House Appropriations and Intelligence Committees. In July, he announced he would not run for reelection. "No one was aware of what Duke was doing," Doc remembered. "Duke came up to me on the House floor one day just before the Thanksgiving recess and said, 'Doc, there's nothing to this.' Then he resigned after pleading guilty in federal court. Before we got back from the break, he was gone."[47]

—

And then in February 2006, right in the middle of the Abramoff and Ney disclosures, a financial watchdog group filed a five-hundred-page ethics complaint against the committee's ranking member, Alan

Mollohan, alleging that he had lied about his assets on his financial disclosure forms and that his real estate holdings and other assets had increased from $562,000 in 2000 to at least $6.3 million in 2004. On April
7, the *New York Times* reported that Mollohan had created non-profit
groups in his West Virginia district in which he was an investor and then
funded the groups with $250 million of federally earmarked funds.[48]

On April 21, minority leader Nancy Pelosi removed Mollohan as
ranking member of the Ethics Committee, but he remained a member
of Congress. She replaced him with Howard Berman of California, who
had served on the committee between 1997 and 2003. "When she asked
me to come back on the committee, it was a difficult moment for me. The
committee is not fun," Berman admitted with an ironic laugh. "It's a terrible job. But I believe in the House as an institution, and the committee
is a part of that, so when I was asked, I did it."[49]

Doc was unable to comment on the Mollohan situation, except to say,
"It is often the case that if the Justice Department has an ongoing investigation, they don't want the Ethics Committee to get involved. [Mollohan's]
constituents kept sending him back until he was defeated in 2010."[50]

—

No sooner had Cunningham, Ney, and DeLay resigned from the
House and Mollohan stepped down from the committee than yet another scandal rocked the Congress. As early as 2003, some congressional staff members became concerned about what they considered to be
unusual, and perhaps inappropriate, relationships between Republican
Mark Foley of Florida and male congressional pages. "Members had observed that he was interacting in what they thought were inappropriate
ways with male pages. It made them uncomfortable. I never observed
any of that at all," Doc remembered.[51]

Foley had been one of Doc's 1994 classmates. As early as November 2005, the *St. Petersburg Times* received copies of sexually suggestive
emails between Foley and former congressional pages but decided to sit
on the story. On Wednesday, September 29, 2006, *ABC News* broke it.
Doc recalled, "The news was all over the Hill on Thursday, and on Friday,

Tom Reynolds of the NRCC confronted Foley about it, and he immediately resigned."[52]

On October 5, Doc and the new ranking member, Howard Berman, held a joint press conference to say the Ethics Committee was launching an immediate and full investigation of the Foley matter and he and Berman would lead the investigative subcommittee, which also included Republican Judy Biggert of Illinois and Democrat Stephanie Tubbs Jones of Ohio. There was little they could do to discipline Foley because he had already left Congress.

In his own statement to the press conference, Berman asserted his independence: "And I want to say that when I was appointed ranking minority member by Leader Pelosi, I indicated at that time I wanted no part of [participating in] an incumbent protection agency.

Then he provided a little badly needed support for Doc:

> After five and a half months of working very closely with Chairman Hastings on a variety of issues—most of which you appropriately do not know anything about, at least at this time—I'm convinced that . . . we all have strong partisan feelings, we have passionate concerns about issues, we have ideological and philosophical differences; but that, on this committee, and for purposes of this investigation, we are going to put those partisan considerations totally aside, as I have seen and witnessed from the chairman during the past five and a half months.[53]

Hastings and Berman did not know each other well before Berman joined the committee. They served on different committees and were in different parties. Berman remembered:

> My remarks were not intended to be taken as either attacking him or defending him for his leadership in the time before I came on the committee, but, hey, I thought we worked pretty well together during that

time. We could look at something a little differently and talk about it.

At this stage, the issue was not the case against Foley. It was an investigation into how this could have happened and [been] dealt with before it ever came to the committee. I vividly remember the two of us talking the night before the recess, and Doc and I agreeing that it should absolutely come to the committee for investigation.[54]

Immediate questions arose about what the Republican leadership knew and when they knew it. Both John Boehner and Tom Reynolds later reported they had notified Hastert about the Foley stories. Hastert came under intense criticism, and there were calls for his resignation. He later claimed he had learned of the story only after it broke in the news. Their conflicting testimony set off a contentious little squabble among the Republican leadership that left Doc in the middle.[55] Doc remembered, "We had all three of them in at different times. I'm not sure if what they said they told Hastert is what Hastert heard. I couldn't draw a conclusion about who was wrong or right."[56]

Coming, as it did, just before the 2006 midterm elections, the scandals added to the Republicans' already considerable problems. "Howard and I were in the middle of reelection campaigns, and we had to run back and forth between our districts and Washington, DC, for the hearings," Doc recalled.[57]

Berman remembered, "I had a safe seat and a weak opponent. For me, it was more about the impact on my quality of life than my reelect. But it certainly had an impact on the 2006 election, broadly speaking."[58]

—

The DeLay-Abramoff scandal had been long and difficult. In the highly charged partisan atmosphere of Washington, DC, it was not hard to conclude that the Republicans had tried to protect their majority leader until they had been forced to take action. But the DeLay scandal had also been about money and influence, something many Americans now took for granted in their elected officials.

The Foley scandal was different. It was about teenagers and about trust and about whether anyone in the Republican leadership had deliberately looked the other way. By the time the Ethics Committee's investigation began, Foley was long gone, and Congress was incapable of dispensing justice. For better or worse, Doc found himself as one of the public faces of an institutional failure.

Three years later, with the Republicans back in control of the House, Speaker Boehner and minority Leader Pelosi agreed to end the House page program due, they said, to costs and technological advancements that had rendered the program no longer essential. Many years after the fact, Doc was of the opinion the Foley matter played a role in their decision.[59]

—

It is hard not to conclude that many of the ethics allegations made against members of Congress were, and are, the result of the intense political divisions that exists between them and, further, that the news of such allegations reinforced the political divide among the public. Wrongdoing by our elected representatives is nothing new, but the use of allegations—proven or unproven—to discredit members of the opposition party has become yet another tool in the political toolbox. Newt Gingrich went after Speaker Jim Wright of Texas. The Democrats went after Gingrich and Tom DeLay in a partisan game of payback.

While only five members have been expelled in the history of the House, Doc Hastings led the subcommittee investigating the last of them, James Traficant, and only a handful more have been censored or reprimanded. Many more have resigned under a cloud or have been defeated for reelection because of their conduct.

The ethics scandals played an important role in the wave election of 2006 in which the Democrats regained control of the House and reinforced a narrative among the public that members of Congress enjoy a sense of privilege that goes beyond the law. A Gallup poll released in 2014, the same year Doc decided not to seek reelection, noted that 61 percent of

Americans rated the honesty and ethics of members of Congress as low or very low, the worst the poll had ever measured for any profession.[60]

In some ways, Doc's newfound notoriety was a welcome change for his staff, who had labored long and hard to make him more visible to the public, but the Foley scandal, on top of everything else, was certainly not the type of visibility they sought. Doc would have preferred much less visibility, but there was simply no way to avoid it under the circumstances.

SERVING AS CHAIRMAN of the Ethics Committee had been an uncomfortable experience. Doc had done it because he had been asked by his leadership to do it and he felt it was his duty to agree. But he was much more comfortable working in near anonymity as an effective insider within the Republican conference, using his influence to advance his conservative philosophy and represent the needs of his district as he did when he obtained a grant to renovate Yakima's historic Capitol Theatre or to fund an English-as-a-Second-Language program. He secured a grant from the Economic Development Administration to help build the Walter Clore Wine and Culinary Center in Prosser and one from another federal agency to turn an old railroad station in Naches into a visitor center. He found $5.12 million in funding to pay for start-of-engineering and design work for a new freeway interchange in Union Gap. Continuing to advocate his small government philosophy, he told a reporter, "A lot of the very best projects start at the local level."[61]

—

On February 1, 2005, Doc and Senator Maria Cantwell reintroduced their legislation to establish the Ice Age Floods National Trail. The House passed Doc's version of the legislation in September, and the Senate, after some initial opposition from the National Park Service, passed its version in October.

Doc continued his efforts to obtain funding for the proposed Black Rock Reservoir. On February 17, the Bureau of Reclamation released the results of the multi-year study that Doc had inserted into legislation as a member of the Rules Committee in 2003. The results were not what he and other supporters had hoped for. The cost of the project had climbed from $1.8 billion to $3.5 billion, raising doubts about the project's feasibility.

Former congressman Sid Morrison, the chairman of the Yakima Basin Storage Alliance, believed the costs could be reduced but estimated the state and local supporters of the project would need to produce an estimated additional $4 million just to study how to reduce the costs.[62] In spite of these setbacks, Doc continued to support the project. Jessica Gleason, his communications director, sent out a release saying, "It would be premature to make a declaration about Black Rock moving forward or not before the feasibility study is completed. We still need water storage, and [Doc's] doing everything he can."[63]

In May, Doc obtained an additional $1.5 million in the House energy and water appropriations bill to continue to study the project.[64] The Senate followed through with an equal amount in the Senate appropriations bill. On July 10, Doc, Sid Morrison, and state representative Shirley Hankins joined about one hundred supporters of the reservoir at a barbecue and rally in Kennewick to generate local support for additional state funding. Senator Patty Murray, a member of the Senate Appropriations Committee, expressed an understandable note of caution about the high cost of the project when compared to the competing demands caused by the war in Iraq and Hurricane Katrina. "Boy, do we have to have our ducks in a row," she said. However, she stayed committed to finishing the $8 million study, which was projected to be completed in 2008.[65]

Washington's governor, Christine Gregoire, visiting Yakima on May 10 to deliver a statewide drought declaration, said she wished the Black Rock reservoir already existed. She announced she would ask the state legislature to provide an additional $8.2 million beyond the existing $1.8 million in the state drought response fund. "I know we are in tough budget times, but that is less significant than the economy."[66]

—

While water was on the minds of many farmers, so was free trade. Apple, cherry, and pear growers supported a new free trade agreement with Central America that would open up new markets in those countries, while asparagus growers pushed for higher tariffs against the competing Peruvian competition. Doc had supported lifting the tariffs on tree fruit since 2003. Apple growers drew a breath of relief when Mexico temporarily removed its 45 percent tariff on apples in June. Exporters responded by shipping 8.4 million boxes to Mexico, only to be caught with millions of boxes in the pipeline when Mexico re-applied the tariffs five months later.[67]

In May, Doc announced the government would help the asparagus growers by purchasing seven million pounds under the federal nutrition program. Growers became concerned again toward the end of the year when the Bush administration approved the Andean Free Trade agreement with Peru. Doc said Rob Portman, the US trade representative and a friend, had assured him that local growers would be consulted before the agreement was negotiated. "That, clearly, didn't happen." He regretted being at odds with the administration's free trade policies but said he would be "hard pressed" to vote for the measure when it came before Congress.[68] He didn't; however, the agreement was ultimately approved by Congress and renewed by the two countries in April 2006.

On June 10, Doc arranged a field hearing in Yakima of the full House Agriculture Committee. He was not a member of the committee but was given a seat on the panel to hear the concerns of Washington farmers prior to the consideration of the next farm bill. Growers of specialty crops opposed price supports or subsidies and asked for more money for research and market access. They also wanted a number of things that were outside the scope of the committee's jurisdiction, including a guest-worker program for immigrant labor, help for the struggling asparagus industry, and money for the proposed Black Rock reservoir."[69]

—

As President Bush promoted comprehensive immigration reform with Congress, those on both sides of the issue in Doc's district made their views known. The number of Latino and Hispanic residents living in Doc's congressional district increased by 135 percent during the twenty years he served in office and, by 2006, represented about 30 percent of his district's population. Most were in the United States legally, but many were not. Their labor was vital to the district's agricultural economy. Doc had always supported a guest-worker program and immigration reform, positions that were not shared by the majority of the Republican Party. Instead, the party focused on border security as the number of illegal immigrants apprehended at the border fluctuated between nine hundred thousand in 2002 and seven hundred thousand in 2006.[70]

On May 2, 2006, between eight and fifteen thousand advocates marched in favor of immigration reform in Yakima. Hundreds of thousands more marched in other cities across the country. The Senate was about to take up the president's immigration reform package. The House had already passed a get-tough bill that would make illegal immigration a felony and called for a seven-hundred-mile wall on the Mexican border. Doc voted against the House bill, saying, "My message in Congress is that the most responsible approach is comprehensive reform that strengthens control over our borders and creates a functional guest-worker program."[71]

The Senate bill passed on May 27 during a two-day visit to Washington State by Mexican president Vincente Fox, who stopped in Yakima long enough to be welcomed by Governor Gregoire and visit a Hispanic-owned apple orchard. In July, Doc suggested that he might be willing to go along with a compromise proposal being discussed by Bush and the House Republicans that would address border security before beginning a guest-worker program, so long as employers "don't have to wait too long for it."[72] Doc cautioned that there were only three weeks left before Congress adjourned for the summer to come to an agreement. When Congress returned, the election season would be in full swing, making any compromise difficult, at best. His observation was prophetic. That was exactly what happened.

—

Although Hanford cleanup was progressing, the large, ongoing problems associated with the construction of the Hanford Waste Treatment Plant continued to receive a lot of publicity. In 2004, Congress had directed the Army Corps of Engineers to study the costs associated with building the Hanford Waste Treatment Plant. At the time, the estimated cost was $5.7 billion. Now, the results of the study found the upper floors of the structure might be subject to earthquake damage, and the project's rapidly escalating cost generated serious doubt about the continued viability of the project. DOE and the state of Washington continued to press their legal battle over the shipment of transuranic waste to Hanford, while DOE's inspector general found that hundreds of unused groundwater monitoring wells had been improperly decommissioned in a way that could spread radioactive contaminants in the groundwater.

In February 2005, the Bush administration released its proposed 2006 budget, which cut Hanford funding by $267 million, or about 12 percent, from the year before. The cuts included a 10 percent cut in funding the WTP, based on the results of the unresolved seismic problems. Doc had been through it all before and was philosophical. "This budget proposal is just that—a proposal—and once again it's only a starting point," he said. "In the months ahead, my colleagues and I will be focused on achieving a funding level that will allow cleanup to continue in a safe and timely manner."[73]

In April, Doc led an effort to get all fourteen members of the Washington and Oregon House delegations to sign on to a request to restore $240 million of the proposed cuts. On May 18, Doc hosted David Hobson of Ohio and Rodney Frelinghuysen of New Jersey, the chairman and Republican senior member, respectively, of the House Energy and Water Appropriations Subcommittee, on a tour of Hanford. Later in the month, the full House Appropriations Committee restored $200 million of the cuts, including all the money requested for the WTP, more money for the HAMMER training facility, new lab space for PNNL, and money to preserve the historic B Reactor.[74] In June, Doc hosted Samuel Bodman, President Bush's energy secretary, and his staff for a tour of Hanford and a private dinner at his home on the Columbia River. Claire kept the thank-you note she received from Bodman shortly thereafter.[75]

Hopes for restoring Hanford funding were dashed in December when a House-Senate conference committee faced the funding realities caused by Hurricane Katrina, the war in Iraq, and the deepening recession by reducing the budget for the Office of River Protection by seventy-three million dollars and the WTP by nearly one hundred million dollars. Scrambling under intense political pressure to find $2.3 billion more in cuts from what were called "unnecessary programs," the White House wanted to rescind one hundred million dollars more of previously budgeted funds to help pay for Hurricane Katrina. "Every American can appreciate the need to prioritize federal spending to pay for hurricane recovery, but it's a total outrage for Hanford cleanup funding to be labeled 'unnecessary,'" Doc said. [76]

In February 2006, the Bush administration proposed a 2007 budget for Hanford of $1.88 billion, an increase from the prior year but still not up to the level of $2.09 billion it had enjoyed in 2005. Meanwhile, the effects to the previous cuts were being felt. By the end of March, Bechtel National, the prime contractor on the WTP, laid off almost a third of the 3,800 workers employed on the project.

In June, all work at the troubled WTP was put on hold while three new studies were ordered and a new senior-level management team was created to oversee work on the project. The cost of the project had escalated to nearly $10 billion. By April 2006, the cost estimate had risen to $11.3 billion. A *60 Minutes* investigative report aired on April 30, drawing national attention to the project. On May 11, the House Energy and Water Subcommittee expressed skepticism about the future of the WTP while approving six hundred million dollars for the project, ninety million dollars less than requested by the administration. The subcommittee made its displeasure plain, saying in its report to the full committee: "Years of revolving-door DOE officials, continual promises to improve management controls and oversight, and sky-rocketing costs have led the committee to the point where it no longer has confidence in the department's estimates in the WTP nor in the department's ability to manage its way back on this project." [77]

Doc agreed with the criticism. "This bill is being written without an official path forward for the vit plant from DOE, and there isn't going to be a final plan for months."[78] In June, the cost of the WTP had climbed to $11.55 billion, assuming an increased expenditure of $800 million a year.

—

And there were other serious problems at Hanford. Fluor Hanford, DOE's contractor responsible for cleaning out the K Basins, missed the deadlines established by the Tri-Party Agreement in 2005. Work lagged on pumping waste from the old single-shell underground tanks. The Justice Department and the state of Washington continued to fight over the constitutionality of Initiative 297, which banned the importation of nuclear waste to Hanford. Its implementation was being appealed to the Ninth Circuit Court of Appeals.

THE 2006 MIDTERM ELECTIONS were difficult for the Republicans. On October 6, according to a Gallup poll, President Bush's approval rating had dropped to 37 percent.[79] When the results of the 2006 national elections were known early on the evening of November 7, the voters had delivered a stinging rebuke to George Bush and the congressional Republicans. In the first wave election since 1994, the Democrats picked up thirty-one seats in the House, giving them a 233 to 202 advantage. They also controlled the Senate because two Independents caucused with the Democrats, and they won most of the state governor's races. For the first time since the creation of the Republican Party in 1860, no Republican captured any House, Senate, or gubernatorial seat that had previously been held by a Democrat.[80] "It was a thumping," the president told a press conference on election night.[81] The next day secretary of defense, Donald Rumsfeld, resigned, a move the president had decided on several weeks earlier.

Dennis Hastert, reelected in his Illinois district, announced he would not be a candidate to become the minority leader in the next Congress. The new Speaker of the House would be Nancy Pelosi, the first woman ever to serve in that position. In the Senate, Harry Reid of Nevada was elected to be the new Senate majority leader, a move that would have long-term consequences for Hanford. For the first time since he had been a member of Congress, Doc would be a member of the minority party. And, more importantly, it ended any possibility he would become the chairman of the Rules Committee.

—

Doc knew his election campaign would be difficult. He would have to swim upstream against the multiple currents of an unpopular Republican president and his administration, which seemed to have trouble getting anything right, a resurgent and energized Democratic base that sensed victory, and his own ability to find time to campaign at all because he was stuck in Washington, DC, with the Foley investigation. His district had already been targeted with "Hear no evil, See no evil, Speak no evil" billboards that advised him to "Quit Messing Around with Tom DeLay. Appoint Outside Counsel Now!"

He beefed up his district staff. In September 2005, he had appointed Barb Lisk, a twelve-year former state legislator, as his new district director. Ellen Howe, his campaign manager for the past two races, left to take a job with the Homeland Security Department in Washington, DC, and was replaced by Tim Kovis, who formerly worked for the state Republican Party.

In late July 2005, an unknown Chelan County resident, Lewis Picton, filed to run for Doc's seat. He lived in Manson but spent most of his time piloting an Alaskan cruise boat. He filed as a Democrat, but his campaign statement sounded libertarian themes of wanting to "dismantle [the government] and return the process and power to the states."[82]

In mid-December, Richard Wright, the Kennewick businessman who had run unsuccessfully in the 2004 Democratic primary, announced his candidacy. Wright said he was filing early "because the pressure's on. The main thing I learned [in 2004] is that the mechanics of [running] take so much time."[83]

On February 9, 2006, Claude Oliver joined the race. A maverick Republican, Oliver had spent the past nine years as a Benton County commissioner and thirteen years before that as the Benton County treasurer. He served for four years in the state legislature from 1977 to 1981. Often controversial, outspoken, and at odds with his fellow commissioners,

Oliver was best known recently for organizing and leading the effort to save the Fast Flux Test Reactor. At the time, he had publically criticized Doc for not trying hard enough to save the reactor. Doc didn't respond publically to Oliver's announcement, but his campaign staff quietly put together and distributed a list of every county commissioner in Doc's district who supported Doc for reelection, including the other two Benton County commissioners who served with Oliver.

Oliver's campaign got off to a rocky start when he sent out a news release that accused Doc of "complacency and lack of backbone" in the DeLay investigation and then another that requested, "Please disregard all previous press releases you may have received regarding my campaign." He said that an unedited version of the release "had got through the printer without his approval."[84] Doc recalled, "Claude's polling numbers were terrible, but he thought he was going to win."[85]

Doc received a boost in February when Speaker Denny Hastert stopped in the Tri-Cities to wish Doc a happy sixty-fifth birthday and kick off his campaign for reelection. "It was not an easy job last year," the Speaker told the several hundred people who gathered for the $150-a-plate reception.[86] Doc knew *that* was right!

Wright formally launched his campaign on March 8, claiming Doc was the worst Ethics Committee chairman in history. "The district doesn't deserve that," he said. Both Oliver and Wright set out on tours of the district.[87] In Yakima on March 22, Oliver accused Doc of letting party loyalty and partisan politics prevent him from doing his job for the Fourth District. He also claimed Doc had done nothing as chairman of the Ethics Committee and was not doing enough to address concerns like water use, light rail, neighborhood crime, and overcrowded courts and jails. "They're not getting addressed," he said.[88]

The major issues in the campaign soon became clear. In May, Wright demanded Doc resign from the Ethics Committee. He criticized Doc's holding the vote open for three hours in the Medicare vote. Both candidates occasionally talked about immigration reform.

But it also became clear how difficult it was to turn issues into the money needed to run the Wright and Oliver campaigns. By June

30, Wright had raised only $111,715, and $63,500 of that was his own money. He had hoped to be able to attract funding from the DCCC, but again, it decided not to oppose Doc in the Fourth District. Oliver had raised only $3,620 by June 30. By comparison, Doc raised $310,000 in the first seven weeks of the campaign and had $350,000 in the bank.[89]

Oliver also pounced on Doc's role in the ethics scandals. He claimed that Doc had refused to open an ethics investigation on DeLay because Doc's campaign had received up to six thousand dollars in contributions from PACs affiliated with DeLay. Doc responded by defending DeLay as a victim of a "political vendetta" against him.[90]

On July 26, Oliver sent Doc a confidential letter citing these allegations and asking Doc to "withdraw from public service." Should he decline, Oliver pledged to "bring this message in a bold and forthright manner to the voters of the 4th district."[91] Doc responded to the letter the next day:

> Dear Claude:
>
> My first reaction upon reading your letter was, "if he doesn't release this to the press, I will."
>
> After all, I think the people of Central Washington are entitled to know exactly what they can expect if they elect you to represent them in Congress. Your letter— riddled with outright lies, distortions, innuendo and deeply offensive attacks on my character and integrity— will give the voters a crystal clear picture.
>
> Frankly, I didn't appreciate being threatened—and I'm confident that the voters won't put their trust in a candidate who would stoop to such shameless tactics.
>
> Needless to say, your threat didn't work. I went ahead and filed for reelection in spite of it—and now I can only hope that you'll continue these kinds of slanderous negative attacks because you're making my campaign this year a whole lot easier.[92]

Doc followed up with a four page rebuttal entitled "Setting The Record Straight: There he [Claude Oliver] goes again" and spent most of the two-week congressional recess in August crisscrossing his district and speaking to voters.[93]

With little money available, Oliver relied on printed cards, flyers, and newspaper advertising to get his message out. In a joint meeting with the editorial board of the *Tri-City Herald*, Oliver restated the consistent themes of his campaign about Doc's leadership of the Ethics Committee, but when the opportunity came to ask Doc one question, it was why Doc had not done more to save the FFTF.[94] In their primary election endorsement of Doc, the paper said that it had no reason to believe that Oliver would have been any more successful in saving the FFTF than Doc had been.[95]

When the results of the September 19 primary election were tallied, Doc received 56.3 percent of the vote to Oliver's 17 percent, while Wright received 22.7 percent to Picton's 4 percent. Ten days later, the Mark Foley story broke, and Doc was required to be back in Washington DC, to lead the investigation, effectively limiting the time he had available to campaign in the final months of the election. The general election campaign was unambiguous: both Wright and Doc ran on Doc's record. Polls showed Doc ahead, and he had more money available. Wright again called on Doc to resign from the Ethics Committee in the wake of the new Mark Foley scandal and said Doc should have been more critical of the Bush administration's handling of the war in Iraq. "I would at least recognize we have a problem," Wright said.[96] In the background, there were whispered allegations of Doc's "protecting a pedophile" that could never be traced to their source. Doc remembered it as the "nastiest campaign I was ever in."[97]

The tensions between Doc and the *Yakima Herald-Republic* that arose in 2004 about their endorsement policies spilled over into 2006. The paper had a policy of interviewing candidates side by side without members of their staff present. In 2004, they endorsed Sandy Matheson, basing their endorsement on issues Doc claimed had not been discussed in the interview.

In 2006, Bill Lee, the paper's editorial page editor, contacted Doc's campaign asking when he might be available for an interview to seek the paper's endorsement. With 2004 fresh in his mind, Doc responded that he chose not to seek their endorsement. "All hell broke loose, but all my grassroots support that didn't like the *Yakima Herald* loved it!"[98]

The paper finally endorsed Doc under a headline that read: "Enthused we're not as we cast our lot with Hastings," writing that "Hastings continues to be less effective than one would expect of a congressman with 12 years on the job."[99]

The *Tri-City Herald* waited until after the only debate of the campaign to endorse Doc but then issued its strongest endorsement of him to date. "After 12 years in the House, Hastings has the experience, knowledge, and influence to be an effective legislator." It also said Wright's "attempt to saddle Hastings with responsibility for the ethical lapses of Congress lacks legitimacy."[100]

Almost everyone was glad to see the campaign end on November 7. Doc felt vindicated by the fact that 60 percent of the voters—his lowest margin of victory since 1996—had voted for him. "I'm pleased with the numbers we had in a tough political environment," he said. Wright remained unavailable for comment.[101] The voters, too, were happy for the negative campaign to end and looked forward to someone cleaning up the ever-pervasive roadside campaign signs.

—

"Life goes on," Doc told a *Yakima Herald-Republic* reporter as they sipped coffee at the Starbucks in Prosser in mid-December after the election. Doc admitted that the past session had been a really difficult one, but "every year has different challenges," he said, conceding that he was happy the past session was over. "We had a real push to get that [Foley report] done toward the end."[102]

On December 8, Doc stood in front of yet another bank of microphones inside the Capitol and announced that his Republican leadership and staff were negligent and in some instances "willfully ignorant" of Mark Foley's improper advances toward male pages, even though the Ethics Committee report found they had broken no House rules. The three-thousand-page report went on to say that the collective failure of some lawmakers and their aides to probe the matter more deeply "is not merely the exercise of poor judgment; it is a present danger to House pages and to the integrity of the institution of the House."[103]

After Congress adjourned, Doc's committee released another report rebuking Washington's Seventh District congressman, Jim McDermott, for violating ethics standards back in 2004 when, as a member of the Ethics Committee, he had leaked an illegally recorded telephone conversation between Newt Gingrich, John Boehner, and several other congressmen who were discussing the political consequences of Gingrich's problems with the Ethics Committee. Boehner sued McDermott as a private citizen and ultimately obtained a large court settlement. The issue had ultimately been referred to and investigated by the Ethics Committee.[104]

McDermott figured indirectly in another incident that occurred as the Republicans were reorganizing for the next term after their disastrous losses in the November election. They would now be in the minority for the first time since 1995. The Republican Steering Committee, which Doc had served on since 2003, was deciding who would be its new ranking members of the various committees. Doc used the occasion to do something he rarely did: get even.

Tom Petri from Wisconsin was a moderate Republican with a strong pro-environmental voting record. He also happened to be John Boehner's pick to become ranking member of the House Transportation Committee. But Doc had a problem with Petri. Several years earlier, Petri had co-sponsored the annual bill introduced by Jim McDermott to breach the lower Snake River dams. Doc recalled: "Tom was senior to me. When you talk member to member with someone, the only thing you have is your word. I went to him and said, 'Tom, that's in my district, and it affects me personally. I understand you may have pressure, but I would appreciate it if you wouldn't co-sponsor that legislation.'"[105]

The next year, McDermott circulated the same bill, and Petri co-sponsored it again. Doc asked him not to do it again. Now, Petri was John Boehner's pick to be ranking member of the Transportation Committee. John Mica of Florida was also running for the job. Doc explained:

So after they both made their case, we sat around and discussed it, and I made the observation that I had a real problem supporting Petri and explained why. When the vote came, Mica won, so I apparently carried the day.

About two weeks later a story came out about the incident involving me and Petri. I never denied it. Tom never came up to me, but John Mica certainly remembers it.

I had to buck Boehner, but there were no repercussions to that. [106]

Doc paused as he looked at the reporter again over his coffee cup: "Yeah," he said, "I'm glad it's done."[107]

CHAPTER THIRTEEN

Into the Wilderness

★

THE DEMOCRATIC VICTORY IN 2006 was the largest wave election since the Republican Revolution of 1994, when the Republicans gained fifty-four seats in the House and nine in the Senate. Now, the Democrats picked up thirty-one seats in the House and five in the Senate. All the congressional levers of power now belonged to the Democrats. Doc recalled: "When you lose, hindsight is 20/20. It was a midterm election, which often tends to favor the party out of power. There were recriminations against the Republican leadership. The Ethics scandals played a role. But most of the blame fell on the president and his policies."[1]

Doc had experienced being in the minority when he served in the Washington legislature. That hadn't been any fun, but this felt even worse. "You don't have control over anything. You're no longer making policy; you're *reacting* to policy." Doc remembered an old saying he had first heard in Olympia: "When you're in the minority, you talk; when you're in the majority, you vote."[2] But he also remembered what Allen Hayward, the Republicans' senior legal counsel in Olympia for thirty-four years, often told his members:

> It is the right of the majority to decide what bills will pass.
> It is the right of the minority to decide how long that will take.
> It is the duty of leadership to avoid irreconcilable conflicts between those rights.[3]

Doc never forgot Hayward's counsel when he presided over the House, as he often did when his party was in the majority. When the reverse was true, as it was now, Doc joined with his Republican colleagues in fully exercising the rights of the minority.

—

In the year leading up to the 2006 election, the House Democrats had stolen a page from Newt Gingrich's playbook and published a six-point plan called "A New Direction for America." It called for a phased redeployment of troops from Iraq, using more special operations forces to kill or capture Osama bin Laden, implementation of the remaining 9/11 recommendations, raising the federal minimum wage, penalizing companies that outsourced jobs to other countries, lower interest rates for college loans, ending dependence on foreign oil by developing alternate energy sources, increasing stem cell research, instituting more ethics reform, and no new deficit spending.[4]

As expected, the Democrats elected Nancy Pelosi as Speaker of the House. She was the youngest of six children born to Italian immigrants who had settled in Baltimore, where her father and one of her brothers had both served as mayor. Her father had also served in Congress. She had interned for Daniel Brewster, a Democratic senator from Maryland, along with Steny Hoyer, who would be her new majority leader.[5] John Boehner, who had been elected as the Republican majority leader after Tom DeLay's resignation, assumed the unaccustomed role of minority leader.

On August 17, 2007, the former Speaker, Dennis Hastert, stood in front of the courthouse in the Illinois town where he had been a high school wrestling coach and announced he was leaving Congress.[6] He was the longest-serving Republican Speaker of the House in history. After his party's stinging defeat in the November midterms, he announced he would not run for minority leader in the new Congress but he continued to serve until his resignation on November 26, 2007. On November 15, he delivered his final speech on the House floor, emphasizing the need for more civility in politics.[78] Doc remembered:

Whenever you have a long-term member die suddenly or leave the institution, it makes an impression on you. I knew Hastert personally. I travelled with him. He was good to me. I got to know him as well as you get to know anyone back there, but life goes on. Life always goes on. Everyone mourns the loss of that person, but everyone's also thinking, do we have a chance to win that seat? That's life going on.[9]

—

On the evening of January 23, 2007, President George Bush delivered his seventh State of the Union address to a joint session of Congress, and he used it to lay out his legislative blueprint for the coming year. But before he did so, he acknowledged the obvious. Turning to Nancy Pelosi sitting behind him, he began, "Madam Speaker," as the audience applauded, and then congratulated the "Democrat majority," unintentionally ruffling some feathers by dropping the "ic" from the end of the word.

Then Bush called for unity. "Our citizens don't much care which side of the aisle we sit on—as long as we're willing to cross that aisle when there is work to be done." He proceeded to call for balancing the budget without raising taxes, cutting back on the practice of congressional earmarks, reducing reliance on foreign oil, and developing new sources of alternative energy. He addressed the need for entitlement reform in Medicare, Medicaid, and Social Security, the reauthorization of his signature No Child Left Behind legislation, new healthcare initiatives, and comprehensive immigration reform.[10] Some of the policies he advocated enjoyed broad, bipartisan support, and he acknowledged that by using some of the same words to describe them that Pelosi had in her "A New Direction for America" document.

The second half of the speech dealt with foreign policy—an area in which he faced serious and growing opposition. He described the expanding threat that had resulted from the policies of his administration. But Congress's lack of resolve in providing adequate oversight had played a role as well.

As far as Iraq was concerned, he conceded: "This is not the fight we entered in Iraq, but it is the fight we're in. Every one of us wishes this war were over and won. Yet it would not be like us to leave our promises unkept, our friends abandoned, and our own security at risk." He repeated his earlier announcement that he was sending an additional twenty thousand soldiers and Marines to Iraq and asked for an increase of ninety-two thousand men in the active duty force, saying, "Our military commanders and I have carefully weighed the options. We discussed every possible approach. In the end, I chose this course of action because it provides the best chance for success."[11]

Many in the room vigorously disagreed with his decision. Doc did not. He just hoped it would work.

—

Since Doc had first visited Iraq in 2005, the sectarian violence there had only increased. The war had destabilized the country's neighbors, and the only winner appeared to be Iran. Syria and Jordan were hosting two million refugees.

During the last half of December 2006, Bush had come to the conclusion that a new policy and a new leadership team were needed in Iraq. After the election was over, he acted. On January 10, 2007, he went on television to announce the surge of twenty thousand troops that had been advised by his new military commander, General David Petraeus.

The new Democratic majority in Congress challenged the decision and sent a resolution opposing it to the floor. Doc, as a member of the Rules Committee, was one of the first to comment on it. He said he shared the frustration of many Americans who wanted the Iraqi government to provide for its own security, "but that is not reality. Withholding military personnel, failing to provide funds for our troops, or pulling out of Iraq with no plan to win the war on terror are not options," Doc told a reporter. "The consequences for failure are simply too dire."[12]

With 168,000 coalition forces now in the country, troops were able to leave their heavily fortified encampments to clear the al-Qaeda members, Sunni insurgents, and Shia militiamen out of Baghdad and Sunni-dominated Anbar Province where most of the violence had taken place. The new policy was called "clear, hold, and build" and involved clearing the insurgents from an area, holding it against recurring attack, and building up trust and relationships with the Iraqis who remained. These were often Sunni Arab tribes who were willing to fight the al-Qaeda insurgents for a price.[13]

At the time, the conventional wisdom was that the surge was a success. Doc agreed: "When you're in a war, you never know what the outcome is going to be. In retrospect, I think we should have done the surge earlier, rather than later. I felt we needed to support our efforts over there because, after all, I had voted for it."[14]

—

The centerpiece of the Bush domestic agenda had been across-the-board tax cuts for all Americans. The savings from his successive tax cuts had added to what Federal Reserve chairman Ben Bernanke called a "global savings glut" in which the increasingly wealthy nations of the world invested huge amounts of capital in the United States simply because it was the safest place in the world for them to invest their money. When US Treasury bonds no longer provided sufficient yields for their investments, they invested in real estate. American banks also participated in the investment binge. They leveraged their capital to invest in risky mortgage-backed securities, and by 2004, with interest rates near an all-time low and credit easy to come by, home ownership in America peaked at 69.2 percent. Between 1993 and 2007, the price of an average American home roughly doubled.[15]

With their newfound wealth, Americans went on a spending spree, running up credit card debt, investing in the stock market, and taking out adjustable rate mortgages. In April 2007, the Dow Jones Industrial Average closed above 13,000 for the first time. In July, it closed above 14,000. After losing almost 400 points on August 9, it rebounded to a new high of 14,164 on October 9. A year later, on September 29, 2008, the market suffered a record-breaking drop of more than 777 points to close at 10,365 and continued to fall until it hit a market low of 6,443.27 on March 6, 2009, having lost over 54 percent of its value since October 9, 2007.[16]

The dire financial situation led the Bush administration to begin working with the Democratic Congress in January 2008 to write legislation providing temporary tax incentives and immediate tax rebates to help stem the onslaught of the approaching recession. The Republican minority spent most of 2008 making difficult decisions about voting for measures to prop up the failing economy, like the Economic Stimulus Act of 2008, which the House passed on January 29, 2008, and supporting their unpopular lame-duck president.

—

In March, one of America's largest investment banks, Bear Stearns, found itself facing a liquidity crisis. President Bush said he had been focusing on jobs and inflation and had not been paying enough attention to problems in the credit markets. The crisis at Bear Sterns came as a complete surprise. His first inclination was to let it fail, but his treasury secretary, Henry Paulson, and others told him that if that happened it would have a domino effect on other failing firms. They devised a thirty-billion-dollar bailout of its mortgage holdings and a sale to JPMorgan Chase.[17]

The crisis continued to grow. The government seized the giant housing finance agencies Fannie Mae and Freddie Mac, and Lehman Brothers filed for the largest bankruptcy in American history. Merrill Lynch was sold in a shotgun marriage to the Bank of America. AIG, the world's largest insurance company, accepted an eighty-five-billion-dollar government bailout. Goldman Sachs and Morgan Stanley, the last two independent investment houses, merged to keep from going under. The government closed Washington Mutual Savings Bank, the largest bank failure in history.

To avert a situation similar to the Great Depression, the government devised a financial bailout plan called TARP—Troubled Asset Relief Program—to guarantee all money market deposits, restart the commercial credit market, ban the short sale of financial stocks, and purchase $3.5 trillion in mortgage-backed securities.[18] Now all they had to do was sell the plan to the Congress and find the estimated seven hundred billion dollars needed to pay for it.

Congress had passed a $250 billion supplemental appropriations bill in June. In July, it passed a $300 billion bill that partially guaranteed sub-prime mortgages in an effort to restore confidence in Fannie Mae and Freddie Mac. Now, the administration was asking for $700 billion for TARP.

—

All this occurred in the middle of the 2008 presidential election campaign. Democrats argued that the government was seizing too much authority. Republicans balked at the cost. On September 24, 2008, President Bush delivered a primetime address to the nation explaining the need to pass the TARP package. Five days later, the House held a vote on the measure, and it failed, 228 to 205. Republican leaders had pushed their reluctant members to vote for the bill, but two-thirds had not, including Doc. Minority leader John Boehner later blamed Republican reluctance to support the bill on House Speaker Nancy Pelosi's "partisan speech" on the House floor during which she had blamed the nation's economic problems on "failed Bush economic policies."[19]

Doc remembered, "Hank Paulson came and briefed the [Republican] conference. I'm no economic specialist, but after I heard what he had to say, my instincts were that this just doesn't sound right to me. I felt instinctively uneasy about the whole thing."[20] Doc told a reporter for the *Yakima Herald-Republic* that he just "couldn't stomach" the idea of the government bailing out Wall Street. "On the question of increased government intervention in the marketplace, I am just plain opposed to such a massive intrusion into the economy. We'll just have to see what happens."[21]

What happened was the 777 point drop in the Dow Jones Industrial Average on September 29 in which the financial markets lost $1.2 trillion in less than three hours.

With no other option available to him in order to avert a catastrophe, Bush was left to convince his fellow Republicans to vote for the measure. The Senate made some slight adjustments to the bill, and perhaps the reaction of the financial markets had shaken some of the bill's opponents, but the Senate voted to approve the TARP, 74 to 25 on October 1. Two days later the House followed suit by approving the Senate version of the TARP by a vote of 263 to 171. Doc voted no a second time. He acknowledged that he was "mad as hell that the reckless actions of Wall Street created this situation, but that doesn't mean that the taxpayers should foot the bill for the risky decisions the financial community had made."[22]

George Bush had the same instinctive attitude about a financial bailout as Doc Hastings had but changed his mind in the face of the potential consequences. He was the president of the United States and had the future of the nation to consider. He told his staff, "If we're really looking at another Great Depression, you can be damn sure I'm going to be Roosevelt, not Hoover."[23] Doc faced no similar burden of responsibility.

—

Against the backdrop of war and recession, Doc began a new phase of his tenure on the House Ethics Committee. With the Democrats now in control of the House, Speaker Pelosi appointed Stephanie Tubbs Jones of Ohio to chair the committee after Howard Berman left it to chair the Intellectual Property Subcommittee of the House Judiciary Committee. A lawyer and former judge, Tubbs Jones had served in Congress since 1999 and had served on the Ethics Committee for several terms. "She came from a very different background than I—her district was in inner-city Cleveland—and, naturally, we saw things very differently, but we got along," Doc said.[24] Doc now became the ranking Republican on the committee. Todd Ungerecht, who had previously served on his congressional staff, rejoined him now to become Doc's staff counsel.

Doc's three terms on the committee were scheduled to end at the end of 2007, and he wanted to move on, but minority leader John Boehner had other ideas. "He told me that he didn't have anyone else and that he wanted me to stay on for another term. I told him that he would have to talk to Claire!"[25]

After what the family had gone through during the last reelect campaign, Boehner was fortunate that Claire wasn't home when he called. He left her a very nice message, explaining that he didn't have anyone else to replace Doc and promising this would be his last term on the committee. Doc recalled, "We talked it over that night. She reluctantly agreed with me, and I agreed to serve one more term."[26]

On August 19, 2008, Tubbs was in Cleveland during the summer recess and suffered a cerebral hemorrhage. She died two days later. She was replaced by Gene Green of Texas. "He was a lawyer from Houston, and being from oil country, we always saw eye to eye on natural resources issues and formed a working, if not close, relationship."[27]

—

On December 7, in the wake of the Democratic victory in the 2006 midterm elections, the Bush Justice Department decided to fire seven US attorneys across the country. The resulting outcry suggested the firings were politically motivated, or worse—payback for the attorneys' lack of vigor in pursuing alleged Democratic voter fraud in the recent elections. With the Democrats now in charge, a Senate investigation ensued. One of the attorneys dismissed was John McKay, the US attorney in Seattle. A member of a prominent Republican family, McKay had been appointed to the job by President Bush in 2001.

On March 6, 2007, McKay testified before the Senate Judiciary Committee that Ed Cassidy—at the time Doc's chief of staff—had called him in the weeks following the 2004 Washington State gubernatorial election to ask whether he was investigating allegations of voter fraud after Christine Gregoire defeated Dino Rossi for governor after a third recount. McKay testified that he stopped the conversation by asking Cassidy whether he was truly asking on behalf of Doc Hastings about a possible internal investigation or whether he was trying to lobby McKay to launch one, which would have been improper. McKay testified that, had he not stopped Cassidy from continuing, he was "certain" Cassidy would have entered into what he called "dangerous territory." Cassidy said the call was a routine effort to determine "whether allegations of voter fraud in the 2004 gubernatorial election were, or were not, being investigated by federal authorities." [28]

The real motivation behind Cassidy's call remains unclear, but given Doc's closeness to Rossi and his strong suspicion of foul play at the time, it would not have been a stretch to imagine that Doc's office might have been trying to light a fire under McKay. Doc steadfastly maintains he was not. "If I would have made the call, it would have been to [Washington's secretary of state] Sam Reed, not McKay."[29] In any event, McKay ultimately decided not to pursue a voter fraud case in the 2004 election, saying there was not sufficient evidence.[30]

By the time of McKay's testimony, Cassidy was serving as a top aide to House leader John Boehner, but the case raised a potential conflict for Doc on the House Ethics Committee. Press reports speculated that, as the ranking Republican on the committee, Doc would certainly play a crucial role in deciding whether to begin an investigation.[31] Both the *Yakima Herald-Republic* and the *Tri-City Herald* editorialized that Doc should welcome an investigation into the matter.[32]

The congressional watchdog group Citizens for Responsibility and Ethics in Washington (CREW) immediately asked the committee to determine whether Cassidy's call had violated congressional rules.[33] The committee took no action on CREW's request because it did not accept complaints from outside groups, and no member had filed a complaint.

By late August, the firings had been exposed as a political witch-hunt of fellow Republicans by an over-zealous attorney general and his staff. The disclosures damaged the reputations of both the attorney general, Alberto Gonzales, a friend and Texan colleague of the president's, and the Republican Party. On September 17, Gonzales and eight other senior staff members of the Justice Department resigned or were fired.

—

The Democrats had made the House Ethics Committee a major campaign issue during the 2006 elections. A number of third-party, public interest groups supported them, like CREW, who frequently attacked Doc and criticized what they called the "culture of corruption" of the House Ethics Committee under his leadership.

In March 2008, Speaker Pelosi and the Democratic leadership decided to create an independent body called the Office of Congressional Ethics (OCE) to investigate allegations of misconduct by members, officers, and employees of Congress. The OCE's mandate, which had jurisdiction only in the House, was to review information from any source and, if it was serious enough, to refer its findings to the Ethics Committee. Only the committee, not the OCE, had the authority to discipline members or staff.[34] Doc and every Republican member voted against the OCE, but the Democrats prevailed. "I felt that the committee already had all the authority it needed. The creation of the OCE was just a nod toward the liberal, third-party outside groups who had been leading the charge against the Republicans in the past Congress."[35]

—

On July 15, 2008, the *Washington Post* reported that Democrat Charles Rangel of New York—first elected to Congress in 1971 and now the chairman of the powerful House Ways and Means Committee—had solicited contributions for the Charles B. Rangel Center for Public Service at City College of New York from corporations with business interests before his Ways and Means Committee and did so using his congressional letterhead.[36] Rangel denied any wrongdoing and asked the House Ethics Committee to look into the allegations. Almost immediately, a string of disclosures revealed other potential ethics violations.[37]

Here was another high-visibility case involving one of the most powerful men in Congress. Doc suggested to committee chairman Gene Green that they lead the investigative subcommittee together, just as Doc and Howard Berman had chaired the Foley investigation. Green agreed. The investigation continued into 2010. Rangel was eventually found guilty by the adjudicatory subcommittee, and two days later, the full committee voted 9-1 to recommend that the House censure Rangel, the strongest possible penalty the committee could invoke short of expelling him from Congress.[38] Rangel remained on the Ways and Means Committee but never again became chairman because the Republicans recaptured the House in the 2010 election. He chose not to run for reelection in 2016.

—

Ed Cassidy, Doc's longtime chief of staff and his key staff member on both the Rules and Ethics Committees, decided to leave Doc's staff at the end of 2006. At the beginning of the new session, minority leader John Boehner approached Doc about hiring Ed as a senior advisor. Doc remembered: "Ed was very professional and had set up a very good office operation for us. We were friends. I had been the best man at his wedding. We worked closely with one another. He had ties to the Ohio delegation dating back to when he had been chief of staff to Martin Hoke. I hated to lose him, but I told John that I didn't have any objections."[39]

Boehner's office announced Cassidy's hiring on February 3, 2007, and Todd Young moved up to take over Ed's position. Although Cassidy was now working for Boehner, he and Doc continued to meet informally from time to time.[40]

On July 25, 2007, the *Wall Street Journal* reported that Don Young of Alaska had been implicated on federal corruption charges involving VECO, an Anchorage-based pipeline services company.[41] The nineteen-term congressman had first been elected in 1973 and was the second longest-serving Republican in the House and the ranking member on the House Natural Resources Committee.

The investigation into Young's activities continued through 2008, and press reports estimated that his campaign spent more than a million dollars defending him. Young was no stranger to controversy. In 2005, he and Alaska senator Ted Stevens had earmarked $223 million to build the famous "Bridge to Nowhere" that later became an issue in the 2008 presidential campaign. At one point, Young threatened to bite a fellow Republican congressman "like a mink" for criticizing one of his earmarks.[42]

On November 14, 2007, Cassidy wrote a memo to his new boss, John Boehner. He said he had met with Doc Hastings and his new chief of staff several weeks earlier and discussed what the impact would be on the House Natural Resources Committee if Young, its ranking member, were forced to step down because of the controversy surrounding him. Cassidy wrote:

> For different reasons, the Members ranking just below Rep. Young have at various times been judged less than ideal candidates for the top Republican seat on the committee. Doc is on leave (with seniority) from

Resources but would be among its most senior Members if he reclaimed his chair. . . .

Doc authorized me to mention . . . that he would be willing to consider returning [to the Natural Resources Committee] if you believe it would be helpful to have him in a position to bid for the ranking position, should it become available either mid-session or at the end of the 110th.[43]

There were, however, some potential complicating factors. A waiver would be necessary if Doc were to return to Natural Resources without giving up his seat on Rules. Everyone realized that Doc's goal was to become chairman of the Rules Committee. If Doc were given some hope that David Dreier would not continue to serve as ranking member's position beyond the current Congress, he could stay on Rules and replace Dreier. If Boehner decided to keep Dreier, Doc would then be willing to return to Natural Resources. Cassidy concluded his memo with the following advice to his new boss:

My recommendation is that the very best way to reward Doc's service and loyalty isn't to appoint him to anything or back him for anything . . . but instead to simply give him a window into your thinking about Dreier and Rules (whether good news for Doc or bad).

John, I can absolutely guarantee that if you confide in him on that subject—let him peek at his hole cards if you will—Doc will never say anything to anyone to make you wish you hadn't.[44]

Boehner listened to Cassidy's advice but saw no reason to replace Young in the middle of the term based on the allegations against which he was actively defending himself. However, he proceeded to have the conversation with Doc that Cassidy had recommended. With the 2008 elections behind them and the end of the current term at hand, the

Republican Steering Committee (on which Doc served) met to organize for the coming session. Young was forced out, and Doc was elected to replace him as the ranking member on the Natural Resources Committee.[45] That required him to give up his seat on the Rules Committee since neither ranking members nor committee chairs of other committees were allowed to serve on that committee.

Doc's appointment to Natural Resources was seen as a good fit. Some back home in the district who had little understanding of how the House actually operated thought that Doc's preference for little-known or poorly understood committee assignments like Rules and Budget suggested a lack of influence in the House. His membership on the Ethics Committee had frequently been used against him during his reelection campaigns. Natural Resources held jurisdiction over many of Doc's favorite hot-button issues, including the Endangered Species Act, Native American policy, federal irrigation projects, public lands, and the Bonneville Power Administration.[46]

As Doc prepared for the new term, he decided on a new look. During the break between sessions, he grew a goatee. "I had always wanted to grow one, and this seemed like a good time to do it." According to Doc, Claire and his staff members viewed his new look favorably, and so did just about everyone else until he happened to run into John Boehner in the halls of the Capitol. Boehner, a meticulous dresser, looked at the goatee and said, "When are you going to shave that thing off?" "When you stop smoking," Doc replied without missing a beat. "That was the end of the conversation."[47]

Doc made some changes to his senior staff. As we have seen, Todd Young was promoted to replace Ed Cassidy as chief of staff and Jessica Gleason was promoted to the communications director's job. He already had a solid district office staff under the leadership of Barb Lisk, backed up by Sharlyn Berger, who had been with him from the beginning in his Pasco office.

—

The Democrats controlled the new Congress, but George Bush remained in the White House. How, many wondered, would the change of congressional leadership and the looming economic crisis influence the issues that were important to the Fourth Congressional District?

Home during the 2007 summer break, Doc made the rounds of the local chambers of commerce and service clubs as he prepared for the remainder of what he knew would be a difficult term. On August 28, he spoke at the Pacific Northwest National Laboratory. The *Tri-City Herald* covered his remarks, providing a good look at his current political state of mind at the time.

He told his audience that after attempts to pass comprehensive immigration reform had failed in the Senate, Doc thought the subject was "dead until after the 2008 presidential election." He didn't agree with Democratic leaders who wanted the government to get involved in expanding healthcare. "People don't make medical decisions like they would if they were paying for it out of their own pocket," he said. He noted that he still wanted Rattlesnake Mountain and the Hanford Reach opened up to the public. Finally, he wanted to make the B Reactor a National Historic Landmark.[48]

Returning back home on November 10, Doc spoke to a group of college students at Columbia Basin College. He criticized the new Democratic leadership for passing only one of twelve spending bills that were required to fund the government. That failure had resulted in the lack of a detailed Hanford budget for the second year in a row.

Again, he promoted Social Security entitlement reform and the use of Personal Retirement Accounts. Finally, he defended the US presence in Iraq, saying that an arbitrary pullout would "provide a sanctuary for terrorists and threaten our security at home."[49]

After a year of being in the minority, Doc shared some thoughts about the experience at a Pasco Chamber of Commerce meeting on January 14, 2008. In response to a question about the previous session, he responded, "What was significant about the [last session] was what [the Democrats] did *not* get done." Years later, he reflected again about being in the minority:

National policies change depending on which party is in control of Congress or the White House, but local issues rarely change. If it was an issue before the election, typically it will still be an issue after the election. For example, nothing much changed with Hanford. Patty Murray and I had been addressing that on a bipartisan basis anyway.

What *can* happen is that different national policies can *influence* local issues.[50]

—

Back on February 7, 2007, the Bush administration had proposed its 2008 Hanford budget. At $1.94 billion, it was higher than the 2007 budget number Congress was expected to pass.[51] Almost immediately, a number of looming uncertainties at Hanford led Congress to lower the amount of money it was willing to make available. Problems included the spiraling higher cost estimates of the Hanford Waste Treatment Plant, the realization that important cleanup deadlines would almost certainly be missed, the retirement of both top DOE managers at Hanford, and uncertainty surrounding the rebid of major Hanford contracts.

In June, the House Appropriations Committee cut $100 million from the WTP budget. Finally, in December with the Christmas recess beckoning, the House and Senate considered an omnibus appropriations bill that provided $1.86 billion for Hanford with $684 million set aside for the WTP.

Doc was happy about the funding level but voted against the bill anyway because it prohibited money from being used for current operations in Iraq. He was on the losing side, and the measure passed by a vote of 253 to 154 and was approved by the Senate on the following day.

In February 2008, the administration presented its proposed 2009 budget for Hanford. It essentially maintained funding at approximately $1.9 billion. Washington's governor, Christine Gregoire, was dismayed at the paucity of the Bush administration's proposal, claiming it was more than $600 million short of what was necessary to achieve even minimal compliance with the Tri-Party Agreement.

Doc didn't believe for a minute that the proposal would be the final amount approved by Congress, but he agreed that the governor had a point. It was "dismaying to see DOE just throw up their hands and say they can't meet legal cleanup milestones," he said.[52]

He joined the state's two senators and two dozen members of Congress in signing letters to the Senate and House Budget Committees, claiming the proposed national cleanup budget was at least $1.1 billion short of what was needed and could cost five hundred jobs at Hanford. He compared the DOE budget to the "tragic story of a jilted bride lured by promises of accelerated cleanup funding, only to be left at the altar, forgotten and neglected"—pretty colorful stuff for Doc.[53]

Doc led the lobbying effort to restore money for nuclear cleanup as the chairman of the Nuclear Cleanup Caucus. In May, he and thirty-six other members sent a letter to the leadership of the House Energy and Water Appropriations Subcommittee. By June, the House Appropriations Committee had restored $24 million of the $58 million Hanford shortfall. After Congress was unable to pass a 2008 budget, they settled on a five-month continuing resolution to carry them over and kick the can down the road into the next year.

Under the circumstances, it was surprising that Doc and his national nuclear cleanup supporters were able to restore any money at all. Their funding request was competing with the bailout of Bear Stearns. Then came the $250 billion supplemental appropriations bill and the $300 billion bill to help restore confidence in Fannie Mae and Freddie Mac. It seemed as if there was a new crisis every day, and Hanford was far from the worst one.

The proposed 2008 budget provided $690 million to construct the WTP, a significant increase over the 2005 funding when 1,700 workers had been laid off. The $690 million figure was the result of smart planning and savvy deal making between Doc, Senator Patty Murray, and the House and Senate appropriators back in 2004. Realizing that funding needs were likely to fluctuate wildly as construction progressed, they agreed on flat-line, annual funding for the project.[54]

In May, high-level negotiations began between DOE, EPA, and the state of Washington over a series of milestones under the Tri-Party Agreement that DOE admitted it was certain to miss. In August, DOE had ordered the restart of construction on the WTP—halted since January 2006—after Samuel Bodman, Bush's energy secretary, signed off on a report regarding earthquake standards. By September 2007, although no agreement on the benchmarks had been reached, the negotiators seemed willing to accept a delay in restarting the construction in return for an increased focus on cleaning up Hanford's contaminated groundwater, but much uncertainty remained.

All through the spring and summer of 2008, the state and federal negotiators tried to reach agreement on new milestones. Twice, Governor Gregoire flew to Washington, DC, to meet with Bodman, but to no avail. By November, DOE's Richland Office had formally notified the state and EPA that twenty-three milestones under the Tri-Party Agreement were at risk due to anticipated federal funding shortages. It asked EPA and the state to "adjust" the milestones to the funding realities, but the milestones remained in place.[55]

In response, on November 26, 2008, the state announced that it planned to file a lawsuit to force DOE to move faster on meeting the milestones. The parties had been negotiating for eighteen months to find a settlement. Doc showed his frustration in a public statement: "We can't afford to put everything on hold and wait for the outcome of a lawsuit." Doc and Patty Murray released a joint statement that called on the parties to resolve the dispute out of court since a lawsuit would make it harder to obtain the federal money needed to address the missed milestones.[56]

—

Doc also battled to retain Battelle Memorial Institute as the operator of the Pacific Northwest National Laboratory in Richland. As 2005 came to a close, DOE had announced it wanted to rebid the PNNL contract and put it out for competitive bids. A major bone of contention between Battelle and DOE was PNNL's unique use permit that allowed it to accept work from private industry as well as the government.[57] The permit had been a staple of PNNL's contract with the government since 1965.

In August 2007, DOE announced it would publish its draft request or proposals before the end of September. Doc was concerned the delay would expose the funding of the lab to the unknown consequences of the 2008 election. However, the uncertainty about the lab's future was eased somewhat by the welcome announcement on August 15 that construction could begin on the new two-hundred-thousand-square-foot, $225 million Physical Science Facility, replacing lab space lost when most of the Hanford 300 area was demolished.[58]

In October, DOE announced the new contract would no longer include the unique use permit, as Doc had feared. The loss of the use permit threatened four hundred jobs and seventy-five million dollars in private contracts. Senator Patty Murray, Doc, and Congressman Norm Dicks released a statement expressing their hope that "DOE does the right thing and restores the use permit."[59] Their efforts were successful. When the omnibus appropriations bill was approved in December, it included language that specifically directed DOE to include the use permit when it rebid the PNNL contract. The Washington delegation had delivered a strong message to DOE: "Leave PNNL alone!"[60] In October 2008, DOE extended Battelle's contract for four years and continued PNNL's controversial special use permit.

—

Doc was able to chalk up several other accomplishments during the year. In June, he freed up $2.25 million in US State Department funds that had been promised to the Volpentest HAMMER training facility in 2005 but then reallocated to other uses. That accomplishment prompted not one but two positive editorials in the *Tri-City Herald*: "Doc Hastings kept faith with Sam Volpentest by doing something Sam would have completely understood, prodding an administration for HAMMER training center money."[61] By June 2008, construction was well underway on a new 6,500-square-foot, $2.25 million building for training US and international border guards to detect nuclear materials.

Doc also worked with the Department of Health and Human Services to get early Hanford workers a one-lump cash settlement of

$150,000 should they contract any of a broad range of cancers. The settlement was announced on September 26, 2007.[62]

In December, more positive news came when the National Park Service's advisory committee recommended that the Hanford's B Reactor be designated a National Historic Landmark.[63] Doc continued to press them for action through the spring, and the formal designation occurred on August 25, 2008.

—

While funding problems played out at Hanford, the new Democratic majority took up a new farm bill. Much of the dryland area in Franklin and Grant Counties produced winter wheat, which was included under the crop subsidy program. In other areas irrigated by the Columbia Basin Project or the region's rivers, specialty crops like apples, wine grapes, and asparagus were produced under free market conditions. Their growers weren't interested in government subsidies, but they were interested in receiving more funding for market research, trade promotion assistance, and protection from the negative impacts of foreign trade deals.

Doc had been through this before in his previous efforts to assist his district's apple and asparagus growers. The two key agricultural committees in Congress were controlled by members from Midwestern and Southern states, whose constituents largely grew program crops. Washington didn't have a member on either committee, and the growers of specialty crops in the state had been largely ignored when the last major farm bill passed in 2002.[64]

By July 2007, the new farm bill was beginning to take shape. Washington's fruit and vegetable growers were hoping to receive five billion dollars in research, state block grants, federal school lunch purchases, and marketing programs over the next five years, but the bill produced by the House Agriculture Committee included only a third of that amount. That wasn't enough to get Doc to vote for it. He and five other members of the Washington delegations voted no.

On May 15, 2008, a new compromise farm bill emerged that provided about $1.3 billion for growers of specialty crops, such as fruits and vegetables, the first time such crops had been included in a farm bill.

With the Bush White House promising a veto in the face of the growing economic crisis, the Senate passed the $289 billion bill by a margin or 81 to 15. The House had passed it by a veto-proof margin of 318 to 106 a day earlier.[65] This time, Doc voted with the majority and against the administration. "Our growers are not looking for direct payments and subsidies," he said, "but the other things . . . are very positive."[66]

The bill had been controversial because it violated the Democratic majority's pay-as-you-go (PAYGO) rule. President Bush vetoed the bill—twice, as it turned out because of an error that had omitted a thirty-four-page section of the bill when it had been sent to him the first time. Congress had to pass and override the president's veto again.[67]

—

Many of Washington's crops required seasonal migrant farmworkers at harvest time. In the Yakima Valley alone, growers relied on a seasonal work force of thirty thousand migrant workers. As many as 70 percent of them were thought to be illegal.[68] An estimated twelve million undocumented immigrants were thought to be living in the United States. Many of these were not farmworkers but individuals who had entered the country legally and overstayed their visas.

Farmers and growers who could afford to provide housing, transportation, and other requirements, employed foreign agricultural workers who held H-2A visas and worked for labor contractors. But most growers could not afford the cost and simply accepted workers' assurances and their identification claiming they were legal. Doc saw the drama play out from all sides. It was the reason he supported a comprehensive immigration plan that tightened border security but expanded the number of guest-worker visas available and went after employers who knowingly hired illegals.

In June, the US Senate again considered comprehensive immigration reform. The measure would have provided a legal path to citizenship for undocumented workers while also tightening border security. But, just as they had in former attempts to pass immigration reform, most of the Republicans in Congress were fixated on border security while a minority of western Republicans tended to support some form of comprehensive reform.

Immigration was a polarizing, hot-button issue across the nation. By August, after a series of amendments and cloture killed the Senate bill, Doc was ready to admit the obvious. "There may be a move to get some sort of a guest-worker program after Labor Day," he told the editorial board of the *Yakima Herald-Republic*, "but any hope of comprehensive reform is dead until after the 2008 presidential election."[69]

—

Like immigration reform, the saga of the Snake River dams continued without any resolution. In March 2007, Doc called on the Bush administration to challenge a ruling by an "activist" Ninth Court of Appeals panel that upheld federal judge James Redden's order to force the dams to spill more water into the Snake River to help migrating salmon. "With the stroke of a pen, judges are overruling science and the efforts of those who actually live in Central Washington who know we can have both salmon and jobs."[70]

—

Most of the day-to-day issues that Doc and his staff dealt with were less visible and controversial than Hanford, the farm bill, or immigration, but they seemed to take just as long to resolve. With each new Congress, Doc would reintroduce some of the same legislation again in the hope that perhaps this would be the year. The 110th Congress was no exception.

One such item of unfinished business involved the proposed Ice Age Floods National Trail. Doc and Senator Maria Cantwell had introduced legislation to create the six-hundred-mile trail in the last session of Congress, but the session ended before differences between the two versions of the bill could be reconciled. Both sponsors were hopeful of quick passage, but it took another year to attain.

—

Another item was public access into the popular seventeen-thousand-acre Juniper Dunes Wilderness Area northeast of Pasco. The dunes area was public lands, but access was limited to a private road, which local farmers blocked off in 2005 because of the hikers, horseback riders, and dirt bikers trespassing on their property. Doc had introduced legislation in 2005 authorizing the Bureau of Land Management to sell 622 acres to the Douglas County PUD with the proceeds of the sale used to open up access to the area, but no action was taken in the Senate. Doc reintroduced his legislation in 2007. The House finally approved it in a vote of 377 to 0 in October 2007. The Senate then passed a similar bill in May 2008. The bills were ultimately included in the 2009 Omnibus Land Management Act, which was signed by President Obama in March 2009.

In October 2010, access to Juniper Dunes appeared to be assured when Franklin County agreed to purchase and improve 2.18 miles of existing road, insuring public access to the area after receiving seven hundred thousand dollars from the Bureau of Land Management. However, in 2012 that plan hit a speed bump when an adjacent landowner expressed concerns that a thirty-inch pressurized water line might be at risk. The cost to replace the line was estimated at more than one million dollars, which the county didn't have.[71]

—

Yet another ongoing issue was Doc's continuing interest in obtaining public access to the Hanford Reach National Monument. In 2006, the Fish and Wildlife Service released a draft plan that looked for alternatives for managing the monument in the future. By June 2007, it was working on its final plan. Doc weighed in with a public statement that included (1) public access to Rattlesnake Mountain, which had been closed since World War II, (2) retention and improvement of the White Bluffs boat launch facility, (3) consolidation on controlled hunting for elk on the Arid Lands Ecology area, and (4) keeping the six McNary Wildlife Refuge islands open to reasonable public use.[72]

—

Yet another ongoing issue was funding the study of the proposed Black Rock Reservoir. The project hit a snag in September when the US Bureau of Reclamation and the state Ecology Department released a study concluding that water seeping through the bottom of the reservoir would raise the water table at Hanford, spreading contamination and threatening the Columbia River. Undeterred, Doc released a statement that "this analysis only forecasts what seepage could occur if nothing was done to stop or confine it. Possible ways to prevent and capture seepage will be coming in the months ahead."[73]

In January 2008, the Bureau of Reclamation released its long-awaited, eight-hundred-page draft environmental impact statement (EIS) for the project. The news it contained was not good. It estimated the project would provide only sixteen cents of benefit for every dollar invested in the six-billion-dollar project. Doc made the best of it, calling on the public to "comment and help shape the final report," but to no avail.[74]

The final EIS was released on December 19, 2008. It recommended against building the massive project. Doc remembered, "It simply cost too much. We were surprised by the figure, but my contention was that everyone needed to have some skin in the game."[75] In April 2009, the Bureau of Reclamation announced that, after thirty years and eighteen million dollars spent on feasibility reports, they were "finished looking at building a reservoir at Black Rock or Wymer because, by themselves, they won't solve all the problems."[76]

MOST EVERYTHING THAT HAPPENED during 2008 occurred against the backdrop of the collapsing economy and the 2008 presidential election. Hillary Clinton was seen by the mainstream Democratic leadership as the heir-apparent to her husband, but Senator Barack Obama of Illinois had excited the party base after his 2004 speech at the Democratic National Convention and had decided to run. Senator John Edwards of North Carolina, John Kerry's 2004 running mate, was also considered a strong contender.

The nomination was sharply contested between Hillary Clinton and Barack Obama, particularly after John Edwards withdrew from the campaign in the midst of a personal scandal. The Democratic establishment applauded Clinton's resume, connections, and the fact that she would become the first female president if elected. Obama was largely untried on the national political stage. He had been elected a US senator only in

2004, but he was a dramatic and accomplished speaker and drew support from younger voters and from the progressive wing of his party. If elected, he would be the nation's first African American president. Other issues involved the uncertainties caused by Obama's relative lack of experience and his huge attraction to independent voters.

Largely unsaid, but hovering over the campaign, was the issue of Clinton's gender and Obama's race. The spirited and sometimes bitter campaign between the two energized the Democratic base. The two fought for every vote, with Obama unable to secure the nomination until June 2008, only five months before the election was to be held. Obama chose an experienced senator, Joseph Biden of Delaware, to be his running mate.

With president George Bush's approval ratings hovering around 37 percent in 2007, the quest for the Republican nomination drew a large field, including senator and war hero John McCain of Arizona, former Massachusetts governor Mitt Romney, former Arkansas governor Mike Huckabee, congressman Ron Paul of Texas, and former New York City mayor Rudy Giuliani.[77] Doc endorsed McCain in mid-February, not long before McCain secured the Republican nomination.[78] The McCain campaign then inexplicably chose the unknown governor of Alaska, Sarah Palin, as his vice-presidential running mate.

To a large degree, the Republican primary campaign was fought over four issues: George Bush's unpopularity, the degree to which McCain could distinguish himself from his predecessor, the unpopularity of the Iraq War, and the extent and causes of the world economic crisis.

When the votes were counted on November 4, Obama won a decisive victory over McCain, receiving the largest percentage of the popular vote cast for a Democrat since Lyndon Johnson in 1964. On election night, 250,000 supporters gathered to hear him speak in Chicago's Grant Park, where Chicago police had clubbed anti-war demonstrators during the 1968 Democratic convention. Obama stated: "If there is anyone out there who still doubts that America is a place where all things are possible; who still wonders if the dream of our founders is alive in our time; who still questions the power of our democracy, tonight is your answer."[79]

Earlier in the evening, after John McCain's gracious concession speech, Obama had thought about what he would do, not on day one but in year one. "What single achievement would most help average Americans?" His answer was healthcare reform, something that hadn't been discussed much during the campaign.[80]

—

The Republican defeat marked the second two-term presidency in a row that had ended badly for the party in power. Bill Clinton's had been weakened by his impeachment and acquittal; George Bush's had been destroyed by the war and the economy. During those sixteen years, the American people had become much more partisan and polarized in their politics. Granted, the degree of their polarization depended on their level of attachment to one of the major parties, how informed they were about politics and public affairs, and whether they voted or not. But to an increasing number of Americans, the level and the tone of the partisan debates in Washington and across the country had become deeply unsettling and led to Gallup poll numbers that equated members of Congress with used car salesmen in terms of their honesty and ethics. Increasingly, the public was being pulled to the ideological left or right, and the new members that they elected to Congress reflected, rather than formed, their views.[81] Would the new Obama administration be able to break the pattern of the past two presidencies?

"WE'VE GOT TO FIGHT THEM there or we'll have to fight them at home," candidate George Fearing said dismissively. "I don't think he's even thought that through," he said, responding to comments about the war that Doc Hastings had made to a November 10 joint appearance before Columbia Basin College and WSU Tri-Cities college students.

A forty-nine-year-old Kennewick attorney, Fearing had lost the one race for the state legislature he had entered. He was well aware that no Democrat had received more than 40 percent of the vote against Doc Hastings in the past ten years. He had heard all the excuses about why he couldn't win, "and then I realized that I was making excuses too."[82]

Fearing announced his candidacy in a four-city swing on February 12, criticizing Hastings for "simply doing the bidding of the president," even if it harmed the district.[83] By the end of April, Fearing was joined by author and radio newsman Don Moody, fifty-six, of Wenatchee, and forty-year-old John Gotts, an internet entrepreneur from White Salmon.[84] Moody withdrew after district Democratic leaders endorsed Fearing, but then Gordon Pross, who had run against Doc in 1998, 2000, and 2004, announced he would run again.

Doc announced his candidacy on April 4 at the Benton-Franklin County Lincoln Day Dinner, taking on believers of global warming "as the same people" who wanted to tear down the dams and prevent a revival of nuclear power and "radical Islamists who want to bring down the entire Western way of life."[85]

Back in Washington, DC, after his announcement, Doc and his family had a pleasant diversion from the upcoming campaign. Doc had never visited the Oval Office. On various occasions, he asked both Josh Bolton, the president's chief of staff, and Karl Rove if they could arrange a visit. It happened that Claire, Kirsten, and Petrina, and Kirsten's oldest son, Ivan, were scheduled to be in town for the First Lady's annual luncheon for members' wives. On April 17, 2008, the family spent a half hour with the president in the Oval Office, during which the president spent most of the time talking with young Ivan. It was his tenth birthday.[86] It was not long before Doc received a handwritten note from Rove telling him that "the President thoroughly enjoyed your family's visit. Glad it all worked out."[87]

Back in Doc's district, the campaign continued its course. By July, it was reported that Doc had raised $480,000 to Fearing's $172,000.

Prior to the August recess, congressional Republicans demanded that the existing ban on drilling oil in Alaska be lifted, and that became the primary subject of Doc's stump speech. He made the rounds of the local service clubs, strongly advocating lifting the moratorium on oil drilling in the Arctic National Wildlife Refuge, "but only to buy time until other sources of energy are more practical," as a means of combating high fuel prices.[88]

In the top-two primary election held on August 19, Doc received 54,847 votes, or 61 percent, while Fearing received 31,375 votes, or 35 percent. Gordon Pross garnered nearly 5 percent of the vote.[89] The next day, former Republican-congressman-turned-Democrat Pete McCloskey was in the district stumping for Fearing and calling attention to Doc's Ethics Committee problems. "They put him as chair of the Ethics Committee for a purpose," McCloskey told the *Yakima Herald-Republic's* editorial board. "They knew he wouldn't allow any investigation of Republicans." From Washington, DC, Doc's chief of staff Todd Young defended his boss, saying, "If he could talk about some things, he'd be a lot better off."[90]

Twelve days after Doc's second vote against the TARP bailout, he debated George Fearing at an event hosted by the League of Woman Voters at CBC. Even though it competed with the final televised presidential debate, more than two hundred attended. Not surprisingly, the subject was the economy. Fearing came out swinging, claiming that Doc was "asleep at the wheel of a car teetering on the brink of a precipice" of economic collapse. Fearing wanted to reduce the federal deficit by bringing the troops home from Iraq and ending special benefits for oil companies. Doc had a list, too, saying the US was spending too much money on the United Nations and the Corporation for Public Broadcasting should be able to exist without government money. He wanted to cut foreign aid with the exception of Israel.[91] It was what local voters wanted to hear.

A day later the *Herald-Republic* reluctantly endorsed Doc again "because we can't in good faith recommend his opponent," but it added a snarky comment that Doc had refused the paper's invitation to interview with its editorial board and didn't seek their endorsement. "We've accepted the fact that Hastings' comfort zone does not stretch much beyond his home base in the Tri-Cities in such matters as endorsements."[92]

On the same day, the *Tri-City Herald* endorsed Doc with perhaps its strongest stamp of approval since 1996. "We're not always happy with his performance. His penchant for the technical details of the legislative process and a tendency to stay behind the scenes have sometimes limited his influence over events, but Doc Hastings has been an effective congressman for the 4th District, even from a seat in the minority caucus."[93]

When the voters went to the polls on November 4, they chose a new president but not a new congressman. Doc received slightly more than 63 percent while George Fearing received almost 37 percent. Doc would now be dealing with a popular new Democratic president and increased Democratic majorities in each branch of Congress. Doc said he shared the country's excitement over the election of the first black president. "This a remarkable county, and this is a historic time."[94]

CHAPTER FOURTEEN

Audacity Meets Reality

★

BARACK OBAMA ESTABLISHED HIS CREDIBILITY as a rising star in the Democratic Party with his keynote speech at the Democratic National Convention in July 2004. In that speech—titled "The Audacity of Hope"—he spoke of the unfulfilled quest for the American Dream that resided in the hearts and minds of millions of Americans: "It's the hope of slaves sitting around a fire singing freedom songs; the hope of immigrants setting out for distant shores . . . the hope of a skinny kid with a funny name who believes that America has a place for him, too. Hope in the face of difficulty. Hope in the face of uncertainty. The audacity of hope!"[1]

Two years later, Obama released a bestselling book that expanded on many of the same themes. It became the blueprint for his 2008 pursuit of the presidency and called for withdrawing American troops from Iraq, increasing energy independence, and universal healthcare.

On the evening of August 28, 2008, Obama accepted his party's nomination for president. Then, before eighty-four thousand people at Denver's Mile High Stadium and an estimated thirty-four million more watching on television, he declared:

> Our government should work for us, not against us. It should help us, not hurt us. It should ensure opportunity not just for those with the most money and influence, but for every American who's willing to work.
>
> That's the promise of America, the idea that we are responsible for ourselves, but that we also rise or fall as

one nation, the fundamental belief that I am my brother's keeper, I am my sister's keeper.

That's the promise we need to keep. That's the change we need right now.[2]

The combination of his optimistic message, his remarkable skills as a campaigner, a record turnout among African American voters, the unpopularity of his predecessor, and a series of self-inflicted campaign errors by John McCain resulted in an Obama landslide victory on November 4. He won the popular vote by almost ten million votes and the Electoral College by nearly two hundred votes. The Democrats picked up twenty-one seats in the House and won all eight contested seats in the Senate. It was the first time since 1930 that the Democrats had picked up substantial numbers of seats in back-to-back elections.[3]

Obama's victory confirmed what many had already believed to be true: the Democratic Party had become more liberal—they preferred to use the term progressive—during the past decade. Hillary Clinton, Obama's primary opponent, had received the support of most of the traditional Democratic establishment, and yet she lost. Obama appealed to the younger, more urban, and highly educated elements of the party. In addition, he attracted 95 percent of African American voters, large numbers of other minorities, the LGBT community, and independent voters. Obama and his advisors truly believed government spending would create new jobs and grow the economy.

The reverse was true for the Republicans. Since 1994, they had become more conservative. Members of Newt Gingrich's Republican Revolution were now considered mainstream, and in their place, an increasingly polarized base was electing Libertarian and even more conservative Republicans to Congress who were denouncing both Obama's overreach and the past spending excesses of the Bush administration in equally strident terms.[4]

From that point on, the stage was set for a battle between two diametrically opposed political philosophies: the liberal policies of Barack Obama and the increasingly conservative Republicans united in their

opposition. Audacity was about to meet the reality of intense and pro-
longed resistance.

—

The country faced an imminent financial catastrophe in the months
between Obama's election and the day he assumed office. Events were
moving so fast that it was nearly impossible to absorb the enormity of
the situation or carefully weigh the responses that needed to be taken.

Bush was still president, but the chairman of the Federal Reserve,
Ben Bernanke, and the treasury secretary, Henry Paulson, were tasked
with dealing with the immediate crises. The new Congress had been in
session for only four days, but the leadership and key committee chairmen found it necessary to stay in nearly constant communication with
the White House, Paulson, and Bernanke.

No president-elect had ever been forced to make so many presiden-
tial-level decisions before being sworn into office than Barack Obama.
Even then, the best he could do was provide policy preferences for the
actions that Congress and the Bush administration were being forced to
take on a daily basis before he was inaugurated. One such proposal was
to go to Congress for another $350 billion in TARP funds. It was rejected
as being political suicide.

On November 24, 2008, the Federal Reserve created the TALF
(Term Asset-Backed Securities Loan Facility), lending one trillion dollars to support owners of securities backed by credit card debt, student
loans, auto loans, and small-business loans. Since the money did not
originate from the Treasury, the program did not require congressional
approval. On December 19, the government used $13.4 billion to bail
out General Motors and Chrysler.

On January 16, 2009, another huge aid package was announced in
order to keep the Bank of America solvent. On March 9, the Dow Jones
hit 6,547, its lowest point during the recession and more than 50 percent
below its high in October 2007. In May, General Motors severed relationships with 1,100 local dealers, including one located in Doc's district.
A month later, the giant automaker filed for bankruptcy, announcing it
would close fourteen plants in the United States. Later that month, the

292 | <small>Congressman Doc Hastings</small>

Great Recession officially ended, but its repercussions would affect the economy and American politics for years. Doc remembered:

> Things were not good nationally, but not so bad in the district. All the decisions were being made by the Democrats. I wasn't on any of the committees that were making them. When they kept spending more and more money, I thought it was just bad policy. These problems in the financial sector had been ignored over time and should have been addressed before crisis occurred. If we had jump-started the economy through regulatory and tax reform earlier, I'm not sure that these problems would have occurred as they did.[5]

—

The new Congress was sworn in on January 6, 2009. In the House, Speaker Nancy Pelosi exercised tight control over her members. Steny Hoyer of Maryland remained the majority leader with Jim Clyburn of South Carolina as majority whip. Democratic committee chairmen without a close relationship with the Speaker were kept on a tight leash. Pelosi made it clear that endless hearings, delayed markups, and other postponing tactics were no longer acceptable when it came to dealing with the financial crisis. She told her caucus, "We're going to do it, not just talk about it and posture."[6]

John Boehner continued to lead the Republicans as minority leader with Eric Cantor of Virginia as minority whip and Mike Pence of Indiana as Republican Conference chairman. Sometimes referred to as a "country club Republican," John Boehner had grown up in modest circumstances far from any toney golf club—the second of twelve children—working in his father's Cincinnati-area bar. As a politician, he paid attention to personal relationships and was generally informal and accessible. He liked to tease his associates—as he had Doc over his new goatee—and enjoyed a glass or two of merlot at the Republican Capitol Hill Club in the evening. His minority whip, Eric Cantor, was a hard-edged workaholic.[7]

—

The two parties had plenty on their plate left over from the previous session, including the $3.1 trillion budget proposal submitted to the previous Congress by George W. Bush. Most pressing was the passage of the stimulus bill, known as the American Recovery and Reinvestment Act. With a price tag of almost eight hundred billion dollars, it consisted of one-third middle-class tax cuts, one-third stabilization funding—to make sure states didn't lay off teachers, firefighters, or other state workers or interrupt unemployment insurance or food stamps—and one-third infrastructure funding, most of which wouldn't kick in until later.

Everyone had ideas about how to spend the money. Washington's senator Patty Murray proposed spending six to seven billion dollars to clean up the nation's nuclear sites. Most members of the Washington delegation supported the proposed stimulus package to some degree—some enthusiastically, some less so—but Doc stood out in his opposition. Joel Connelly, a political writer for the *Seattle Post-Intelligencer*, wrote that "no Northwest congressman churned out more boilerplate press releases denouncing President Obama's economic stimulus package" than Doc Hastings, yet "the reckless spending," as he called it, "pumped more money into his district than any other place in America." A Brookings Institution report issued in 2014 said the stimulus package spent $3,750 per constituent in Doc's District for a total of $2.678 billion dollars.[8]

Doc told the *Tri-City Herald*, "I don't believe that spending billions more in federal taxpayer dollars for new government programs or to fill state coffers is the way to get our economy on track." Instead, he called for "tax relief that creates jobs and helps businesses expand, approval of pending trade agreements, and more exploration, drilling, and production of domestic energy sources."[9]

—

Barack Obama was sworn in on January 20, 2009. Chief Justice John Roberts botched the oath of office after Obama began to repeat the words faster than Roberts had anticipated. Because of the confusion over the original oath and the concerns voiced by many conservatives that Obama was not a US citizen, Roberts administered the oath again at the White House a day later.[10]

The president's first week in office achieved real, immediate change. Obama signed the Lilly Ledbetter Fair Pay Act for women and reauthorized the Children's Health Insurance Program (CHIPRA), which had passed the House and Senate after they reconvened in January.

But it was the looming stimulus bill that held everyone's attention. Obama and the Democratic congressional leadership had agreed on a one-trillion-dollar ceiling—unless more was needed. Added to the $700 billion TARP program, the $800 billion stimulus bill meant that Obama's new administration would start $1.5 trillion in the hole. Doc was aghast at the magnitude of the deficit spending. "I would just point out that this was the first time in history when the annual deficit exceeded one trillion dollars," Doc recalled.[11]

Before the financial crisis escalated, Republicans had agreed to support a "timely, temporary, and targeted" stimulus package to address what they thought was going to be a short and shallow recession, but the proposed package of new spending and proposed tax cuts went far beyond anything the Republicans could support. Obama made a highly unusual trip to Capitol Hill to talk directly to the House Republican Conference, but John Boehner instructed his members not to vote for the bill, regardless of what the president said to them.[12]

To peel off some votes, Obama tried removing items the Republicans objected to, like reseeding the National Mall. "It was death by a thousand cuts," George Miller of California told an Obama biographer. "As soon as we take out contraceptives, they say, 'Take out the Mall.' When we take out the Mall, [they say] 'Take out the honeybees.'"

Was the president being naïve? He told a biographer that while he had expected plenty of partisanship, the *intensity* of the Republican intransigence took him by surprise: "There's a sense on the part of a big chunk of the Republican Party that they have no responsibility to govern right now. From their perspective, they may just see this as payback."[13]

The House passed another stimulus bill on January 28, 2009, in what was essentially a party line vote of 244 to 188. Eleven Democrats voted against it. This time, no Republicans voted for it. Eric Cantor believed the Democrats had badly overplayed their hand. "You really could've gotten some of our support," Cantor later told Obama's chief of staff, Rahm Emanuel. "You just refused to listen to what we were saying."[14]

Doc opposed the House version of the stimulus bill. "A massive expansion of the federal government is not the way to get our economy back on track," he said. "In fact, the vast majority of spending in this bill is wholly unrelated to creating jobs or growing our economy." Instead, Doc called for what he described as "fast-acting tax cuts for small businesses and families," things like "trade policies that support Washington agriculture," and protecting dams that provide "lower cost power."[15]

On February 10, the Senate voted 61 to 37 to approve a slightly different version of the bill. Only three Senate Republicans voted for it.[16] Obama felt the lack of Republican support "set the tenor for the whole year."[17]

The bill went back to the House with the changes from the Senate. With Patty Murray on the Senate Appropriations Committee, Washington State would receive almost seventy-six billion dollars, including almost two billion dollars for Hanford cleanup, enough to create an estimated four thousand jobs. On February 13, the House considered the legislation again. Doc again voted no in a 246-183 mostly party-line vote in which seven Democrats also voted no. As far as the money for Hanford cleanup was concerned, Doc argued, "Cleanup obligations should come first, and meeting the federal government's cleanup commitments at Hanford and other sites need not cost American taxpayers the trillion-dollar price of the stimulus bill.[18]

At the start of the session, the Democrats in the Senate had only fifty-eight votes while they awaited the results of a recount in a tight Minnesota senatorial election. Ultimately, Democrat Al Franken was declared the winner, and Republican Arlen Specter switched to the Democrats, providing the needed sixtieth vote to ensure passage of the stimulus bill, but then Ted Kennedy of Massachusetts died, leaving the Democrats again one vote short for passage. Unable to turn any moderate Republicans, the Democratic leadership had to wait until Paul Kirk had been appointed to succeed Kennedy in order to pass the final version of the bill by a vote of 60 to 38. All Democrats and Independents voted for it, along with three Republicans, and on February 17, 2009, President Obama signed the American Recovery and Reinvestment Act into law.[19]

—

With the divisive vote on the stimulus bill now behind him, Obama dealt with the leftover 2009 budget because Congress had failed to pass any appropriations bills by the time he took office. Moreover, the presence of thousands of earmarks—the practice of including money in a budget for pet projects—in the budget made it even more problematic. The twenty thousand earmarks in the original budget had been reduced to nine thousand, a number Obama still considered unacceptable. But in light of the Republican opposition to the stimulus, he made a practical decision: The earmarks could remain in the 2009 budget but would be prohibited in the 2010 budget.

On March 11, 2009, Congress passed the $410 billion Omnibus Appropriations Act. It included four hundred earmarks worth $377 million inserted by members of Washington's congressional delegation alone, including twenty-four projects worth $54.9 million that Doc had inserted. Assuming the bill would pass without his vote, Doc voted no. "I had some stuff in there, but the Democrats were in control, and it passed on pretty much a straight party line vote."[20]

The decision to let the earmarks remain in the 2009 budget may have contributed to the rousing welcome the president received for his first address to the Congress on February 24. Striking an optimistic tone that had been absent in his recent public remarks, Obama said, "The weight of this crisis will not determine the destiny of this nation. The answers to our problems don't lie beyond our reach. They exist in our laboratories and universities, in our fields and our factories, in the imaginations of our entrepreneurs and the pride of the hardest-working people on Earth."[21]

Obama also delivered the opening salvos of the healthcare debate: "Let there be no doubt: Healthcare reform cannot wait, it must not wait, and it will not wait another year." He promised his 2010 budget would serve as a new "vision for America—as a blueprint for our future."[22]

The speech certainly drew a sharp distinction with the past. In the face of the worst recession in modern times, Obama proposed to overhaul an entrenched healthcare system, reverse global warming, and expand education. Doc and other Republicans condemned his priorities. "More spending, bigger government, and endless government-run bailouts financed by raising taxes and forcing future generations to foot the bill is not the solution," Doc said.[23] He also noted that the budget assumed significantly higher economic growth in future years than most economists thought possible.

On April 2, after weeks of acrimonious debate, both the House and Senate passed different versions of their own 2010 budget along straight party-line votes. No Republican voted for either version of the bill.[24] On April 29, 2009—Obama's one-hundredth day in office—the Senate approved a $3.5 trillion budget settled by a House-Senate conference committee. The two budgets had significantly increased the federal deficit, setting off continuing political arguments over which president did more to increase the federal deficit.

—

Many of the spending cuts proposed in that 2010 budget were designed to free up funding for the president's landmark healthcare overhaul. Nothing the president sought to achieve was greater or more difficult than overhauling the American healthcare system. Obama knew the recent costly bailouts and high unemployment had soured the public mood, but he deeply believed the American healthcare system was simply unsustainable. He told Speaker Pelosi this was their only chance. If they didn't get this done now, it "was not going to get done."[25]

To signal the importance of the issue, Obama addressed a joint session of Congress on February 24, 2009. With supportive Democratic majorities in both houses of Congress, healthcare bills began working their way through the legislative process. Republicans uniformly opposed them, supported by various vested interests, which helped organize and fund public opposition.

Obama hoped to reach out to at least some Republicans. In July, the Senate's Health, Education, Labor and Pensions Committee passed the Affordable Health Choices Act. The bill included more than 160 Republican amendments accepted during a month-long markup. Later that month, the House Energy and Commerce Committee passed the bill, although crucial time had been lost during which opponents were able to negatively influence public opinion while Congress deliberated.

Republicans were particularly opposed the provision known as the "public option," which would provide government-run health insurance to those not covered by private health insurance companies. In addition, the administration faced a serious messaging problem. The Affordable Care Act (ACA) had a thousand moving parts, and it was hard to explain to the public. All that most people knew was their healthcare was going to change and they would be stuck paying for those who could not afford coverage.

—

In August, Congress adjourned for summer recess. Members were immediately confronted by waves of angry constituents, aroused by fears of the unknown regarding the future of their healthcare and fueled by negative advertising and the nearly non-stop dire predictions of pundits on conservative talk radio. One concern was the legislation might create "death panels" that would determine who would and would not receive treatment for their illnesses. The conservatives came out in full force, concerned about the cost of the program and government overreach.

Doc spent his recess telling his constituents, "I am opposed . . . to a government-run healthcare plan." He told the Hispanic Chamber of Commerce in Pasco, "I think we have a very good healthcare system in this country." He touted the traditional patient-physician relationship and said a government-run plan would put bureaucracy between the people and their doctors. He believed the so-called public option would eventually squeeze private insurance providers out of the marketplace.[26] Still, it was hard to escape the reality that family insurance premiums had more than doubled in Washington State over the past ten years, rising five times as fast as salaries, according to a study released by a consumer health organization.[27]

Intense partisanship surrounded the issue and consumed the daily news. Various proposals and compromises came and went. Many conservatives felt that John Boehner's finest hour had come when he opposed the ACA in a fiery speech on the House floor. "Look at how this bill was written. Can you say it was done openly? With transparency and accountability? Without backroom deals struck behind closed doors? Hell no, you can't!"[28] Finally, on November 7, the House barely passed its version of the healthcare bill by a vote of 220 to 215, but the Democrats had to compromise on insurance coverage for abortions in order to get enough votes for passage. Doc voted no.

The Senate passed its version of healthcare on December 19, 2009, when conservative Democrat Ben Nelson of Nebraska became the sixtieth vote needed to overcome a Republican filibuster. Another roadblock occurred on January 29, 2010, when Republican Scott Brown won the special election to replace Ted Kennedy, who had died of brain cancer. Brown opposed the healthcare bill. Now, without the sixty votes needed to overcome a filibuster, the legislation appeared to be dead. Harry Reid, a feisty former boxer who was the Senate majority leader, announced he would use the reconciliation process to pass the measure with a simple majority, a move he had hoped to avoid when the Obama budget had been passed a year earlier.

On March 21, 2010, in a rare Sunday vote, many watched from home on C-SPAN and live network TV as the House passed the bill that overhauled the American medical system by a vote of 219-212. Democratic members shouted, "Yes, we can!" on the floor of the House. All 178 Republicans opposed it, along with 34 Democrats. The projected cost of the plan, which would extend insurance coverage to roughly thirty-two million additional Americans, was $940 billion. Obama signed the bill two days later.

—

Just as the Republicans had overreached with their 1995 government shutdown, the Democrats overreached with the passage of the Affordable Care Act. America's healthcare system was broken and needed fixing, but the way in which the legislation was pushed through Congress by the Democrats left memories that the Republicans would not soon forget. The event would mark the beginning of the unraveling of the national Democratic Party. The mind-boggling complexity of the new law confused voters and made criticism of it easy. It became a rallying cry for Republicans who regained control of Congress in 2010 and went on to gain increasing majorities in the lion's share of state legislatures and an overwhelming number of state governorships.

In 2014, Chuck Schumer of New York, by then the Senate minority leader, told the National Press Club that Democrats "blew the opportunity the American people gave them" by passing healthcare reform in 2009 and 2010 instead of working on economic legislation designed to help middle-class voters. At the time, House minority leader Nancy Pelosi disagreed. "We come here to do a job, not keep a job. There are more than 14 million reasons why that's wrong," Pelosi said in a written statement, referring to people who gained health coverage through the law.[29] As time went on, the internal recriminations inside the Democratic Party subsided, in public at least, and the law became more popular as Americans got used to it. Republicans attempted for the next seven years to repeal and replace the ACA without success. Unfortunately, parts of America's healthcare system remain broken and cry out for bipartisan solutions.

The Republicans were frustrated and angered by their inability to stop the Affordable Care Act from being implemented. With the public deeply divided about the new law, they looked forward to the upcoming midterm elections. Doc remembered: "In the first six months, with the huge majorities they had, I don't think any Republican thought that we had a chance of winning in 2010. But with all that spending, economic recovery stalled, and the spontaneous rise of the Tea Party, everything started to pick up for us."[30]

—

The other major piece of legislation from Obama's first term was the Wall Street Reform and Consumer Protection Act, commonly referred to as "Dodd-Frank" after Chris Dodd, senator from Connecticut and the chairman of the Senate Banking Committee, and Barney Frank, the acerbic but brilliant congressman from Massachusetts who served as the chairman of the House Financial Services Committee. The legislation called for the consolidation of regulatory agencies, a new oversight council to evaluate systemic risk, comprehensive regulation of financial markets, consumer protection reforms, and tightened regulation of credit rating agencies.[31]

The initial version of the bill passed the House largely along party lines in December 2009, and the conference committee reconciled the House and Senate versions on June 25, 2010. The House passed the conference report by a vote of 237 to 192 on June 30, 2010, and the Senate followed fifteen days later by a vote of 60 to 39. The president signed the bill on July 21, 2010. It was the last major piece of legislation to be signed before the upcoming 2010 midterm elections.

To most people, Dodd-Frank was far too complicated to understand, but its implications were profound, decreasing the possibility of another Great Recession. It was not without its detractors, however, and Doc was one of them. He had once served on the board of the Yakima Federal Savings and Loan Association. "The people who got hurt were the small community bankers. They can't make character loans anymore. If the loan doesn't pencil, you can't make it."[32]

—

A third major Obama financial initiative—deficit reduction—never made it to the point where it could be considered by Congress. With the leftover 2009 budget and the new 2010 budget generating huge deficits, the president's economic advisors hit upon an idea that had first been promoted by Democratic Senator Kent Conrad of North Dakota: Create a bipartisan fiscal commission that would be charged with creating a plan to cut the federal deficit by 3 percent by 2015.

On February 18, 2010, Obama signed an executive order creating an eighteen-member National Commission on Fiscal Responsibility and Reform with the members appointed equally by the president, the House and the Senate. The commission would be led by Erskine Bowles, President Clinton's former chief of staff, and by the maverick seventy-eight-year-old former Republican senator from Wyoming, Alan Simpson.

Simpson, who had served for eighteen years in the Senate with Vice President Joe Biden, demanded that all options for reducing the deficit be on the table, including heathcare spending and reforms. "Is it all on the table?" he asked the president. "Yes," Obama responded.[33]

The commission met six more times during 2010, receiving testimony from government officials, business and labor leaders, and numerous special interest organizations. Simpson and Bowles gave so many press interviews that Simpson, at least, developed something of a cult following. A draft report was issued on November 10, eight days after the Republicans' stunning victory in which they regained control of the House.[34]

The president had set December 1, 2010, as the deadline for the Simpson-Bowles Commission to vote on its draft report. The fifty-page draft outlined measures to cut four trillion dollars from the federal deficit over ten years through a combination of spending cuts and higher taxes. It also provided several suggestions for major tax reform, including an option for dramatically simplifying the tax code. The proposal left Obama's Affordable Care Act in place but called for reduced Medicare payments to doctors and the creation of a government-run health insurance plan that would compete with private insurers under the law's healthcare exchanges.

There was something in the Simpson-Bowles report for everyone to hate. "Simply unacceptable," said outgoing Speaker Nancy Pelosi. Grover Nordquist, the leader of Americans for Tax Reform, an anti-tax group, warned the 275 members of Congress who had signed his Taxpayer Protection Pledge that if they supported the plan they would face immediate retaliation in their next election.[35]

After the Republicans won the November elections, the president tried to reach out to the Republican leadership but was rebuffed by Eric Cantor and other conservatives who instead urged Obama to immediately extend the Bush-era tax cuts.[36] Three Republican members of the Simpson-Bowles Commission, Dave Camp of Michigan, who would become the chairman of the House Ways and Means Committee in the new Congress, Jeb Hensarling of Texas, the Republican conference chairman, and Paul Ryan of Wisconsin, refused to support the draft plan when it was brought to a vote during the lame duck session on December 1. Only eleven of the eighteen members supported the plan, ensuring that it would not be sent to Congress for consideration. Three Republicans and four Democrats voted against it. Simpson had been right. "Everyone had to agree to shoot one of their favorite cows," and they had simply been unable or unwilling to do it.[37] Doc recalled: "Obama understood that his position on spending was totally different from the Republicans in the House and Senate. The easiest way out is to appoint a commission and then go find Republicans to serve on it. I can count the votes. Obamacare was going to survive in their report. I think Alan [Simpson] was hoodwinked on that one."[38]

—

The president had unveiled his 2011 budget proposal back on February 1, 2010, approximately two weeks before he created the Simpson-Bowles Commission. It had called for $3.8 trillion in spending and would have added another $1.3 trillion to the deficit. While Simpson-Bowles was on the table, lawmakers failed to pass an appropriation bill by September 30, the end of the fiscal year, and the issue was punted forward to the new Republican-controlled Congress.[39]

During the lame duck session, with only a month left in the majority, the Democrats in the House pushed through legislation extending the Bush tax cuts on lower- and middle-income individuals but letting the tax cuts for the wealthy—vitally important to the Republicans—expire. "I'm trying to catch my breath," Boehner told a reporter, "so I don't refer to this maneuver . . . today as chicken crap, all right?" The House bill failed to pass the Senate because of a Republican filibuster. The mood for the next session of Congress had been established.

—

The divisive fights over healthcare reform, Dodd-Frank, deficit reduction, and the budget couldn't hide the fact that the country was still at war. Barack Obama favored a reset in Iraq, and the success of the Bush administration's surge allowed him to begin rotating troops out of the country.

Although Obama favored a smaller military footprint overseas, he was no pacifist. By the end of 2009, he had been briefed on the CIA's use of Predator drones against al-Qaeda targets and individuals. He authorized more drone strikes in his first year than Bush had in his entire presidency. At the same time, he refrained from using the terms "terrorism," "terrorist," or "war on terror" because he felt it needlessly inflamed the Arab world. Rather, his purpose was to subvert the sources of Islamic extremism that he believed were responsible for the terrorism in the first place.[40]

Afghanistan was another matter. When Obama was inaugurated, there were approximately thirty-five thousand US troops in that country and nearly the same number of NATO troops. The mind-numbing corruption of the Karzai government and its reluctance to hold scheduled elections were allowing the Taliban to grow again in influence and power with the support of its counterparts in Pakistan. US casualties were rising, and a counter-insurgency strategy like the one implemented in Iraq didn't seem to be working. As a result, Obama removed General David McKiernan after less than a year on the job—a highly unusual step in the US military. He was replaced by General Stanley McChrystal, who promptly asked for more troops and then promptly got himself in trouble by telling a reporter he couldn't support a strategy that didn't include those troops. Obama felt he was being jammed by his generals and his own secretary of defense, Robert Gates. He called them in to receive what one author called "the most direct assertion of presidential authority over the US military since President Truman fired General MacArthur."[41]

Between June and the end of 2009, Obama sent forty thousand more US troops to Afghanistan, matched by an almost equal number of NATO troops. Then he called in David Petraeus, the architect of the proposed surge, and laid down the law: "The only way we'll consider this is if we get the troops in and out in a shorter time frame." The time frame he had in mind was 2011, just before the end of his first term in office.[42]

Doc had been at odds with Barack Obama on just about everything, but on Afghanistan, they agreed. "While long overdue, [this surge] is a concrete step forward toward securing Afghanistan and, in turn, our nation. Our military commanders on the ground know what it takes . . . and I am encouraged the president took their advice to increase troop levels."[43]

—

While all this was going on, a quiet scandal was brewing in the background. As early as March 2010, the Internal Revenue Service began more careful scrutiny of what appeared to be political organizations applying for tax-exempt status. It was an indication of the highly charged political climate in the nation. Organizations that appeared to be affiliated with the Tea Party, USA Patriot, or other conservative causes were singled out for more intense scrutiny, although some liberal organizations were placed on the watch list as well.[44] Lois Lerner, IRS's director of Exempt Organizations, retired but the congressional Republicans believed they had uncovered a major political scandal and called for public hearings as a means of both getting to the truth and embarrassing the Obama administration. As a member of the House Oversight Committee, Doc would later become involved.

—

Now the longest serving Republican member of Congress from the Pacific Northwest, Doc reacquainted himself with the issues being considered by the House Natural Resources Committee in his capacity as its new ranking member. The committee was a fairly large committee in 2009, consisting of approximately twenty-five Democrats and eighteen Republicans. Nick Rahall of West Virginia chaired the committee. First elected to Congress in 1976, Rahall had been an early supporter of Barack Obama's but opposed the administration's clean energy proposals, particularly as they related to the coal industry. Doc remembered:

> Nick and I got along well. His chief of staff and Todd Young forged a good relationship, so they pretty much worked everything out before we had to deal with it.
>
> Being from West Virginia, Nick wasn't a great fan of the administration's cap and trade proposals. I always had the feeling that the Democrats' caucus loaded up

his committee with enough Democrats who supported cap and trade so that the combination of conservative Democrats and Republicans on the committee couldn't muster enough votes against the program.[45]

Doc's initial job as the committee's ranking member was to interview the staff and assign Republican members to the various subcommittees created by the majority, a job made much easier because Doc already served on the Republican Steering Committee.

Doc recalled two anecdotes from his first term back on the Natural Resources Committee. In August 2007, he had introduced a bill to relocate a portion of the road that had washed out in 2003 from the tiny lakefront town of Stehekin in Chelan County to the North Cascades National Park. Rebuilding the road required encroaching on a wilderness area, which was an anathema to environmentalists. But Doc prevailed and sponsored a bill that had the support of Jay Inslee, who was by then representing Washington's First Congressional District and a member of the committee.

Inslee was anxious to claim some credit for the bill, which awaited markup by the committee, but he was habitually late to the committee's meetings, something that annoyed chairman Rahall. Knowing that Inslee would probably be late, Rahall told Doc that he was going to put Doc's Stehekin bill first on the agenda. "You can talk about it if you want, but if not, we'll just pass it quickly." Rahall gaveled the committee to order and called up Doc's bill. He asked Doc if he supported it. He did. So did the majority, and they quickly moved on to the next agenda item. Inslee arrived some minutes later and asked what had happened to the Stehekin bill, concerned that he might miss an opportunity to comment and take some credit for his efforts. Rahall told him the bill had already been considered, "but you weren't here." Point made.[46]

Another anecdote involved a piece of proposed legislation, which had been floating around Congress for several sessions that would grant Native Hawaiian peoples the same rights of self-determination and self-governance afforded to American Indian tribes. Doc opposed the legislation and took delight in filibustering the bill in committee for so long that the time available for consideration ran out.

—

The most important piece of natural resources legislation voted on during that session of Congress was never sent to the committee. The Omnibus Public Land Management Act of 2009 was a jumble of 159 separate bills that had been passed by the Senate. They included Doc's Ice Age Floods National Geologic Trail and funding for the road into the Juniper Dunes Wilderness Area.

After receiving the legislation from the Senate, the House leadership tried to pass the bill on the suspension calendar, which required a two-thirds vote to pass, but the measure failed by two votes. They sent it back to the Senate where the Omnibus language was stripped from the Senate bill and attached it to a convenient House bill being considered by the Senate. The Senate then sent the revised House bill back to the originating chamber where it passed in its amended form by a majority vote. Doc had voted against it, even though it contained his Ice Age Floods Trail proposal. "It was a large Christmas tree of a bill, about 1,100 pages. No one ever read most of it, nor did it get any scrutiny in the House. I had some things in it, but I still voted against it."[47]

In May, Doc joined Maria Cantwell and Gary Kleinknecht, the president of the Ice Age Floods Institute, for a press conference at the trailhead on Badger Mountain in Richland to celebrate the passage of the legislation authorizing the Ice Age Floods National Geologic Trail.

ONE ISSUE THAT WAS SURE TO GET DOC'S attention at the start of each new Congress was the annual struggle to find funding to clean up the nation's nuclear sites and, in particular, Hanford. The 2009 omnibus budget included Hanford spending of almost two billion dollars, more for Hanford than the Bush administration had asked for. The Obama administration's 2010 budget proposal was delayed while Congress passed the stimulus bill and the 2009 budget. Doc organized two dozen House members from eight states to sign a letter to the new energy secretary,

Steven Chu, saying it would be "extremely harmful" if stimulus funding for cleanup was used as an excuse to reduce regular DOE funding.[48] By the end of April, the appropriations bill had passed and been signed into law, increasing Hanford funding to about $2.1 billion. At the same time, the nearly $2 billion in stimulus funding allowed new hiring to begin. It was estimated the money would create or save four thousand jobs. By June, stimulus funding had created more than fourteen thousand jobs in Washington State.[49]

In August 11, 2009, Chu visited Hanford, touring the Hanford Waste Treatment Plant, the B Reactor, and the HAMMER training facility. He was joined by the governors of Washington and Oregon and Senators Murray and Cantwell in announcing a tentative agreement on new deadlines for cleaning up Hanford's worst waste after two years of negotiations and lawsuits. In October 2010, the parties finally reached agreement on the deadlines for disposing of tank wastes, which now relied on a consent decree enforced by the federal court.[50]

In February 2010, the Obama administration released its 2011 budget request, which proposed an increase of twenty-two million dollars over 2010. The administration had considered cutting the overall cleanup budget nationally by 20 percent, but Murray intervened with the White House budget office in a display of her growing power as a member of the Senate Appropriations Committee. Doc, for once, was satisfied. "This request is a marked improvement over where this administration started last year. Overall, it is a positive step in the right direction at Hanford."[51]

—

The Obama administration's 2011 budget proposal dramatically cut funding for the Yucca Mountain nuclear depository, undercutting a decision about where the glass logs from Hanford's waste treatment plant would be stored. In June 2009, Doc and twenty-five congressmen had sent a letter to DOE asking it to continue funding the Nuclear Regulatory Commission (NRC) licensing review of the Yucca Mountain site.

The government had spent $13.5 billion on the Yucca Mountain project since 1983, but Harry Reid, the senior senator from Nevada, was now the Senate majority leader and had promised to shut down Yucca Mountain. Obama had committed to appoint a blue ribbon committee to look at other disposal solutions. On October 20, Doc wrote to the president asking where the blue ribbon committee was. He already knew the answer. The committee had not yet been appointed. Finally, in February 2010, the committee was named but told not to consider Yucca Mountain as an option.

On March 4, 2010, the administration withdrew its license application to the NRC for Yucca Mountain. Doc's reaction was predictable. "A unilateral decision to abandon Yucca Mountain without any justification and blocking it from ever being considered in the future is simply indefensible," he said in a statement. He was backed up by other members of the Washington delegation and state elected officials.[52]

In April, the state of Washington filed a lawsuit in federal court to prevent DOE from closing down the Yucca Mountain facility. A federal appeals court in Washington, DC, struck it down, ruling the state had not proven that "irrefutable harm" would occur if the facility were to be shut down and holding off a final decision until after the NRC reached a conclusion.

The outcome looked hopeless until three Tri-Cities civic leaders stepped in. Bob Ferguson had been a government manager in the nuclear industry for years and a successful entrepreneur. He recruited Bill Lampson, the president of Lampson International, a worldwide leader in the crane and rigging business, and Gary Petersen, the vice president of government programs for TRIDEC, the regional economic development agency. Both Lampson and Ferguson were former TRIDEC board chairmen. They contracted with Tim Peckinpaugh, a Tri-Cities native, former staffer to Congressman Sid Morrison, and longtime attorney in the Washington, DC, office of K&L Gates, with many clients in the Tri-Cities. In what appeared to be a David versus Goliath mismatch, they filed a lawsuit to stop the closure of Yucca Mountain with the US Court of Appeals in Washington and sent out an appeal to the community for contributions to help them pursue their case.

Soon, they got some help from America's voters. The 2010 midterm elections swept the Republicans back into control of the House. Doc enlisted Darrell Issa of California, the new chairman of the House Oversight and Government Reform Committee, to press the NRC to release its decision. Meanwhile, it appeared the chairman of the commission had intentionally delayed announcing the commission's Yucca Mountain decision. Doc continued to press his point with anyone who would listen. "Congress designated Yucca Mountain as the national repository. The designation is in the law. This president, in my estimation, is unilaterally changing that," Doc said.[53]

The Yucca Mountain saga was just beginning.

—

As the Yucca Mountain controversy spun up, several other Hanford-related projects were winding down. The National Park Service (NPS) study that Doc and Senator Maria Cantwell had commissioned in 2004 was released in December 2009. NPS looked at several options for preserving the B Reactor but rejected the possibility of including it in the national park system. That was not what Doc wanted to hear. He immediately criticized the "vague assertions and conclusions" in the study. DOE had already proven it was feasible and safe to conduct public tours of the reactor. "Those realities are not reflected in the draft study," Doc wrote in his response.[54]

As he had on many other occasions, Doc sought the help of his congressional colleagues. On March 3, 2010, nine members of the Washington delegation sent a letter to Jon Jarvis, the director of the NPS. They noted: "None of the draft alternatives as written fully provide for the preservation and interpretation of the Hanford's B Reactor. We believe that the most unique and historically compelling technical facilities at all of the sites under consideration must be incorporated into any final National Park Service plan." They also noted that DOE-sponsored tours of the reactor sold out within minutes of being announced on the internet.[55]

In May, the Department of Energy officially got behind the effort to preserve the Manhattan Project facilities at Oak Ridge, Los Alamos, and

Hanford, committing to "maintain them, preserve important resources at these sites, ensure visitor and employee safety, and request the necessary funding from Congress to do so in the future."[56]

A revised and final report including recommendations on the B Reactor was expected to be delivered to Congress by the end of January 2011. By then, Doc would be chairman of the Natural Resources Committee.

—

Another Hanford-related issue was Doc's continuing effort to expand the public access to the 196,000-acre Hanford Reach National Monument, which had been created over his objections in 2000. On May 27, 2010, he introduced legislation directing the US Fish and Wildlife Service to provide public access to the top of 3,600-foot Rattlesnake Mountain, the tallest point in the mid-Columbia and the western boundary of the Hanford Site. While his legislation did not mandate how or when public access should occur, its clear intent was to allow access in a timely manner. "This is about making sure that land the American people own is accessible to them," he said in a statement.

The Fish and Wildlife Service was concerned about the deteriorating condition of the one-lane road to the top of the mountain, the long-expressed cultural concerns of local Native American tribes, as well as protecting the unique plant ecosystem at the top of the mountain where 100-mph winds were not uncommon. Under the pressure of Doc's legislation, the Fish and Wildlife Service announced it planned to conduct limited guided tours of the mountain in the future when funds became available.[57] The issue would continue into the next Congress.

—

Another issue in which Doc intervened proactively concerned the skyrocketing fees the US Forest Service charged the owners of cabins located on its land. Since 1915, the agency had charged owners a fee equal to 5 percent of the assessed valuation of the cabin. However, as the market values of cabins grew along with their popularity, some owners had seen their annual fees jump from $1,400 to as much as $17,000 a year.

On March 19, 2010, Doc introduced the Cabin Fee Act of 2010 to change the fee structure from a percentage of assessed value to a tiered fee structure based on inflation. The bill was still working its way through the House when the session of Congress ended.

—

Doc also continued his efforts to market Washington apples. The crop in 2008 had been a bumper one, and fruit was backing up in the warehouses. In May 2009, Doc and Democrat Eric Massa of New York persuaded forty other members to sign a letter to the agriculture secretary, Tom Vilsack, asking him buy an extra million boxes of apples for the federal nutrition programs. In January 2010, Doc got sixty-six legislators to sign another letter to Vilsack urging him to approve two hundred million dollars in market access funding prior to an announced federal spending freeze the president had announced in his 2010 State of the Union speech. Vilsack approved the funding.

Unfortunately, apple exports took another unexpected hit when Mexico imposed tariffs on a long list of American agricultural exports after Congress killed a pilot program to allow Mexican trucks on US highways. The Republicans claimed the congressional action stemmed from objections from the Teamsters union, an important ally of the Democrats. The action contributed to a $19.7 million decline in Washington State exports, mostly apples, to Mexico in 2009. Doc complained to the administration in August 2009 after the tariff was first proposed, saying Washington growers could not sustain an estimated forty-four million dollars in losses. "Now it is almost a year and a half later, there is no end in sight, no plan, and little public effort by the administration to protect the number one industry in our entire state. It's time for the administration to stand with our farmers—not special interest groups."[58]

Doc considered the lack of a response from the Obama administration to be par for the course when dealing with Congress. "The administration never so much as gave us the light of day," he said.[59]

In July 2011, the two countries reached an agreement to eliminate the 20 percent tariff on tree fruit in return for allowing Mexican trucking firms to make deliveries within the United States.[60]

—

Doc was even more frustrated by what he considered the politically motivated decision by a Portland federal judge and his environmental supporters to breach the Snake River dams. In 2007, a panel of the Ninth Circuit Court of Appeals had upheld federal judge James Redden's order to force the dams to spill more water into the Snake River to help salmon migrate. After that, a fragile truce had been agreed to by the stakeholders. Then, in May 2009, Judge Redden ruled that any salmon recovery plan must include contingencies to study "specific alternative hydro actions . . . as well as what it will take to breach the lower Snake River dams if all other measures fail." The judge's comments were guaranteed to get Doc's attention. In a public statement of the kind that congressional staffers must love to write for their bosses, Doc said: "Instead of moving forward with a plan supported by nearly all parties involved, the judge has chosen to fight for the interests of the dam removal extremists. Federal law doesn't allow dam removal and no Democrat-politician-turned-activist-judge can rewrite the law. Only Congress has the authority to authorize dam removal."[61]

In August, twenty-three Democrats, led by Jim McDermott of Washington, introduced legislation for the fifth time that required the Corps of Engineers to investigate the issue of breaching the dams. Doc countered with a statement that promised a fight when their bill reached the House Natural Resources Committee where he was ranking member.[62] The *Tri-City Herald*'s editorial board compared the controversy to an "Old West Shootout."[63] It was not the first time, nor would it be the last, that Doc would express his frustration with another member who intruded onto his turf. McDermott responded by comparing Doc and his Eastern Washington constituents to members of the Flat Earth Society.[64]

By April 2010, the Obama administration essentially agreed with the findings of the study under the Bush administration that dam removal "was a contingency of last resort and would be recommended to Congress only when the best scientific information available indicates dam breaching would be effective and is necessary." Doc said the option should never have been included in the report in the first place and the Corps of Engineers "should file away the study in a locked drawer and be prepared to resist those who will push for the work to begin," a pointed reference to Judge Redden and his supporters.[65]

—

Efforts to design a path to citizenship for the roughly twelve million immigrants living in the United States illegally—a large number of them in Doc's district—surfaced again in 2009 and continued to be a contentious and politically polarizing issue through the end of the 111th Congress and beyond.

Supporters of immigration reform argued it would be nearly impossible to deport that many people and providing them a path to citizenship would have social and economic benefits. Critics claimed any such program rewarded illegal immigration and encouraged more of it. A particular problem concerned children of illegal immigrants who had been brought to the United States by their parents, or who had been born here and were legal citizens.

Legislation called the DREAM Act had been introduced in Congress on a bipartisan basis since 2001 but had failed to pass. In 2009, the DREAM Act legislation was introduced again, with thirty-nine senators and 128 House members co-sponsoring the legislation.

Doc supported comprehensive immigration reform that secured the border and allowed a functional guest-worker program to support the agriculture industry. But now he was pressured from Latino groups in the Yakima Valley to go beyond his previous position and support the DREAM Act. On December 9, 2010, the legislation came before the House. Doc voted no.

He justified his position in a prepared statement he sent out to the local press:

> Many children were brought here through no fault of their own at a very young age. They did not choose to break the law and they deserve a chance at a brighter future.

But this bill goes far beyond providing children with an opportunity. It provides a special avenue for illegal immigrants as old as 30 to become citizens.

Rewarding parents who have broken the law and allowing some to jump ahead of those waiting to enter the U.S. legally is not a fair solution.[66]

THE MIDTERM ELECTIONS WERE HELD on November 2, 2010. Although it is common for the president's party to lose seats in its first midterm election, the results of the 2010 midterms were historic. The Republicans picked up sixty-four seats in the House—recapturing the majority—and six in the Senate, where the Democrats barely retained their majority. The election resulted in the largest change between the two parties in the House since 1948 and in any midterm election since 1938. It was also the third major wave election since 1994. The eagerness of the voters to change their representatives in Congress seemed to confirm the unpopularity of Congress as an institution and the inability of either party to steer the nation on what the public felt was the right track.

After spending much of election night and part of the next day offering condolences to defeated Democrats, Obama admitted to his staff that he had taken "a shellacking." It was particularly painful to him because he knew many of those who lost did so because of their support for him and his programs.[67]

The voters' disdain for their elected representatives had been growing for decades but accelerated during the Bush and Obama administrations. Residual anger lingered over the Great Recession and the bailouts of the financial and automobile industries. Obama had inherited a disaster, but it seemed his priorities had done little to help the many Americans who were still trying to recover from the Great Recession. At the time of the election, the national unemployment rate was still more than 9 percent, and the federal debt had climbed dramatically. The public wasn't interested in hearing that the recession was officially over or how much worse it could have been; people knew only how bad it had been for them.

Many Americans were uncomfortable with the administration's advocacy of social issues like the DREAM Act, criminal sentencing standards, LGBT rights, and importantly, the role that race played in American life. They were also confused and distrustful of Obama's sweeping reform of the healthcare system. A fourth factor had been the rise of the Tea Party. The nativist and quasi-libertarian movement focused on tax rates and the size of the federal deficit and became a vocal force in mobilizing voters to cast their ballots for Republican candidates.[68]

For all the enthusiasm and motivation on the right, the Democrats suffered from a lack of enthusiasm among their own progressive base who felt the new president had not done enough to keep his promises to them. To be sure, most of the broken promises were the result of Obama's decision not to push Congress while he still believed he might receive some bipartisan support for his healthcare and energy proposals, but that hadn't mattered to key elements of his base. He also waited too long to call the Republicans out for their almost uniform opposition to his proposals. "They drove us into the ditch; don't give them back the keys," he would finally say during a late campaign rally.[69] By then it was far too late.

—

Doc's 2010 reelection campaign began when Jay Clough, a thirty-three-year-old former Marine from Kennewick, announced he was running as a Democrat on November 10, 2009. A graduate of Central Washington University, Clough had earned degrees in Pacific Asian studies and Chinese. After four years in the Marine Corps, he had lived in China, Korea, and Japan, where he met his wife and taught school for three years before going to work for a Hanford contractor.[70] He criticized Doc for not doing more to promote trade, not supporting clean energy jobs, and not getting around the district more to "listen to the people's concerns." Jessica Gleason, Doc's communications director, countered with a statement noting that Doc had recently hosted a telephone town hall in which he had discussed his views on healthcare with fifty thousand voters.[71]

Another former Marine joined the race on March 2, 2010, when Mary Ruth Edwards, a forty-nine-year-old teacher and single mother of two, announced she would run for Doc's seat as a member of the Constitution Party, which believed in a strict, originalist interpretation of the Constitution and in state sovereignty. "Our constitution has been virtually shredded," she announced in a phone interview with the *Yakima Herald-Republic*. Her website said she would repeal all legislation dealing with education and stood against any effort to register guns or ammunition.[72] And while the Tea Party had not yet fielded a candidate, it held a rally in Yakima that attracted more than a hundred supporters.[73]

By the end of the filing deadline in June, the field of candidates swelled to six. Leland Yialelis was a sixty-two-year-old state transportation worker from East Wenatchee. Rex Brocki of Union Gap filed as a Tea Party candidate. Shane Fast was a former reserve Pasco police officer who supported the Tea Party but was running as a Republican. Yialelis said his politics were similar to the Libertarian Party, "but I'm not a Libertarian. That's why I'm not running as one. Party labels make me somewhat nervous. That's why I'm running as an Independent."[74] Brocki, a retired business owner, had run for Doc's seat in 2008. Fast supported term limits and wanted to replace Obama's healthcare plan with "something about ten pages long that makes prescriptions and healthcare for seniors and veterans more accessible." He supported Arizona's recent anti-immigration laws.[75]

With Doc in Washington, tied up in the House by consideration of the Dodd-Frank legislation, Jay Clough crisscrossed the district during June and July, appearing in twenty-two communities. None of the other candidates did much campaigning. However, they all accused Doc of reneging on a pledge to serve no more than five terms when he was elected in 1994. Doc claimed the story was Fourth District folklore. "In 1994, there was a tremendous push by term limits people to sign a term limits pledge," he said. "I never did and was criticized for not signing. That's one of the ironies of this. I have never considered my service here as being a lifetime job, and I don't take a congressional pension." If reelected, he promised to control congressional spending and reduce the deficit, calling the current deficit "unprecedented in our history."[76]

When the primary election was held on Tuesday, August 17, Doc and Jay Clough were the victors with Doc receiving more than 58 percent of the vote to Clough's 23 percent.

In the general election contest that followed, Clough tried to paint Doc as a career politician whose votes in Congress had helped cause the Great Recession. "It is career politicians like himself who got us to the point of needing bailouts," he told the *Tri-City Herald*'s editorial board. Doc ran on his record. "I have a record, and I'm proud of that record,"[77] he said. He pointed out that he had voted against every bailout, both Obama's and Bush's. He believed the election was about the policies and actions of the Obama administration and its Democratic supporters in Congress. "I respect the choices the people made in 2008, but I think the people didn't expect the massive change they've seen, the massive intrusion of government into their lives."[78]

Doc enjoyed an overwhelming advantage in campaign contributions. By the end of July, Doc had raised $813,000 while spending only $333,000. Clough had raised about $49,000. Doc sensed that the Republicans had a good chance of winning in November and was looking ahead. For his ninth term, he said he wanted to elect John Boehner Speaker of the House, repeal Obamacare, extend the Bush-era tax cuts, and repeal any remaining bits of the government stimulus packages. The *Tri-City Herald* endorsed Doc, but he again declined to seek the editorial support of the *Yakima Herald-Republic*.

It was not surprising, then, that Doc Hastings cruised to another easy victory on November 2, winning by a margin of 68 percent to 32 percent. As much as he enjoyed his victory, he enjoyed his party's victory even more. "This election was a referendum on the first two years of the Obama presidency. Obamacare was passed, really, over the objections of the American people."[79]

Back in Washington after their election victory, House Republicans met to organize their conference prior to taking over control of the House in the next session of Congress. It was clear Doc was the odds-on favorite to become the next chairman of the House Natural Resources Committee, but since leaving the Ethics Committee, he needed to choose a second committee. Doc recalled: "The Republican Steering Committee was responsible for making the appointment. Because of the outcome of the election, there were lots of new Republicans to find committee appointments for, as well as lots of openings, but whatever committee I chose, I was going to have seniority. From a list of possible committees, I chose the Committee on Oversight and Government Reform."[80]

With the Republicans back in charge of the House, the committee's aggressive new chairman, Darrell Issa of California, called for multiple investigations of the Obama administration. He told the press he intended to hold "seven hearings a week, times forty weeks."[81] As it turned out, Doc would not be a very active member. "I was focusing everything on my chairmanship," he said.[82]

That focus created an uncharacteristic flap when Doc sent a letter to each member of the House Republican Conference proposing that the energy portfolio of the House Energy and Commerce Committee be transferred to the Natural Resources Committee.[83] It was a surprisingly brash move for a man who had labored in the partisan shadows of the Rules, Budget, and Ethics Committees for the past sixteen years, but he had given his action careful consideration.

The four major House committees are Ways and Means, Appropriations, Energy and Commerce, and Rules. All except Rules had specific responsibility for the formation of public policy. In some policy areas, like healthcare, multiple committees share overlapping jurisdiction. Doc believed there should be a single committee in the House with oversight over Medicare and Medicaid, which together represented almost half of the federal budget. This had become even more important after the passage of the Affordable Care Act. In another example, the Senate had an Energy and Natural Resources Committee, and Doc thought that it provided a good model for the House to follow as well.

In his letter to the conference, Doc referred to the House Energy and Commerce Committee, which had broad jurisdiction over healthcare, telecommunications, technology, and consumer protection, in addition to energy and environment concerns, as a "Goliath" that should be cut down to size in the interest of "leveling" the distribution of power in the chamber, and he proceeded to draft rule effecting the transfer.

The Republicans had picked up eighty-six new members after the 2010 elections, and very few freshmen were going to be assigned to a major committee. By increasing the scope and responsibility of his committee, it would increase the ability of at least some of these new members to serve on a major committee. "My God, the timing is right," Doc thought. "I believed that I had the tacit approval from [Speaker-designate John] Boehner to do it. He didn't discourage it, but he didn't endorse it, either."[84] One press report suggested Doc's action would have impacted the jurisdictions of half the committees in the House in some way.

Doc's proposal drew immediate fire from Fred Upton of Michigan, who was vying with Joe Barton of Texas to become the chairman of the House Energy and Commerce Committee, who responded that "this ill-advised proposition could not come at a worse time and would have dire consequences."[85] Dave Camp of Michigan, the chairman of the Ways and Means Committee, which would also be impacted, had been a classmate of Boehner's and might have weighed in on the proposal. Boehner never spoke to Doc about his proposal, but he didn't need to. Doc remembered what happened next:

> Barry Jackson, Boehner's chief of staff at the time, came up to me and said, "Doc, can we talk?"
>
> I said, "Sure."
>
> So we went into the back room, and he said, "It would be very good if you did not offer that amendment."
>
> I said, "Barry, I think I can probably carry the day, and I think I have a pretty good chance."
>
> "I think it would be better if you didn't offer it."
>
> And I said, "OK."[86]

"In retrospect," Doc recalled, "my only regret is that I should have pushed it harder. With that many new members, I'm sure I could have carried the day, but that's water under the bridge now."[87] On December 8, Doc was duly elected by the Republican conference as chairman of the House Natural Resources Committee.

Two years later, when the Republicans organized for the 113th Congress, Doc raised the issue of creating a single healthcare committee again. He organized a group of what by then were second-termers who had been elected in the 2010 election, some of whom had supported his attempt to transfer the energy portfolio to Natural Resources. "We decided that we were going to try to change the rules and create a health committee. I offered an amendment to change the rules to create the committee and got the crap kicked out of me. Every committee chairman with jurisdiction stood up and implied that 'Oh my God, that's a terrible idea, and the world's going to come to an end.' That was that!"[88]

THE PATIENT PROTECTION AND AFFORDABLE CARE ACT (ACA) would forever be called Obamacare. It was the defining event of Barack Obama's first term and one of the most bitterly polarizing events of his presidency. Whether Republican or Democrat, the political party out of power had once been known as the loyal opposition; now it was simply the total opposition. When there had been a political center, the party in power could count on finding at least some willing partners with which to work out a compromise. Now, both the center and any thought of compromise were gone. Obama made his job more difficult with his disdain for "grin and grip" politics. In remarks delivered near midnight following the vote, a relieved president said: "We pushed back on the undue influence of special interests. We didn't give in to mistrust or to cynicism or to fear. Instead, we proved that we are still a people capable of doing big things. This isn't radical reform, but it is major reform."[89]

But it was also reform that deeply divided the American public. In July, the Pew Research Center reported that Americans disapproved of the ACA by a margin of 47 to 35 percent. Seventeen percent had no opinion or refused to answer. By November, just before the election, the number who disapproved remained the same, but those approving had moved up to 43 percent and those with no opinion had shrunk to 10 percent. It would take until November 2016 for the percentage of Americans who approved of the ACA to outnumber those who disapproved—by one percentage point.[90]

The failure of the Simpson-Bowles Commission was, likewise, another major setback for the Obama administration. It proved that any good-faith effort to find a compromise had become nearly impossible in the polarized atmosphere of the nation's capital. More Democrats had opposed the compromise plan than had Republicans. Both sides realized they could not successfully face their constituents in the next election if they voted for the plan.

The intensity of the Republican opposition set a pattern for the rest of the Obama presidency. In October 2010, Mitch McConnell, the Senate minority leader, had told the National Journal, "The single most important thing we want to achieve is for President Obama to be a one-term president."[91] From that point forward, Obama believed that trying to find bipartisan solutions was useless and began to rely more and more on executive orders to run the government.

CHAPTER FIFTEEN

Demands of Leadership

★

Doc Hastings remembered that the 112th Congress didn't begin well when it convened on January 5, 2011. Prior to the traditional turning over of the gavel to John Boehner, the new Speaker of the House, Nancy Pelosi, had made "a hell of a long speech . . . that was not received well by our side. It was ridiculous. She'd just lost sixty-three seats, and she's talking to us about adopting the Democratic agenda."[1]

The election of 2010 was the third major wave election since 1994. The second had occurred only four years before when the Democrats had gained control of the House. With the addition of his newly elected members, John Boehner enjoyed the largest Republican majority the House had seen since 1947, but they were hardly a cohesive group. Many of the new members came from districts that reflected America's growing political divide. Dozens of the new Republicans identified themselves with the anti-tax, anti-big government Tea Party movement, moving the already conservative, but broader, Republican conference even farther to the right. Leader Pelosi faced similar problems. Nineteen members of her caucus had voted against her as the leader of the Democrats in the House.[2]

The Democrats retained control of the Senate but with a reduced majority, marking the first time since 2001 that the two houses of Congress were controlled by different parties. The Gallup job approval poll of Congress rose slightly after the election but then dropped down over the next two years to a point where only 14 percent of Americans approved of the job their elected representatives were doing.[3]

One of the first official acts of the new Congress was to read the US Constitution aloud for the first time in history. The new conservative majority was also successful in getting a new rule passed requiring that each new piece of legislation cite the part of the Constitution that justified its existence.[4]

"I just read the First Amendment!" Gabrielle Giffords, a three-term Democrat representative from Arizona, said as she exited the floor. "Reflecting on the Constitution in a bipartisan way is a good way to start the year."[5] Two days later, she would be seriously wounded at a Tucson, Arizona, shopping center, shot along with nineteen others at a meeting outside a shopping center by a mentally disturbed constituent. Six others, including one of her aides and a federal district judge, would die. Her Arizona district had been one of the toss-up districts that had been targeted by both parties, resulting in a particularly toxic political atmosphere there. Doc was sympathetic but philosophical. "I don't mean to be cavalier about it, but when you are in public life, you assume that those things can happen. I never dwelt on it."[6]

—

President Obama delivered his State of the Union address on January 25, just seventeen days after the shooting. A suggestion had been made to have Republicans and Democrats sit together during the speech, and Doc and Democrat Norm Dicks did so. The president proposed a five-year freeze in domestic spending projected to save four hundred billion dollars over the next decade, renewed his call for passage of a variety of energy conservation proposals, and suggested eliminating the tax breaks for oil and gas companies that had so infuriated the Republicans in the last session.[7] The speech provided little in the way of compromise aimed at solving the twin financial crises that had been kicked down the road by the Democrat-controlled lame duck session—the 2011 budget and the federal debt ceiling.

—

By April 2011, two starkly different visions of the federal budget were under consideration. The first was last year's Obama administration budget, which had gone nowhere in the past Congress, even though it was controlled by the Democrats. Instead of approving the necessary appropriations bills, lawmakers had passed six short-term continuing resolutions (CRs), allowing the government to operate at current funding levels.

The second was a budget proposal called the "Path to Prosperity," released by Republican Paul Ryan of Wisconsin, the new chairman of the House Budget Committee. It claimed to reduce the deficit by $4.4 trillion and create a budget surplus by 2040, largely by reforming Medicare and turning Medicaid into a block grant program. Ryan's plan wagered that higher healthcare costs for the elderly and the poor would be offset by an economic renewal spurred by lowering the federal deficit and cutting taxes.[8]

Efforts by the House leadership to pass Ryan's proposal were complicated by the newly elected conservatives, who said it didn't go far enough to meet their goal of cutting domestic spending by one hundred billion dollars in 2011. "The Tea Party reflected the growing conservatism of the Republican conference," Doc recalled. "They had a chance to offer their amendments, just like the Black Caucus or any other group did. And, frankly, I didn't think their requests were out of line."[9]

In response, the House Appropriations Committee prepared a new CR that cut spending more aggressively.[10] On April 4, the White House reached out to Speaker Boehner in an effort to open negotiations on another short-term budget extension. Intense negotiations continued late into the early hours of April 8, 2011—the day the existing CR was set to expire—primarily over the issue of funding Planned Parenthood. The Republicans demanded that it be cut. Obama was adamant that it stay. It remained in return for budget cuts in other areas. Finally, they agreed upon a seventh short-term CR that funded the government through September 30, 2011.[11] Both parties had agreed to kick the can down the road again.

A long-term budget agreement proved to be much more difficult to achieve. The federal debt limit, set at $14.7 trillion, would need to be raised in late spring or summer if the government were to keep from defaulting on its obligations. The debt limit had been raised regularly by both parties in the past but had not been raised since the Simpson-Bowles negotiations. Finding the votes to raise it now would be even more difficult because of the influence of the House conservatives who demanded cuts in government spending equal to any increase in the debt limit. Doc agreed. "I felt like everyone else. I wasn't going to vote to raise the debt ceiling without spending cuts," he said.[12]

Everyone understood that the Republicans had enough leverage to force the administration to make significant spending cuts. Vice President Joe Biden was charged with convening a group of top Democrats and Republicans to hammer out an agreement on what those cuts would be. By May 10, 2012, the task force had identified $123 billion in cuts, but the hardline conservatives didn't think that number was anywhere near large enough. Nor were they intimidated by the potential of a government default. "My guys don't even believe default is a problem," majority leader Eric Cantor said.[13]

The president and Boehner had already been quietly negotiating an even bigger deal than the Biden group was discussing. When they had played golf together in mid-June, Obama had proposed three options: a smaller budget deal with roughly $1 trillion in cuts, a medium-sized deal of about $2.4 trillion in cuts, and a big deal that would cut $4 trillion over ten years. Boehner wanted to go for the big deal. It was a game-changing proposal with the potential to lower the deficit by shrinking the size of government, overhauling the tax code, and instituting changes to Medicare and Social Security. It was a once-in-a-decade chance.[14]

But it was not to be. The big budget plan quickly ran into the political reality of a starkly divided, highly partisan Congress that was unwilling to compromise on the White House's insistence the big deal include additional revenue. Unable to make the sale, Boehner called the president and told him the Republicans would have to walk away from the discussions "right now."[15]

The president was unhappy but faced similar problems. Many in his party would rather fight to save their pet programs than compromise on a deal. But as president of the United States rather than the leader of the Democratic Party, Obama believed he had a responsibility to avert another financial crisis:

My interest in not playing chicken or seeing any miscalculation here that leads to a default, was profound.

What's already becoming apparent is that this new House is not feeling a similar sense of urgency. And you have very prominent members of the House Republicans who are not only prepared to see a default, but in some cases are welcoming the prospects of a default.

So I'm already at the point [where I'm] getting concerned that Boehner may miscalculate and not be able to deliver on his caucus even if we wind up striking a deal.[16]

On July 13, various credit rating agencies placed the US government on their credit watch lists. A series of almost non-stop meetings between the principals on both sides and their staffs ensued. Boehner brought Cantor into the discussions in spite of the majority leader's deep distrust of the president. The details of the negotiations that took place over the next eighteen days were so arcane and complicated that it took author Bob Woodward 167 pages to describe them in his best-selling account of the crisis, *The Price of Politics*.

On July 17, it appeared the two sides had reached a deal. Unaware that a deal was imminent, a group of six powerful senators developed their own plan. In response, a group of Tea Party conservatives in the House, led by Jim Jordan of Ohio, fashioned a piece of legislation they called the Cut, Cap, and Balance Act of 2011, which required current spending cuts, a cap on the level of future spending, and the passage of a balanced-budget amendment by Congress before the federal debt ceiling could be extended. Boehner privately derided the proposal by referring to it as "Snap, Crackle and Pop," but the House passed it in mid-July with Doc voting for it.[17] To Boehner, it was a futile strategy leaving him with few cards to negotiate with. As he expected, it was rejected out of hand by Obama and the Republican-led Senate. Doc lamented what might have been:

In 1995, the legislation creating the Balanced Budget Amendment to the Constitution failed by one vote in the Senate. Had it passed, presumably thirty-eight states would have ratified the amendment and it would have become law.

Then, when 9/11, the question of going to war, or how to respond to the recession would have forced us to make hard decisions about spending money we didn't have or, by a super-majority vote, to decide to do something different.

It is likely that the stimulus would never have taken place.[18]

Boehner remained under intense pressure from the conservative members of his conference. Why compromise, they reasoned. They would almost certainly win the 2012 presidential election. On July 22, Boehner was forced to walk away from the negotiations again. Obama was furious. Now he believed that the Republicans didn't want a deal, saying, "I couldn't get a phone call returned. I've been left at the altar a couple of times."[198]

On July 25, 2011, Boehner and the Senate majority leader Harry Reid unveiled competing budget plans. Boehner's plan passed the House only after he included a provision that required a balanced budget amendment to the Constitution before extending the debt ceiling through the end of 2012. The Democratic Senate refused to consider it. In partisan payback, the House then refused to consider the Senate bill. August 2—the day the government would run out of money—was only two days away.

But in the end, neither party wanted to be blamed for a governmental default and shutdown. Exhausted, the two sides announced a complicated two-stage agreement on July 31, known as the Budget Control Act of 2011. In the first stage, $917 billion in spending cuts would be imposed over ten years in return for a $900 billion increase in the debt ceiling. In the second stage, a special joint committee of Congress—a so-called "super committee"—would be created to recommend a plan to further reduce the deficit by at least $1.2 trillion by November, 23, 2011. If the super committee failed to come up with a plan, it would trigger across-the-board spending cuts beginning in March of 2013 that would reduce discretionary spending every year for the next ten years to produce the $1.2 trillion in spending cuts.

The Budget Control Act passed the House on August 1 by a vote of 269 to 161 with sixty-six Republicans and ninety-five Democrats voting against it. The Senate passed it the following day. No one liked the legislation, but everyone realized there was no alternative.[20] Doc, who presided over part of the House debate, told the *Tri-City Herald* that he voted for it only because it "has no tax hikes, includes more cuts in spending than increases to the debt limit, paves the way for a balanced budget amendment, and averts a credit default."[21] It passed the Senate on the following day. The stock market didn't appear to have much confidence in Congress's ability to successfully implement the act. On August 4, the Dow dropped 500 points, the steepest decline since before Obama took office. Many of his own staffers believed he had reached the lowest point in his presidency.[22]

—

The difficult job of identifying $1.2 trillion in spending cuts now fell to the super committee that had been created under the Budget Control Act. Speaker Boehner appointed Jeb Hensarling of Texas, a close associate of Ryan's and the chairman of the Republican Conference. Senate majority leader Reid chose Washington's senior senator, Patty Murray, as the other co-chair. She was chair of the Senate Veterans' Affairs Committee and secretary of the Senate Democratic Conference.

Beginning in September 2011, the committee organized and then held a series of five public hearings in addition to seeking recommendations from industry groups, federal agencies, and congressional committees, including Doc's House Natural Resources Committee. On October 14, Doc provided his recommendations for reducing the deficit in letters to Hensarling and Murray. They included increasing energy production on the North Slope of Alaska, lifting the ban on offshore drilling, selling off surplus federal facilities and land, and increasing access to resources located on federal lands.[23]

Unfortunately, the differences between the two sides were simply too great. Two days before the super committee's November 23 deadline, the co-chairs issued a statement that concluded that "it will not be possible to make any bipartisan agreement available to the public before the committee's deadline."[24] The headline in the *New York Times* read, "Failure Is Absorbed With Disgust and Fear, but Little Surprise." The first line of the story echoed what many were thinking, "Does the American political system even work anymore?"[25]

—

The failure of the super committee to agree on spending cuts was one factor in what would become known as the fiscal cliff of 2013. But there were two others. The first was the inconclusive results of the 2012 national election. The second was the issue of whether—or how—to extend the 2001 Bush tax cuts.

On February 17, 2012, faced with the expiration of the Bush payroll tax cut, Congress agreed to extend it again, but the cuts were not offset by budget cuts or tax increases elsewhere. Both the payroll tax rates and Bush income tax rates, which had been extended for two years by the 2010 Tax Relief Act, were now set to expire on December 31, 2012. Until that time, the full attention of both parties was focused on winning the 2012 national election.

Neither party received a mandate in the 2012 national election. Obama was reelected, and while the Democrats picked up seats in both the House and the Senate, they were not enough to overcome the Republican majority in the House guaranteeing that major policy initiatives would remain deadlocked. Congress reconvened on November 13, right after the elections, and negotiations between the parties began again.

In the lame duck session that followed the election, both parties agreed on an extension of the Bush income tax cuts. The Republicans wanted to extend them for everyone. The Democrats wanted to extend them for all but the top 2 percent of taxpayers. A divided Congress compromised by extending the cuts for all but the top 1 percent of earners and providing additional unemployment benefits in a new piece of legislation called the American Taxpayer Relief Act of 2012. Many Republicans balked at even this compromise, and Boehner needed Pelosi's Democrats to pass the measure in the House. It passed just before midnight on December 31, 2012—New Year's Eve—by a vote of 257 to 167 with Speaker Boehner and Doc voting for the bill and 151 Republicans voting against it. The Senate passed it two hours later, at 2:00 a.m., by a vote of 89 to 8, and President Obama signed it the next day.[26]

The deal delayed, but did not cancel, the spending cuts triggered by the failure of the super committee. Sequestration—the across-the-board spending cuts mandated by the Budget Control Act—began in March 2013. Payroll taxes were allowed to increase after the temporary payroll tax cut expired, further delaying the economic recovery, but it was enough to temporarily avoid a default and government shutdown. Obama considered it a badly needed short-term win. Doc wasn't so sure. "I was nervous about it when we voted on New Year's Eve," Doc remembered:

> But that was the price of getting the deal. Spending is always problematic, but the part that made some of those tax rates permanent was very good policy. Some of those tax provisions should have been permanent all along.
> The White House had the megaphone, and when you have political differences, the party with the megaphone's always going to win.[27]

———

The debt limit crisis was a period of real peril for the United States. A government default and shutdown would have been catastrophic for the nation's economy. It is hard not to conclude that in their unwillingness to compromise, our leaders largely failed their obligations to govern. The congressional Republicans believed that President Obama had been so wounded by his healthcare proposal that they would win the 2012 election and didn't need to compromise. Obama complained that the Republicans were "never on the level" during the negotiations and offered only a deliberate pattern of partisan obstruction.[28] On the other hand, many Washington, DC, observers, like author Bob Woodward, have concluded Obama failed to exercise the kind of leadership that a Ronald Reagan or Bill Clinton would have exhibited in similar circumstances.[29] Doc remembered that Boehner told his conference Obama kept moving the goal posts during the negotiations. "I don't know if that was true or not."[30]

The fiscal cliff negotiations diminished John Boehner's standing as Speaker of the House and probably set in motion his ultimate demise a year later. Doc remembered:

> In retrospect, it was probably not a good strategy on [Boehner's] part to sit down and try to negotiate [with] President Obama. He should have said, "We have a regular process that we're going to go through. If you want to veto what comes out of that process, fine, but there's no way I can assure you that I'm going to have 218 people [the number of members needed to pass a bill] following me.[31]

What the American people thought of their actions was reflected in the 14 percent congressional approval rating in the Gallup Poll.

—

Few Americans understood the intricacies and the political maneuvering involved in the budget negotiations. Most of their television screens were tuned to images of the demonstrations occurring throughout the Middle East or to the never-ending series of debates between an ever-changing field of Republican candidates as they jockeyed to become the 2012 Republican presidential nominee.

In 2011, the United States had been continuously engaged in military operations in the Middle East for ten years. Most were unaware that President Obama had quietly, but dramatically, increased US special operations against al-Qaeda and its leaders. On May 1, 2011, he was able to announce that US forces had killed Osama bin Laden during an attack on his compound in Pakistan. On June 22, Obama announced that ten thousand troops would be withdrawn from Afghanistan by the end of 2011 and an additional twenty-three thousand troops would leave by the summer of 2012. In December, he could announce that the last US combat forces had left Iraq.

Beginning in late 2010, a pro-democracy movement known as the "Arab Spring" began to sweep the Middle East. Starting in Tunisia, more or less spontaneous demonstrations against authoritarian regimes spread to Oman, Yemen, Egypt, Syria, and Morocco. At first, the most important of these was in Egypt, a key American ally, run by Egyptian president Hosni Mubarak. The Obama administration was torn between the views of older foreign policy advisors like secretary of state Hillary Clinton, secretary of defense Robert Gates, and CIA director Leon Panetta, who counseled caution, and the president's younger advisors who felt demonstrations represented a potential shift to more democratic regimes in the region. Obama sided with his younger advisors and advised Mubarak to resign.

In March 2011, demonstrations broke out against Muammar Gaddafi in Benghazi, Libya. The United States had participated in a NATO-led military intervention to impose a no-fly zone in Libya in order to help the rebel groups take over the Libyan government. Gaddafi had long been a problem but in 2003 had pledged to get rid of his weapons of mass destruction after witnessing the fate of Saddam Hussein in Iraq. By August, Gaddafi was gone, but his country remained a no-man's zone of various tribal factions.

By January 2012, the government of Bashar al-Assad began to wage war on those elements opposed to him in a conflict that would ultimately turn into a long-running Syrian Civil War.

—

With the Republicans in control of the House, Doc Hastings assumed his position as the chair of the House Natural Resources Committee, whose offices and committee room were located in the familiar confines of the Longworth House Office Building. With his new position came some staff changes. With three small children, Jessica Gleason, Doc's chief of staff, stepped down to work on Hanford issues from home.

She was replaced by Jenny Gorski, who had worked in Doc's congressional office and on the Rules Committee since 2001.

His staff presented him with a handsome gavel, and several of them joined him on the committee. Todd Young became the committee's majority staff director in 2011, and Todd Ungerecht became senior counsel to the chairman after the 2010 election. Doc hired Jill Strait, a veteran of Cathy McMorris Rodgers's office, as the committee's communications director. She sent out a regular stream of press releases in his name.[32]

The Democratic ranking member on the committee was Edward J. Markey of Massachusetts. First elected in a special election in 1976, Markey had served as the chairman of the Select Committee on Energy Independence and Global Warming and on the House Energy and Commerce Committee, where he was chairman of the Subcommittee on Energy and the Environment. Markey had a strong environmental record in Congress, and some saw his appointment by minority leader Pelosi as a counterbalance to Doc's pro-business, anti-environmentalist positions. Doc remembered:

> You could hardly imagine two people farther apart politically than Ed Markey and myself, but we got along well. He had this wonderful way of saying things. I used to think that he had a damn good speechwriter, but I learned that his synonyms and metaphors all came from him.
>
> When I took over the committee, I invited him and his top staff to come in and told him that I was going to respect his turf and I hoped we could work together. If not, well, that was just the way it was going to be.
>
> The work of the committee was overseen by Todd Young and Jeff Duncan, Markey's top guy, with whom he had some problems.[33]

Doc was by now a recognized leader in the Republican conference because of his position as a committee chairman, his time in office, and his close relationship with Speaker Boehner. As a committee chairman, he could no longer serve on the Rules Committee, although he tried to attend the weekly meetings of committee chairmen sponsored by majority leader Eric Cantor. Doc was also one of a select group of committee chairmen and other members invited to informal luncheons by Speaker Boehner, a practice started by Dennis Hastert.

While considered more pragmatic than former committee chairmen Richard Pombo of California and Don Young of Alaska, Doc Hastings intended to reshape the priorities of the committee. He recalled, "The first thing I wanted to do was increase energy development. Gas prices were sky high. Oil was at $150 a barrel. We had jurisdiction over drilling on federal lands and in the oceans." Other important priorities included dealing with the California water crisis, changing the Endangered Species Act and the Antiquities Act, reversing the Obama administration's anti-coal regulations, and reforming the role of the Bureau of Reclamation.[34] He also made it very clear that no bill related to breaching the Snake River dams would ever see the light of day in his committee while he was its chairman.

He was proud of his lifetime average score of 3 (out of 100) in the League of Conservation Voters' scorecard of environment votes in the House.[35] He enjoyed a lifetime rating of 96 from the US Chamber of Commerce. "On environmental issues broadly, he's really just about one of the worst, easily," said Leda Huta, executive director of the Endangered Species Coalition. Business interests couldn't disagree more. "I can tell you we are excited about him taking over the committee and think he'll do an outstanding job," said Dan Naatz, vice president for federal resources at the Independent Petroleum Association of America.[36] When confronted with criticism from environmentalists, Doc pointed to his record of trying to clean up Hanford: "If you can't say that is being environmentally sensitive, then I don't know what your definition of environmentally sensitive is. When people try to characterize me as being against the environment, I honestly have to shake my head."[37]

Within two months of taking over the committee, Doc was supporting legislation to remove the gray wolf from the endangered species list and introducing bills with catchy titles to expand offshore energy production. The Putting the Gulf Back to Work Act reversed the Obama administration's de facto moratorium on oil drilling in the Gulf of Mexico. A second bill, the Restarting American Offshore Leasing Now Act, ordered the secretary of energy to conduct three lease sales in the Gulf of Mexico and one off the coast of Virginia. The third, the Reversing President Obama's Moratorium Act, lifted the long-standing moratorium on offshore drilling.

Doc increasingly used the committee's oversight functions to call administration officials before the full committee to testify on their environmental actions amid what were always tough questions. The committee also subpoenaed government documents from agencies, which rarely responded in a timely manner, if at all. "They ignored us as much as possible," Doc said of the Obama administration.

—

His three oil-drilling bills passed the House during the first two weeks of May on largely bipartisan votes, although Doc was not there to participate in the debate. [38] He had been home for the weekend when he was hospitalized with diverticulitis, a painful swelling of the intestinal wall. Claire spent Mother's Day in Richland's Kadlec Medical Center with him. Doc was recovering at home when he received the following from Ed Markey:

> Doc went to the Doc
> He was feeling quite ill
> For his three drilling bills?
> And the Doctor told Doc
> Leave those Fools on the Hill
> You've lined up the votes
> For your three drilling bills.
> And Doc told the Doc
> Guess I'll just have to wait
> I do like to win
> But I'll miss the debate!

At the bottom of the page, Markey wrote in longhand: "I hope you're feeling better. Look forward to having you around for the next drilling debate. Your friend, Ed Markey." All three of the bills Doc had introduced later stalled in the Senate.[39]

—

In July, Doc introduced the Cutting Red Tape to Facilitate Renewable Energy Act, one of a series of four bills passed out of the committee to increase energy production of federal lands. He continued to spar with Portland federal judge James Redden regarding the Snake River dams:

> Judge Redden has explicitly ordered federal agencies to consider dam removal. Not only is dam removal an extreme action that would be devastating to the Pacific Northwest's economy and is not proven to recover fish, Judge Redden has zero authority to order the removal of dams and the agencies have no authority to breach dams. Only Congress can authorize removal of the Northwest's federal dams and I can definitively state that this will not happen on my watch.[40]

In August, Doc again introduced his Rattlesnake Mountain Public Access Act. Previously, the legislation had failed to advance in the Democrat-controlled House. But now, he was chairman of the Natural Resources Committee. The committee passed his bill on a unanimous vote on November 17, and the full House followed suit on December 14, but the matter died in the Senate.

On October 4, 2011, Doc opposed an Obama administration plan that called for "zoning the oceans." Democrats asserted that zoning would provide more certainty on how Americans could use public waters. Doc feared the planning process would lead to new regulations on lands next to rivers and watersheds that drained into the oceans. Ed Markey likened the idea to planning for the use of air space. "Opposing ocean planning is like opposing air-traffic control," he quipped.[41] In November, Doc called the secretary of the interior, Ken Salazar, before the committee to challenge the Obama administration's five-year plan to limit offshore drilling. He asked the administration to open up part of Arctic National Wildlife Refuge (ANWR) to energy exploration.

—

On January 8-15, 2012, Doc and Claire took a break and joined Speaker Boehner and six other members and their wives on a CODEL to Brazil, Columbia, and Mexico, three of the largest US export markets in Central and South America. With a population of 195 million, Brazil was a major importer of Washington State hops and pears. Doc also met with Brazilian officials to learn how they handled offshore oil drilling. The second stop on the tour, Columbia, had recently adopted a free-trade agreement with the United States. In Mexico, Doc talked with high-level officials about the recently resolved dispute over cross-border trucking and issues related to potato exports."[42]

Claire had a wonderful time, visiting Copacabana Beach and the local botanical gardens in Rio de Janeiro, taking a historical tour in Bogotá, and touring the National Palace and the Metropolitan Cathedral in Mexico City. Her summation: "Great trip. Learned a lot."[43]

—

Back in Washington, DC, on January 30, Doc's committee marked up the energy portion of an important piece of Republican legislation, the American Energy and Infrastructure Jobs Act, which involved the jurisdiction of several House committees. He framed the energy portion of the legislation this way:

> Energy "resources" are what you potentially think you may have in the ground. "Reserves" are what you have proven that you have in the ground. Counting Alaska and offshore, the United States has more proven reserves than any other country in the world. Most of these are on public lands. Those reserves that are on private lands are being developed, depending on market conditions.
>
> The problem was the length of time it takes the federal government to permit development. Our legislation

would have fast-tracked the permitting. It didn't remove any of the environmental requirements.[44]

The legislation opened up part of the ANWR for energy exploration and removed the Obama administration moratorium on offshore oil drilling. Doc continued:

> The Democrats' argument was that OPEC would just increase production. My response has always been that the way to beat a cartel is to out-produce it.
>
> The political fight revolved around the fact that the environmentalists were trying to dry up the Alaskan pipeline. If they drilled less oil, the pipeline wouldn't work as effectively. Alaskans understandably wanted to utilize some of these reserves for their own purposes but couldn't because the federal government owns almost all the land. I think they have a point. The environmentalists say it's pristine, and that's bullshit.[45]

The House passed the legislation in February 2012, but it, too, stalled in the Senate. Later, opponents noted that Doc had received more money for his 2012 reelect campaign from oil and gas interests than from any other lobbying group.

—

Another important issue was the need for a federal response to the recurring California droughts. The state had suffered extensive droughts in both 2009 and 2010. "I had lived and worked in the area and felt a special affinity for it," Doc remembered.[46]

The problem was not new. Similar droughts had occurred at least twelve times since 1850. In response, the state and federal government had developed a complex system of reservoirs and delivery canals that allowed water to be transferred from northern California to where it was needed in the central and southern parts of the state. That system was already under pressure to meet the needs of the state's rapidly expanding population when, in 1995, federal court rulings—particularly those involving the endangered delta smelt in the estuaries of the Sacramento and San Joaquim Rivers—made things worse. In an effort to save the fish, badly need water was being diverted from the farmers and irrigators and causing economic chaos in the areas receiving less water. It was another instance of "farmers versus fish," Doc said.

The California congressional delegation was badly split on the issue because many of the state's Democratic lawmakers had close ties to the environmental community. As a result, no federal fix had been pursued while the Democrats controlled the House.

Doc took a similar position to those he had taken when dealing with competing stakeholders on issues in his district. He met with six Republican members who represented areas impacted by the problem: "You guys need to come to some agreement and work this out. Let me know what that agreement is, and I'll try to pass federal legislation to help you," he said. "It was very tough for some of them politically, but they finally worked it out," Doc recalled.[47]

As a part of his agreement with the California delegation, the staff scheduled a field hearing in April 2011 in Fresno to take testimony from stakeholders prior to developing legislation to fix the problem. Doc and seven members, mostly Republicans, participated in the hearing. In early 2012, Devin Nunes, one of the California Republicans Doc had worked with and a senior member of the Ways and Means Committee, sponsored legislation that resolved the differences between northern California, other watershed areas, and the San Joaquin Valley. It passed the House in spite of the overwhelming opposition of California's Democratic delegation and a presidential veto threat, but the Senate declined to take up the measure. Instead, Senator Diane Feinstein inserted a number of short-term measures that facilitated water transfers into the Energy and Water Appropriations bill.

—

On June 21, 2012, the House passed the Domestic Energy and Jobs Act, which included five bills that had originated in Doc's committee. The legislation also died in the Senate. On the same day, Doc and Ben

Lujan, Democrat of New Mexico, introduced legislation to create the Manhattan Project National Historic Park, which included Hanford's historic B Reactor and other facilities at Oak Ridge, Tennessee, and Los Alamos, New Mexico, but it, too, died in the Senate.

The hard work of developing legislation in his committee and having it pass the House, only to die or not be considered at all by the Democratic majority in the Senate was a recurring source of frustration for Doc. Former Washington Democratic congressman Al Swift is credited with having coined the phrase, "the Republicans are the opposition; the Senate is the enemy." Now, Doc and other frustrated Republicans turned it around to target the Democratic Senate.[48]

Maria Cantwell was the ranking member on the Senate Energy and Natural Resources Committee and often Doc's contact on his counterpart committee. She remembered:

> Doc was pretty determined about what he wanted to see done, particularly after he had an oversight role on energy issues.
>
> I would call him and say, "Can you help me over here, or he'd call me and say, "Can't you get anything done over there in the Senate? Don't think I'm just going to go for this and this and this. I'm not going to just go for that."

On other occasions, Cantwell would become a messenger from powerful senators to Doc:

> I can remember Carl Levin [chairman of the Senate Armed Services Committee] coming to me and saying, "You've got to call Doc Hastings. I'm not going to do this." I'd call Doc and he'd go ballistic . . . and I thought, OK, you guys need to work this out." I felt like I was the go-between. I remember that I had to go into the Senate cloakroom and do a lot of calling.[49]

—

In August, Doc introduced the Saving Our Dams and New Hydro-power Development and Jobs Act that he claimed would "eliminate government roadblocks and frivolous litigation, which . . . come with the expansion of new hydropower." A field hearing of the committee was scheduled in Pasco to take testimony in support of the legislation. The Pasco Chamber of Commerce organized a rally to coincide with the field hearing, during which one demonstrator handed out twenty-year-old signs shaped like lightning bolts that had been used at the original Save Our Dams rally. This time, the rally was much smaller, drawing about one hundred demonstrators to the TRAC facility in Pasco. The Save Our Wild Salmon organization held a press conference nearby.[50] The bill failed to pass the House. Doc was philosophical. "Rarely does anything pass the first time it's introduced."[51]

In September, while the presidential campaign was entering its final stages and the campaign was rhetoric strong, Doc introduced HR 3409, the Stop the War on Coal Act. It passed the House on September 21, 2012. It then went to the Senate where it was referred to the Senate Environment and Public Works Committee, where it died. Doc was philosophical about the fate of all of the legislation he and his colleagues had developed in committee and shepherded through the House, only to see it die in the hands of the Democratic-controlled Senate. "That's just the legislative process," he said.[52]

> Besides, we were coming up to an election year in 2012. I fully expected [Mitt] Romney to win and that we would win the Senate. All the numbers were on our side. So we were setting the stage for that.
>
> After we won the Senate and the presidency, we'd dust all that stuff off, pass it again, and "boom," we'd send it over to the Senate, and President Romney would sign it and it would become law.[53]

With nearly two million dollars in economic stimulus funding due to expire in 2011, Doc focused on an orderly transition for the nearly 1,600 Hanford workers who would be laid off during the coming year. It had been hoped that a special voluntary retirement program could be created for them, but the Department of Energy refused to go along. Doc believed DOE was being shortsighted and the process of laying off that many people would itself cost seventy-one million dollars. "Layoffs like this are obviously harmful to workers and are counterproductive to efforts to hire and retain new workers, as many at Hanford near retirement. This is the direct result of poor decisions and poor planning by DOE, and I couldn't be more disappointed by their decision."[54]

He was more pleased by the Obama administration's proposed 2012 budget for Hanford, rolled out in February, which increased funding from $2.18 billion in 2010, the last year a budget had been approved, to $2.37 billion. The increase, however, was all in the budget of the Office of River Protection, which was responsible for the management of tank wastes and the construction of the waste treatment plant. Funding for other Hanford programs, including the operation of the tank farms, was in jeopardy. The president's budget proposal also did not contain any funding for Yucca Mountain in Nevada, the remote desert site that had been chosen in 1987 as the long-term depository for the nation's nuclear waste. The site had been shut down in March 2010, after the Obama administration took office and Harry Reid of Nevada became the Senate majority leader, leaving Doc and most of the state's congressional delegation at odds with the Obama administration.

The lawsuit brought by the state of Washington and three Tri-City businessmen had been tossed out by the District of Columbia Circuit Court of Appeals on the procedural technicality.[55] The House partially removed that obstacle when it passed the 2013 Energy and Water Appropriations Bill on June 6 by approving an amendment that added ten million dollars to the NRC budget so it could no longer claim budget constraints for its failure to act on DOE's request to withdraw Yucca Mountain's license. Still, the Obama administration refused to proceed with licensing. The state and the local businessmen filed a second lawsuit and, this time, prevailed in obtaining an extraordinary judicial remedy that compelled the administration to proceed with licensing the facility.[56] The lawyer for the Tri-City businessmen, Tim Peckinpaugh, remembered, "The extraordinary remedy we won in the second lawsuit, a writ of mandamus, was a big deal. Courts seldom resort to this remedy, which underscores how outrageous the administration's non-compliance was."[57]

—

Doc applauded DOE's decision to create an Asset Revitalization Task Force to study requests and make recommendations on the release of DOE lands at Hanford. Energy Northwest, the operator of the Columbia Generating Station, was interested in 300 acres of land, and TRIDEC, the regional economic development entity, requested 1,341 acres located just north of Richland for future industrial purposes.[58] In June, Doc was successful in amending the 2012 National Defense Reauthorization Bill (NDAA) to extend the Office of River Protection at Hanford through 2019.

—

In November, with last-minute negotiations to avoid the fiscal cliff underway, DOE announced that the Hanford Waste Treatment Plant was again in jeopardy of missing the court-mandated construction deadlines. A review indicated that the project's cost had climbed to $12.3 billion. Obviously, the previous estimate of $5.5 billion in 2003 was far too low. Since the necessary appropriations bill for 2012 had not yet passed the Congress, and Doc warned that DOE's decision to move away from steady annual funding would create endless cycles of layoffs and expensive rehiring. "The department needs to stop adding risk and uncertainty to [the WTP] by planning for a funding cycle that will not happen—and will have inevitable detrimental impacts on other cleanup priorities," he wrote in a letter to the agency. DOE responded that it was studying the matter.[59]

—

On September 19 and 20, interior secretary Ken Salazar visited Doc's district, following up on an invitation he had received when Doc first became chairman of the Natural Resources Committee. In Yakima, Salazar discussed water issues with Doc, Senator Maria Cantwell, Governor Christine Gregoire, and a group of tribal leaders, irrigators, local governmental leaders, and environmentalists who had developed a five-billion-dollar plan to improve the basin's water storage needs. The plan included expanding Bumping Lake in the Chinook Pass area and creating another reservoir in the Yakima River Canyon. Doc emphasized the need for everyone to stick together and "speak with one voice."[60]

Salazar then moved on to Richland, where he toured the historic B Reactor later the same day. Back on June 14, 2012, Washington senators Maria Cantwell and Patty Murray had introduced legislation creating the Manhattan Project National Historic Park in the Senate. Doc followed suit by introducing companion legislation in the House on June 21, which passed out of committee without opposition. Expecting no opposition on the floor, Doc's legislation was placed on the suspension calendar, which requires a two-thirds vote to pass. He was surprised when Democrat Dennis Kucinich of Ohio unexpectedly decided to oppose it on moral grounds. "The bill is about graveyards, not national parks," Kucinich said during the debate.[61] His argument convinced enough Democrats to vote against the bill, and it was defeated on a vote of 237 to 180, less than the two-thirds required to pass. Doc remembered that Kucinich had come up to him on the floor and told him that he was going to oppose the bill:

> Afterward, he came up and offered a slight apology.
>
> We could have gone back and gotten a rule to bring it up before the House when all it would have needed was a simple majority. We could have sent it over to the Senate after it passed, but it would have been a very small bill and would have faced mixed support. There was just a couple of months left before they adjourned for the [2012] campaign.
>
> We made a conscious decision to wait and include it in next year's NDAA [National Defense

Authorization Act]. Kucinich also got defeated when he got redistricted.[62]

—

Immigration remained as difficult and contentious an issue for Republicans as it had been for Democrats. In June 2011, House Republicans unveiled a bill that would have required employers nationwide to use the federal E-Verify system to check the employment eligibility of job applicants. A week earlier, the city of Yakima had voted 4 to 3 to make E-Verify mandatory for city employees and contractors. Doc was not so sure about that approach. "There has to be special consideration for the agriculture community," he said.[63] His concerns were validated when the bill never made it out of committee. Doc knew that immigration reform would be highly unlikely in a presidential election year.

IT SEEMED AS IF THE 2012 presidential election had been going on for two years. Senate majority leader Mitch McConnell had vowed to make Barack Obama a one-term president at the beginning of the new Congress in 2011, and the president had been surprised—shocked even—by the depth of the Republican opposition to him ever since. Republicans believed they faced a vulnerable opponent, badly wounded by his unpopular healthcare plan and a still-struggling economy.

Republicans widely believed they would win the 2012 election. Almost since Barack Obama had arrived on the political stage, right-wing conspiracy theorists had been spreading rumors that Obama was a Muslim or that he had not been born in the United States. Unfortunately, many Republicans were only too happy to play along with their rabidly anti-Obama base. A *Time* magazine poll reported that 46 percent of Republicans believed Obama was a Muslim. Another showed that 51 percent of Republicans planning to vote in Republican primaries believed Obama had not been born in the United States.[64]

Another concerning issue was that a number of state legislatures had passed restrictive new voting laws they claimed combatted voter fraud. Many others felt the new laws had been designed to suppress the ability of presumably Democratic voters to cast their ballots. A number of these laws were later found to be unconstitutional, but they concerned Obama's campaign team during the election.[65]

A third concern was the emergence of Super PACs (political action committees). A Supreme Court case, *Citizens United v. Federal Election Commission*, had opened the doors to unlimited political contributions by labor unions and corporations, and *SpeechNow.org v. Federal Election Commission* allowed groups to spend unlimited amounts of money on advertisements endorsing political candidates. Labor unions had discovered ways to take advantage of the first ruling early on, so it was Republican-leaning corporations and interest groups that gained an advantage from the decisions as they quickly learned to catch up to and even exceed organized labor's contributions. Among the Super PACs were Karl Rove's American Crossroads and Crossroads Grassroots Policy Strategies. Americans for Prosperity, formed by David and Charles Koch, and John Boehner's American Action Network were also notable for the amount of outside money funneled into the campaigns of Republican candidates. Democratic activists created similar PACs.

After the drubbing the Democrats had suffered in the 2010 midterms, Obama expected a flood of Super PAC money to be unleashed against him. And then he caught a break.

So confident were the Republicans of victory that ten Republicans announced their candidacy for president by May 2011. The first Republican debate was held on May 5 in Greenville, South Carolina, and nineteen more followed.

An indication of just how conservative the Republican Party had become occurred during the third debate held in Ames, Iowa, on August 11, 2011, when *Fox News* anchor Bret Baier asked the candidates the following question: "Say you had a deal, a real spending cuts deal, 10-1, spending cuts to tax increases. . . . Who on this stage would walk away from that deal? Will you raise your hand if you feel so strongly about not raising taxes, you'd walk away on the 10-1 deal?" All eight candidates raised their hands. Each of them—if offered a debt-reduction deal that was 10-1 in their favor—would refuse it. Former Democratic

Pennsylvania governor Ed Rendell responded by calling the Republican field a "clown car."[66]

—

The Republican primaries began in January 2012 with Mitt Romney, the former governor of Massachusetts; Ron Paul, a congressman from Texas; and former Speaker Newt Gingrich each winning one of the first three contests. That had never happened before. Instead of being spent against Obama, the Republicans' Super PAC money was being directed toward fighting each other. Through the debates and the primaries that followed, the anti-Romney candidates peaked and flamed out with incredible regularity until just two remained to oppose Romney: former senator Rick Santorum and Newt Gingrich. Added public scrutiny led to both of them coming up short, leaving Romney, who chose Paul Ryan, the chairman of the House Budget Committee, as his running mate. Doc immediately endorsed the ticket.

Obama always thought Romney would win. Romney had served as a moderate governor of Massachusetts in 2002 but had morphed into a mainstream conservative before becoming chairman of the Republican Governors Association and running for president, eventually losing to John McCain in 2008. During the primaries, Romney had been forced to adopt more and more conservative positions, but many on the far right doubted his authenticity as a hardline conservative.

But the president had his own problems. At the end of 2011, Obama's approval ratings were in the mid-forties. Polls showed his support among white working-class men plummeting, from 39 percent in 2008 down to the mid-twenties. Less than a third of the country felt the country was headed in the right direction.[67] If the campaign was going to be about the past four years, Obama would lose. Obama's advisors decided they would change the question before the voters. With whom would they be better off over the next four years—Obama or Romney?[68]

On September 8, 2011, Obama addressed a joint session of Congress to promote the American Jobs Act, a collection of bipartisan bills designed to get Americans back to work, which he claimed would be fully paid for. Three months later, he delivered a nationwide address in small Osawatomie, Kansas, the place where Theodore Roosevelt had first declared his New Nationalism in 1910. Obama used the speech to frame his vision of the future to the American people in terms similar to what Roosevelt had used: "I'm here in Kansas to reaffirm my deep conviction that we're greater together than we are on our own. I believe that this country succeeds when everyone gets a fair shot, when everyone does their fair share, when everyone plays by the same rules. These aren't Democratic values or Republican values. They're American values."[69]

Mitt Romney was untouchable from a personal standpoint, but he had a habit of aggravating his weaknesses. He often made off-hand references to his personal wealth and multiple homes. He seemed tone-deaf to the lives of average Americans. On September 17, 2012, speaking at a high-dollar fundraiser in a private home in Boca Raton, Florida, Romney made a comment about the president's supporters that was secretly recorded and then went viral:

> There are 47 percent of the people who will vote for the president no matter what. All right, there are 47 percent who are with him, who are dependent upon government, who believe that they are victims, who believe the government has a responsibility to care for them, who believe that they are entitled to healthcare, to food, to housing, to you name it. That that's an entitlement. And the government should give it to them. And they will vote for this president no matter what.[70]

In spite of repeated efforts to walk the gaffe back, the damage had been done. Romney had called nearly half the electorate deadbeats. Earlier, on June 28, 2012, Republicans had received more bad news. The Supreme Court ruled 5 to 4 that the individual mandate of the Affordable Care Act was constitutional because it was considered a tax. The decision came as a blow to the Republicans.

And then it was time for the national conventions. The Republicans largely wasted theirs. For the second time in four years, the first day was scrapped because of a hurricane. It was clear that many Republicans were not enthusiastic about Mitt Romney. Their passion came from despising Barack Obama. By contrast, the Democratic convention was tightly controlled and capped off by the candidate's acceptance speech to eighty thousand enthusiastic supporters at Denver's Mile High Stadium.

Neither political convention produced the post-convention bounce that normally followed such events, and since Romney was already trailing in the polls, the lack of voter excitement following the convention hurt him more than Obama. A polarized electorate had already made up their minds. As the election neared, Obama led by four or five points in most of the swing states. The only way to close the gap was to win the three presidential debates. Obama lost the first one but won the next two.

On Election Day, black and Hispanic voters turned out for Obama in even higher numbers than they had in 2008, particularly in those states that had tried to suppress the vote. A larger percentage of black voters cast ballots than white voters for the first time. Younger voters between eighteen and twenty-nine—19 percent of the electorate—voted for Obama by a margin of 60 to 37 percent. Obama became the first incumbent since Franklin Roosevelt in 1944 to win reelection with fewer electoral votes and a lower popular vote percentage, but he won the popular vote by five million votes, the Electoral College vote by a margin of 332 to 206, and he carried every battleground state except North Carolina.[710] Democratic voters failed to show the same level of enthusiasm for their down-ballot candidates, however, and the Republicans picked up eight seats in the House to ensure a continuation of divided government.

—

By contrast, Doc's ninth reelection was a walkover. On April 19, 2011, Jay Clough, Doc's 2010 opponent, announced another run at the incumbent. The former Marine said he hoped to ride a pro–middle class platform and a different political landscape to victory in 2012. Ten months later, he opted instead to run for state representative.[72]

Doc announced his candidacy for a tenth term on March 30 in a prepared statement that hit on nearly all his talking points: "America deserves a more efficient, less intrusive government that spends less and serves better. As I travel throughout Central Washington, I hear constant encouragement to keep up the fight to end President Obama's out-of-control spending, to eliminate the national debt, to fix the tax code, and to repeal the illegal government takeover of your health care."[73]

Five days later, he had his first opponent. Mohammed H. Said, a seventy-three-year-old physician from Ephrata, announced his candidacy as a member of the American Centrist Movement, which he claimed to have founded. Said supported medical marijuana, universal healthcare, and a unified secular state combining Palestine and Israel and opposed US involvement in Iraq and Afghanistan. He had previously run for both governor and the US Senate, attracting less than 1 percent of the primary vote.

Doc attracted a more serious candidate ten days later when Yakima businesswoman, community organizer, and horse breeder Mary Baechler joined the race. She was best known for having invented the baby jogger but was a champion of many liberal causes. "I'm the little engine that could," she said. "It's time to speak out."[74]

Enthusiasm was noticeably lacking at the party caucuses held in April. Only 158 Democrats showed up at nineteen caucus sites in Yakima County, and the Republicans ended up supporting Ron Paul instead of frontrunner Mitt Romney. When the filing date arrived in May, Doc and Baechler filed, but so did Mohammad Said, who filed as a Democrat, and Tea Party activist Jamie Wheeler of Kennewick, who filed as a Republican. She said Doc was not conservative enough to make the needed cuts to government spending.

Doc's war chest contained more than one million dollars, with most small contributions coming from donors in Washington State. The *Yakima Herald-Republic* reported that only six contributions of $2,500 or more came from statewide donors, while many of the larger donations were from PACs affiliated with the oil and gas industry. Doc hardly needed the money. The last time he had run a TV ad was in 2004. What he didn't spend was sent to the National Republican Campaign Committee. Wheeler came up with a unique twist to fundraising.

She deliberately capped her campaign donations at $4,995 to avoid the federal reporting requirement.[75]

When the results of the August 7 primary were counted, Doc received more than 59 percent of the vote, with 26.5 percent going to Baechler, 11 percent to Wheeler, and almost 3 percent to Said.

Doc and Baechler squared off in a debate in Pasco on October 15 and before the *Yakima Herald-Republic*'s editorial board two days later. Baechler argued that Doc's focus had been on special interests and far-right policies that either didn't affect or failed to meet the needs of the district. Doc countered that the election had national implications, as he desired to repeal Obama administration policies and programs such as the Affordable Care Act. The *Tri-City Herald* again endorsed Doc.[76]

The election result was never in doubt. Doc headed into his tenth term with a majority of more than 66 percent.

When the House Republican Conference met on November 14, 2012, John Boehner, Eric Cantor, and Kevin McCarthy were reelected to their previous positions. Cathy McMorris Rodgers of Washington was elected as Republican conference chair, the number four leadership position, over conservative favorite Tom Price of Georgia, who had been endorsed by Paul Ryan.

On Thursday, November 15, 2012, it was announced that Pete Sessions of Texas would become the chairman of the House Rules Committee and that Doc would again assume the chairmanship of the Natural Resources Committee.

But behind that announcement was one of the most significant events in Doc's congressional career.

Doc enjoyed a close relationship with John Boehner. They had socialized and travelled together. Doc would occasionally bring him back a bottle of wine from his district, as he had after the two returned from their CODEL to South America in January, and Boehner would always respond with a personal note.

It had always been Doc's ultimate goal to serve as chairman of the House Rules Committee. He had almost succeeded in 2010 when Republicans regained the majority, but Boehner had asked David Dreier to serve another term in the hope of retaining his seat in his California swing district. That strategy had succeeded, and Doc assumed the chairmanship of the Natural Resources Committee. When Dreier announced his retirement at the end of that term, Doc expected he would move over and become chairman of the Rules Committee in the next Congress.

Pete Sessions of Texas was junior to Doc on Rules but had been instrumental in winning back the majority for the Republicans in 2010 and picking up eight more seats in 2012 as chairman of the National Republican Campaign Committee. He wanted the chairmanship of the Rules Committee, and many of the rank and file believed he deserved it, lobbying Boehner on his behalf. Boehner now had a problem. He had already promised the job to Doc. Hastings recalled:

> I got a call from John and went to his office—just the two of us—and he said, "Doc, I'm going to have to not let you have the Rules Committee chairmanship. I've decided to give it to Pete. He got us the majority, and he deserves something."
>
> I said, "Well, is there anything I can say?"
>
> And he said, "No, there really isn't."
>
> I thanked him for telling me straight up, and that's the way it went. It was his appointment to make.[77]

John Boehner corroborated Doc's story:

> There are a handful of conversations I've had to have with members over the years that were just downright AWFUL. Just awful.
>
> There were two people vying to be chairman of the Rules Committee, Doc Hastings and Pete Sessions of Texas. Pete was also the chairman of the NRCC, and

Doc was about to be chairman of the Natural Resources Committee. I had asked Doc to be chairman of the Natural Resources Committee, and he asked me if this would preclude him from being chairman of the Rules Committee, and I told him no.

Sometime prior to the 2010 election—maybe six months out—I told Doc, "You're my guy. I want you to be chairman of the Rules Committee."

Unfortunately, Boehner was not able to follow through on his promise.

Sessions was chairman of the NRCC and brought us into the majority in 2010. He had a lot of support among a lot of members, and as much as I felt that Doc would do a better job—and I had told Pete that I was going to give it to Doc—I got a couple of phone calls from some members that caused me to think pretty seriously about this. The more I thought about it, the more I came to the conclusion that I didn't have a choice but to make Pete the chairman.

I called Doc in and told him straight up, "Doc, I know I promised you the Rules Committee, but I can't keep my promise." It was one the hardest things I ever had to do.[78]

It had not been Doc's primary motivation, or even more than a passing thought, but had he been selected by Boehner to chair the Rules Committee, he would have been one of only a handful of members in the history of the Congress to chair three major committees.[79]

CHAPTER SIXTEEN

Dean of the Delegation

★

WHEN THE HOUSE CONVENED at noon on Thursday, January 3, 2013, for the first session of the 113th Congress, it reflected the nation's growing diversity. Among the eighty-two new members were the first Hindu to serve in Congress, the first openly bisexual congresswoman, the first openly gay lawmaker of color, four African Americans, ten Latinos, and five Asian Americans. Eighteen percent of the new members were women. [1]

John Boehner and Nancy Pelosi were reelected Speaker and minority leader, respectively, again by wide margins, but much of the press coverage focused on how many members of their own parties had opposed their leadership. Representative Jim Jordan of Ohio and other hardline conservative members organized a coup to keep Boehner from becoming Speaker. Twelve Republicans actually voted against Boehner, the most since 1997, but at one point there had been as many as seventeen, which would have been enough to keep him from being elected on the first ballot. One of the coup leaders, Walter Jones of North Carolina, told *The Hill* that they "just decided they couldn't go through with it."[2] Boehner, who had a history with Jordan going back to Ohio, later would later refer to him as "a legislative terrorist."[3]

Nancy Pelosi fared a little better. Only eight Democrats voted against her leadership, down from the twenty who had voted against her in 2011.

Many of the Republicans still had a bitter taste in their mouths from the dramatic and highly divisive New Year's Eve vote that avoided the fiscal cliff. Doc was one of them, even though he had been on the winning side. In a telephone interview with the *Yakima Herald-Republic*, he said: "What we have is a spending problem and not a revenue problem. The national debt is up by fifty percent in four years. You simply can't keep kicking that ahead to future generations. If we are going to raise the debt limit, we need a commitment of at least that much, if not more, in spending cuts." He blasted President Obama for his refusal to link the debt issue to spending cuts. "For the president to suggest as he did that he would not engage in that discussion is absolutely irresponsible," Doc said.[4]

Doc's comments now carried more weight than they once had. He had won his 2012 reelect with 66 percent of the vote. He was a respected senior member of the Republican conference, a full committee chairman, a close friend and associate of Speaker Boehner's, and the senior Republican in Washington's congressional delegation. Because of his willingness to mentor younger members, Doc was sometimes called the "dean of the delegation."[5] His staff was recognized as one of the best in the House. That staff, and its counterpart at the House Natural Resources Committee, worked to improve Doc's visibility, sending out a virtual stream of press releases and position statements. Even those who opposed his politics grudgingly respected his growing stature as one of the few members who had chaired two full committees and who often presided over the House when it considered important legislation.

—

Monday, January 21, 2013, dawned bitterly cold in the nation's capital. Just before midday, Barack Obama joined only sixteen men in history who had twice been elected president of the United States. A crowd estimated at more than one million people crowded the National Mall to witness the event. Doc listened as Obama laid out his ambitious agenda.

Throughout the hard-fought presidential campaign, Obama predicted the Republicans who fought him so fiercely throughout his first term would now recognize the voters had spoken and it was time to work together. With a sense of renewed confidence, Obama called on Congress to combat climate change, enact immigration reform, and tighten gun control. More progress needed to be made on human and civil rights for racial minorities, women, and members of the LGBT community. "Just send me a bill," he said.[6] Doc remembered how he had felt when he had heard that: "He hadn't shown any indication in his first term that he was willing to work with us. The only major thing that he had accomplished was the Affordable Care Act, and it was terribly unpopular. Many of those things, like climate change and gun control, were simply dead on arrival in the House."[7]

On February 12, Obama's State of the Union speech contained an even more aggressive list of proposals. Addressing the deficit was first among them. It had been reduced by more than $2.5 trillion in the past several years, mostly through spending cuts but also by raising tax rates on wealthy Americans. "Now," he said, "we need to finish the job . . .the question is, how?" His answer included increasing the federal minimum wage, finding market-based solutions to climate change, using oil and gas revenues to fund clean tech research, providing free pre-school for all, immigration reform, and gun control.[8]

The last issue was personally significant to the president. After the December 14, 2012, shooting of twenty first-graders at Sandy Hook Elementary School in Connecticut, Obama couldn't get the children out of his mind. He mounted a vigorous effort to pass gun control and tasked Joe Biden with the new initiative.

Obama knew gun control legislation in the Republican-controlled House was a non-starter, but he believed he could put together a modest proposal that could pass the Senate with a little Republican help. Once again, Obama's past unwillingness to reach out to even lawmakers of his own party and the influence of the National Rifle Association in both parties doomed the effort. Four Democrats voted against the motion to proceed, and only two Republicans voted for it—five votes short of the sixty votes needed to consider the legislation.

—

Another bipartisan issue Obama pursued was immigration reform. He had received 71 percent of the Hispanic vote in 2012. Latinos were becoming an ever-greater percentage of the electorate in Republican states like Georgia and Texas. Obama thought Republicans could benefit by reaching out to a large voting bloc they were clearly losing.

Immigration reform had been a wedge issue within the Republican Party since 1986 when Ronald Reagan signed a comprehensive overhaul that provided amnesty to millions of undocumented immigrants. The issue had split George Bush from his party's conservatives in 2005. John Boehner and Eric Cantor recognized their problem soon after the 2012 election and called for a Republican version of immigration reform that emphasized border security and a multi-step process that could end in citizenship, but without amnesty—a position similar to the one Doc had been proposing.

Again, the action was in the Senate. A "Gang of Eight," led by Arizona Republican John McCain and New York Democrat Chuck Schumer, developed a comprehensive reform bill that would put eleven million illegal immigrants on a thirteen-year path to citizenship once the southern border was secured. On June 26, the Senate voted 68-32 to approve the measure. Fourteen Republicans crossed the aisle to vote in favor.

In the House, however, conservatives blocked Boehner from even bringing immigration reform to a vote. They were concerned the proposed pathway to citizenship might survive in a compromise with the Senate.[9] Others were unwilling to risk being primaried or defeated by even more polarized Republicans in the next election. Boehner was boxed in. He wanted immigration reform and didn't personally object to a path to citizenship, particularly for the children who had been brought to the country through no fault of their own, but he realized the conservatives would never forgive him if he didn't listen to the vast majority of his membership. He would later tell a reporter that not solving immigration was his second-greatest regret.[10] On June 30, President Obama announced the death of immigration reform. "I believe Speaker Boehner when he says he wants to pass an immigration bill," Obama declared from the White House. "But last week, he informed me that Republicans will continue to block a vote on immigration reform at least for the remainder of this year." As a result, Obama said he would take executive action where possible on immigration policy.[11]

Doc recalled that Obama "might have been able to find some common ground on immigration, but it was his way or the highway, and that was it. It didn't sound like he was serious in terms of a compromise."[12]

Chuck Todd, author and moderator of *Meet the Press*, described the situation in his book about the president, titled *The Stranger*: "Obama couldn't understand it: why wouldn't Republicans act in their own self-interest? But what he didn't understand was that Republicans were acting in their near-term self-interest, and in this case self-interest had become opposing him."[13]

When Doc read Todd's analysis, he agreed: "There's probably some truth to that. We look at our self-interest in terms of election cycles. I had the benefit of being able to look a little farther out. It's part of the polarization of the country. When we won all those seats in 2010 and 2012, I have no doubt that in every district where a Republican won Obama was the main whipping boy with Nancy Pelosi right behind him."[14]

—

On August 28, 2013, Doc spoke at a meeting of the Tri-City Regional Chamber of Commerce. One of the four hundred attendees asked him about the level of political polarization in Washington, DC, and the differences between prominent Republicans. Doc responded:

> There's no question that the country largely is divided philosophically. And both parties have factors in their party that don't see eye to eye. The differences in our party are largely about the degree and process of how you're going to accomplish an end.
>
> I don't see a schism [in our party]. What I see is a robust discussion about how we should be moving. . . . If you want to see divisions in politics, you should look at the other party. I think sometimes they have more problems than we have.[15]

By advocating for gun control and immigration reform, Obama had almost guaranteed he would start out his second term with a pair of losses. With nothing to show for their efforts of reaching out to Republicans, Obama's advisors decided to recalibrate in order to save his legacy.[16] A new approach was evident when Obama spoke to reporters on January 14, 2014. His tone had changed:

> We are not just going to be waiting for legislation in order to make sure that we're providing Americans the kind of help that they need. I've got a pen, and I've got a phone. And I can use that pen to sign executive orders and take executive actions and administrative actions that move the ball forward in helping to make sure our kids are getting the best education possible, making sure that our businesses are getting the kind of support and help they need to grow and advance, to make sure that people are getting the skills that they need to get those jobs that our businesses are creating.[17]

Doc remembered how put off he was by the president's comments and recalled what his philosophical idol, Ronald Reagan, had said under similar circumstances: "Die-hard conservatives thought that if I couldn't get everything I asked for, I should jump off the cliff with the flag flying—go down in flames. No, if I can get 70 or 80 percent of what it is I'm trying to get . . . I'll take that and then continue to try to get the rest in the future."[18]

But this was a different Republican Party from the one Ronald Reagan had led. These Republicans were not particularly interested in compromise and continually used the threat of shutting down the government to demand new spending cuts from what they perceived was a weakened president.

—

The ceiling on the national debt had technically been reached at midnight on December 31, 2012, when the Treasury Department began to use what it called "extraordinary measures" to keep the government in operation. On January 15, 2013, the credit rating agencies again warned that delays in raising the debt ceiling could result in downgrading the credit rating of government bonds.[19] Fundamental disagreement continued as the two sides fought over the next budget. In February, the House and Senate passed the No Budget, No Pay bill, which suspended the debt ceiling through May 18 in order to give the House and Senate time to pass a budget and temporarily withheld the pay of members of Congress if they did not produce a budget plan by April 15.

On March 1, the $1.2 trillion in mandatory budget cuts over the next decade that had been imposed by the Budget Control Act finally went into effect. In response, the House Budget Committee reported out its budget plan on March 15. It revised the tax code to create only two income tax brackets, ended the alternative minimum tax on high-income corporations and individuals, and reduced the corporate tax rate. It also repealed the Affordable Care Act and converted Medicare into a system incorporating private insurance plans. The Republican plan passed the House on March 21, 2013, on an almost straight party-line vote of 221 to 207.[20] Doc voted yes.

It was a different story in the Senate. It hadn't passed a budget since 2009. But on the same day the House passed its budget, the Senate Budget Committee introduced its budget resolution. The Democratic proposal called for $3.7 trillion in federal spending and increased taxes and assumed the federal deficit would continue to grow.[21] The Senate narrowly passed its own budget resolution by a vote of 50 to 49.

On May 19, the debt ceiling was reinstated, and the Treasury managed to keep the government open, although it warned the money would run out on October 17. Another short-term CR, which would have delayed the implementation of the Affordable Care Act for a year and fast-tracked construction of the controversial Keystone XL Pipeline, was floated by Texas senator Ted Cruz and his conservative supporters in the House. Boehner objected. Not only would the Democrats never go for it, but also the Republicans would be blamed again for precipitating another government shutdown. Boehner later recalled: "I told them. 'Don't do this. It's crazy. The president, the vice president, Reid, Pelosi, they're all sitting there with the biggest shit-eating grins on their faces that you've ever seen, because they can't believe we're this f****** stupid."[22]

—

Boehner's warnings to his conference fell on deaf ears. The government had reached the edge of the fiscal cliff again, and this time, it fell over it. An automatic government shutdown began on October 1, 2013, when eight hundred thousand federal workers were told to stay home and another 1.3 million were required to report to work but without any assurance of when, or if, they would be paid.[22] Doc agreed with his Speaker and recalled, "While I agreed with repealing Obamacare, I was not in favor of the shutdown, and I argued against it. I believe that approach always causes more problems than it's worth."[23]

In fact, during the sixteen-day shutdown, Doc used his essential staff in his personal and committee offices to continue to conduct official business, including legislative and oversight hearings. When the Obama administration began to draw public fire for erecting metal barricades around national parks and memorials to dramatize their closure during the partial government shutdown, Doc organized a joint oversight hearing on October 16, 2013, between his committee and the House Oversight Committee entitled, "As Difficult As Possible: The National Park Service's Implementation of the Government Shutdown," and called in the director of the National Park Service to testify.[24]

To no one's surprise, the government shutdown—coming as it did right before the holidays—was immensely unpopular. The public wondered why lawmakers couldn't reach a compromise. As Doc and Boehner had forecast, the conservative Republicans, who had been the loudest voices calling for the shutdown, were blamed for the inconvenience. By the morning of October 16, Republican lawmakers had heard enough from their constituents and were ready to give the president almost exactly what he had requested months earlier—a clean bill to fund the government and increase the debt limit with no strings attached.

Under the terms of the agreement, a joint budget conference was created—led by Paul Ryan and Patty Murray—to iron out a compromise on their budget programs. On December 10, 2013, they announced a compromise between the two versions of the budget that became known as the Bipartisan Budget Act of 2013. It increased discretionary spending over the next two years, eliminated some of the forced budget cuts that had been scheduled over the next two years, and made up for the increases with long-term cuts in mandatory spending.[25]

The Senate overwhelmingly ratified the deal, 81 to 18, with more than half of the Senate's Republicans voting yes, but the House was another matter. Boehner had argued against shutting down the government but tried to appease the conservatives in his conference who wanted to continue their fight. Moderates argued that the Senate would never accept the conservative demands. With the House Republicans bitterly divided and Boehner himself badly weakened, the effort collapsed. Boehner was forced to reach out and negotiate a deal with Senate majority leader Harry Reid. The House reluctantly followed the Senate in approving the measure 285 to 144, with Doc presiding over the tough vote. Only eighty-seven Republicans joined the united Democrats in voting for the measure, and Doc was one of them. Speaker Boehner put the best face on the situation he could: "We've been locked in a fight over here, trying to bring government down to size, trying to do our best to stop Obamacare. We fought the good fight. We just didn't win."[26]

He had a different message for Doc. On February 24, he sent Doc this short note:

> Dear Doc,
>   It took courage to vote for the debt ceiling increase. It was the right thing to do for the country and the conference. Look forward to working with you on other equally important issues. Thank you.[27]
>
> —

While the budget battle raged at home, a very real catastrophe was growing in the Middle East. The Syrian Civil War was yet another manifestation of the Arab Spring movement. Like Iraq, modern Syria was a result of the redrawing of the Ottoman Empire's boundaries at the end of World War I. But even more so than Iraq, Syria was a hodge-podge of different religions, ethnic factions, and urban-rural divides that had been held together by a brutal dictatorship. The country's strategic position ensured that Turkey, Lebanon, Jordan, Israel, Iraq, and the Gulf States were involved in Syria's future, and Russia maintained an active naval base there.

The anti-government demonstrations in 2011 grew into a full-fledged civil war that pitted multiple religious sects and urban and tribal factions against the government and each other. The war attracted into the void outside groups like Hezbollah, a Shia Islamist militant group based in Lebanon, Sunni al-Qaeda militants, and their offspring, ISIS (the Islamic State in Iraq and Syria).

Having made a campaign pledge to get American soldiers out of Iraq and Afghanistan, Obama was in no mood to intercede in the Syrian morass, but he was understandably concerned about President Assad's stockpile of chemical weapons. At a White House press briefing on August 20, 2012, he issued a warning: "We have been very clear to the Assad regime, but also to other players on the ground, that a red line for us is we start seeing a whole bunch of chemical weapons moving around or being utilized. That would change my calculus."[28]

The US military developed plans to train anti-Assad fighters in Jordan and other countries, but again the White House was conflicted. Obama's older national security advisors—secretary of state Hillary Clinton and CIA director Leon Panetta—supported more aggressive action against Assad, but they were again overruled by the president's younger advisors and his own instinctive caution. The thought of another attack on an Arab country that posed no immediate threat to the United States after a decade of war in Afghanistan, Iraq, and Libya was simply unpalatable.[29]

A year after Obama drew his red line, Assad launched a large-scale poison gas attack on a suburb of Damascus that brutally killed hundreds of civilians, all caught on video and immediately streamed around the world. Again, the president couldn't get the pictures of the children out of his mind and prepared to intervene. And then he pulled back.

Doc presides over the vote on Medicare prescription drugs on November 23, 2003. He kept the vote open for two hours and fifty-three minutes until there were enough Republican votes to pass it. The vote resulted in ethics charges against minority whip Tom DeLay. *Hastings family*.

Doc visits a Franklin County asparagus farm to show his support during trade negotiations with Peru that devastated Washington asparagus producers, March 3, 2004. *Hastings family*.

Claire writes in her journal while Doc looks on after their visit to Egypt, Jordan, Iraq, Israel, Lebanon, Cyprus, and Belgium, April 2, 2005. *Hastings family*.

Doc (*second from left*) and other members of congressional delegation led by David Dreier, chairman of the House Rules Committee, are briefed by a Marines Corps officer in Fallujah, Iraq, on March 26, 2005. Their visit came only a month after the battle for Fallujah had ended. *Hastings family*.

Doc loved all sports, but he particularly loved NASCAR. Here he is after taking a test run at the Rockingham, North Carolina, track. *Hastings family*.

Ed Cassidy (*right*) served as Doc's first chief of staff and then as staff on the House Rules and Ethics Committees. *Getty Images/Bloomberg/Ken Cedeno.*

Doc holds a press conference to announce his willingness to begin an investigation of minority leader Tom DeLay if the Democrats would allow the committee to convene under the GOP-backed House rules, April 20, 2005. With Doc are the Republican members of the committee (*left to right*), Judy Biggert of Illinois, Melissa Hart of Pennsylvania, and Tom Cole of Oklahoma. *Hastings family.*

Doc and Democratic ranking member Howard Berman (*left*) of California hold a press conference to announce the start of an ethics investigation into Congressman Mark Foley of Florida, October 5, 2005. *Getty Images/MCT.*

The troubled Hanford Waste Treatment Plant under construction in April 2006. Prime contractors had changed, 3,800 workers were laid off, and the cost had skyrocketed from $5 billion to more than $11.2 billion. Construction on part of the facility was shut down so that the problems could be addressed. *US Department of Energy.*

Speaker Dennis Hastert stopped by the Tri-Cities to wish Doc a happy birthday in February 2006. *Hastings family.*

"Quit Monkeying Around with Tom DeLay" billboards showed up in Doc's district during his 2006 re-election campaign. *Hastings family.*

Doc always tried to debate his opponents during each election cycle. For all the smiles in this picture, his re-election against Richard Wright in 2006 was the most unpleasant of his career. *Tri-City Herald/Bob Brawdy.*

President George W. Bush congratulates Nancy Pelosi, the first female Speaker of the House, at the State of the Union Speech on January 23, 2007. *Library of Congress.*

Doc and his family visit the White House on April 17, 2008. *Left to right*: Petrina, the president, Doc's grandson Ivan Lancaster, Claire, Doc, and Kirsten. It was Ivan's tenth birthday. *Hastings family.*

A giant television screen captures the scene as Barack Obama accepts the Democratic nomination in front of eighty thousand supporters at Denver's Mile High Stadium, August 28, 2008. *Wikipedia Commons.*

In September 2008, with the election in full swing, the Bush administration proposed a seven-hundred-billion-dollar Troubled Asset Relief Program (TARP). Doc voted against it twice. The Dow fell 777 points, the largest drop in its history. The Great Recession was underway. *PicQuery.com*.

Vice president Joe Biden looks on as President Obama signs the $787 billion economic stimulus bill in Denver on February 17, 2009. Doc and every other Republican voted against the bill. *White House Press Office/Pete Souza*.

Doc and Senator Maria Cantwell hold a press conference in Richland marking the passage of legislation authorizing the Ice Age Floods National Geologic Trail, May 2009. *Gary Kleinknecht*.

Doc argues on the floor of the House against the passage of the Omnibus Public Land Management Act on March 11, 2009. Doc voted against it, even though it included several of his pet projects. *Hastings family*.

President Obama celebrates with his White House staff as the House passes the Affordable Care Act, March 21, 2010. *White House Press Office/Pete Souza.*

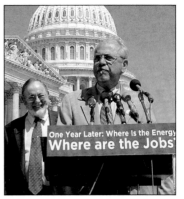

Doc and Don Young of Alaska hold a press conference leading up to the 2010 midterm elections to complain about the lack of stimulus jobs in the energy field. Doc wanted to increase the jobs by opening up energy development offshore and on federal lands. *House Committee on Natural Resources.*

DOE had spent $13.5 billion on the Yucca Mountain, Nevada, nuclear repository. In March 2010, the Obama administration decided to shut it down. Doc immediately fought the action. *US Department of Energy.*

Doc and Gene Green of Texas chaired the investigative subcommittee of the Ethics Committee that found Charlie Rangel, the chairman of the House Ways and Means Committee, guilty of eleven of the thirteen counts against him on November 20, 2010. *Hastings family.*

Doc's name familiarity was so high in his Central Washington district that his blue-and-white campaign signs didn't have to say "re-elect" on them. Claire came up with idea of just using his well-known nickname. *Hastings family.*

Doc surprised many with his unsuccessful attempt to absorb the energy portfolio of the House Energy and Commerce Committee into the Natural Resources Committee in November 2010. *House Committee on Natural Resources.*

Doc and ranking member Ed Markey of Massachusetts enjoy a lighthearted moment during a hearing of Doc's committee on the Deepwater Horizon disaster on January 26, 2011. The two cooperated on legislation that sold off the National Helium Reserve to make the gas available to high tech industry. *House Committee on Natural Resources.*

Speaker John Boehner, vice president Joe Biden, President Obama, and Senate majority leader Eric Cantor try to negotiate a budget deal in the White House in July 2011. *White House Press Office/Pete Souza.*

Pitching the American Energy and Infrastructure Jobs Act in February 2012. *Left to right*: Jeb Henserling of Texas, Doc, Speaker Boehner of Ohio, and Fred Upton of Michigan. Like much of the legislation passed in the House, the measure died in the Senate. *House Committee on Natural Resources.*

Standing in front of the start of the Alaska Pipeline at Prudhoe Bay, Alaska, in 2012. Doc continued to fight to open up Alaska for more energy exploration. *Left to right*: Don Young of Alaska, Doc, and committee staffers Todd Young and Tim Charters. *House Committee on Natural Resources.*

Doc and Natural Resources committee members review documents during a committee hearing in 2013. *Left to right*: Don Young of Alaska, Doc, ranking member Peter DeFazio of Oregon, and David Watkins, chief minority counsel. *House Committee on Natural Resources.*

Doc speaks to President Obama about energy policy after the president met with the Republican conference on January 14, 2013, to talk about raising the debt limit. *Hastings family.*

Doc's district staff was the foundation of his excellent constituent relations. Long-time staffer Sharlyn Berger (*front row, far left*) and district director Barb Lisk (*front row, second from left*) appear in October 2014. *Sharlyn Berger.*

Doc and his family walk from his Pasco office to a nearby hotel to announce that he will not seek re-election, February 13, 2014. *Tri-City Herald/Bob Brawdy.*

Doc speaks to a water rights rally of three thousand farmers in Fresno, California, in conjunction with a field hearing of the Natural Resources Committee that would lead to legislation to free up water supplies held up by a smelt listed on the Endangered Species Act, March 19, 2014. *House Committee on Natural Resources.*

Doc presides during House debate over the Concurrent Resolution of the 2015 budget as budget chairman and future Speaker Paul Ryan compliments him on his twenty years of service, April 10, 2014. *Hastings family.*

Doc speaks to colleagues, staff, family, and friends in the Natural Resources Committee hearing room during the formal unveiling of his official portrait on November 19, 2014. *House Committee on Natural Resources.*

Doc, Senator Maria Cantwell, a National Park Service ranger, and local school children raise the American and National Park Service flags over the B Reactor, November 11, 2015. *National Park Service.*

Doc enjoys his retirement from the deck of his Pasco, Washington, home overlooking the Columbia River with the broad expanse of the Hanford Site and Rattlesnake Mountain in the background. *House Committee on Natural Resources.*

Author C. Mark Smith (*right*) conducted approximately 150 hours of recorded interviews with Doc in the office of his Pasco home between January 2016 and August 2017 for this book. *C. Mark Smith.*

Eighty percent of Americans believed the president should seek congressional authorization to go to war. On August 31, 2013, Obama went on television declaring that he would seek approval from Congress before taking action. His threat of force had energized the Russians to negotiate on behalf of their client state. For the second time in two weeks, Obama went on television to ask Congress to postpone its vote authorizing force in order to give diplomacy a chance.

Doc told the *Tri-City Herald* that with the House in summer recess, he "had not had a chance to see the classified briefings, and I'm going to withhold judgment publically until I have that opportunity."[30] He had supported the invasion of Iraq in 2003, as well as the 2007 troop surge there. In 2007 and 2009, he co-sponsored legislation that would have tightened economic sanctions on Syria, but that legislation never came to a vote on the House floor. In 2011, he joined a bipartisan majority who voted against a bill authorizing military intervention in Libya. "They're all different," he told the *Herald*: "Getting involved in foreign affairs is a constant struggle. We do have a responsibility as one of the most prominent countries in the world. But there has to be a plan and an end game, and I need to know what that is."

—

While Obama won reelection by a smaller margin than he had in 2008, the American people gave him a solid victory in 2012. He defeated Mitt Romney by five million votes and carried the Electoral College by 126 electoral votes. With his powerful communications skills and a Democratic Senate, Obama had the best opportunity to pursue the Democratic agenda since Lyndon Johnson's presidency in the 1960s.

But in fact, Barack Obama's second term was largely one of missed opportunities. His cautious, judicial mind lacked what some biographers have called the "schmooze gene."[31] He also faced a resentful and intransigent Republican House whose base back home was more interested in opposing Obama than in compromising with him. As a result, Obama largely decided to ignore and to try to work around Congress in his second term.

In their deep distaste of the president, the congressional Republicans continued to overreach. They spent the first half of his second term hunting for a scandal when they could have simply chipped away at the administration's credibility by arguing it was either incompetent or incapable. They overreached again when their refusal to agree to a budget compromise resulted in the sixteen-day government shutdown.

The public believed that both Congress and the president had failed them. A Gallup Poll, released in November 2013, showed that a whopping 86 percent of respondents disapproved of the job Congress was doing. Another 5 percent had no opinion, leaving only 9 percent of respondents who approved of the job their elected representatives were doing. Their disapproval cut both ways. In 2014, President Obama also recorded the lowest approval ratings of his presidency—41 percent.[32]

—

Doc looked forward to his second term as chairman of the Natural Resources Committee. From the start of the new session, there were rumors that Doc would soon have a new ranking member on the committee.

In December 2012, Ed Markey announced his candidacy to fill John Kerry's seat after President Obama nominated the Massachusetts Democrat to be secretary of state. Markey won the special election primary on April 30, 2013, and went on to defeat his Republican opponent by ten percentage points. Doc recalled:

> He was there, but pretty much in name only, during his campaign. He was probably using our accomplishments on the committee as campaign fodder in his election. On a personal basis, I was pleased that he won, but we didn't need another Democrat in the Senate.
>
> I was also really pleased when it was announced that DeFazio had been picked to move up to ranking member. He was from the Pacific Northwest, and he knew the natural resources issues really well.[33]

While they had disagreed on many things, Doc and Markey had worked well together and found common ground on eliminating the Federal Helium Reserve in Texas, operated by the Bureau of Land Management (BLM). The huge, underground rock dome held half of the nation's and 30 percent of the world's supply of helium. Created in 1926 to store helium for military airships, it continued to be maintained long after it became obsolete. By 1996, the program was $1.3 billion in debt.

On February 6, 2013, Doc and Markey, along with several co-sponsors, introduced HR 527, the Helium Stewardship Act of 2013, which eliminated the helium reserve program by authorizing BLM to sell the helium on the open market where there was a growing demand from high-tech companies. The bill passed the House on April 26. With Markey now in the Senate, the measure passed that body by unanimous consent on September 26 and was signed by the president on October 2.[34]

—

Doc's new ranking member, Peter DeFazio of Oregon, had been elected from Oregon's Fourth Congressional District in 1986 and was the longest serving member of the Oregon delegation. A liberal populist, DeFazio was one of only four Democrats to vote against the stimulus bill because the legislation included tax cuts for the wealthy. He called for ending the Bush tax cuts on the wealthy and supported the Occupy Wall Street movement.[35] During the 2012 Democratic primaries, DeFazio, along with fellow congressman Dennis Kucinich of Ohio and Bernie Sanders, the Independent senator from Vermont, argued that President Obama should face tougher primary opposition "where all the issues would be aired out."[36]

With one short exception, DeFazio had served on the Natural Resources and its predecessor committees since he was elected to Congress. Once Markey was elected to the Senate, DeFazio won a contested election in the Democratic House Steering and Policy Committee to become the new ranking member. He admitted he wasn't expecting much under Doc's chairmanship:

I found that during the times when the Republicans had the majority, the committee was generally one of the most partisan and least productive committees in Congress, and that didn't change much when Doc was chair.

Some of the previous [Republican] chairmen had more extreme views than Doc, but Doc was quite conservative on land and environmental issues. There were times when I would have chosen a different path, but he had a majority and his leadership to deal with.[37]

The two men hadn't known each other well prior to Doc's joining the committee in 2011, but for all their policy differences, the two developed a special bond. "When you're a member from the Pacific Northwest, it's kind of like being in a club," Doc said. DeFazio agreed. "We found common ties in working on Northwest issues. Doc and I worked on issues related to the Bonneville Power Administration and on the Columbia River Treaty, which is really a big deal."[38]

Their relationship allowed for good-natured banter and an occasional story at the other's expense, such as DeFazio told at the unveiling of Doc's official portrait on November 14, 2014. "Why did Doc have such an aversion to bills creating new wilderness areas?" he asked. "We didn't approve any of the eighty-nine [areas] that were introduced since Doc became chairman of the committee." He offered an explanation:

It goes back to his childhood, actually. It's something Doc doesn't like to talk about. Traumatic instances in our lives are often like that.

Doc was on a camping trip with his family when he was very young, and they were adjacent to a wilderness area. Doc wandered off and got lost. And so ever since then, Doc has had this kind of prejudice against unroaded areas.[39]

When several Republicans asked him if the story were true, De-Fazio replied: "Doc and I had a relationship where I could joke around like that with him. But it is true that no new wilderness bills were passed while Doc was chairman."[40]

In truth, it made little difference who the ranking member was. The committee's direction and agenda were solidly under Doc's control as chairman, and he had some priorities he wanted to address before he retired. Although he'd pushed a lot of legislation through his committee and through the House in the past session, his bills died—or weren't considered at all—by the Democratic Senate. Doc intended to dust off the legislation, reintroduce it in the next Congress, and have it ready to send to a Republican Senate and president after they won in 2016.

—

Doc's decision to retire at the end of his current term introduced a new sense of urgency and purpose into his final year as chairman of the committee. Doc and his staff redoubled their efforts to accomplish the remaining priorities that needed to be addressed before Doc retired. One of those was Hanford's historic B Reactor and the proposed Manhattan Project National Historical Park. Legislation had been introduced into both the House and the Senate in the previous session, but the session had ended before they could pass.

On March 7, 2013, senators Maria Cantwell and Lamar Alexander of Tennessee reintroduced their legislation creating the national park. A week later, Doc introduced similar legislation in the House. His committee would have jurisdiction over the bill.[41] On April 24, the bill passed out of the Natural Resources Committee. In May, it passed the Senate Energy and Natural Resources Committee with the help of its chairman, Ron Wyden, of Oregon, who was a supporter of the project, and Maria Cantwell. On June 15, the measure passed the House on a vote of 315 to 108. Assuming the Senate would pass authorizing legislation, Doc and Ron Wyden came up with a novel solution to fund the project. They would attach the park legislation to the separate versions of 2014 Defense Appropriations Act making their way through both houses of Congress.

Doc also included a provision that required DOE to transfer approximately 1,600 acres of Hanford land to Tri-Cities entities and provide limited access to Rattlesnake Mountain. On December 10, 2013, Doc and DeFazio toured Hanford while in town for a hearing on the Columbia River Treaty while the Senate considered its version of the bill. "I'm always cautiously optimistic. Sometimes the process slows down. We have to keep working it," Doc said.[42]

Tim Peckinpaugh believes that the three land access bills—the Manhattan Project National Historic Park, the Rattlesnake Mountain access, and the land transfer to the local community were among Doc's greatest legislative achievements and formed some of the most positive aspects of Doc's legislative legacy.[43]

—

But it was not to be—at least not in 2014. The Senate passed its version of the NDAA but excluding the national park provision. Two other paths remained to fund the project. The first was the conventional, but more uncertain, legislative path. The second, preferred alternative was to attach the park, the Rattlesnake Mountain access, and land transfer language to the new 2015 NDAA bill. The third time proved to be the charm, and all three provisions were included in the 2015 NDAA that was passed by the House and Senate in December 2014 and signed almost immediately by President Obama.

Peter DeFazio recalled how it happened, a story little known in the Tri-Cities: "There was a major public lands bill in the Senate that they wanted to insert into the NDAA, and so we negotiated from the House side, and Doc got the Manhattan Project National Historic Park for the B Reactor, and I got a badly needed expansion of the Oregon Caves National Monument."[44]

The Senate public lands bill included a twenty-two-thousand-acre expansion of the Alpine Lakes Wilderness in Eastern King County, which Doc had resisted in committee, just as he had most other new or expanded wilderness areas His resistance drew the ire of the Seattle newspapers, particularly the *Seattle-Post Intelligencer*, for several years.[45] Doc reluctantly agreed to the compromise that added the new national parks, wilderness areas, and heritage sites—the first lands-protection bills to be approved since 2009 and the most significant expansion of the national parks system in decades—in return for the three provisions.[46]

———

Another of Doc's remaining goals was passing his Cabin Fee Act. A previous version of the bill had passed the House in 2012 but was not considered in the Senate. On June 19, 2013, Doc tried again. This time, it passed both the Natural Resources Committee and the full House by unanimous consent, and it too was included in the 2015 NDAA.

———

Yet another of Doc's goals involved the Healthy Forests for Healthy Communities Act, which required each national forest to designate "forest revenue reserves" and set harvest volumes. Doc introduced his bill on April 12, 2013. Doc and the committee staff worked with DeFazio on the legislation to include a provision sought by DeFazio to manage Bureau of Land Management forest lands in Oregon (called "O&C" lands) as well as other provisions. It passed out of committee on November 17 and then passed the full House two days later by a vote of 244 to 173, with DeFazio and sixteen other House Democrats supporting it. The Senate did not act on the measure.

———

More unfinished business involved the federal response to the recurring California droughts. In 2012, Doc had introduced legislation to solve the problem that had been hammered out by the members of the California House delegation. It had passed by the House but was not taken up by the Senate. Legislation was introduced again at the beginning of the new session. On February 5, 2014, the House passed HR 3964, the Sacramento-San Joaquin Valley Emergency Water Delivery Act, which would restore badly needed water supplies to farmers and communities. Unfortunately, it stalled in the Senate again.

Frustrated, a giant rally was held in Fresno on March 19 to put pressure on the Senate. "We did our job; now you do your job!" he remembered telling the participants. "Pass a bill so we can go to conference!"

Doc's frustration with the Senate was palpable. "The House is passing legislation, and the Senate isn't," he told the Columbia Basin Badger Club in Pasco in March 2014. He was referring to the legislation to fend off the California water shortage, but he could have been talking about any number of bills that had gotten hung up in the Senate. "It takes two to tango," he said.[47] "Nothing got resolved before I left Congress," said Doc, recalling his frustration.[48]

—

Doc continued his long-standing objection to the Endangered Species Act (ESA) and was particularly critical of how the Obama administration ran the program. At a field hearing of the Natural Resources Committee held in Pasco on August 2, 2013, the subject was the White Bluffs bladderpod, a small yellow-flowering plant that, according to Fish and Wildlife Service studies, grew only on the northern slope of portions of Hanford Reach National Monument, as well as state and private farmland in Franklin County.

A year before, the Fish and Wildlife Service had proposed listing the species under the ESA without telling Franklin County or affected landowners. When locals learned about it, the local farmers worried that a government declaration of critical habitat on their land would result in restrictions on irrigation and land use. After Doc's intervention during the review and comment period, the government decided to implement its critical habitat declaration only on federally owned lands. Doc responded that the forty-year-old law needed reform. "I look forward to considering common-sense reforms to the ESA in the months ahead," he said.[49]

When a study did genetic testing on the bladderpod in Franklin County versus samples taken in Oregon and Idaho, it found them to be identical. A frustrated Doc Hastings remembered, "We brought that up at a committee hearing. I asked them, 'In view of that evidence, is that going to change your thinking?' And they said no! What are you going to do?"[50]

Doc stepped up the pressure on the agency, demanding that it turn over the unpublished data that the Fish and Wildlife Service used to justify the plant's listing, but it ignored the subpoena and finalized the listing and critical habitat designation in December 2013.

By early February 2013, Doc had assembled a group of thirteen Republicans who called for an update to the ESA, which had not been reauthorized since 1988. A year later in 2014, following a series of hearings, letters, and comments, they released a report proposing more than two dozen "targeted reforms" that included such things as more accurate economic impact studies, safeguards for private landowners, target population goals set up front to define "recovery" for delisting, and more transparency about the scientific data. "The way the act is written, there is more of an effort to list [species as endangered or threatened] than to delist," Doc claimed. Peter DeFazio told the *Yakima Herald-Republic* that he believed a balanced modernization of the law could probably find bipartisan support, but that was not what was in the Republicans' report:

> If this so-called report issued by a partisan task force is any indication, we will likely spend time debating legislation that will be cast as common-sense reforms, but will actually gut the law that has prevented the extinction of iconic American animas such as the bald eagle and the gray wolf. Because these "reforms" will only appeal to the radical, tea-party wing partisans, it will go nowhere in the Senate.[51]

On April 30, 2014, the committee approved four bills to improve and modernize the ESA, including requiring transparency of data and science used in federal listing decisions, ensuring that data from states, tribes and local governments was factored into ESA listing decisions, requiring federal government to track attorneys' fees paid as a result of ESA litigation, and capping the statutory reimbursable attorneys' fees for ESA litigation at the same rate that Social Security or veterans benefit litigants would recover from the government.

The committee approved HR 4315, the Endangered Species Transparency and Reasonableness Act. Field hearings were held in four states on steps needed to modernize the ESA. The legislation followed the reforms that had been recommended in the GOP task force report. The full House passed the legislation on July 29, 2014, with the support of several Democrats, but as Congressman DeFazio had predicted, it was not taken up by the Senate.[52]

—

Another area Doc and DeFazio agreed on was the potential negative impacts of renegotiating the 1964 Columbia River Treaty with Canada. The treaty was a result of the 1948 floods that had devastated the Tri-Cities and wiped out the city of Vanport in Oregon. At the time, the Columbia River dams had too little storage capacity to control the vast amount of water generated by an unusually harsh winter.

Doc and DeFazio reviewed a draft of American recommendations as the treaty approached the deadline for review, and they had concerns. In particular, Doc was worried about provisions that would expand the scope of the treaty to include protection of endangered species and climate change. Of even greater concern to both was their desire to reduce Canada's share of the hydropower that was produced downstream by American dams. On December 9, 2013, Doc and DeFazio organized a field hearing in Pasco to hear testimony.[53] Those concerns remained following the hearing. Formal negotiations to extend the treaty began in 2016.

—

Doc understandably devoted most of his time and effort to the Natural Resources Committee, but in his final term, he was named a member of the House Oversight and Government Reform Committee and participated in two notable hearings.

On May 8, 2013, the committee held a hearing into the attacks on the US diplomatic compound in Benghazi, Libya, in 2012 that resulted in the deaths of US ambassador Chris Stevens and three others. Carried out just weeks before the presidential election, the attacks were politicized almost immediately by Republican nominee Mitt Romney. In the year that followed, the incident became a highly partisan political issue. Republicans claimed the Obama administration had tried to cover up the causes of the attack and mistakes made during the attempted rescue, and Democrats reflexively defended Obama and then–secretary of state Hillary Clinton, the presumed Democratic presidential candidate in 2016.

At the hearing, the committee's attention focused on the testimony of Gregory Hicks, a career foreign service officer who was the chargé d'affaires of the US mission in Libya and one of thirty Americans that had escaped or been rescued. Hicks's testimony was thought to be critical of the administration's procedures to provide adequate safety for the diplomats in Benghazi, and Doc joined in the questioning, mostly clarifying points made earlier by Hicks. It was a high-visibility hearing on a politicized issue, but subsequent investigations revealed little could have been done differently to change the tragic outcome.[54]

Two weeks later Doc participated in another highly charged hearing involving the Internal Revenue Service. Following the disclosures in 2010 that the IRS had delayed processing applications for tax-exempt status by conservative political organizations, the director of the office, Lois Lerner, retired, and several internal investigations ensued. Following the release of the IRS inspector general's report, the Oversight Committee announced it would hold hearings on the matter.

On May 22, 2013, Lerner created a firestorm by pleading the Fifth Amendment after making a brief opening statement to the committee. Doc voted with the rest of the Republicans to hold her in contempt of Congress.[55] The full House agreed with the committee's action when the matter came before them, but the Justice Department determined she had not waived her constitutional rights by making her statement. Republicans used the issue to try to embarrass the Obama administration.

—

During his last term—and particularly during his last year in office—Doc and Claire took advantage of the opportunity to travel abroad on several CODELs to various parts of the world. Doc justified the trips on the basis that "you learn a lot of things on these trips so that when you have to make decisions, you have some idea of what's going on."[56]

On June 28, 2013, Doc and Claire joined an old friend, Senator Roger Wicker of Mississippi, on an eight-day CODEL to Turkey, Azerbaijan, and Hungary. Wicker had served in the House from 1995 to 2007 and was a 1995 classmate of Doc's. The two had become good friends. The trip was sponsored by the Commission on Security and Cooperation in Europe (CSCE), which was holding its annual meeting in Istanbul, Turkey. Four other members of Congress joined Doc and Wicker on the trip. Two stayed in Istanbul to attend the meeting, while Wicker, Doc, and Senator Mike Crapo of Idaho took a side trip to meet with US troops manning a Patriot missile battery and to hold a town hall meeting with refugees from the Syrian Civil War at a camp near Gaziantep on the Syrian border.

The next stop was Baku, Azerbaijan, the newly oil-rich country on the Caspian Sea in Central Asia. The country was a close ally of Israel's and surrounded by hostile neighbors like Russia and Iran. The final stop was Budapest, Hungary, to meet with leaders of the Hungarian Parliament. Claire spent the time sightseeing and sketching the sights of the historic city.

Between April 11 and April 20, 2014, Doc and Claire joined a large CODEL led by Speaker Boehner on a trip to the United Arab Emirates, Afghanistan, Turkey, and Portugal. In Abu Dhabi, the delegation had a private audience with a member of the Al Nahyan royal family. "It was a very interesting discussion because it showed me the divisions within the Arab world," Doc shared. "He was guarded, but frank. The UAE is probably our most valued ally in the Middle East."[57]

The wives stayed in Abu Dhabi while the delegation flew around Iran to Kabul, Afghanistan. They received high-level briefings from the American ambassador and General Joseph F. Dunford, the commander of all coalition troops in the country, before staying overnight and flying back to the UAE early the next morning. The next day they were off to Ankara, Turkey, for meetings with the Speaker of the Turkish Parliament and a meeting with the president of Turkey. They spent several days in

Istanbul and then fit in a quick stop in Lisbon, Portugal, before returning to the United States.

In early June, they visited Guam, Vietnam, and Singapore as a part of a CODEL led by John Kline, a congressman from Minnesota, who had also been on the trip to the Middle East. On Guam, Doc met with the governor, lunched with airmen at Anderson Field, and toured the THAAD anti-missile defense battery on the island. Then it was off to Hanoi, the capital of Vietnam, where Doc visited the famous Hanoi Hilton prison complex where American servicemen had been held during the Vietnam War. The trip concluded with a quick stop in Singapore.

Doc and Claire led their final CODEL to Australia and New Zealand in August. Seven other members and their wives joined them. In New Zealand, they visited a geo-nuclear power plant where water flowed from high-temperature geothermal fields with such force that it turned into steam to power the turbines. Doc was interested in the potential of such technology for producing power in the Rocky Mountain region.

They then flew to Darwin in Northern Australia, where they visited a plant producing helium gas as a by-product of the natural gas that was pumped from huge offshore deposits. Doc's interest had been sparked by the legislation he had co-sponsored to sell the US strategic helium reserve, which had allowed helium to find its market price and made it possible for this plant to be profitable. Doc was delighted: "Ed Markey and I developed legislation to sell off the US helium reserve and let the free market take its course, and here was a private company taking advantage of what we had done."[58] It was a rare example of Doc's being able to see his political philosophy play out in actual practice.

As Doc began his last term in office, he faced new problems at the Hanford Site. One of the single-shell underground nuclear waste tanks built during World War II was leaking several hundred gallons of liquid sludge a year. The automatic sequestration mandated by the Budget Control Act had kicked in as planned in March 2013, and 250 Hanford workers lost their jobs. DOE was so short of funds that it proposed transferring money from the Hanford Waste Treatment Plant's pre-treatment facility to other Hanford work or meeting critical needs at other cleanup sites because work on the pre-treatment facility was shut down due to technical issues.

Frustrated by DOE's lack of progress, Washington's governor, Jay Inslee, proposed a new set of deadlines that would amend the court-ordered consent decree issued in 2010. To no one's surprise, DOE announced in June that it would miss two of the environmental cleanup deadlines. DOE claimed the reason was Congress's failure to approve a budget for 2013. Doc claimed the reason was largely incompetence.[59] New testing had identified that at least six of the old single-wall tanks were now leaking. DOE's new secretary, Ernest Moniz, visited Hanford on June 19, saying he would have a new plan for Hanford cleanup by the end of summer.

Released in September, Moniz's plan recommended that some of Hanford's radioactive waste could be treated without sending it to the troubled pre-treatment plant. However, each alternative the plan suggested had added costs and regulatory problems. Doc was frustrated by the response and issued a statement: "DOE needs to provide information on the schedule and the cost for the report's recommendations and their effects on court-enforced deadlines."[60]

—

On August 13, 2013, Doc received good news. The US Court of Appeals ruled 2-1 that the Obama administration needed to respect the fact that Congress had designated Yucca Mountain, Nevada, as the site of the nation's nuclear waste repository. About ten billion dollars had been spent on preparing the site before the Nuclear Regulatory Commission discontinued its licensing process.[61]

—

By October, the government floundered in the middle of its self-inflicted budget crisis, and 2,300 Hanford workers were expected to be furloughed from their Hanford jobs. TRIDEC estimated that as many as nine thousand workers at Hanford and Pacific Northwest

National Laboratory could be sent home. Luckily, a budget compromise was reached on October 16, 2013, before many jobs were affected. Doc had not yet announced his retirement, but he must have looked forward to not having to put up with the annual funding and regulatory battles at Hanford anymore. Of course, he couldn't really escape them. His home on the Columbia River overlooked the Hanford Site to Rattlesnake Mountain, and he would be reminded of them every day.

—

Doc made one last attempt to improve water storage in the Yakima Basin before he retired. On February 5, 2014, he issued discussion drafts of three bills that required the federal government to set aside a fund for new and expanded water storage projects whose cost was beyond the financial capacity of the state and local authorities. Under his proposal, money would be taken from existing Bureau of Reclamation funds newly dedicated to general water storage projects in the Yakima Basin. "In these fiscal times, it is going to require creativity and new ideas to achieve needed water solutions," he said.[62] On June 18, Doc's bill was approved by the House Energy and Water Appropriations Committee, but again, the legislation failed to be considered by the Senate.

—

Another issue that remained up in the air was the continued need for agricultural research and trade assistance for farmers in Doc's district. The previous farm bill had expired in 2012. Efforts to craft a new one were hampered by bickering between Republicans in the House and between the House and the Senate.

On July 11, the House voted on a new farm bill that included crop subsidies and other farm benefits, but in an effort to mollify conservative Republicans, it excluded food stamps, which had been an important part of the legislation. Dozens of Republicans opposed their party and voted against the bill. Doc voted for it, saying the bill "made clear the House's commitment to farms, while working to bring fiscal sense to government."[62] But when the House bill arrived in the Senate, it replaced most of the House language with its own, which included the nutrition programs. The Senate passed its version of the bill by unanimous consent on July 18, and the bill went to conference. It authorized $958 billion to fund everything from food stamps to crop insurance over the next five years. It doubled funding for programs that benefited specialty crops like tree fruit, wine grapes, and hops. Doc claimed victory by saying the new bill "eliminates or consolidates more than one hundred programs and saves taxpayers twenty-three billion dollars of their hard-earned money."[64]

—

Doc and Claire had periodically talked about their life after Congress—just conjecture over a glass of wine—over the past two or three years. It became more serious after Doc was elected to his tenth term. He was seventy-two years old and would be seventy-four at the end of that term. It had been a great ride. He believed his presence in Congress had made a difference. He was happy with what his committee had achieved during his chairmanship.

But there had also been disappointments. The Republicans had been unable to implement their policy agenda under a president who ruled by executive order and a Senate controlled by Democrats. Doc would later say that President Obama's election in 2012 was his greatest disappointment during his time in office.[65] But he was speaking in political terms. His greatest personal disappointment in Congress was not becoming chairman of the Rules Committee. Looking back, he recalled, "Listen, on a personal note, sure, I would have liked to be chair of the Rules Committee. I spent twelve years there and felt that I was imminently qualified to do it."[66]

He would certainly not miss being alone during the week in Washington, DC, or the long, almost weekly cross-country flights back and forth to Pasco, a trip that averaged eight hours each way, counting the layovers in Salt Lake City or Minneapolis. That got old really fast, even if he did get upgraded to first class. In the old days, some members would pass the time with more than a few drinks, but that didn't work for Doc. Nor would he miss having to raise money for the next reelect—never one of his favorite activities.

He also believed the organization of the House could be improved, particularly in terms of the jurisdictions of the House committees. He had made that clear when he tried to engineer the transfer of the energy portfolio to his Natural Resources Committee. Many were concerned about the internal divisions within the Republican conference. Doc, not so much: "That didn't bother me. I viewed these differences as a matter of degree and tactics. Those were there for the whole twenty years I served in Congress. That didn't change. We're all Republicans, and our views are a lot closer to each other than they are to the Democrats.'"[67]

Doc spent almost a year considering his decision to retire without telling anyone. Then, just before he left for the 2013 Christmas recess, he called Todd Young, Jessica Gleason, and Jenny Gorski into his office and broke the news. Gorski recalled the meeting: "I didn't think Doc was going to tell us he was retiring when he wanted to meet. I was surprised and wanted him to think it over during the recess to make sure that was really what he wanted—not just a bad reaction to the government shutdown, which was so depressing."[68]

Jessica Gleason was working from home at that point, her twins just about one year old. Todd called and told her Doc wanted to talk with her. She said:

> [I] knew right away that he was either retiring or firing me—and the latter was the more unlikely.
>
> I always figured that at most it would be two more years. It was bittersweet news—happy for him but a loss for the people he represented, for Congress, and for those of us who were privileged enough to work with him for so long.
>
> My next thoughts were (1) relief we didn't have to raise more money and (2) how much of the stuff he wanted to get done and the bills he wanted to pass could we as staff get done for him before he actually retired.[69]

Todd Young, not surprisingly, thought of Doc's decision in terms of an opportunity to use his political capital to achieve his policy goals and pet projects while he still had the political capital to do so. Gorski explained: " Once you announce you're retiring, people start writing you off, and Todd wanted to make sure that we had everything moving full-speed ahead so that Doc could accomplish all he had set out [to do] for Central Washington. In that last year, Doc got a lot of legislative priorities signed into law."[70]

Doc held off making a formal announcement until he was in the district with his family at his side. He called a press conference on February 13, 2014, at the Pasco Best Western hotel. A photograph in the *Tri-City Herald* showed Doc and his family walking from his office to the hotel. Serving as congressman "had been a great privilege," Doc said and then framed his announcement in terms of his wife. "My wife has been the greatest pillar of support, and it will be twenty years, and if you add the eight years I was in the legislature, I think she deserves to have a husband that's here more often than not."[71]

Almost immediately, the comments started pouring in from friends, political supporters, and former adversaries. Jay Inslee, Doc's first opponent and Washington's new governor, issued a statement that said: "Despite the fact that we each beat the other once, we had a good working relationship, could enjoy a laugh together and swapped plenty of basketball tales. I appreciate Claire's contribution to this state too, and on behalf of all Washingtonians wish them both good luck in retirement."[72]

John Boehner noted the pending loss of one of his closest supporters in the House: "I'm grateful for Doc's service to our institution and our nation, and for his friendship and support throughout our many years together in the House."[73]

The papers carried extensive analyses of his past accomplishments and future legacy.

Those same papers and many of the district's voters had once written him off as a partisan cypher, a congressman of limited accomplishment because he was rarely seen on the national news. When he did break into the national spotlight, it was over his controversial leadership of the Ethics Committee. It was not until later—after he became the chairman of the Natural Resources Committee—that his growing clout began to draw national attention.

Others commented that for a fiscal conservative, Doc didn't mind spending billions of dollars a year on Hanford. But it was consistent with his political philosophy. The government had created the problem; it had an obligation to fix it. Spending more money now, if it could be spent in a steady and responsible manner, saved money in the future. Although he was a partisan Republican, he was pragmatic enough to know that some issues required bipartisanship to find the best solution.

Much of the strongest criticism levelled at him over the years came from environmentalists. His views that the Endangered Species Act was flawed and his belief that government lands ought to be used for the benefit of all the people who owned them had been formed before he was ever elected to Congress and never changed.

—

Doc's political hero and role model was Ronald Reagan, and if he lacked the Gipper's talent for turning a phrase, he shared his small-town, business-friendly, positive view of America, its people, and its future. John DeVaney, one of Doc's former staffers, now a successful association executive, commented on Doc's similarities to Reagan:

> Like Reagan, Doc had thought deeply about his political philosophy and knew what he wanted to accomplish, where he stood on issues, and why. It was this more intellectual and ideological approach to politics that was sometimes mistaken as political rigidity. I think this view is mistaken.
>
> Too many elected officials know only that they want to be elected officials and have some vague tribal affiliation with one party or the other. This kind of legislator will often take one side of an issue based on what their opponents are doing—if they're for it, I must be against it.

Doc was different. His political beliefs were firmly rooted in his personal values and what he believed was best for the country, making them very hard to change.

> The fact that Doc had thought about what he wanted to accomplish, and knew what he could and couldn't accept, meant that he was open to working with anyone and everyone on areas of common interest. It meant that he could strike principled compromises, because he knew what was negotiable and what was, for him, a matter of principle.
>
> By the end of his time in Congress, he was often being criticized by those on the right, not for any policy differences, but because he wasn't spending enough time counting coup on TV and on radio talk shows.[74]

Doc was an institutionalist, deeply respectful of the traditions of the House. He felt a keen sense of honor every time he was given the opportunity to preside over the House. Doc was always willing to take on the tough assignments. Some ascribed it to his loyalty to his Republican leadership. One of his early staff members, Jeff Markey, saw it differently:

> He played an important role in the institution. Not because he was always in the public eye, but because he wasn't. Perhaps because he had the good fortune to represent a safe seat, he willingly agreed to take on the hard jobs that no one else wanted to do, with fairness and generally without controversy.[75]

—

While Doc's political views and the way he approached his job changed little, if at all, during the time he served in Congress, the politics of those who served around him— particularly the newer members of the Republican conference—had changed considerably. When Doc was first elected to Congress in 1994 as a part of Newt Gingrich's Republican Revolution, he was a part of a new influx of conservative Republicans. Even as late as 2009, the National Journal rated him as the seventy-second most conservative member of the House. Four years later, the magazine rated 103 of Doc's Republican colleagues as being more conservative.[76]

—

Naturally, speculation abounded concerning Doc's successor. By the end of the filing period on May 16, 2014, a dozen congressional hopefuls had filed for Doc's seat, including one Independent, two Democrats, and nine Republicans. With Washington's unusual top-two primary system, the race boiled down to Sunnyside farmer, former state legislator, and state Department of Agriculture director Dan Newhouse and Eltopia farmer and Tea Party favorite Clint Didier, a former tight end for the Washington Redskins. Doc withheld his endorsement of Newhouse until it could be used to maximum advantage, given the fact that Didier had outpolled Newhouse in the Republican primary. With Doc's endorsement in hand, Newhouse went on to defeat Didier in a tough and spirited election.

—

Doc enjoyed some special occasions that marked the end of his congressional career. A longstanding tradition in Congress is that departing committee chairs donate a portrait of themselves so their leadership could be remembered in future years. Many such portraits hang on the walls of their main or subcommittee hearing rooms or, as in the case of some of the older committees dating back to the nineteenth century, in the library or committee offices.

On November 19, 2014, Doc, his family and friends, members of the leadership, other members of Congress, and his congressional and committee staffs gathered near the dais in the Natural Resources Committee Room for the formal unveiling of Doc's official portrait, some fellowship, and a little Washington wine.

Claire had selected the artist, Michele Rushworth, who lived on Camano Island in Washington State, after reviewing her portraits of former Washington governors Gary Locke and Christine Gregoire. The portrait was of Doc sitting, surrounded by symbols of his legislation career—a bust of Ronald Reagan, for whom Doc was a delegate in 1976, his

1994 Contract with America class ring, and the committee chairman's gavel his staff had given him.

Congresswoman Cathy McMorris Rogers, the chairman of the Republican conference, served as the master of ceremonies. She kept the event light and informal, recognized Doc's family, and mentioned that Doc was not above counselling her when she made a mistake when chairing the conference meetings. She was followed by ranking member Peter DeFazio, who got a laugh with his "Doc getting lost in the wilderness" story.

Then, it was John Boehner's turn to accept the portrait on behalf of Congress. He thanked Ed Cassidy, who had worked for both of them, and kidded Claire about the color of her hair. Then, he discussed Doc's contributions to the House:

> Now, here is a guy who never asks for anything. He only asks to help. He will do all the tough stuff, the thankless tasks, whatever it takes.
>
> You know, we needed somebody to be the Ethics Committee chairman, really at a time, really the most awful time over the last twenty years, and, of course, Doc was there to take on the job. We needed somebody on Rules who knew what they were doing, and so I want[ed] and got Doc. You need somebody to preside over a tough debate on the floor of the House—we [would] go get Doc. And so now after coming here to work on the issues that he deeply cares about, Doc begins a retirement that he so richly deserves and has earned.

Boehner unsuccessfully fought back tears as he said:

> And that means we are going to have to figure out how in the hell to run this place without you.

But all of you know how I can get [beginning to cry]. Doc's a good guy and, kind of like everything that is right about public service, right here.

You know, he has had a long political career. He is a decent guy; [he's] done a good job. Doc, it has been an honor to serve with you, and now these official words: it is my honor to accept your portrait into the House collection.[77]

Visibly moved, Doc embraced the Speaker as Cathy McMorris Rogers interjected a bit of humor, saying, "Yeah, leave it to the Speaker to make us cry!"[78]

Finally, the majority leader, Kevin McCarthy of California, told a story about Doc's skill as a politician. McCarthy had a dinner group—a diverse selection of older and younger members, along with some committee chairs—which met periodically to touch base about the mood and potential strategy of the Republican conference. It fell to McCarthy to pay for it, and he noted that, somehow, they (referring to Doc) always ended up drinking Washington instead of California wines.

Doc's remarks were short and heartfelt. He thanked his family, particularly his two brothers, Robert and Regan, who had travelled there, and then, characteristically, he thanked his staff: "Whatever success I have had . . . wouldn't have happened were it not for the staff . . . that I have had over the years. I am blessed to have staff that have stayed with me for a long time, and I know I have told you hopefully enough times that I know that. I really appreciate the work you do. I get to have the portrait, but I know where all the hard work came from.

Showing a flash of his sense of humor, he quipped about how the portrait had been paid for by voluntary contributions from industries that had business before his committee and from his left-over campaign war chest: "I find it very ironic that you give money to a fund that I pay for, for a portrait of me that I turn back to the government. That is somewhat contrary to what I thought government was all about.[79]

—

On April 10, 2014, Doc was presiding over the House during the debate over the concurrent resolution on the 2015 budget, as he had often done before. Toward the end of the debate, there was a short recess to allow the members to return to the floor for the final vote. Doc recognized Paul Ryan, the chairman of the Budget Committee, who rose to say:

> Mr. Speaker, I yield myself the balance of the time. Let me first start off by saying, Mr. Chairman [addressing his remarks to Doc Hastings], that you have presided over this budget [resolution] for many years. You have set a great example for the rest of us. This is your last year serving, and I want to thank you for what you have done for this institution. Thank you for setting such a great example.[80]

The House assembled, stood, and gave Doc a rousing round of applause.

—

The local weather was partly cloudy with temperatures in the mid-fifties on December 10, 2014, better-than-normal weather for nation's capital on a mid-winter day. Unfortunately, the members of the House were unable to enjoy it. They spent the long day considering homeland security legislation and the early evening listening to an extended tribute to California Democrat Henry Waxman who was retiring. It was getting late when Cathy McMorris Rogers, Washington congresswoman and Republican conference chairman, requested an hour's time under a Special Order to honor Doc Hastings who had also announced his retirement.

Beyond the normal kind of compliments people say on such occasions, McMorris Rogers related a personal anecdote about the first time she had returned to the floor of the House with her newborn baby boy who had recently been diagnosed with Down syndrome. Doc had asked to be recognized to welcome her back to the House and to introduce her son, Cole, to the members.

Hal Rogers of Kentucky, the chairman of the House Appropriations Committee and a close friend of Doc's, rose to say that there was nobody more knowledgeable about politics than Doc: "He knows every congressional district. He knows the politics of that district, and that makes for some great, great conversation. But I think the most important thing that I could say about Doc Hastings is about his character, the character that he possesses. Someone once said, 'Character is doing what's right when no one is looking.'"[80]

Newly elected Washington Democrat Denny Heck and Republican Jaime Herrera Buetler added their own kind words. Heck had served with Doc in the Washington legislature and said that Doc had been the first member to visit his office when he arrived in Washington, DC. Buetler, Washington's Third District congresswoman, said she would never forget how Doc had willingly provided advice every time she asked for it. She recounted one of Doc's favorite quotes: "It is amazing what you can accomplish if you are not worried about who gets the credit."[81]

Doc sat there, listening to the comments with mixed emotions of embarrassment, appreciation, and maybe more than a little pride because he knew that at least some of what they were saying about him was true.

—

The final incident occurred on December 11, 2014, late at night, when the 113th Congress was getting ready to adjourn. The last vote of the evening was on a motion to suspend the rules and pass the John Muir National Historic Site Expansion Act, sponsored by Doc's old adversary George Miller of California. By prior agreement, Doc left the dais before the vote was concluded, and another member assumed his place.

Earlier in the evening, Doc had found Speaker John Boehner at his normal place on the left side of the chamber and asked him if he would be hosting members for a glass of wine in his office after the session ended, as was his custom. Boehner answered, "Sure."

After leaving the dais, Doc walked to the Speaker's office, where he found the Speaker and several other members conversing about the close of the session and enjoying a glass of wine. As the others left, one by one, it finally became Doc's turn to say goodbye. He shook Boehner's hand, left the office, and walked back toward the House Chamber through Statuary Hall, which had been the location of the original House Chamber. Doc was all alone. His footsteps on the marble floor echoed throughout the empty hall. He thought to himself, "You know, I may be walking out of here for the last time."[82]

As Doc approached the House Chamber, he made a right, then a left, and then another right, arriving at the elevators, which took him down to the sub-basement of the Capitol. He walked through security to where the tram normally transported members to the Rayburn House Office Building. It was not running that late at night, so he walked through the tunnel to the Rayburn Building basement and into the parking garage where his car was parked. He drove through the dark night across the Potomac River on I-395 to his condominium in Pentagon City.

Several days later, Doc was back home in Pasco.

EPILOGUE

★

DOC HASTINGS RETIRED TO HIS HOME on the Columbia River, where the view from his deck looks out over the Hanford Site and the sun sets behind Rattlesnake Mountain in the west. He's been working on improving his golf score with old friends and political supporters.

On October 14, 2015, about seventy-five people joined Doc and his family at the dedication of an interactive display of his congressional memorabilia, including his desk, office door plaque, member's pin, voting card, and committee gavel, at the Franklin County Historical Society in Pasco.[1]

A month later, he joined Senator Maria Cantwell, National Park Service officials, community leaders, and local schoolchildren as they helped to raise the National Park Service's flag above the historic B Reactor for the first time. Cantwell was impressed that Doc had cared enough to attend the ceremony. "He could easily have said, 'I'm not involved in this anymore,' but he came, and you could really see that he cared about the history and the legacy of the region."[2]

On February 3, 2016, DOE and local officials signed the documents transferring 1,631 acres of the Hanford Site over to local control, one of the three major land bills involving Hanford that had passed during his last year in office. A year later, the French solar energy company Neoen announced plans to build a twenty megawatt solar power installation on one hundred of the three hundred acres of property the community received from DOE next to the Columbia Generating Station.[3]

Doc remained intensely interested in the federal government's relationship with the region he once represented. He joined a group that is advocating for the return of thirty-four miles of Columbia River shoreline to local Tri-Cities governments. The Corps of Engineers acquired the land after the 1948 flood and during the construction of McNary Dam for flood control purposes. Since then, the government has largely thwarted local efforts to improve the riverfront while the communities pay out hundreds of thousands of dollars each year to maintain some of it as public parks.

Doc, TRIDEC, the regional economic development entity, and the local communities argued that returning the valuable shore land to local control would improve access and recreation, allow for planned development, and give local jurisdictions control over one of their most important assets.[4] With Doc's urging, Congress mandated that the Corps release data on how it acquired the land and what it paid for it. When the data was released on June 13, 2017, local leaders said it was incomplete, but Doc is optimistic the issue may be resolved soon.[5]

Doc continued his ongoing battle with environmentalists, Indian tribes, and federal judges in Oregon to save the lower Snake River dams. In May 2016, Michael Simon, the US District Court judge who replaced retired judge James Redden, issued an opinion that sided with fishing groups, environmentalists, the state of Oregon, and the Nez Perce tribe in finding the latest federal plan to protect endangered species of Columbia River salmon was inadequate. He ordered the Army Corps of Engineers to prepare a new one by early 2018. Representatives Cathy McMorris Rogers and Dan Newhouse have introduced legislation directing the Corps to maintain the current salmon protection plan until 2022.[6]

Two issues that clearly won't be resolved anytime soon are the cleanup of the Hanford Site and a long-term resolution of the Yakima Basin water storage problem. Over the next five years, DOE will be entering into another round of rebidding of the major contracts at Hanford. DOE has set a goal of starting to process low-activity radioactive waste at the Hanford Waste Treatment Plant by 2022, and the current, court-enforced deadline for processing high-level nuclear waste is 2036. Deadlines have come and gone in the past. Local parties, formerly at odds with each other, have come together to support the he Yakima Basin Integrated Plan, a $4 billion combination of water storage and conservation, improved fish passage, habitat restoration and other initiatives. But while the state of Washington has committed over $130 million in funding for the plan, complete implementation depends on federal funding, which has remained elusive.

One activity that Doc certainly didn't anticipate in retirement was any more involvement with congressional ethics—probably the most difficult experience of his congressional career—but when the call came to serve, he again answered it.

The Office of Congressional Ethics (OCE) had been created by the House Democratic leadership in 2008 to supplement the work of the House Ethics Committee, which they thought had been too protective of Republicans under Doc's chairmanship. At the time, Doc and every other Republican voted against the creation of the OCE, but the Democrats prevailed. Unlike the Ethics Committee, the OCE is authorized to investigate allegations of misconduct from any source and, if they are considered to be serious enough, to refer them to the Ethics Committee for disposition. OCE consists of four members and two alternates, appointed equally from each party, plus a professional investigative staff. Two members, one from each party, serve as co-chairs. Current members of Congress and lobbyists are excluded, but former members are allowed to serve.

In the years that followed, OCE operated largely under the radar screen, as had been intended. In 2015, before he resigned as Speaker, John Boehner nominated Doc to serve as one of the co-chairs. "I didn't seek the position, but he asked, and I felt obligated to accept," Doc recalled.[7] Doc later learned that minority leader Nancy Pelosi had objected to him on the grounds that he had engaged in "hyper-partisan" behavior when he had chaired the Ethics Committee while still in Congress.[8] Doc believed that issue had gone away.

Then, in late 2016, as the majority Republicans organized the 115th Congress, they once again reviewed the issue and created a new rule that substituted the word "consult" for "concur" in the selection of new OCE chairpersons and members, meaning that one party only had to tell the other whom it intended to appoint, rather than obtain its approval. At that point, the new Speaker, Paul Ryan, contacted Doc and asked him again to serve as OCE's co-chair. On February 15, 2017, Speaker Ryan announced that Doc had agreed to become the Republican co-chair of the committee. Once again, Doc had agreed to accept the more or less thankless task. Characteristically, he noted he had not sought the post. "If the Speaker felt that I was able to do that, then I was proud to say I would," Doc said.[9] He has since resumed his long, eight- to ten-hour flights back and forth to Washington, DC, but on a monthly basis instead of a weekly one.

As this book was going to press, a nationwide flood of allegations of sexual impropriety surfaced against well-known entertainment and network news figures, corporate executives, and not surprisingly, members and potential members of Congress. Sexual abuse by powerful people is nothing new. It has been going on forever and has certainly been a staple of cocktail hour speculation in Washington, DC, and elsewhere. But it now appears that public attitudes may be changing in the way that such allegations are received and addressed—yet another of the cultural shifts our nation has experienced in recent decades. Doc will almost certainly be involved with some of these matters as the co-chairman of the OCE.

IT WAS DIFFICULT TO SEPARATE cause and effect, but the widening of America's partisan divide—the result of more than twenty years of nearly endless political controversy—was clear enough. In Congress, it had become more difficult—often impossible—for the two parties to compromise when trying to pass key legislation. In an attempt to break the impasse, voters changed the political composition of the body in three national wave elections in 1994, 2006, and 2010.

After each new wave election, the majority party overreached in passing key parts of its policy agenda over the nearly united opposition of the other party—because it could. Unrewarded by success, both parties searched within themselves for solutions amid a mutual identity crises in which the Democrats moved farther to the left and the Republicans moved farther to the right. By the close of 2017, the tribal nature of the political divide had become so intense that many Republicans claimed they would prefer to vote for an accused child molester than to vote for a Democrat in a special election for a US Senate seat from Alabama.[10]

Two years after Doc Hastings left office, another national election was held. A record seventeen Republican candidates competed in the various debates held during the 2016 presidential campaign. An even dozen of them went on to compete in the primaries. The Republicans' record of overpromising and under-delivering ultimately enabled Donald J. Trump, a real estate developer and reality-TV star—a man with no governmental experience and with serious questions about his personal character and business integrity—to bully and bluster his way past his ineffectual opposition to win his party's nomination and then the presidency in a victory that few, including Trump, believed was possible to win.

Trump won by taking advantage of the voters' disdain for the past performance of both major parties. Trump employed a kind of reverse identity politics, promoting a populist-nationalist agenda that spoke to the needs and fears of mostly white voters who felt they had been left behind, "flown over," and ignored. A gifted salesman, Trump convinced them he alone could "make America great again."

In a campaign that featured two candidates with the lowest voter approval ratings in history, Trump defeated Hillary Clinton, whose traditional campaign was run as if she were entitled to the victory. At a time when many were still reeling from the Great Recession, she failed to mount an economic argument for why she should be elected. Still, she beat Trump by three million in the popular vote, but he carried the most states and, therefore, won victory in the Electoral College.

As this book is being written, Trump has proven to be as unorthodox a president as he was a candidate—the ultimate disrupter—with his resulting public approval ratings hovering somewhere in the high 30 percent range, the lowest of any president in history at this point in his presidency.[11] A federal Special Counsel and at least four congressional committees are investigating the involvement of the Russian government in the election, and at least two grand juries have been impaneled to look into the matter.[12]

The Republican Party, split apart by internal factions, has been unable to pass the national agenda it has advocated for the past seven years, even though it controls both houses of Congress and the presidency. On December 20, 2017, the Republican Congress successfully passed a massive tax bill, which had been rushed to consideration—its major legislative achievement of the year. It passed the House with no Democrats voting for it and a dozen GOP members voting against it and passed the Senate along straight party lines using the same process of reconciliation the Democrats had used to pass the Affordable Care Act.[13]

The Democratic Party is equally immobilized, still relitigating and recovering from its 2016 election loses. It remains to be seen if Trump's lack of popularity and the internal conflicts within the Republican Party will result in another wave election in 2018.

In a strange way, Donald Trump's presidency may be what is needed to disrupt the partisan divide and force both parties to find ways of working together for the common good.

In the days and months following the announcement of his retirement, Doc received scores of calls, notes, and letters from members of Congress, cabinet members, friends, and constituents. He kept each of them, just as he had others he had received over the years. Tom Cole, who had assumed J. C. Watts's Oklahoma House seat, was and is the chairman of a House Appropriations Subcommittee. His note reflected the thoughts of many of Doc's Republican colleagues:

> While I respect your decision to leave the House at the end of this session, I want to let you know how much I will miss serving with you. You're a remarkable member—principled, thoughtful, civil, and [a] credit to our country, the House, and our party. If there were more people like you in the House, America would be better off.[14]

And, as a reminder that the House of Representatives is a melting pot of differing political beliefs and viewpoints, Democrat Raúl Grijalva of Arizona, a member of the Natural Resources Committee, sent a simple note along with a parting gift for Claire because his Tucson district included the area in which she had lived and gone to high school: "Enjoy your lives and be proud of your work (and know, someone like me is always here trying to undo it). Peace, my friend."[15] Almost three years after Doc left the Capitol Building late at night on December 11, 2014, he has had time for introspection. Often asked to evaluate his time and accomplishments in office, he has given a lot of thought to his answer, which rarely varies:

> I always considered it a privilege to serve the district that I represented, simply because I was a member of a pretty unique club—four hundred and thirty-five out of a population of over three hundred million—for a given two-year period.
>
> As far as accomplishments are concerned, each term is different with different challenges. I'll leave it to others to make that determination. The bottom line is that I had the privilege of serving in Congress for twenty years and eight years in the legislature before that, representing the views of the people who elected me. It was an honor and a responsibility that I took very seriously, and from my point of view, I think I was successful in that effort.[16]

APPENDIX A

Washington State Congressional District Boundaries, 1993–2013

Fourth District, 1993–2002

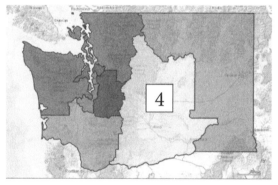

Fourth District, 2003–2013

Fourth District, 2003 to present

Source: https://en.wikipedia.org/wiki/Washington%27s_congressional_districts.

APPENDIX B

Representatives of Washington's Fourth District, 1915–2017

William LaFollette	R	**March 4, 1915–March 3, 1919 Served in Congress from March 4, 1911. Redistricted from WA-3.**
John William Summers	R	**March 4, 1919–March 3, 1933**
Knute Hill	D	March 4, 1933–January 3, 1943
Hal Holmes	R	**January 4, 1943–January 3, 1959**
Catherine Dean May	R	**January 4, 1959–January 3, 1971**
Mike McCormack	D	January 4, 1971–January 3, 1981
Sid Morrison	R	**January 4, 1981–January 3, 1993**
Jay Inslee	D	January 4, 1993–January 3, 1995
Doc Hastings	R	**January 4, 1995–January 3, 2015**
Dan Newhouse	R	**January 4, 2015–present**

Source: https://en.wikipedia.org/wiki/Washington%27s_4th_congressional_district.

APPENDIX C

Presidents of the United States, 1932–2017

Franklin D. Roosevelt   D   March 4, 1932–April 12, 1945
Died in office

Harry S. Truman   D   April 12, 1945–January 20, 1953

Dwight D. Eisenhower   R   January 20, 1953–January 20, 1961

John F. Kennedy   D   January 20, 1961–November 22, 1963
Died in office

Lyndon Johnson   D   November 22, 1963–January 20, 1969

**Richard M. Nixon   R   January 20, 1969–August 9, 1974
Resigned from office**

Gerald R. Ford   R   August 9, 1974–January 20, 1977

Ronald Reagan   R   January 20, 1977–January 20, 1989

George H. W. Bush   R   January 20, 1989–January 20, 1993

Bill Clinton   D   January 20, 1993–January 20, 2001

George W. Bush   R   January 20, 2001–January 20, 2009

Barack Obama   D   January 20, 2009–January 20, 2017

Source: https://en.wikipedia.org/wiki/President_of_the_United_States

APPENDIX D

Partisan Representation in Congress, 1995–2017

House				Senate			
104th Congress (1995–1997)							
Democrats		Republicans	Other	Democrats		Republicans	Other
204		230	+54	1	47		53	+10	

105th Congress (1997–1999)							
207	+3	226		2	45		55	+2	

106th Congress (1999–2001)							
211	+4	223		1	45		55		

107th Congress (2001–2003)							
212	+1	221		2	50	+4	50–49		1[1]

108th Congress (2003–2005)							
205		229	+7	1	48		51	+2	1

109th Congress (2005–2007)							
202		231	+2	1	44		55	+4	1

110th Congress (2007–2009)							
236	+34	199			49	+4	49		2

111th Congress (2009–2011)							
257	+21	178			56–58	+7	40–42		2

112th Congress (2011–2013)							
193		242	+64		51		47	+5	2

113th Congress (2013–2015)							
201	+8	234			53	+2	45		2

114th Congress (2015–2017)							
188		247	+13		44		54	+9	2

[1] Independent candidates caucus with the Democrats

Source: https://en.wikipedia.org/wiki/Party_divisions_of_United_States_Congresses

APPENDIX E

Voter Outcomes in Washington's Fourth District, 1994 to 2012

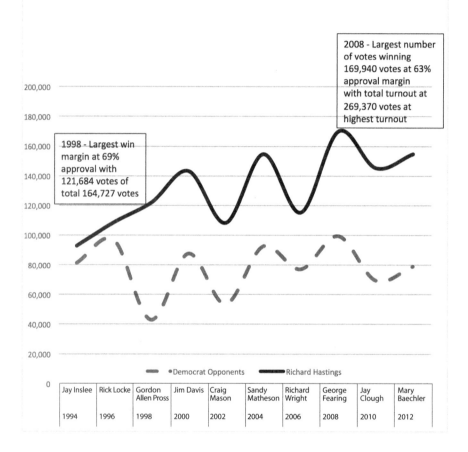

Source: Washington Secretary of State

APPENDIX F

Congressional and Presidential Approval Ratings Compared to Doc Hastings Election Results, 1994–2012

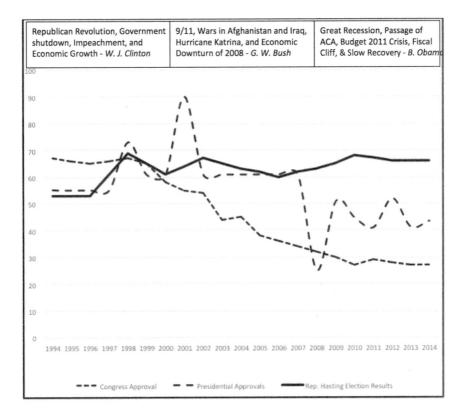

| Republican Revolution, Government shutdown, Impeachment, and Economic Growth - *W. J. Clinton* | 9/11, Wars in Afghanistan and Iraq, Hurricane Katrina, and Economic Downturn of 2008 - *G. W. Bush* | Great Recession, Passage of ACA, Budget 2011 Crisis, Fiscal Cliff, & Slow Recovery - *B. Obama* |

Sources: Gallup Polls, Approval ratings for President W. J. Clinton, G. W. Bush, and B. Obama, 1992 to 2016. Averages for each term are shown between congressional election years.

Washington State Election Results, US Congressional District 4, 1994 to 2012. Percentage averages are shown in odd-numbered non-election years. Rep. Hastings won with 53% of the votes in 1994, then 69% in 1998, and finally 66% in 2012.

Pew Trust Surveys through 2015 reflect the approval ratings of Congress from 1994 to 2014, from 67% in 1994 to 27% in 2012.

NOTES

Introduction

1. Washington State Legislature, Members of the Washington State Legislature 1889-2014 (Olympia, WA: Legislative Information Center, 2014). http://leg. wa.gov/History/Legislative/Documents/MembersOfLeg2014.pdf

2. "Washington 4th District," *2012 Census of Agriculture, Congressional District Profile*, February 21, 2016, http://www.agcensus.usda.gov/Publications/2012/ Online_Resources/Congressional_District_Profiles/cd5304.pdf.

3. US Census Bureau, Population Estimates for Counties by Race and Hispanic Origin, June 1, 1994.

4. US Census Bureau, Population Estimates for Counties by Race and Hispanic Origin, June 1, 1994; Population Estimates, Current Estimates, Data for Counties by Age, Sex, Race and Hispanic Origin, July 1, 2014; Fast Facts for Congress, 2014 American Community Survey 1-Year Estimates, February 11 and 20, 2016, http://www.census.gov/fastfacts.

5. 1994 Estimate extrapolated from 1990 and 2000 Census, Fast Facts for Congress, 2014 American Community Survey 1-Year Estimates, February 20, 2016, http://www.census.gov/fastfacts.

6. "Views of Race Relations," Pew Research Center, June 27, 2016, accessed September 25, 2017, http://www.pewsocialtrends.org/2016/06/27/2-views-of-race-relations.

7. "Partisanship and Political Animosity in 2016," Pew Research Center, June 22, 2016, accessed September 25, 2017, http://www.people-press.org/2016/06/22/ partisanship-and-political-animosity-in-2016.

8. Carol Doherty, "7 things to know about polarization in America," *Pew Research Center*, June 12, 2014, accessed August 18, 2017, http://www.pewresearch.org/ fact-tank/2014/06/12/7-things-to-know-about-polarization-in-america.

9. Dictionary.com defines gerrymandering as "the dividing of a state, county, etc., into election districts so as to give one political party a majority in many districts while concentrating the voting strength of the other party into as few districts as possible." The name comes from Massachusetts governor Elbridge Gerry whose party redistricted the state in 1812.

10. Doc Hastings, interview by the author, March 8, 2016.

Chapter 1

1. Timothy Egan, *Breaking Blue* (Seattle: Sasquatch Books, Reprint Edition, 2004).

2. *Great Depression*, video, 2:55, December 15, 2008, accessed March 21, 2016, http://www.spokesman.com/video/2008/dec/15/great-depression.

3. Ester M. J. Froistad, "Family Chronicle" (Mukilteo, WA: self-published, 1976).

4. Ibid., 25.

5. "A Look at the 1940 Census," *US Census Bureau*, March 31, 2016, https://www.census.gov/newsroom/cspan/1940census/CSPAN_1940slides.pdf.

6. Melissa O'Neil, "Businesses Grew with Mid-Columbia," *Tri-City Herald*, August 16, 1997, A3.

7. Ibid.

8. Click Relander, *Drummers and Dreamers*, paperback ed. (Seattle: Northwest Interpretive Association, 1986), 296.

9. Gary E. Moulton, ed., *The Journals of Lewis & Clark Expedition*, 12 volumes (Lincoln, NE: University of Nebraska Press, 1883-2001), 5:276-277.

10. "Ainsworth, Washington," February 15, 2016, https://en.wikipedia.org/wiki/Ainsworth,_Washington; "Franklin County," April 2, 2016, https://www.sos.wa.gov/legacy/cities_detail.aspx?i=34.

11. "1880s!" *Washington State Railroads Historical Society*, April 3, 2016, http://www.wsrhs.org/date1880s.htm.

12. Walter A. Oberst, *Railroads, Reclamation and the River: A History of Pasco* (Pasco, WA: Franklin Country Historical Society, 1978), 102.

13. Harry Thayer, *Management of the Hanford Engineering Works in World War II* (New York: ASCE Press, 1996), 16.

Chapter 2

1. Dallas Barnes, interview by the author, April 28, 2016.

2. Paul Rogat Loeb, *Nuclear Culture: Living and Working in the World's Largest Atomic Complex* (Gabriola Island, BC, Canada: New Society Publishers, 1986), 122-123.

3. C. Mark Smith, *Community Godfather: How Sam Volpentest Shaped the History of Hanford and the Tri-Cities* (Richland, WA: Etcetera Press, 2013), 59-60; Elizabeth Gibson, "Flood inundates Kennewick and Richland on May 31, 1948," March 31, 2004, accessed April 7, 2016, http://www.historylink.org/index.cfm?DisplayPage=output.cfm&file_id=5675.

4. Judy Mosebar, interview by the author, April 5, 2016.

5. Ibid.

6. Doc Hastings, interview by the author, March 24, 2016.

7. Ibid.

8. Doc and Claire Hastings, interview by the author, May 24, 2016.

9. Roger Hastings, interview by the author, April 11, 2016.

10. LaMar Palmer, interview by the author, April 13, 2016.

11. Ibid.

12. Doc and Claire Hastings, interview, May 24, 2016.

13. Ibid.

14. Janice and George Ling, interview by the author, April 14, 2016.

15. Ibid.

16. Ibid.

17. Linda Yamauchi Atkinson, interview by the author, April 14, 2016.

18. "Yen from 1890s Found behind Mural in Demolished Pasco Building," *Tri-City Herald* online, December 10, 2014, accessed April 24, 2016, http://www.tri-city herald.com/latest-news/article32208789.html.

19. Ibid.

20. Palmer, interview.

21. Barnes, interview.

22. Ling, interview.

23. Roger Hastings, interview, April 11, 2016.

24. Ibid.

25. Ibid.

26. Roger Hastings, interview, April 11 and May 25, 2016.

27. Ron Grey, interview by the author, April 29, 2016.

28. Duane Taber, interview by the author, April 25, 2016.

29. Harry S. Truman, Public Papers of the President, May 10, 1950, accessed March 3, 2017, https://books.google.com/books?id=AzzeAwAAQBAJ&pg=PA355&lp-g=PA355&dq=harry+truman+dedicates+pasco+elks+lodge+in+1950&-source=bl&ots=phcJ0CnAVJ&sig=XVWoluAwYZ8DrlWmgJgNYEG7QA-A&hl=en&sa=X&ved=0ahUKEwjx2Iy0u7vSAhVK72MKHbMlB2MQ6AEI-HjAB#v=onepage&q=harry%20truman%20dedicates%20pasco%20elks%20lodge%20in%201950&f=false.

30. Taber, interview.

31. Petrina Hastings Zusy, interview by the author, July 12, 2016.

32. Roger Hastings, email to the author, July 17, 2016.

33. Roger Hastings, email to the author, July 18, 2016.

34. Atkinson, interview.

35. Ling, interview.

36. Mosebar, interview.

37. Ibid.

38. Barnes, interview.

39. Doc and Claire Hastings, interview, April 19, 2016.

40. Ibid.

41. Grey, interview.

42. Ibid.

43. Claire Hastings, interview by the author, April 7, 2016.

44. Doc and Claire Hastings, interview by the author, May 12, 2016.

Chapter 3

1. "New Mail Center Will Be in Pasco," *Tri-City Herald*, January 14, 1964, 1.

2. Brad Saunders, "The Town That Wouldn't Die," *Pageant Magazine,* February 1971, 139.

3. Roger Hastings, interview by the author, May 2, 2016.

4. Doc and Claire Hastings, interview, April 19, 2016.

5. Sharlyn Berger, interview by the author, June 29, 2016.

6. Doc and Claire Hastings, interview by the author, April 7, 2016.

7. Doc and Claire Hastings, interview, April 19, 2016.

8. Ibid.

9. Ibid.

10. George W. Scott, a very perceptive historian who served for fourteen years as a representative and senator in the Washington legislature, described this phenomenon in his book, *A Majority of One: Legislative Life.* "Politics fascinates because it is literally larger than life otherwise lived. Are you excited by overload? Imagine a new scenario every hour. Do you want to look beyond your class . . . and rub shoulders with every kind of person?" George W. Scott, *A Majority of One: Legislative Life* (self-pub., Xlibrus Corporation, 2010), 378.

11. Doc and Claire Hastings, interview, April 19, 2016.

12. Ibid.

13. Doc and Claire Hastings, interview, May 3, 2016.

14. Doc Hastings, interview, October 1, 2017. Doc became a close friend and political admirer of Dunn. At her funeral, there were four eulogies. They were delivered by her two sons; by William Ruckelshaus, the former EPA administrator, lawyer, and environmental activist; and by Doc Hastings.

15. Doc and Claire Hastings, interview, May 3, 2016.

16. Ibid.

17. Slade Gorton, interview by the author, May 4, 2016.

18. Remarks at the 1976 Republican Convention by Ronald Reagan, August 19, 1976, https://reaganlibrary.archives.gov/archives/reference/8.19.76.html.

19. Craig Shirley, *Reagan Rising* (New York: HarperCollins Publishers, 2017), 4.

20. Ibid., 5.

21. Thomas M. DeFrank, *Write It When I'm Gone: Remarkable Off-the-Record Conversations with Gerald R. Ford* (New York: G. P. Putnam's Sons, 2007), 109.

22. Doc and Claire Hastings, interview, April 19, 2016.

23. Kirsten Hastings Lancaster, interview by the author, July 13, 2016.

24. Zusy, interview.

25. Colin Hastings, interview by the author, August 8, 2016.

26. Zusy, interview.

27. Lancaster, interview, July 13, 2016.

28. Ibid.

29. Doc and Claire Hastings, interview by the author, June 9, 2016.

30. Berger, interview.

31. Ibid.

32. Tri-City Herald Staff, "Hastings leads GOP legislative victory," *Tri-City Herald*, November 8, 1978, 1.

Chapter 4

1. Don Brazier, *History of the Washington Legislature 1965-1982* (Olympia, WA: Washington State Senate, 2007), 35, accessed June 11, 2016, http://leg.wa.gov/ History/Legislative/Documents/HistoftheLeg1965-82.pdf.

2. Doc and Claire Hastings, interview by the author, May 26, 2016.

3. Shirley Hankins, interview by the author, May 18, 2016.

4. Doc and Claire Hastings, interview, May 12, 2016.

5. William Polk, interview by the author, May 14, 2016.

6. Doc and Claire Hastings, interview, May 12, 2016.

7. Doc and Claire Hastings, interviews, May 3 and 26, 2016.

8. David Ammons, interview by the author, July 2, 2016.

9. Larry Ganders, interview by the author, June 2, 2016.

10. Ibid.

11. Wayne Ehlers, interview by the author, June 9, 2016.

12. Walgren was indicted later that year in the same FBI sting operation that forced co-speaker John Bagnario to resign, but Walgren won his primary that November.

13. "Baggy at the Bat," collection of miscellaneous digital files, papers, DVDs, and ephemera in the possession of Richard "Doc" Hastings.

14. Doc and Claire Hastings, interview, May 3, 2016.

15. Brazier, 40.

16. Denny Godfrey, "Nuclear Power Faces 'Battle of Life' in Legislature," *Tri-City Herald*, January 13, 1980, 3.

17. Ronald Reagan, "Election Eve Address 'A Vision for America,'" *The American Presidency Project*, UC Santa Barbara, May 19, 2016, http://www.presidency. ucsb.edu/ws/?pid=85199.

18. John C. Hughes, *Slade Gorton: A Half Century in Politics* (Olympia, WA: The Washington State Heritage Center Legacy Project, The Gorton Center, National Bureau of Asian Research, 2011), 154.

19. Ammons, interview.

20. William M. Polk, interview by the author, May 14, 2016.

21. Brazier, 43.

22. Ray Moore, interview by Sharon Boswell, *Ray Moore, An Oral History* (Olympia, WA: Washington State Oral History Program, Office of Secretary of State, 1999), 87, accessed May 9, 2016, apps.leg.wa.gov/oralhistory/moore.pdf.

23. Ibid., 90.

24. Ehlers, interview, June 9, 2016.

25. Allen Hayward, email to the author, July 5, 2017.

26. Polk, interview, May 21, 2016.

27. Doc and Claire Hastings, interview, May 12, 2016.

28. Lancaster, interview, July 13, 2016.

29. Zusy, interview.

30. Ibid.

31. Hankins, interview, May 18, 2016.

32. Doc and Claire Hastings, interview by the author, August 11, 2016.

33. Lyle Burt, "New Taxes Loom as Legislature Convenes," *Seattle Times*, January 10, 1983, A1.

34. Lyle Burt, "Spellman Calls for Education Funds, Jobs Legislation, Tax Increases," *Seattle Times*, January 11, 1983, B2.

35. Daniel Jack Chasan, *Speaker of the House: The Political Career and Times of John L. O'Brien* (Seattle: University of Washington Press, 1990), 69.

36. Doc and Claire Hastings, interview, June 9, 2016.

37. Ehlers, email to the author, July 27, 2016.

38. Doc and Claire Hastings, interview, May 26, 2016.

39. Ibid.

40. Hankins, interview, May 18, 2016.

41. Doc and Claire Hastings, interview, April 26, 2016.

42. William Polk, email to the author, June 5, 2016.

43. Doc and Claire Hastings, interview, April 26, 2016.

44. Lyle Burt, "'Not a great session,' says Spellman," *Seattle Times*, March 9, 1984, B2.

45. "Republican Party Platform of 1984," *The American Presidency Project*, August 20, 1984, accessed June 25, 2016, http://www.presidency.ucsb.edu/ws/?pid=25845.

46. Doc and Claire Hastings, interview, June 23, 2016. Clark Durant founded the Cornerstone charter and independent schools in inner-city Detroit and was an unsuccessful candidate for the US Senate in Michigan in 1990 and 2012.

47. John D. Spellman, interview by John D. Spellman, "Inside Olympia," KTW-TV, May 11, 2000.

48. Larry Ganders, "Lawmakers Convene amid Pomp, Issues," *Tri-City Herald*, January 15, 1985, A1.

49. Moore, 90.

50. Larry Ganders, "Gardner to Call Special Session of Legislature," *Tri-City Herald*, April 29, 1985, 1.

51. Smith, *Community Godfather*, 272.

52. Larry Ganders, "Legislature Off to Quick Start," *Tri-City Herald*, January 14, 1986, A1.
53. Larry Ganders, "Republicans at Bottom of Governor's Chart of Support," *Tri-City Herald*, March 13, 1986, A2.
54. Doc and Claire Hastings, interview, April 19, 2016.
55. Doc and Claire Hastings, interview by the author, July 7, 2016.
56. Dave Hoover, "Jesernig Joins Fray as Hastings Retires," *Tri-City Herald*, April 23, 1986, A1.
57. Doc and Claire Hastings, interview, June 23, 2016.
58. Doc Hastings, remarks made at a press conference announcing his retirement from serving in the Washington legislature, April 23, 1986, unknown producer (1986), videotape, Hastings collection.
59. Doc Hastings's last floor speech of the Washington legislature, August 1, 1986, unknown producer (1986), videotape, Hastings collection.
60. Doc and Claire Hastings, interview, April 19, 2016.
61. Doc and Claire Hastings, interview, April 26, 2016.
62. Ibid.
63. Editorial, "Will the 16th District Lose Its Tri-City Seat?" *Tri-City Herald*, April 24, 1986, A4.

Chapter 5
1. Hughes, *Slade Gorton*, 285.
2. Wanda Briggs, "Pasco's Hastings Eyes Congressional Campaign," *Tri-City Herald*, November 21, 1991, A1.
3. Doc Hastings, remarks made at a press conference announcing his candidacy for Congress at the Pasco Red Lion Hotel, February 13, 1992, unknown producer (2002), videotape, Hastings private collection; Pat Moser and Erik Smith, "Hastings Joins Race to Replace Morrison," *Tri-City Herald*, February 14, 1992, A9.
4. Doc and Claire Hastings, interview by the author, May 26, 2016.
5. Berger, interview.
6. Doc and Claire Hastings, interview, May 26, 2016.
7. Berger, interview.
8. Jim Jesernig, interview by the author, June 19, 2016.
9. Jay Inslee, interview by the author, June 20, 2016.
10. Doc Hastings, League of Woman Voters candidate forum, KYVE-TV, September 10, 1992, (Yakima, WA: KYVE-TV, 2002), videotape, Hastings collection.
11. The northern spotted owl was listed as a threatened species under the 1973 Endangered Species Act throughout its range of northern California, Oregon, and Washington on June 23, 1990, citing loss of old growth timber habitat as the primary threat. Harvests of timber in the Pacific Northwest were

reduced by 80 percent, decreasing the supply of lumber and increasing prices. "Northern spotted owl," November 1, 2016, https://en.wikipedia.org/wiki/Northern_spotted_owl.

12. Erik Smith, "Jesernig, Hastings Lead Field in 4th District," *Tri-City Herald*, October 17, 1992, A2.

13. Editorial, "For Congress, we endorse . . .," *Tri-City Herald*, September 13, 1992, A4.

14. Inslee, interview, June 20, 2016.

15. Editorial, "For Congress: Jay Inslee," *Tri-City Herald*, October 25, 1992, D2.

16. Ibid.

17. Doc and Claire Hastings, interview by the author, June 9, 2016.

18. "The Man in the Arena," *Almanac of Theodore Roosevelt,* excerpt from Theodore Roosevelt's "Citizenship in a Republic" speech delivered at the Sorbonne, Paris, France, April 23, 1910, accessed June 12, 2016, http://www.theodore-roosevelt.com.

19. "5 Things You May Not Know about Gingrich," NPR, June 9, 2016, http://www.npr.org/2011/11/19/1424990/5-things-you-may-not-know-about-gingrich.

20. Jon Meacham, *Destiny and Power: The American Odyssey of George Herbert Walker Bush* (New York: Random House, 2015), 339.

21. Meacham, 447.

22. David Horsey, "Republicans Unresponsive to a Speech They Could Have Written," *Seattle Post Intelligencer*, January 25, 1995, A13.

23. "1993 Omnibus Budget Reconciliation Act," Berkeley Library UC, September 10, 2016, http://bancroft.berkeley.edu/ROHO/projects/debt/1993reconciliationact.html.

24. Doc and Claire Hastings, interview, June 9, 2016.

25. Associated Press, "Big Bucks: Congressional Campaigns Top $13 million," *Tri-City Herald*, November 5, 2004, A1.

26. Erik Smith, "Inslee Wants Debate on Women's Issues," *Tri-City Herald*, September 2, 1994, A2.

27. Doc and Claire Hastings, interview by the author, March 8, 2016.

28. Isolde Rafter, "Jay Inslee's Uphill Battle," *Seattle Business* online, June 2012, accessed June 12, 2016, http://www.seattlebusinessmag.com/article/jay-inslees-uphill-battle.

29. Erik Smith, "Stumble over Acronym Heats Up House Race," *Tri-City Herald*, September 9, 2004, A4.

30. Gary Peterson, interview by the author, November 14, 2012. Enhanced LIGO facilities at Hanford and in Louisiana ultimately picked up a signal that resulted from the collision of two black holes on September 14, 2015, thus confirming Einstein's theory of relativity.

31. Erik Smith and Wanda Briggs, "Hastings Outpolls Inslee in Primary," *Tri-City Herald*, November 21, 1994, A1.

32. Gary Bullert, email to the author, July 7, 2016. At the time, Bullert was a political science professor at Columbia Basin College in Pasco, and Doc came to his class to discuss the 1994 campaign. Bullert said Doc would win because of the larger voter turnout in the general election.

33. John Boehner, interview by the author, September 8, 2016.

34. Erik Smith, "Dole Tells Doc to Pack Up (for Congress)," *Tri-City Herald*, September 8, 1994, A1.

35. Ibid.

36. Erik Smith, "'Doc' Says He'll Reject Pension if He Wins," *Tri-City Herald*, November 4, 2004, A3.

37. Editorial, "Jay Inslee," *Tri-City Herald*, November 6, 1994, D4.

38. Editorial, "Our Recommendation's for Tuesday's Election," *Yakima Herald-Republic,* November 6, 1994, F6.

39. Mark Walker, "4th District Race Getting Animated," *Yakima Herald-Republic*, October 29, 1994, A1.

40. Mark Walker, "High-Profile Race Is Inslee's to Lose: Morrison," *Yakima Herald-Republic*, October 30, 1994, A1.

41. Jay Inslee, interview by the author, August 8, 2016.

42. Erik Smith, "Pasco's 'Doc' Hastings Topples Inslee," *Tri-City Herald*, November 9, 2004, A1.

43. Doc and Claire Hastings, interview, June 9, 2016.

44. Dan Balz, "Party Controls Both Houses for First Time Since '50s," *Washington Post*, November 9, 1994, A1.

45. Ed Gillespie and Bob Schellhas (ed.), *Contract with America: The Bold Plan by Rep. Newt Gingrich, Rep. Dick Armey, and the House Republicans to Change the Nation* (New York: Time Books, a division of Random House, 1994), 4.

46. Ibid.

47. Major Garrett, "Beyond the Contract," *Mother Jones* online, March/April 1995, accessed June 8, 2016, http://www.motherjones.com/politics/1995/03/beyond-contract.

48. Doc and Claire Hastings, interview, June 9, 2016.

49. Ibid.

Chapter 6

1. Doc and Claire Hastings, interview, June 23, 2016.

2. Ibid.

3. Ibid.

4. Doc and Claire Hastings, interview, March 8, 2016.

5. Cassidy went on to serve on the staffs of the House Rules and Ethics Committees, on the staff of House minority leader, and then as director of House Operations under Speaker of the House John Boehner. He then served as the chief administrator of the House until his retirement in December 2015.
6. Doug Riggs, interview by the author, August 5, 2016.
7. Ibid.
8. Todd Ungerecht, interview by the author, August 9, 2016.
9. David A. Fehrenhold, "The Ins and Outs of the Capitol Hill Office Lottery," *Washington Post* online, November 18, 2010, accessed July 31, 2016, http://www.washingtonpost.com/wp-dyn/content/article/2010/11/18/AR2010111806561.html?sid= ST2010111902338.
10. Upon his retirement, Doc opted to purchase his desk and ship it to its new location as the centerpiece of the Doc Hastings exhibit at the Franklin County Historical Museum in Pasco.
11. Ibid.
12. Ibid.
13. The Republican conference chairman (the Democrats call theirs the caucus chairman) has a position roughly the same as the caucus chairman in the Washington legislature. He or she presides over the meetings of the various party membership in the Congress and is also responsible for developing and managing the messaging that goes out to the members about the leadership's position on various bills and issues before the Congress.
14. John Boehner, interview, September 8, 2016.
15. Doug Riggs, email to the author, August 21, 2016.
16. Doc and Claire Hastings, interview by the author, July 14, 2016.
17. Ibid.
18. 100 Days: Contract with America Celebration (Washington, DC: National Republican Campaign Committee, 1995), DVD.
19. "Oath of Office," *History, Art & Archives*, February 15, 2016, http://history.house.gov/Institution/Origins-Development/Oath-of-Office/.
20. Doc Hastings, interview, March 8, 2016.
21. For simplicity's sake, the author will use "Speaker," the commonly used abbreviation of the term, Speaker pro tem, for the remainder of the book.
22. Doc Hastings, interview by the author, February 1, 2016.
23. Doc and Claire Hastings, interview, June 23, 2016.
24. Claire Hastings, interview by the author, June 23, 2016.
25. Doc and Claire Hastings, interview, June 23, 2016.
26. Ilene Clauson, email to the author, June 2, 2017.
27. Ibid.
28. Polk, interview, May 14, 2016.
29. Doc and Claire Hastings, interview, June 23, 2016.

30. Riggs, interview.
31. Todd Young, interview by the author, February 17, 2017.
32. Doc and Claire Hastings, interview, June 23, 2016.
33. Norm Dicks, interview by the author, March 8, 2016.
34. Doc and Claire Hastings, interview, May 26, 2016.
35. Ilene Clauson, email to the author, February 21, 2017.
36. Doc and Claire Hastings, interview, May 26, 2016.
37. Lindsey Graham, interview by the author, September 7, 2016.
38. Doc and Claire Hastings, interview by the author, September 29, 2016.
39. Doc and Claire Hastings, interview, July 14, 2016.
40. Gary Petersen, email to the author, July 21, 2016.
41. Doc and Claire Hastings, interview, July 7, 2016.
42. Doc and Claire Hastings, interview by the author, September 15, 2016.
43. Ibid.
44. Cathy McMorris Rogers, remarks made at the unveiling and presentation of the official portrait of the Honorable Doc Hastings, Washington, DC, November 19, 2014.
45. Doc and Claire Hastings, interview, July 7, 2016.
46. Doc and Claire Hastings, interview, July 14, 2016.
47. Doug Riggs, email to the author, August 16, 2017.
48. Graham, interview.
49. Jon DeVaney, email to the author of May 7, 2017.
50. Finley Peter Dunne was an American humorist from Chicago who published *Mr. Dooley in Peace and in War* in 1898. Speaking with a thick Irish accent, the fictional Mr. Dooley expounded upon political and social issues of the day from a Chicago Irish pub.
51. Polk, interview, May 14, 2016.
52. Graham, interview.
53. Doc and Claire Hastings, interview, March 8, 2016.
54. Doc and Claire Hastings, interview by the author, October 6, 2016.
55. Ungerecht, interview.
56. Todd Young, interview by the author, January 31, 2017.
57. Rogers remarks, November 19, 2014.
58. "The Eleventh Commandment" was a phrase used by Ronald Reagan during his 1966 campaign for governor of California. The Commandment reads: "Thou shalt not speak ill of any fellow Republican." "The Eleventh Commandment (Ronald Reagan)," Wikipedia, https://en.wikipedia.org/wiki/The_Eleventh_Commandment_(Ronald_Reagan), accessed November 4, 2017.
59. Doc and Claire Hastings, interview, September 29, 2016.
60. Doc and Claire Hastings, interview, June 23, 2016.
61. Ibid.

62. Ibid.
63. Ibid.
64. Jon DeVaney email, May 7, 2017.
65. Riggs, interview.

Chapter 7
1. Denny Hastert, *Speaker: Lessons from Forty Years in Coaching and Politics* (Washington, DC: Regnery Publishing, 2004), 116.
2. Graham, interview.
3. Alice A. Love, "Republican Halftime Show," *Roll Call*, February 23, 1995, 1.
4. Gloria Borger, "Halfway There," *U.S. News & World Report*, March 6, 1995, 10-11.
5. Hastert, 117-119.
6. Jennifer Babson, "Armey Stood Guard over Contract," *Congressional Quarterly*, April 8, 1995, 987.
7. It was common for Speaker Gingrich to sign and date copies of important legislation on the day it passed and send them to members as a memento of the occasion. In Doc's files, there are two copies of the budget that passed on May 18, 1995, signed and dated by the Speaker. Hastings collection).
8. Doc and Claire Hastings, interview, September 29, 2016.
9. Todd Ungerecht, email to the author, August 29, 2016.
10. Doc Hastings, interview by the author, October 27, 2016.
11. Hastert, 126-127.
12. William E. Leuchtenburg, *The American President* (New York: Oxford University Press, 2015), 756-757.
13. Deroy Murdock, "Newt Gingrich's Implosion," *National Review* online, August 28, 2000, accessed August 24, 2016, http://www.nationalreview.com/article/204716/newt-gingrichs-implosion-deroy-murdock.
14. Tim J. Christie, "Hastings: Time to Switch Focus," *Yakima Herald-Republic*, January 5, 1996, A1.
15. Doc and Claire Hastings, interview by the author, August 18, 2016.
16. "Blame for Both Sides as Possible Government Shutdown Approaches," Pew Research Center, September 23, 2013, accessed May 29, 2017, http://www.people-press.org/2013/09/23/blame-for-both-sides-as-possible-government-shutdown-approaches.
17. Sally Bedell Smith, *For Love of Politics: Bill and Hillary Clinton; The White House Years* (New York: Random House, 2007), 213.
18. Doc Hastings, interview, October 27, 2016.
19. Barbara Vobejda, "Clinton Signs Welfare Bill amid Division," *Washington Post*, August 23, 1996, A1.
20. Doc and Claire Hastings, interview, September 15, 2016.

21. Doc and Claire Hastings, interview, August 18, 2016; Doc Hastings, interview by the author, October 27, 2016.

22. Doc Hastings, interview by the author, September 9, 2016.

23. Smith, *Community Godfather*, 334-335.

24. Doc and Claire Hastings, interview, March 8, 2016.

25. Ibid., 341-342.

26. John Carlson, "Doc Hastings: Hidden Star in the State's Delegation," op-ed, *Seattle Times* online, August 15, 1995, accessed October 5, 2016, http://community.seattletimes.nwsource.com/archive/?date=19950815&slug=2136527.

27. Wanda Briggs, "Final Hanford Budget to Cut Job Loss," *Tri-City Herald*, December 9, 1995, A1.

28. Petersen, interview.

29. Hughes, *Slade Gorton*, 305.

30. Joel Connelly, "Gorton Called 'An Anti-Environmental Zealot' Republican Senator Scores Zero; Nethercutt, Hastings at Low End," *Spokesman-Review* online, February 3, 1998, accessed October 18, 2016, http://www.spokesman.com/stories/1998/feb/03/*gorton*-called-an-anti-environmental-zealot.

31. Doc Hastings, email to the author, October 19, 2016.

32. Moulton, *The Journals of the Lewis & Clark Expedition*, 5:216.

33. Although inadequate, fish ladders were provided for all the dams on the Columbia below Grand Coulee and for the lower Snake River dams.

34. Cassandra Tate, "Army Corps of Engineers abandons plans for Ben Franklin Dam on November 2, 1981," HistoryLink.org, August 24, 2005, accessed October 26, 2016, http://www.historylink.org/File/7440.

35. Nicholas K. Gerandios, "Project May Tame Last Free-Flowing Stretch of the Columbia River," *Los Angeles Times* online, August 14, 1988, accessed December 8, 2016, http://articles.latimes.com/1988-08-14/news/mn-642_1_columbia-river.

36. Eric Gerber, interview by the author, December 7, 2016.

37. Timothy Egan, "Ringold Journal: A Stretch of River That Time Forgot," *New York Times* online, May 3, 1989, accessed December 8, 2016, http://www.nytimes.com/1989/05/03/us/ringold-journal-a-stretch-of-river-that-time-forgot.html.

38. Gerber, interview.

39. Doc Hastings, interview, October 27, 2016.

40. Todd Ungerecht, email to the author, February 27, 2017.

41. Brad Knickerbocker, "A River 'Saved' by the Bomb," *Christian Science Monitor* online, August 20, 1998, accessed October 30, 2016, http://www.csmonitor.com/1998/0820/082098.feat.feat.2.html.

42. Doc and Claire Hastings, interview, March 8, 2016.

43. Doc and Claire Hastings, interview, July 7, 2016.

44. Erik Smith, "Doc Gets First Challenger," *Tri-City Herald*, October 5, 1995, A5; "House Candidate Rails about 'Dictator' Gingrich," *Tri-City Herald*, October 6, 1995, A3.

45. Editorial, "This Campaign Is a Real Loser," *Tri-City Herald*, October 8, 1995, D2.

46. Colin Hastings, interview by the author, August 8, 2016.

47. Doc Hastings letter to Martin Frost, September 8, 1995, Doug Riggs collection.

48. Ken Robertson, email to the author, October 4, 2016.

49. Boehner, interview, September 8, 2016.

50. Editorial, "For Congress: Doc Hastings," *Tri-City Herald*, November 3, 1996, D2.

51. Erik Smith, "Hastings Wins Second Term," *Tri-City Herald*, November 6, 1996, A1.

52. Adam Clymer, "GOP Pushes Congress Strategy That Shuns Dole," *New York Times* online, October 23, 1996, accessed October 9, 2016, http://www.nytimes.com/1996/10/23/us/gop-pushes-congress-strategy-that-shuns-dole.html.

Chapter 8

1. *NBC Nightly News,* privately recorded, January 27, 1998, unknown location, NBC, DVD, Hastings collection.

2. William E. Leuchtenburg, *The American President* (New York: Oxford University Press, 2015), 744-745.

3. Doc kept his copy as a highly unusual historical artifact. He made it available to the author during his research. The online document can be found at http://www.washingtonpost.com/wp-srv/politics/special/clinton/icreport/icreport.htm.

4. "Live Coverage of the Rules Committee Vote," privately recorded, September 10, 1998, unknown location, CNN, DVD, Hastings collection.

5. *CBS News,* "A Clinton Timeline," January 8, 2001, accessed September 24, 2016, http://www.cbsnews.com/news/a-clinton-timeline.

6. David Greenberg, *Republic of Spin,* (New York: W. W. Norton, 2016), 423.

7. Doc and Claire Hastings, interview by the author, September 1, 2016.

8. Philip Klein, "Starving Obama Care," *American Spectator* online, August 6, 2010, accessed September 15, 2016, http://spectator.org/39324_starving-obamacare.

9. John E. Yang, "House Reprimands, Penalizes Speaker," *Washington Post*, January 27, 1997, A1.

10. Denny Hastert, *Speaker: Lessons from Forty Years in Coaching and Politics* (Washington, DC: Regnery Publishing, 2004), 128.

11. James Carney, "Attempted Republican Coup: Ready, Aim, Misfire," CNN online, July 28, 1997, accessed October 10, 2016, http://www.cnn.com/ALLPOLITICS/1997/07/21/time/gingrich.html.

12. Boehner, interview, October 12, 2016.

13. Dick Armey letter to Doc Hastings, July 22, 1997, Hastings collection.

14. Hastert, 150.

15. Doc and Claire Hastings, interview, September 1, 2016.

16. Les Blumenthal, "Hastings Touts New Influence," *Tri-City Herald*, December 5, 1996, A1.

17. Doc and Claire Hastings, interview, July 7, 2016.

18. Jeff Markey, interview by the author, January 13, 2017.

19. Ibid.

20. Boehner, interview, September 8, 2016.

21. Graham, interview.

22. Doc once asked the architect of the Capitol to compute the size of fifty-three million gallons of nuclear waste in comparison to the size of the House Chamber. The answer came back that it would fill up the House Chamber twenty-one and a half times.

23. Vitrification is the transformation of a substance into glass.

24. Doc and Claire Hastings, interview, July 14, 2016.

25. Riggs, interview; Doug Riggs email to the author, September 16, 2016.

26. Riggs, interview.

27. Doc and Claire Hastings, interview, July 7, 2016.

28. Doc and Claire Hastings, interview, September 29, 2016.

29. Ibid.

30. Doc and Claire Hastings, interview, August 18, 2016.

31. Doc and Claire Hastings, interview by the author, June 8, 2017.

32. Ben Pershing, "Ethics Chairman Admired in GOP," *Roll Call*, February 3, 2005. 19.

33. Ibid.

34. Doc and Claire Hastings, interview, September 29, 2016.

35. Ibid.

36. Annette Cary, "Tribes Return Ancient Kennewick Man to the Ground," *Tri-City Herald* online, February 19, 2017, http://www.tri-cityherald.com/news/local/article133780309.html.

37. Doc Hastings, interview, October 27, 2016.

38. Ibid.

39. *Local News at Six*, privately recorded, March 10, 1998, Yakima, WA, KAPP-TV, DVD, Hastings collection.

40. Scott Sonner, "Salmon Issues Split NW Delegation—Gorton Squares off with Murray on Bill," *Seattle Times* online, April 12, 1998, accessed October 22, 2016, http://community.seattletimes.nwsource.com/archive/?date=19980412&slug=2744720.

41. Kim Bradford, "National Marine Fisheries Service Draws Heavy Fire at Pasco Hearing," *Tri-City Herald*, September 3, 1998, A1.

42. Nancy Gibbs and Michael Duffy, "Fall of the House of Newt," *Time* online, November 16, 1998, accessed September 27, 2016, http://content.time.com/time/magazine/article/0,9171,989559,00.html.

43. Doc and Claire Hastings, interview, September 29, 2016.

44. Associated Press, "The Speaker Steps Down," *New York Times* online, November 8, 1998, accessed September 27, 2016, http://www.nytimes.com/1998/11/08/us/the-speaker-steps-down-excerpts-from-phone-call-about-gingrich-s-future.html?_r=0.

45. Hastert, 161-164.

46. Doc and Claire Hastings, interview, September 29, 2016.

47. "Coverage of the Republican Leadership Press Conference and Analysis," privately recorded, November 18, 1988, unknown location, *CNN Live*, DVD, Hastings collection.

48. Howard Kurtz, "Report of Hyde Affair Stirs Anger," *Washington Post*, September 17, 1998, A15.

49. Hastert, 167.

50. Ibid.

51. Ibid.

52. Doc and Claire Hastings, interview, September 1, 2016.

53. Hastert, 169.

54. Robert T. Nelson, "No Longer a Wasteland for Democrats?" *Seattle Times*, September 20, 1998, B1.

55. Ibid.

56. "1998 Washington State Video Voter's Pamphlet," featuring video presentations of Gordon Allen Pross and Peggy McKerlie (privately recorded, unknown location, 1998, Office of the Secretary of State), DVD, Hastings collection.

57. Editorial, "Congress: 4th District: Re-elect Hastings," *Tri-City Herald*, October 18, 1998, D2.

58. Editorial, "Congressional Contest Falling to Doc Hastings/YHR endorses Doc Hastings," *Yakima Herald-Republic*, October 27, 1998, A4.

59. Doc and Claire Hastings, interview, September 29, 2016. The phrase originated from when the Deep South was solidly Democratic and voters claimed they would rather vote for a yellow dog than a Republican.

60. Doc and Claire Hastings, interview, September 1, 2016.

61. Keating Holland, "A Year after Clinton Impeachment, Public Approval Grows of House Decision," CNN online, December 16, 1999, accessed May 29, 2017, http://archives.cnn.com/1999/ALLPOLITICS/stories/12/16/impeach.poll.

62. Associated Press, "Gingrich, Clinton Had Stormy Partnership," December 22, 2011, accessed May 30, 2017, http://www.foxnews.com/us/2011/12/22/gingrich-clinton-had-stormy-partnership.html.

Chapter 9

1. Federal News Service, "House Speaker Dennis Hastert's Opening Remarks to the 106th Congress," *Washington Post* online, January 6, 1999, accessed October 25, 2016, http://www.washingtonpost.com/wp-srv/politics/govt/leadership/stories/haserttext010799.htm.

2. Andrew Johnson, who was impeached and acquitted by one vote in 1868, had been elected as vice president but became president after Abraham Lincoln's assassination.

3. Doc and Claire Hastings, interview by the author, October 6, 2016.

4. Sally Bedell Smith, *For the Love of Politics* (New York: Random House, 2007), 372.

5. Doc and Claire Hastings, interview, October 6, 2016.

6. Smith, 381; Associated Press, "NW Lawmakers Split on Speech," *Tri-City Herald*, January 28, 2000, A3.

7. John F. Harris, *The Survivor: Bill Clinton and the White House* (New York: Random House, 2005), 431-437.

8. Doc and Claire Hastings, interview, September 1, 2016.

9. "Public Views about Guns," Pew Research Center, August 26, 2016, accessed June 1, 2017, http://www.people-press.org/2016/08/26/public-views-about-guns/#total.

10. Tom DeLay, *No Retreat, No Surrender: One American's Fight* (New York: Sentinel, 2007), 90.

11. Ibid., 104.

12. Mike Lee, "Doc Becomes Assistant GOP Whip," *Tri-City Herald*, January 27, 1999, A4; "Appointment Helps Strengthen Hastings' Hand," *Yakima Herald-Republic*, February 1, 1999, B1.

13. Lee Blumenthal, "French company shows interest in Hanford project," *Tri-City Herald*, April 28, 2000, A1.

14. Robert Ferguson, interview by the author, July 31, 2013.

15. "KNDU Local News," privately recorded October 19, 2000, Pasco, WA, KNDU-TV, DVD, Hastings collection.

16. "Hastings: More Study Needed Before Removing Dams," *Yakima Herald-Republic*, January 18, 1999, B1.

17. Mike Lee and Kim Bradford, "Thousands Rally to Save Snake Dams," *Tri-City Herald*, February 19, 1999, A1.

18. Annette Cary, "Legislators Quiz Experts at Pasco," *Tri-City Herald*, April 28, 2000, A1.

19. Smith, *Community Godfather*, 409.

20. Doc Hastings, interview, October 27, 2016.

21. Doc Hastings, interview by the author, January 26, 2017.

22. Gerber, interview.

23. Eric Gerber, *Save the Hanford Reach Timeline* (Boston: Boston Productions, 2013), interactive video at the Reach Interpretive Center, Richland, WA.

24. Lynda V. Mapes, "Babbitt to Tour Hanford Reach," *Seattle Times* online, May 16, 2000, accessed November 14, 2016, http://community.seattletimes.nwsource.com/archive/?date=20000516&slug=4021167.

25. Les Blumenthal, "Monument Status Advised for Reach," *Tri-City Herald*, June 1, 2000, A1.

26. Hughes, *Slade Gorton*, 330.

27. Les Blumenthal, "Monument Status," *Tri-City Herald*, June 1, 2000, A1.

28. Doc and Claire Hastings, interview, October 6, 2016.

29. Mike Lee, "A Monumental Decision," *Tri-City Herald*, June 10, 2000, A1.

30. Ibid.

31. Department of Energy, *US Department of Energy Response to the 24 Command Fire on the Hanford Reservation June 27-July 1, 2000*, October 2000, https://energy.gov/sites/prod/files/2014/04/f15/0011hanf.pdf.

32. Associated Press, "Hanford Fire Out; No Signs of Radiation," *Los Angeles Times* online, July 1, 2000, accessed November 5, 2016, http://articles.latimes.com/2000/jul/01/news/mn-46850; "Live at 6," privately recorded July 1, 2000, Pasco, WA, KEPR-TV, DVD, Hastings collection.

33. "Live at 6," privately recorded July 1, 2000, Pasco, WA, KEPR-TV, DVD, Hastings collection.

34. Mike Lee, "Congress Passes Bailout Bill for Farmers," *Tri-City Herald*, May 26, 2000, A1.

35. "November 19, 1999, Press Conference," privately recorded November 19, 1999, Yakima, WA, Y-Pac Public Television, DVD, Hastings collection.

36. Doc and Claire Hastings, interviews by the author, August 18 and November 10, 2016.

37. Marvin Olasky, *Compassionate Conservatism: What It Is, What It Does, and How It Can Transform America* (New York: Free Press, 2000).

38. Annette Cary, "Bush Bullish on Snake Dams," *Tri-City Herald*, February 29, 2000, A1; Linda Ashton, "Bush Says Breaching Not Option," *Yakima Herald-Republic*, February 29, 2000, A1.

39. Doc and Claire Hastings, interview, November 10, 2016.

40. Smith, 420.

41. "The National Mood, *CBS 60 Minutes*, November 6, 2016, accessed August 21, 2017, https://www.cbsnews.com/videos/the-national-mood.

42. Hughes, 334.

43. Ibid., 335.

44. Doc and Claire Hastings, interview, November 10, 2016.

45. Michael Sear, "Coulee City Wheat Farmer Takes on Hastings," *Columbia Basin Herald*, October 8, 1999, A1.

46. Jim Davis, interview by the author, November 21, 2016.

47. "YD Picnic July 14, 2000," privately recorded July 14, 2000, Richland, WA, unknown producer, VCR, Hastings collection.

48. Davis, interview.

49. Tom Roeder, "Election 2000—Doc Stays in D.C.—Congressman Cancels Debate with Challengers to Say in Capital Because of Budget Logjam," *Yakima Herald-Republic*, October 31, 2000, A1.

50. Editorial, "It's Time for a Change; Davis Deserves a Shot," *Yakima Herald-Republic*, October 27, 2000, A4.

51. Editorial, "Congress, 4th: Hastings," *Tri-City Herald*, November 5, 2000, D2.

52. Doc and Claire Hastings, interview, November 10, 2016.

53. Davis, interview.

Chapter 10

1. Jesse A. Hamilton, "Lincoln Day Banquet: Hastings Likes Bush's Work So Far," *Yakima Herald-Republic*, March 4, 2001, C1.

2. George W. Bush, "Address in Austin Accepting Election as the 43rd President of the United States," *The American Presidency Project*, December 13, 2000, http://www.presidency.ucsb.edu/ws/?pid=84900.

3. Doc and Claire Hastings, interview by the author, December 8, 2016.

4. Stuart Rothenberg, "Speaker Hastert Finding It's Hard to Do More Than Play Defense," *Roll Call*, May 27, 1999, 10.

5. "Congress and the Public," Gallup, accessed May 31, 2017, http://www.gallup.com/poll/1600/congress-public.aspx.

6. "No Child Left Behind Act," Wikipedia, accessed May 31, 2017, https://en.wikipedia.org/wiki/No_Child_Left_Behind_Act.

7. Tim Alberta, "John Boehner Unchained," *Politico Magazine*, November-December 2017, accessed November 5, 2017, https://www.politico.com/magazine/story/2017/10/29/john-boehner-trump-house-republican-party-retirement-profile-feature-215741.

8. Doc and Claire Hastings, interview by the author, March 15, 2016.

9. George W. Bush, "Remarks by the President in Tax Cut Bill Signing Ceremony," website for *The White House*, June 7, 2001, https://georgewbush-whitehouse.archives.gov/news/releases/2001/06/20010607.html.

10. Doc and Claire Hastings, interview, August 18, 2016.

11. Doc and Claire Hastings, interview by the author, December 1, 2016.

12. Ungerecht email, January 3, 2017.

13. Tom Roeder, "America at War—Terrorist Attacks Put Cramp on Doc Hastings," *Yakima Herald-Republic*, October 27, 2001, C1.

14. Doc Hastings, interview by the author, January 26, 2017.

15. Doc and Claire Hastings, interview, December 1, 2016.

16. Annette Cary, "Energy Chief Says Cleanup Funds Fine," *Tri-City Herald*, May 11, 2001, A1.

17. Markey, interview.

18. Doc and Claire Hastings, interview by the author, November 17, 2016.

19. *Rep. Traficant Ethics Inquiry, Day 4 Part 2*, video, 01:11:43, C-SPAN, July 28, 2002, accessed January 30, 2017, https://www.c-span.org/video/?171335-2/rep-traficant-ethics-inquiry-day-4-part-2.

20. Doc and Claire Hastings, interview, December 1, 2016.

21. David Halberstam, *War in a Time of Peace* (New York: Scribner, 2001), 491-493.

22. Doc and Claire Hastings, interview, December 1, 2016.

23. Ilene Clauson, email to the author, January 31, 2017.

24. Doc and Claire Hastings, interview, December 1, 2016.

25. Markey, interview; Young, interview, January 31, 2017.

26. Markey, interview.

27. Clauson email, January 31, 2017; Young, interview, January 31, 2017.

28. Reuters, "US: George Bush Aide Releases 'We Are at War' Handwritten Notes from 9/11," *The Indian Express*, updated September 9, 2016, accessed December 5, 2016, http://indianexpress.com/article/world/world-news/us-george-bush-aide-releases-we-are-at-war-handwritten-notes-from-911-3022235.

29. *CNN—Ex-President George W. Bush's Post 9/11 Speech*, video, 04:23, CNN, November 11, 1999, uploaded October 15, 2006, accessed December 15, 2016, https://www.youtube.com/watch?v=YMiqEUBux3o.

30. Tom Roeder, "Attack on America—Doc Hastings Says Congress Willing to Declare War," *Yakima Herald-Republic*, September 13, 2001, A11.

31. Ungerecht email, January 30, 2017.

32. George W. Bush, *Decision Points* (New York: Crown Publishers, 2010), 158 (footnote).

33. Ron Fournier, "State of the Union—A Wartime State of the Union—President Pledges to Battle Twin Enemies of Terrorism Abroad, Recession at Home," *Yakima Herald-Republic*, January 30, 2002, A1.

34. "2002 State of the Union Address," Wikipedia, accessed January 3, 2017, https://en.wikipedia.org/wiki/2002_State_of_the_Union_Address.

35. Doc Hastings, interview by the author, January 24, 2017.

36. Ibid.

37. Denny Hastert, *Speaker* (Washington, D.C.: Regnary Publishing, Inc., 2004), 231.

38. Shan Carter and Amanda Cox, "One 9/11 Tally: $3.3 Trillion," *New York Times* online, September 8, 2011, accessed December 15, 2016, http://www.nytimes.com/interactive/2011/09/08/us/sept-11-reckoning/cost-graphic.html?_r=0.

39. Doc and Claire Hastings, interview of December 1, 2016.

40. Bush, 165.

41. Doc Hastings, interview, January 26, 2017.

42. Ibid.

43. Bob Woodward, *Bush at War* (New York: Simon & Schuster, 2002), 87.

44. Bob Woodward, *Plan of Attack* (New York: Simon & Schuster, 2004), 26.

45. Leah Beth Ward, "Doc Hastings: Prepare for War," *Yakima Herald-Republic*, October 5, 2002, A1.

46. John Stang, "Congressman Speaks about Pro-War Vote," *Tri-City Herald*, October 15, 2002, A1.

47. Tom Roeder, "Apple Aid Inches Closer to Growers' Pocketbooks," *Yakima Herald-Republic*, March 3, 2001, A1.

48. Tom Roeder, "Apple Bailout Trimmed to $75 Million," *Yakima Herald-Republic*, November 9, 2001, A1.

49. Doc Hastings, interview, January 26, 2017.

50. Jesse A. Hamilton, "Checks in the Mail for Growers," *Yakima Herald-Republic*, March 23, 2002, C1.

51. Tom Roeder, "Hastings: Feds Will Give Relief," *Yakima Herald-Republic*, April 18, 2001, B1.

52. "Thirty Mile Fire," *Wikipedia*, accessed January 5, 2017, https://en.wikipedia.org/wiki/Thirty_Mile_Fire.

53. Young, interview, January 31, 2017.

54. Tom Roeder, "Congress Probes Fatal Thirtymile Fire," *Yakima Herald-Republic*, October 17, 2001, A1; Jessie A. Hamilton, "Thirtymile Hearing Postponed/No new date scheduled by U.S. Senate panel," *Yakima Herald-Republic*, October 18, 2001, A1; Jessie A. Hamilton, "Hearing on Fire Set for Wednesday," *Yakima Herald-Republic*, November 11, 2001, A1.

55. Tom Roeder, "Fire-Probe Bills Sails through House," *Yakima Herald-Republic*, June 24, 2002, A1.

56. Bill Gabbert, "Update on the condition of the firefighters who deployed fire shelters on the Cedar Fire," Wildfire Today, June 29, 2016, access July 2, 2017. http://wildfiretoday.com/2016/06/29/update-on-the-condition-of-the-firefighters-who-deployed-fire-shelters-on-the-cedar-fire.

57. David Lester, "Pasco Representative Requests $300,000 for Reservoir Study," *Yakima Herald-Republic*, April 20, 2002, C1; David Lester, "Where to Tap Funds? Black Rock Backers Say Reservoir Can Solve a Variety of Irrigation, Recreation and Habitat Needs," *Yakima Herald-Republic*, July 24, 2002, A1.

58. Doc Hastings, interview, January 26, 2017.

59. Leah Beth Ward, "Hastings Don't Have to Wait for Gov. Locke," *Yakima Herald-Republic*, November 22, 2002, C3.

60. Annette Cary, "FFTF Loses Restart Fight," Tri-City Herald, December 20, 2001, A1.

61. John Stang, "Vit Construction Gets Go-Ahead," *Tri-City Herald*, July 10, 2002, B1.

62. Tom Roeder, "Democrat Davis Won't Challenge Hastings Again," *Wenatchee World*, January 7, 2002, 3.

63. Tom Roeder, "Rep. Hastings Will Run for Fifth Term," *Yakima Herald-Republic*, February 20, 2000, C1.

64. Chris Mulick, "Hastings' Challenger Mason Makes His Pitch," *Tri-City Herald*, August 3, 2002, B1; Graham Black, "College Instructor Tosses Hat in for Doc Hastings' Seat—Craig Mason," *Yakima Herald-Republic*, August 3, 2002, B1.

65. Chris Mulick, "General Election Race Is On," *Tri-City Herald*, September 19, 2002, B1; Leah Beth Ward, "Doc Hastings, Craig Mason Will Face Off for Seat in Congress," *Yakima Herald-Republic*, September 18, 2002, B1.

66. Leah Beth Ward, "Doc Hastings: Statement about Enron PAC Money Is Lie," *Yakima Herald-Republic*, October 6, 2002, C1.

67. Editorial, "Congress, 4th District: Re-elect Doc Hastings," *Tri-City Herald*, October 17, 2002, A12.

68. Jon DeVaney, email to the author, May 7, 2017.

69. Leah Beth Ward, "Callers Ring in Debate—Hastings, Mason Spar over Handful of Issues in 4th District Race," *Yakima Herald-Republic*, November 1, 2002, C1.

70. Chris Mulick, "Hastings, Nethercutt Win Re-election to Congress," *Tri-City Herald*, November 6, 2002, A4.

71. Doc Hastings, interview, January 26, 2017.

Chapter 11

1. George W. Bush, "First Inaugural Address," Bartleby, January 20, 2001, accessed January 22, 2017, http://www.bartleby.com/124/pres66.html.

2. Doc Hastings, interview, January 26, 2017.

3. George W. Bush, "Second Inaugural Address," Wikisource, January 29, 2005, accessed January 22, 2017, https://en.wikisource.org/wiki/George_W._Bush's_Second_State_of_the_Union_Address.

4. Les Blumenthal, "Powell Made Strong Case, State Lawmakers Say," *Tri-City Herald*, February 6, 2003, B3.

5. Woodward, *Plan of Attack*, 150.

6. Les Blumenthal, "Hastings Bullish on U.S. Progress in Iraq," *Tri-City Herald*, March 26, 2004, B1.

7. "Timeline of the Iraq War," Wikipedia, accessed February 12, 2017, https://en.wikipedia.org/wiki/Timeline_of_the_Iraq_War#September.

8. Jessica Gleason, interview by the author, February 24, 2017.

9. "Hastings Elected to Steering Committee," *Yakima Herald-Republic*, November 15, 2002, C1.

10. Doc Hastings, interview, January 26, 2017.

11. Doc and Claire Hastings, interview by the author, February 13, 2017.
12. Doc and Claire Hastings, interview by the author, February 28, 2017.
13. Doc and Claire Hastings, interview, March 8, 2016.
14. Alex Fryer, "Doc Hastings' Low-Key Style Earns Respect," *Seattle Times* online, October 26, 2003, accessed January 20, 2017, http://community.seattletimes.nwsource.com/archive/?date=20031026&slug=hastings26m0
15. Ibid.
16. Markey, interview.
17. Thomas E. Mann and Norman J. Ornstein, *The Broken Branch: How Congress Is Failing America and How to Get Back on Track* (Oxford, United Kingdom: Oxford University Press, 2006), 1-3.
18. Los Angeles Times and Washington Post, "Doc Gets It Wrong, and Bush Gets His Bill," *Yakima Herald-Republic*, November 23, 2003, 13.
19. Doc Hastings, interview, January 26, 2017.
20. Carl Hulse, "Fight to Pass Medicare Measure Raised House Speaker's Profile," *New York Times* online, December 6, 2003, accessed February 14, 2017, http://www.nytimes.com/2003/12/06/us/fight-to-pass-medicare-measure-raised-house-speaker-s-profile.html.
21. Doc Hastings, interview, January 26, 2016.
22. When the GOP regained control of the House after the 2010 election, Doc found himself again presiding over another late-night session. In the course of presiding over a series of votes on amendments, the clerks use a stopwatch to keep track of the time taken for each vote. Doc beat the previous record for ending a vote by one second. John Sullivan, the parliamentarian that night, had a dry sense of humor. He looked over and said, "Doc, you now hold the record for the shortest and the longest votes in history."
23. Doc Hastings, interview, January 26, 2017.
24. Carl Hulse, "Inquiry Sought in House Vote on Drug Plan for Medicare," *New York Times* online, February 2, 2004, accessed February 14, 2017, http://www.nytimes.com/2004/02/02/us/inquiry-sought-in-house-vote-on-drug-plan-for-medicare.html?_r=0.
25. Doc and Claire Hastings, interview, December 1, 2016.
26. Charles Babington, "Ethics Panel Rebukes DeLay," *Washington Post*, October 1, 2004, A1.
27. Doc and Claire Hastings, interview, December 1, 2016.
28. Charles Babington, "DeLay Draws Third Rebuke," *Washington Post*, October 7, 2004, A1.
29. Doc and Claire Hastings, interview, August 18, 2016.
30. Doc and Claire Hastings, interview, March 8, 2016.

31. "Political Polarization in the American Public," Pew Research Center, June 12, 2014, accessed May 31, 2017, http://www.people-press.org/2014/06/12/political-polarization-in-the-american-public.

32. Tim Peckinpaugh, email to Jeff Markey and Todd Young, January 8, 2003, C. Mark Smith private collection; John Stang, "Hanford cleanup budget unveiled," *Tri-City Herald*, February 4, 2003, A1.

33. Leah Beth Ward, "Hastings Bucks GOP on Drug Bill," *Yakima Herald-Republic*, August 7, 2003, B1.

34. Associated Press, "11 Disciplined in Thirtymile Fire," *Tri-City Herald*, February 13, 2003, A4.

35. Associated Press, "Federal Spending Bill Includes $1 Million for Dam Study," NewsEdge Insight, February 13, 2003; David Lester, "State House Gives Black Rock Study Cash," *Yakima Herald-Republic*, February 14, 2003, C1; "House Bill Includes $1.5 Million in 2005 Funding for Black Rock," *Yakima Herald-Republic*, June 27, 2004, C1.

36. John Stang, "Regulators Say DOE Waste Plans in Disarray," *Tri-City Herald*, March 18, 2003, B3.

37. John Stang, "DOE Halts Major Cleanup at Hanford," *Tri-City Herald*, May 10, 2003, A1.

38. Lisa Stiffler, "Congress, DOE at Odds over Hanford Cleanup," *Seattle Post-Intelligencer* online, July 17, 2003, accessed February 8, 2017, http://m.seattlepi.com/news/article/Congress-DOE-at-odds-over-Hanford-cleanup-1119629.php.

39. Editorial, "Hastings; Indecision Comes Late in Dispute," *Tri-City Herald*, October 1, 2003, A10; editorial, "Hastings Takes Stance," *Tri-City Herald*, October 3, 2003, A14.

40. Doc and Claire Hastings, interview of February 13, 2017.

41. Oregon Department of Energy, *Hanford Cleanup: The First 25 Years* (Salem, OR: Oregon Department of Energy, 2014), 128.

42. Benjamin Romano, "Asparagus Industry Gets Help," *Yakima Herald-Republic*, March 13, 2004, A1; Leah Beth Ward, "More Funding for Asparagus Harvester Research," *Yakima Herald-Republic*, November 24, 2004, C1.

43. Doc and Claire Hastings, interview, February 13, 2017.

44. Ibid.

45. Annette Cary, "Bush's Visit to Tri-Cities Latest of 6 Presidents in Last Century," *Tri-City Herald*, August 22, 2003, B1.

46. Young, interview, February 17, 2017.

47. Leah Beth Ward, "Bush Reiterates: Dams Stay," *Yakima Herald-Republic*, August 23, 2003, A1.

48. Chris Mullick, Anna King, and Jeff St. John, "Bush Touts Region's Dams," *Tri-City Herald*, August 23, 2003, A1.

49. Doc and Claire Hastings, interview, February 13, 2017.

50. Young, interview, February 17, 2017

51. "Bovine spongiform encephalopathy," Wikipedia, accessed February 16, 2017, https://en.wikipedia.org/wiki/Bovine_spongiform_encephalopathy; Associated Press, "Officials Trace 5 Cows to Connell Herd," *Tri-City Herald*, January 17, 2004, A1.

52. Leah Beth Ward, "Cheney Fires Up Faithful at Rally," *Yakima Herald-Republic*, July 31, 2004.

53. Bob Woodward, *State of Denial* (New York: Simon & Schuster, 2006), 348-350.

54. "Washington gubernatorial election, 2004," Wikipedia, accessed February 18, 2017, https://en.wikipedia.org/wiki/Washington_gubernatorial_election,_2004.

55. Doc and Claire Hastings, interview, February 13, 2017.

56. Annette Cary, "HEHF Chief Matheson Leaving, Ready for Change," *Tri-City Herald*, November 31, 2000, A3.

57. Editorial, "Prospect of Competition for Congress Appealing," *Tri-City Herald*, February 29, 2004, F2.

58. Sandy Matheson, interview by the author, April 3, 2017.

59. Chris Mullick, "Matheson to Make Candidacy Official," *Tri-City Herald*, March 24, 2004, B1.

60. Jack Briggs, email to the author, March 9, 2017.

61. Leah Beth Ward, "Mason Says He's Aiming at Hastings," *Yakima Herald-Republic*, June 22, 2004, C1; Leah Beth Ward, "Political Novice Joins the Race for Congress," *Yakima Herald-Republic*, July 1, 2004, B1.

62. Editorial, "Congressional Primary, 4th District: Matheson," *Tri-City Herald*, August 26, 2004, A12.

63. Leah Beth Ward, "Challenger Says Doc Puts His Party First," *Yakima Herald-Republic*, October 17, 2004, A1.

64. Chris Mullick, "Hastings Defeats Matheson for House, *Tri-City Herald*, November 3, 2004.

65. Sandy Matheson, email to the author, April 4, 2017.

66. Doc and Claire Hastings, interview by the author, August 10, 2017.

67. Chris Mullick, "Hastings, Matheson Civil in Debate," *Tri-City Herald*, October 19, 2004, A1.

68. Riggs, interview.

69. Ken Robertson, email to the author, June 1, 2016.

70. Mike Shepard, interview by the author, June 20, 2016.

71. Bill Lee, interview by the author, June 20, 2016.

72. Editorial, "Endorsements," *Yakima Herald-Republic*, October 27, 2004, A4; editorial, "Change in the 4th," *Seattle Times* online, October 22, 2004, accessed February

20, 2017, http://old.seattletimes.com/html/endorsements/2002069187_four-thed22.html; editorial, "4th District: Hastings," *Tri-City Herald*, October 21, 2004, A10.

73. Chris Mullick, "4th District Confronts Philosophical Choice," *Tri-City Herald*, October 23, 2004, A1.

Chapter 12

1. George W. Bush, "President Bush's Second Inaugural Address," NPR.org, January 20, 2005, accessed March 4, 2017, http://www.npr.org/templates/story/story.php?storyId=4460172.

2. George W. Bush, "Text of President Bush's 2005 State of the Union Address," *Washington Post* online, courtesy of FDCH E-Media, February 2, 2005, accessed March 4, 2017, http://www.washingtonpost.com/wp-srv/politics/transcripts/bushtext_020205.html.

3. Bush, *Decision Points*, 298-304.

4. Ibid., 298.

5. Doc and Claire Hastings, interview by the author, March 19, 2017.

6. Bush, *Decision Points*, 300.

7. Doc and Claire Hastings, interview, March 19, 2017.

8. Bush, *Decision Points*, 302-304.

9. "Hurricane Katrina," Wikipedia, accessed March 6, 2017, https://en.wikipedia.org/wiki/Hurricane_Katrina.

10. Bush, *Decision Points*, 310.

11. Dean Baker, "Recession Looms for the U.S. Economy in 2007," Center for Economic and Policy Research, November 2006, accessed March 6, 2017, http://cepr.net/documents/publications/forecast_2006_11.pdf.

12. Doc Hastings, interview, October 27, 2916.

13. "United States housing bubble," Wikipedia, accessed March 6, 2017, https://en.wikipedia.org/wiki/United_States_housing_bubble.

14. Doc and Claire Hastings, interview, March 19, 2017.

15. Leah Ward, "Hastings Still Supports Iraq's 'Nation-Building,'" *Yakima Herald-Republic*, August 17, 2005, B3.

16. Woodward, *State of Denial*, 409.

17. Mike Allen, "GOP Shifts Gears on Ethics Rule," *Washington Post*, January 5, 2005, A15.

18. Carl Hulse, "After Retreat, GOP Changes House Ethics Rule," *New York Times* online, January 5, 2005, accessed March 7, 2017, http://www.nytimes.com/2005/01/05/politics/after-retreat-gop-changes-house-ethics-rule.html?_r=0.

19. Ben Pershing, "Ethics Chairman Admired by GOP," *Roll Call*, February 3, 2005, 19.

20. John Bresnahan, "Democrats Slam Pick for Ethics," *Roll Call*, February 3, 2005, 1.

21. Alicia Mundy, "Rep. Hastings to Head House Ethics Committee," *Seattle Times* online, February 3, 2005, accessed March 4, 2017, http://www.seattletimes.com/seattle-news/rep-hastings-to-head-house-ethics-committee.

22. Doc and Claire Hastings, interview, August 18, 2016.

23. Ibid.

24. Doc and Claire Hastings, interview, December 1, 2016.

25. Susan Ferrechio, "Hastert Replaces Three Members of Panel That Repeatedly Rebuked Delay," *CQ Today*, February 3, 2005, 26.

26. Jim Camden, "Rocky Start for the New Ethics Chief," *Spokesman-Review* online, February 20, 2005, accessed March 8, 2007, http://www.spokesman.com/stories/2005/feb/20/rocky-start-for-the-new-ethics-chief.

27. Susan Ferrechio, "Standoff Leaves House Ethics Panel Out of Business, *CQToday*, March 11, 2005, 2.

28. Les Blumenthal, "Ex Hastings Aide Won't Get Panel Post," *Tri-City Herald*, April 28, 2005, B1.

29. Les Blumenthal, "Washington Group Calling for Hastings' Resignation," *Tri-City Herald*, June 10, 2005, B3.

30. Doc Hastings, interview by the author, March 16, 2017.

31. Doc and Claire Hastings, interview by the author, February 28, 2017.

32. Sheryl Gay Stolberg, "After Ethics Rebukes, DeLay's Fortunes May Lie with His Party's," *New York Times* online, October 8, 2004, accessed December 15, 2016, http://www.nytimes.com/2004/10/08/politics/after-ethics-rebukes-delays-fortunes-may-lie-with-his-partys.html.

33. Christine Bourge, "Analysis: House GOP Ethics Gambit Fails to Impress Dems," UPI, April 20, 2005, accessed March 15, 2017, http://www.upi.com/Defense-News/2005/04/20/Analysis-House-GOP-ethics-gambit-fails-to-impress-Dems/78311114045927/.

34. Susan Ferrechio, "Offer to Probe DeLay Quickly Rejected, *CQToday*, April 21, 2005, 1.

35. Carl Hulse, "House Overturns New Ethics Rule as G.O.P. Relents," *New York Times* online, April 28, 2005, accessed March 8, 2017, http://www.nytimes.com/2005/04/28/us/front%20page/house-overturns-new-ethics-rule-as-gop-relents.html.

36. Sharon Theimer, "Hastings Linked to Lobbyist in Delay Probe," *Yakima Herald-Republic*, June 10, 2005, A1.

37. "DeLay Hammered by Campaign Finance Indictment, Steps Down as House Majority Leader," Democracynow.org, September 29, 2005, accessed March 8, 2017, https://www.democracynow.org/2005/9/29/delay_hammered_by_campaign_finance_indictment.

38. Leah Ward, "Doc Feels the Heat," *Yakima Herald-Republic*, October 7, 2005, A1.

39. Alicia Mundy, "Hastings Says Ethics Panel Won't Investigate DeLay," *Seattle Times* online, October 6, 2005, accessed March 22, 2017, http://www.seattle-times.com/seattle-news/hastings-says-ethics-panel-wont-investigate-delay.

40. Ward, "Doc Feels the Heat."

41. "The Abramoff Affair: Timeline," *Washington Post* online, December 28, 2005, accessed March 8, 2017, http://www.washingtonpost.com/wp-dyn/content/custom/2005/12/28/CU2005122801176.html.

42. Leah Ward, "Congressman Hastings' Job Gets Tougher," *Yakima Herald-Republic*, January 14, 2006, A1.

43. "Boehner, Blunt Seek to Replace DeLay," CNN online, January 8, 2005, accessed March 17, 2017, http://www.cnn.com/2006/POLITICS/01/08/house.majorityleader/index.html.

44. Doc Hastings, interview, March 16, 2017.

45. "Roy Blunt," Wikipedia, accessed March 17, 2017, https://en.wikipedia.org/wiki/Roy_Blunt#cite_note-32.

46. David Espo, "DeLay Announces Resignation from House," *Chicago Tribune* online, April 4, 2006, accessed March 8, 2017, http://www.chicagotribune.com/sns-ap-delay-story.html.

47. Doc and Claire Hastings, interview, December 1, 2016.

48. "Local Projects: Federal Funds," *New York Times* online, April 7, 2006, accessed March 9, 2017, http://www.nytimes.com/imagepages/2006/04/07/washington/20060408_EARMARK_GRAPHIC.html.

49. Howard Berman, interview by the author, March 29, 2017.

50. Doc and Claire Hastings, interview, March 19, 2017.

51. Doc and Claire Hastings, interview, February 28, 2017.

52. Doc and Claire Hastings, interview, March 19, 2017.

53. CQ Transcripts Wire, "House Ethics Committee Holds a News Conference," *Washington Post* online, October 5, 2006, accessed March 17, 2017, http://www.washingtonpost.com/wp-dyn/content/article/2006/10/05/AR2006100500972.html.

54. Berman, interview.

55. "Mark Foley Scandal," Wikipedia, accessed March 9, 2017, https://en.wikipedia.org/wiki/Mark_Foley_scandal#cite_note-washpostkolbe10-18-7; Jonathan Weisman and Charles Babington, "GOP Leader Rebuts Hastert on Foley," *Washington Post* online, October 1, 2006, accessed March 9, 2017, http://www.washingtonpost.com/wp-dyn/content/article/2006/09/30/AR2006093001265_pf.html.

56. Doc and Claire Hastings, interview by the author, April 6, 2017.

57. Doc Hastings, interview, March 16, 2017.

58. Berman, interview.

59. Doc Hastings, interview by the author, April 22, 2017.

60. Jennifer Harper, "Whoops: Congress Gets the Nation's Lowest Rating for Honest and Ethical Standards," *Washington Times* online, December 20, 2014, accessed June 1, 2017. http://www.washingtontimes.com/news/2014/dec/20/naughty-list-congress-gets-nations-lowest-rating-h.

61. Charlene Koski, "Hastings Gets Funding for Naches Depot," *Yakima Herald-Republic*, April 26, 2006, A1.

62. David Lester, "Black Rock Cost Put at $3.5 Billion," *Yakima Herald-Republic*, February 9, 2005, A1.

63. Leah Beth Ward, "Feds: State and Local Resources Needed to Pay for Black Rock," *Yakima Herald-Republic*, April 22, 2005, A1.

64. Leah Beth Ward, "Black Rock in Line for $1.5 Million," *Yakima Herald-Republic*, May 25, 2005, A1.

65. Leah Beth Ward, "Hopes for Black Rock Grow Darker," *Yakima Herald-Republic*, October 11, 2005, B1.

66. David Lester, "It's Official—Drought Declared," *Yakima Herald-Republic*, March 11, 2005, A1.

67. Lia Steakley, "Mexico Imposes Tariff on Apples," *Yakima Herald-Republic*, October 6, 2005, A1.

68. Leah Beth Ward, "Hastings Sounds Off on Peru," *Yakima Herald-Republic*, December 10, 2005, B1.

69. Leah Beth Ward, "House Ag Panel Gets an Earful," *Yakima Herald-Republic*, June 11, 2006, C1.

70. Ana Gonzalez-Barrera, "Apprehensions of Mexican Migrants at U.S. Borders Reach Near-Historic Low," Pew Research Center, April 14, 2016, accessed May 13, 2017, http://www.pewresearch.org/fact-tank/2016/04/14/mexico-us-border-apprehensions.

71. Leah Beth Ward, "Message of the March," May 3, 2006, *Yakima Herald-Republic*, A1.

72. Leah Beth Ward, "Hastings Considers Immigration Enforcement Compromise," *Yakima Herald-Republic*, July 7, 2006, C1.

73. Annette Cary, "Bush Budget Proposes Hanford Cuts," *Tri-City Herald*, February 8, 2005, A1.

74. Annette Cary, "Committee Restores Hanford Money," *Tri-City Herald*, May 19, 2005, B1.

75. Samuel W. Bodman, note to Claire Hastings, June 17, 2005, Hastings collection.

76. Oregon Department of Energy, *Hanford Cleanup: The First 25 Years* (Salem, OR: Oregon Department of Energy, 2014), 132.

77. Annette Cary, "House Calls for Reform at Vit Plant," *Tri-City Herald*, May 12, 2006, A1.

78. Ibid.

79. "Presidential Approval Ratings—George W. Bush," Gallup, accessed March 21, 2017, http://www.gallup.com/poll/116500/presidential-approval-ratings-george-bush.aspx.

80. David R. Jones, "Why the Democrats Won," CBS News, November 8, 2006, accessed March 22, 2017, https://en.wikipedia.org/wiki/United_States_elections,_2006#cite_note-7.

81. "Bush Transcript, Part 3: Election Loss a 'Thumping,'" CNN online, November 8, 2006, accessed March 23, 2017, http://www.cnn.com/2006/POLITICS/11/08/bush.transcript3.

82. Mike Federman, "4th District—Lewis Picton," *Yakima Herald-Republic*, August 27, 2006, B1.

83. Chris Mulick, "Paperwork Filed to Challenge Hastings' Spot," *Tri-City Herald*, April 20, 2006, B1.

84. Leah Beth Ward, "Challenger Tones down News Release," *Yakima Herald-Republic*, March 22, 2006, B1.

85. Doc and Claire Hastings, interview, April 6, 2017.

86. Annette Cary, "Hastert Makes Stop in Tri-Cities," *Tri-City Herald*, February 23, 2006, A1.

87. Annette Cary, "Candidate Criticizes Hastings Performance," *Tri-City Herald*, March 8, 2006, B3.

88. Ed Stover, "Challenger to Hastings Comes Out Swinging." *Yakima Herald-Republic*, March 22, 2006, B3.

89. Chris Mulick, "Hastings' Rivals Not Bringing In Funds," *Tri-City Herald*, May 3, 2006, B1.

90. Leah Beth Ward, "Hastings Supports Delay as Victim of 'Political Vendetta,'" *Yakima Herald-Republic*, October 4, 2005, B1.

91. Claude L. Oliver, letter to Richard "Doc" Hastings, July 26, 2006, Hastings collection.

92. Richard "Doc" Hastings letter to Claude Oliver, July 26, 2006, Hastings collection.

93. "Setting the Record Straight: There he (Claude Oliver) goes again," Hastings collection.

94. Chris Mulick, "Republicans Duke It Out in 4th District," *Tri-City Herald*, September 3, 2006, B1.

95. Editorial, "4th District Congress: Hastings and Wright," *Tri-City Herald*, September 17, 2006, F2.

96. Chris Mulick, "Wright, Hastings Contend for 4th," *Tri-City Herald*, October 22, 2006, A1.

97. Doc and Claire Hastings, interview, March 19, 2017.

98. Doc and Claire Hastings, interview, April 6, 2017.

99. Editorial, "Enthused We're Not as We Cast Our Lot with Hastings," *Yakima Herald-Republic*, October 23, 2006, C8.

100. Editorial, "4th District, Congress: Doc Hastings," *Tri-City Herald*, November 1, 2006, A10.

101. Leah Ward, "Hastings Wins, But Chairman Hopes Are Gone," *Yakima Herald-Republic*, November 8, 2006, C1.

102. Patrick D. Muir, "Hastings Keeps Low Profile in Valley Visit," *Yakima Herald-Republic*, December 14, 2006, B1.

103. David Stout, "Panel Finds Negligence but No Violations in Foley Case," *New York Times* online, December 8, 2006, accessed June 1, 2017, http://www.nytimes.com/2006/12/08/washington/09foley.html.

104. Alicia Mundy, "Ethics Panel Rebukes McDermott," *Seattle Times* online, September 12, 2006, accessed April 8, 2017, http://www.seattletimes.com/seattle-news/panel-rebukes-mcdermott-in-ethics-case.

105. Doc and Claire, interview, July 14, 2016.

106. Ibid.

107. Muir, "Hastings Keeps Low Profile in Valley Visit."

Chapter 13

1. Doc Hastings, interview, April 6, 2017.

2. Ibid.

3. Allen Hayward, *My Ride* (Centralia, WA: Gorham Printing, 2014), 36.

4. "A New Direction for America," Office of the House Democratic Leader, Nancy Pelosi, July 2006, accessed March 27, 2017, http://www.washingtonpost.com/wp-srv/special/politics/political-rallying-cry/new-direction-for-america.pdf.

5. "Nancy Pelosi," Wikipedia, accessed March 27, 2017, https://en.wikipedia.org/wiki/Nancy_Pelosi.

6. "Rep. Dennis Hastert Says He Will Not Seek Re-election," website for FOX News, August 19, 2017, accessed March 27, 2017, http://www.foxnews.com/story/2007/08/19/rep-dennis-hastert-says-will-not-seek-re-election.html.

7. "Dennis Hastert," Wikipedia, accessed March 27, 2017, https://en.wikipedia.org/wiki/Dennis_Hastert.

8. After his resignation, Hastert became a successful lobbyist and consultant. It was later disclosed that he made millions in real estate while serving in Congress. In 2015, after Hastert had been indicted for illegally structuring financial transactions, it was disclosed that Hastert had paid $1.7 million to a man that he had sexually abused as a high school wrestling coach. In September, Hastert pleaded guilty to illegally withdrawing funds from his bank and lying to the FBI. He was released from federal prison to a halfway house on July 17, 2017.

9. Doc Hastings, interview, April 6, 2017.

10. An earmark is a provision attached to a discretionary spending bill that directs funding of a specific project or activity, often unrelated to the spending bill itself.

11. George W. Bush, "2007 State of the Union Address," website for *The White House*, January 23, 2007, accessed March 27, 2017. https://georgewbush-white-house.archives.gov/news/releases/2007/01/20070123-2.html.

12. Les Blumenthal, "Hastings to Oppose Resolution Challenging Troop Surge in Iraq," *Tri-City Herald,* February 14, 2007, B4.

13. "Iraq Troop Surge of 2007," Wikipedia, accessed March 28, 2017, https://en.wikipedia.org/wiki/Iraq_War_troop_surge_of_2007.

14. Doc Hastings, interview, April 6, 2017.

15. Michael Giusti, "Homeownership Rate Plunges," BankRate.com, accessed April 29, 2017, http://www.bankrate.com/finance/money-guides/homeownership-rate-plunges-1.aspx.

16. "United States Bear Market of 2007-2009," Wikipedia, accessed April 15, 2017, https://en.wikipedia.org/wiki/United_States_bear_market_of_2007%E2%80%9309.

17. Bush, *Decision Points*, 452-453.

18. Ibid., 458.

19. Chris Isidore, "Bailout Plan Rejected—Supporters Scramble," CNN Money online, September 29, 2008, accessed August 11, 2017, http://money.cnn.com/2008/09/29/news/economy/bailout.

20. Doc Hastings, interview by the author, April 18, 2017.

21. Dave Leder, "Hastings Joins GOP Rebellion against Bill," *Yakima Herald-Republic*, September 30, 2008, A1.

22. Les Blumenthal, "Washington House Members Maintain 'No' Votes," *Tri-City Herald*, October 4, 2008, B1.

23. Bush, *Decision Points*, 440.

24. Doc Hastings, interview by the author, April 6, 2017.

25. Ibid.

26. Ibid.

27. Ibid.

28. Susan Crabtree, "Senior Aide Implicated," *The Hill* online, March 6, 2007, accessed April 14, 2017, http://thehill.com/homenews/news/11231-senior-aide-implicated.

29. Doc and Claire Hastings, interview by the author, May 18, 2017.

30. Charles Pope, "McKay Tells of GOP Call in 2004-05," *Seattle Post-Intelligencer* online, March 6, 2007, accessed April 15, 2017, http://www.seattlepi.com/local/article/McKay-tells-of-a-GOP-call-in-2004-05-1230365.php.

31. Larry Margasak, "Republicans Could Face New Ethics Probes," *Washington Post* online, March 7, 2007, accessed April 14, 2017, http://www.washingtonpost.com/wp-dyn/content/article/2007/03/06/AR2007030600381_pf.html.

32. Editorial, "Hastings Should Welcome Investigation," *Tri-City Herald*, March 11, 2007, F2; editorial, "Congress Must Probe Mass Firings," *Yakima Herald-Republic*, March 12, 2007, A4.

33. Alicia Munday, "Group Wants Ethics Probe of Hastings, Former Aide," *Seattle Times* online, March 9, 2007, accessed April 14, 2017, http://www.seattletimes.com/seattle-news/group-wants-ethics-probe-of-hastings-former-aide/.

34. "About," website for the Office of Congressional Ethics, accessed April 13, 2017, https://oce.house.gov/about.

35. Doc Hastings, interview by the author, April 6, 2017.

36. Christopher Lee, "Rangel's Pet Cause Bears His Own Name," *Washington Post* online, July 15, 2008, accessed April 13, 2017, http://www.washingtonpost.com/wp-dyn/content/article/2008/07/14/AR2008071402546.html.

37. Daphne Retter, "Big Wheel Benz the Rules," *New York Post* online, September 18, 2008, http://www.washingtonpost.com/wp-dyn/content/article/2008/07/14/AR2008071402546.html; Isabel Vincent and Susan Edelman, "Tricky Charlie's Carib Hideaway," *New York Post* online, August 31, 2008, http://nypost.com/2008/08/31/tricky-charlies-carib-hideaway; David Kocieniewski and David M. Halbfinger, "Interest Was Waived for Rangel on Loan for Villa," *New York Times* online, September 5, 2008, http://www.nytimes.com/2008/09/06/nyregion/06rangel.html; David Kocieniewski and David M. Halbfinger, "Rangel Owes U.S. Back Taxes, Lawyer Says," *New York Times* online, September 9, 2008, http://www.nytimes.com/2008/09/10/nyregion/10rangel.html.

38. Paul Kane and David A. Farentholt, "House Censures Rep. Charles Rangel in 333-79 vote," *Washington Post* online, December 1, 2010, accessed April 13, 2017, http://www.washingtonpost.com/wp-dyn/content/article/2010/12/02/AR2010120201626.html?hpid=topnews.

39. Ibid.

40. Cassidy later went on to become the administrator of the US Capitol when Boehner served as Speaker of the House.

41. John R. Wilke, "Alaska's Young, Stevens Face Inquiry," *Wall Street Journal* online, July 15, 2007, accessed April 29, 2017, https://www.wsj.com/articles/SB118531999682776863.

42. Rachel Weiner, "Don Young: No Stranger to Controversy," *Washington Post* online, March 29, 2013, accessed April 29, 2017, https://www.washingtonpost.com/news/the-fix/wp/2013/03/29/don-young-no-stranger-to-scandal/?utm_term=.8b0a821caf9c.

43. Ed Cassidy, memo to John Boehner, November 14, 2007. Hastings collection.

44. Ibid.

45. Leah Ward, "Hastings Is Eyeing a Return to the House Natural Resources Panel," *Yakima Herald-Republic*, December 11, 2008, C2; Les Blumenthal, "Hastings Named to Resource Panel," *Tri-City Herald*, December 12, 2008, A1.

46. Editorial, "Hastings Named to Resource Committee," *Tri-City Herald*, December 12, 2008, A1.

47. Doc Hastings, interview, April 6, 2017.

48. Mary Hopkin, "Hastings Shares His Opinions While on Break with Congress," *Tri-City Herald*, August 29, 2007, B3.

49. Annette Cary, "Hastings Fields Questions from Public," *Tri-City Herald*, November 27, 2007, B1.

50. Doc Hastings, interview by the author, April 6, 2017.

51. Annette Cary, "$1.94 Billion 2008 Hanford Budget Proposed," *Tri-City Herald*, February 6, 2007, A1.

52. Annette Cary, "Jobs Could Get Axe under Budget," *Tri-City Herald*, February 5, 2008, A1.

53. Annette Cary, "Plan to Accelerate Cleanup 'Abandoned,'" *Tri-City Herald*, February 36, 2007, B1.

54. Doc Hastings, interview, April 6, 2017.

55. Annette Cary, "DOE: 23 Cleanup Deadlines at Risk," *Tri-City Herald*, November 7, 2008, A1.

56. Annette Cary, "State to File Suit against DOE," *Tri-City Herald*, November 26, 2008, A1.

57. John Trumbo, "Contract Extended," *Tri-City Herald*, August 2, 2007, A1.

58. John Trumbo, "Construction to Start Today on PNNL Lab," *Tri-City Herald*, August 15, 2007, B1.

59. John Trumbo, "PNNL Contract to Disallow Private Work," *Tri-City Herald*, October 26, 2007, A1.

60. Annette Cary, "Hanford Budget, PNNL Lab Use Permit Gets OK'd," *Tri-City Herald*, December 20, 2007, A1.

61. Editorial, "HAMMER victory," *Tri-City Herald*, June 21, 2007, A8.

62. Anette Cary, "Government OKs Health Payments for Early Workers," *Tri-City Herald*, September 2, 2007, B1.

63. Les Blumenthal, "Reactor Gets Nod for New Status," *Tri-City Herald*, December 6, 2007, A1.

64. Les Blumenthal and Anna King, "A Focus on Farming," *Tri-City Herald*, February 11, 2007, A1.

65. Les Blumenthal, "Farm bill cruises through Senate," *Tri-City Herald*, May 16, 2008, A1.

66. David Lester, "Farm Bill Sidebar," *Yakima Herald-Republic*, May 15, 2008, A3.

67. "Food, Conservation, and Energy Act of 2008," Wikipedia, accessed April 27, 2017, https://en.wikipedia.org/wiki/Food,_Conservation,_and_Energy_Act_of_2008.

68. Leah Ward, "More Fruit Growers Ready to Use Guest-Worker Program," *Yakima Herald-Republic*, February 26, 2007, A1.

69. Leah Ward, "Hastings Says Congress Might Look Again at Guest Workers," *Yakima Herald-Republic*, August 18, 2007, B1.

70. Andrew Sirocchi, "Hastings Wants Bush Administration to Challenge 9th Circuit Salmon Decision," *Tri-City Herald*, April 11, 2007, A1.

71. John Trumbo, "Juniper Dunes Access Project Hits $1M Snag," *Tri-City Herald*, August 26, 2012, B1.

72. Annette Cary, "More Public Access to Monument Sought," *Tri-City Herald*, June 21, 2007, B1.

73. David Lester, "Reservoir Could Spread Hanford Pollution," *Yakima Herald-Republic*, September 19, 2007, A1.

74. David Lester, "Black Rock Report Is Bad News," *Yakima Herald-Republic*, January 30, 2008, A1.

75. Doc and Claire Hastings, interview by the author, May 11, 2017.

76. John Trumbo, "Reclamation Ends Water Storage Studies," *Tri-City Herald*, April 4, 2009, B1.

77. "President George W. Bush Presidential Job Approval," Gallup, accessed April 28, 2007, http://www.gallup.com/poll/116500/presidential-approval-ratings-george-bush.aspx; "United States Presidential Election 2008," Wikipedia, accessed April 28, 2007, https://en.wikipedia.org/wiki/United_States_presidential_election,_2008.

78. Barbara Serrano, "Hastings Gives Support to McCain," *Yakima Herald-Republic*, February 6, 2008, C2.

79. Jonathan Alter, *The Promise* (New York, Simon & Schuster, 2010), 38-39.

80. Ibid., 39.

81. Thomas E. Mann and Norman J. Ornstein, *It's Even Worse Than It Looks: How the American Constitutional System Collided with the New Politics of Extremism* (New York: Basic Books, 2013), 45-46.

82. Patrick D. Muir, "Ready to Race against Doc," *Yakima Herald-Republic*, November 19, 2007, C1.

83. Annette Cary, "Kennewick Attorney Fearing to Run against Rep. Hastings," *Tri-City Herald*, February 13, 2008, B4.

84. Patrick D. Muir, "Old, New Media Personalities Strive to Overthrow Hastings," *Yakima Herald-Republic*, April 24, 2008, C4.

85. Patrick D. Muir, "Doc," *Yakima Herald-Republic*, April 5, 2008, A7.

86. Doc and Claire Hastings, interview by the author, June 8, 2017.

87. Karl C. Rove, handwritten note to Doc Hastings, April 26, 2008. Hastings collection.

88. Joshi Pratik, "Hastings Says Drilling the Answer," *Tri-City Herald*, August 14, 2008, B6.

89. "Election Results," *Tri-City Herald*, August 20, 2008, A1.

90. Patrick D. Muir, "McCloskey," *Yakima Herald-Republic*, August 22, 2008, B1.

91. Annette Cary, "Candidates Divided on Fixing Economy," *Tri-City Herald*, October 16, 2008, A1.

92. Editorial, "4th District House of Representatives: It's Hastings by Default, Again," *Yakima Herald-Republic*, October 17, 2008, A4.

93. Editorial, "4th Congressional District: Re-elect Doc Hastings," *Tri-City Herald*, October 16, 2008, A8.

94. Leah Ward, "Election Hastings," *Yakima Herald-Republic*," November 4, 2008, C1.

Chapter 14

1. FDCH E-Media, "Transcript: Illinois Senate Candidate Barack Obama," *Washington Post* online, July 27, 2004, accessed May 8, 2017, http://www.washingtonpost.com/wp-dyn/articles/A19751-2004Jul27.html.

2. Barack Obama, "Transcript: 'This is your victory,' says Obama," CNN online, August 28, 2008, accessed May 8, 2017, http://edition.cnn.com/2008/POLITICS/11/04/obama.transcript.

3. "United States Elections, 2008," Wikipedia, accessed May 8, 2017, https://en.wikipedia.org/wiki/United_States_elections,_2008.

4. "Tea Party Movement," Wikipedia, accessed May 8, 2017, https://en.wikipedia.org/wiki/Tea_Party_movement.

5. Doc and Claire Hastings, interview, May 11, 2017.

6. Jonathan Alter, *The Promise* (New York: Simon and Schuster, 2010), 81.

7. Bob Woodward, *The Price of Politics* (New York: Simon & Schuster, 2012), 62.

8. Joel Connelly, "The 'Colossal Failure' That Helped Doc Hastings' District," *Seattle Post Intelligencer* online, March 20, 2014, accessed June 26, 2017, http://blog.seattlepi.com/seattlepolitics/2014/03/20/the-colossal-failure-that-helped-doc-hastings-district.

9. Les Blumenthal, "Economy a Priority for State's Delegation," *Tri-City Herald*, January 4, 2009, A1.

10. Josh Clinton and Carrie Roush, "Poll: Persistent Partisan Divide over 'Birther' Question," NBC News online, August 10, 2016, accessed May 9, 2017, http://www.nbcnews.com/politics/2016-election/poll-persistent-partisan-divide-over-birther-question-n627446.

11. Doc and Claire Hastings, interview, August 10, 2017.

12. Alter, *The Promise*, 84, 117.

13. Ibid., 118.

14. Woodward, *The Price of Politics*, 21.

15. Les Blumenthal, "House Approves Economic Stimulus Bill," *Tri-City Herald*, January 29, 2009, A1.

16. "American Recovery and Reinvestment Act of 2009," Wikipedia, accessed May 8, 2017, https://en.wikipedia.org/wiki/American_Recovery_and_Reinvestment_Act_of_2009.

17. Alter, *The Promise*, 120.

18. Annette Cary, "Hastings Says 'No' to Stimulus Bill," *Tri-City Herald*, February 14, 2009, B1.
19. "American Recovery and Reinvestment Act of 2009," Wikipedia, accessed May 8, 2017, https://en.wikipedia.org/wiki/American_Recovery_and_Reinvestment_Act_of_2009.
20. Doc and Claire Hastings, interview, May 11, 2017.
21. Michael D. Shear and Anne E. Kornblut, "In Speech to Congress, Obama Outlines His Plans for Economic Recovery," *Washington Post* online, February 25, 2009, accessed May 10, 2017, http://www.washingtonpost.com/wp-dyn/content/article/2009/02/24/AR2009022401832.html?sid=ST2009022402300.
22. Emily Smith, "Timeline of the Health Care Law," CNN online, June 2, 2012, accessed May 13, 2017, http://www.cnn.com/2012/06/28/politics/supreme-court-health-timeline.
23. Frank Purdy, "Hastings says Obama Taking Country in Wrong Direction," *Yakima Herald-Republic*, February 25, 2009, A1.
24. Carl Hulse, "Budgets Approved, with No GOP Votes," *New York Times* online, April 2, 2009, accessed May 13, 2017, http://www.nytimes.com/2009/04/03/us/politics/03budget.html?_r=0.
25. Alter, *The Promise*, 244-246.
26. Drew Foster, "Hastings Opposes Government-Run Health Care," *Tri-City Herald*, August 19, 2009, B3.
27. Les Blumenthal, "Fiery Debate Won't Sway Lawmakers," *Tri-City Herald*, September 7, 2009, A1; Les Blumenthal, "Health Insurance Premiums Skyrocket," *Tri-City Herald*, September 16, 2009, A4.
28. Alberta, "John Boehner Unchained."
29. Alexander Bolton, "Dems on ObamaCare: Was It Worth It?" *The Hill* online, December 4, 2014, accessed August 23, 2017, http://thehill.com/homenews/senate/225959-dems-on-o-care-was-it-worth-it.
30. Doc and Claire Hastings, interview, May 11, 2017.
31. "Dodd–Frank Wall Street Reform and Consumer Protection Act," Wikipedia, accessed May 14, 2017, https://en.wikipedia.org/wiki/Dodd%E2%80%-93Frank_Wall_Street_Reform_and_Consumer_Protection_Act.
32. Doc and Claire Hastings, interview, May 11, 2017.
33. Woodward, *The Price of Politics*, 45.
34. "National Commission on Fiscal Responsibility and Reform," Wikipedia, accessed June 20, 2017, https://en.wikipedia.org/wiki/National_Commission_on_Fiscal_Responsibility_and_Reform.
35. Woodward, *The Price of Politics*, 60.
36. Ibid., 62.
37. Ibid., 66.
38. Doc and Claire Hastings, interview by the author, June 22, 2017.

39. Samantha Dana and Mattea Kramer, "History of the U.S. Federal Budget, 2011 –2013," National Priorities Project, February 12, 2014, accessed June 21, 2017, https://www.nationalpriorities.org/analysis/2014/history-us-federal-budget-2011-2013.

40. Alter, *The Promise*, 347-348, 350.

41. Ibid., 379.

42. Ibid., 387.

43. Les Blumenthal, "Democrats Not Sold on War Decision," *Tri-City Herald*, December 6, 2009, A1.

44. Shushanna Walsh, "IRS Scandal Stretches across US," ABC News online, May 14, 2013, accessed July 26, 2017, http://abcnews.go.com/politics/t/blogEntry?id=19178678.

45. Doc and Claire Hastings, interview, May 18, 2017. "Cap and trade" is a system for controlling carbon emissions released into the environment by placing a cap on the amount that can be released by a given company but which also allows that company to purchase the ability to release more emissions from another company that has not reached its full allowance.

46. Doc and Claire Hastings, interview, May 18, 2017.

47. Ibid.

48. Annette Cary, "Senate Panel Seeks More Funding," *Tri-City Herald*, March 31, 2009, B1.

49. Les Blumenthal, "Stimulus at work—Economic Stimulus Money That Went to Small-Business Owners Largely Overlooked," *Tri-City Herald*, August 9, 2010, A1.

50. Oregon Department of Energy, *Hanford Cleanup: The First 25 Years* (Salem, OR: Oregon Department of Energy, 2014), 178, 183-184.

51. Annette Cary, "2011 Hanford Budget Bump Proposed," *Tri-City Herald*, February 2, 2010, A1.

52. Annette Cary, "DOE Files to End Yucca Mountain," *Tri-City Herald*, March 4, 2010, A1.

53. Annette Cary, "Hastings Gets Key Aid in Nuclear Waste Battle," *Tri-City Herald*, November 20, 2010, A1.

54. Annette Cary, "Hastings Calls for Another Look at B Reactor," *Tri-City Herald*, January 30, 2010, B1.

55. Annette Cary, "Congressional Leaders Support B Reactor Park," *Tri-City Herald*, March 4, 2010, A1.

56. Letter from energy assistant secretary Ines Triay to Jon Jarvis, director of the National Park Service, May 13, 2010, Oregon Department of Energy, *Hanford Cleanup: The First 25 Years* (Salem, OR: Oregon Department of Energy, 2014), 189.

57. Annette Cary, "Hastings Introduces Bill to Open Rattlesnake Mountain," *Tri-City Herald*, May 28, 2010, A1; Annette Cary, "Officials Plan Tours of Rattlesnake Mountain," *Tri-City Herald*, July 9, 2010, B1.

58. Michelle Dupler, "Growers Seek End to Mexican Tariffs," *Tri-City Herald*, September 9, 2010, A1.

59. Doc and Claire Hastings, interview, May 18, 2017.

60. David Lester, "Northwest Produce Now Tariff-Free," *Yakima Herald-Republic*, October 22, 2011, B1.

61. Editorial, "Salmon Aren't Helped by Revival of Dam Debate," *Tri-City Herald*, May 29, 2009, A8.

62. Pratik Joshi, "Bill Opens Possibility of Dam Removal," *Tri-City Herald*, August 1, 2009, B1.

63. Editorial, "Old West Melodrama on the Snake River Dams," *Tri-City Herald*, August 9, 2009, E2.

64. Les Blumenthal, "McDermott Again Seeks Dam Breaching Study," *Tri-City Herald*, August 20, 2009, A1.

65. Kevin McCullen, "Plan Outlines Dam Removal Steps," *Tri-City Herald*, April 1, 2010, A1.

66. Patrick D. Muir, "DREAM Act," *Yakima Herald-Republic*, December 10, 2010, A1.

67. Peter Baker, *Obama: The Call of History* (New York: Callaway, 2017), 85.

68. "United States elections, 2010," Wikipedia, accessed May 25, 2017, https://en.wikipedia.org/wiki/United_States_elections,_2010.

69. Jonathan Alter, *The Center Holds* (New York: Simon and Schuster, 2013), 4.

70. Philip Ferolito, "Democrats Take on Doc Hastings," *Yakima Herald-Republic*, November 10, 2009, B1.

71. Drew Foster, "Kennewick Ex-Marine to Challenge Hastings," *Tri-City Herald*, November 10, 2009, B1.

72. Patrick D. Muir, "Conservative Sets Sights on Unseating Doc Hastings," *Yakima-Herald Republic*, March 2, 2010, A12.

73. Leah Ward, "Tea Party Looks to Get Active Politically," *Yakima Herald-Republic*, March 17, 2010, B1.

74. Patrick D. Muir, "Yialelis/Filings," *Yakima Herald-Republic*, June 10, 2010, B2.

75. Patrick D. Muir, "Anti-incumbent Mood Unlikely to Dislodge Doc Hastings," *Yakima Herald-Republic*, August 8, 2010, C1.

76. Michelle Dupler, "Hastings Faces 5 in Fourth District," *Tri-City Herald*, August 15, 2010, B1.

77. Patrick D. Muir, "ELECTION Hastings/Clough," *Yakima Herald-Republic*, October 3, 2010, B1.

78. Michelle Dupler, "Newcomer Tried to Point Hastings as Insider," *Tri-City Herald*, October 18, 2010, A1.

79. Patrick D. Muir, "Hastings Clough," *Yakima Herald-Republic*, November 3, 2010, A5.
80. Doc Hastings, interview by the author, July 25, 2017.
81. Jake Sherman and Richard E. Cohen, "Issa Plans Hundreds of Hearings," *Politico* online, November 8, 2010, accessed July 27, 2017, http://www.politico.com/story/2010/11/issa-plans-hundreds-of-hearings-044850.
82. Doc Hastings, interview by the author, July 25, 2017.
83. "Ranking Member Hastings Proposes Creation of Energy and Natural Resources Committee," House Committee on Natural Resources Press Release, accessed June 7, 2017, https://naturalresources.house.gov/newsroom/documentsingle.aspx?DocumentID=215332.
84. Doc and Claire Hastings, interview by the author, May 29, 2017.
85. Margaret Kriz Hobson, "A Burst of Energy for Natural Resources?" *CQ* online, November 29, 2010, accessed June 7, 2017, https://robbishop.house.gov/news/documentsingle.aspx?DocumentID=215783.
86. Doc and Claire Hastings, interview, May 29, 2017.
87. Doc and Claire Hastings, interview, August 10, 2017.
88. Doc Hastings, interview by the author, November 28, 2017.
89. Robert Pear and David M. Herszenhorn, "Obama Hails Vote on Health Care as Answering 'the Call of History,'" *New York Times* online, March 21, 2010, accessed May 14, 2017, http://www.nytimes.com/2010/03/22/health/policy/22health.html?pagewanted=all&_r=0.
90. "Support for 2010 Health Care Law Reaches New High," Pew Research Center, February 23, 2017, accessed June 3, 2017, http://www.pewresearch.org/fact-tank/2017/02/23/support-for-2010-health-care-law-reaches-new-high.
91. Woodward, *The Price of Politics*, 70.

Chapter 15

1. Doc and Claire Hastings, interviews by the author, June 8 and July 20, 2017.
2. Jonathan Allen and John Bresnahan, "19 Democrats Vote against Pelosi," *Politico* online, January 5, 2011, accessed July 16, 2017. http://www.politico.com/story/2011/01/19-democrats-vote-against-pelosi-047081.
3. Congress and the Public, Gallup, accessed July 21, 2017, http://www.gallup.com/poll/1600/congress-public.aspx.
4. Jennifer Steinhauer, "Constitution Has Its Day (More or Less) in House," *New York Times* online, January 6, 2011, accessed June 20, 2017, http://www.nytimes.com/2011/01/07/us/politics/07constitution.html.
5. Ibid.
6. Doc and Claire Hastings, interview, June 22, 2017.
7. "2011 State of the Union Address," Wikipedia, accessed June 20, 2017, https://en.wikipedia.org/wiki/2011_State_of_the_Union_Address.

8. "The Path to Prosperity," Wikipedia, accessed July 8, 2017, https://en.wikipedia.org/wiki/The_Path_to_Prosperity.

9. Doc and Claire Hastings, interview by the author, June 29, 2017.

10. Carl Hulse, "Republican Leaders Yield to a Push for More Budget Cuts," *New York Times* online, February 10, 2011, accessed June 21, 2017, http://www.nytimes.com/2011/02/11/us/politics/11congress.html?_r=0.

11. Carl Hulse, "Budget Deal to Cut $38 Billion Averts Shutdown," *New York Times* online, April 8, 2011, accessed June 21, 2017, http://www.nytimes.com/2011/04/09/us/politics/09fiscal.html.

12. Doc and Claire Hastings, interview, July 20, 2017.

13. Woodward, *The Price of Politics*, 122.

14. Carl Hulse, "For Boehner, Lofty Budget Goals Checked by Realit," *New York Times* online, July 10, 2011, accessed June 22, 2017, http://www.nytimes.com/2011/07/11/us/politics/11boehner.html.

15. Alter, *The Center Holds*, 165.

16. Ibid., 189.

17. Alberta, "John Boehner Unchained."

18. Doc and Claire Hastings, interview by the author, July 13, 2017.

19. Alter, *The Center Holds*, 166-167.

20. Ibid., 171.

21. Rob Hotakainen, "Plan Wins Mostly Bipartisan Support," *Tri-City Herald*, August 2, 2011, A1.

22. Alter, *The Center Holds*, 175.

23. Final Recommendations to the Joint Select Committee on Deficit Reduction, House Committee on Natural Resources, October 14, 2011, accessed July 22, 2017, https://naturalresources.house.gov/uploadedfiles/nrdeficitreductionrecommendations-10.14.11.pdf.

24. Woodward, *The Price of Politics*, 363.

25. Alter, *The Center Holds*, 370.

26. American Taxpayer Relief Act of 2012, Wikipedia, accessed July 22, 2017, https://en.wikipedia.org/wiki/American_Taxpayer_Relief_Act_of_2012.

27. Doc and Claire Hastings, interview, July 13, 2017.

28. Peter Baker, *Obama: The Call of History* (New York: Callaway, 2017), 99.

29. Woodward, *The Price of Politics*, 379; Alter, *The Center Holds*, 167.

30. Doc and Claire Hastings, interview, June 22, 2017.

31. Ibid.

32. Todd Ungerecht, email, June 26, 2017.

33. Doc and Claire Hastings, interviews, June 22, 2017 and August 10, 2017.

34. Doc and Claire Hastings, interview, June 29, 2017.

35. Joel Connelly, "Rep. Doc Hastings, State's Most Conservative Congressman, to Retire," *Seattle Post-Intelligencer* online, February 13, 2014, accessed

June 26, 2017, http://blog.seattlepi.com/seattlepolitics/2014/02/13/rep-doc-hastings-to-retire-states-most-conservative-congressman.

36. Rob Hotakainen, "Conservationists Fear Hasting Will Lean to Businesses," *Tri-City Herald*, January 10, 2011, A1.

37. Ibid.

38. Audrey Hudson, "Setting New Energy Agenda: Republicans Will Challenge Obama's Policies One Subpoena at a Time," *Human Events*, April 16, 2012, 12.

39. Hastings collection.

40. "Chairman Hastings' Statement on Judge Redden Ruling," press release, House Natural Resources Committee, September 8, 2011, accessed June 27, 2017, https://naturalresources.house.gov/newsroom/documentsingle.aspx?DocumentID=254871.

41. Bob Hotakainen, "Congress Spars over 'Ocean Zoning' Plan," *Tri-City Herald*, October 5, 2011, A1.

42. Michelle Dupler, "Doc Hastings Returns for S. America Trip Touting Opportunity for Farmers, *Tri-City Herald*, January 18, 2012, B2.

43. Claire Hastings, trip notes, Hastings collection.

44. Doc and Claire Hastings, interview, July 13, 2017.

45. Doc and Claire Hastings, interview by the author, May 28, 2017.

46. Doc and Claire Hastings, interview, June 29, 2017.

47. Doc and Claire Hastings, interview, August 10, 2017.

48. Barry Popik, "The Senate is the enemy, July 6, 2014, accessed August 15, 2017, http://www.barrypopik.com/index.php/new york city/entry/the senate is the enemy.

49. Maria Cantwell, interview by the author, August 14, 2017.

50. Annette Cary, "Hearing Draws Demonstrators," *Tri-City Herald*, August 16, 2012, A1.

51. Doc Hastings, interview by the author, July 5, 2017.

52. Doc and Claire Hastings, interview, June 29, 2017.

53. Doc Hastings, interview, July 5. 2017.

54. Annette Cary, "1,600 Layoffs in the Works at Hanford," *Tri-City Herald*, January 20, 2011, A1.

55. Annette Cary, Court Tosses Lawsuit," *Tri-City Herald*, July 2, 2011, A1.

56. Barry M. Hartman, Tim L. Peckinpaugh, Christine A. Jochim, and Christopher R. Nestor, "US Court of Appeals Orders the Nuclear Regulatory Commission to Resume Yucca Mountain Licensing Proceeding, Upholding Rule of Law Over Politics," K&L Gates *Stay Informed,* August 15, 2013, accessed November 19, 2017, http://klgates.com/us-court-of-appeals-orders-the-nuclear-regulatory-commission-to-resume-yucca-mountain-licensing-proceeding-upholding-rule-of-law-over-politics-08-15-2013; In re Aiken County, 725 F.3d 255 (D.C. Cir. 2013), decided August 13, 2013, reh'g en banc denied (Oct. 28, 2013).

57. Tim Peckinpaugh, email to the author, November 21, 2017.

58. Annette Cary, "DOE Developing Policies for Reuse of Hanford Land," *Tri-City Herald*, February 22, 2011, A1.

59. Annette Cary, "Some Vit Plant Deadlines at Risk," *Tri-City Herald*, November 22, 2011, A1.

60. David Lester, "Salazar Offers Support for Yakima Basin Water Projects," *Yakima Herald-Republic*, September 19, 2011, A1.

61. Annette Cary, "House Debates B Reactor Park," *Tri-City Herald*, September 20, 2012.

62. Doc Hastings, interview, July 5, 2017.

63. Mike Faulk, "Hastings Unsure if He Will Support New E-Verify Bill," *Yakima Herald-Republic*, June 18, 2011, A12.

64. Chuck Todd, *The Stranger*, (New York: Little, Brown and Company, 2014), 255.

65. Michael D. Regan, "GOP Voting Restrictions Struck Down in Three States," *PBS NewsHour* online, July 30, 2016, accessed July 7, 2017, http://www.pbs.org/newshour/rundown/gop-voting-restrictions-struck-three-states.

66. Seung Min Kim, "Rendell Amazed by GOP 2012 'Clown Car,'" *Politico* online, January 26, 2012, accessed July 7, 2017, http://www.politico.com/blogs/on-congress/2012/01/rendell-amazed-by-gop-2012-clown-car-112391.

67. Alter, *The Center Holds*, 269.

68. Todd, 325-326.

69. "Read the Full Text of President Obama's Economic Speech in Kansas," *Los Angeles Times* online, December 6, 2011, accessed July 15, 2017, http://articles.latimes.com/2011/dec/06/news/la-pn-text-obama-speech-kansas-20111206.

70. Molly Moorehead, "Mitt Romney Says 47 Percent of Americans Pay No Income Tax," Politifact, September 18, 2012, accessed July 7, 2017, http://www.politifact.com/truth-o-meter/statements/2012/sep/18/mitt-romney/romney-says-47-percent-americans-pay-no-income-tax.

71. Alter, *The Center Holds*, 559.

72. Mike Faulk, "Jay Clough Ready to Challenge Doc Hastings Again," *Yakima Herald-Republic*, April 19, 2011, A10; Mike Faulk, "Clough Quits Second Bid to Oust Doc," *Yakima Herald-Republic*, February 3, 2012, B1.

73. Mike Faulk, "Doc Hastings to Seek Another Term in 4th District," *Yakima Herald-Republic*, March 31, 2012, B1.

74. Mike Faulk, "Community Activist to Challenge Incumbent Congressman," *Yakima Herald-Republic*, April 10, 2012, A12.

75. Mike Faulk, "Longtime 4th District Congressman to Face Two Democrats and One Republican," *Yakima Herald-Republic*, July 22, 2012, B1.

76. Editorial, "Doc's Experience Qualifies Him to Get Things Done," *Tri-City Herald*, October 23, 2012, A6.

77. Doc and Claire Hastings, interview, August 18, 2016.

78. John Boehner, interview, September 8, 2016.

79. Doc Hastings, interview, July 22, 2007.

Chapter 16

1. Emily Feldman, "113th Congress Sworn in Thursday," *NBCNew5, Chicago* online, January 3, 2013, accessed July 16, 2017, http://www.nbcchicago.com/blogs/ward-room/113th-Congress-Sworn-in-Thursday-Meet-Your-Leaders-185533312.html.

2. Russell Berman, Erik Wasson, and Molly K. Hooper, "Failed Coup Effort against Boehner Highlights House GOP Divisions," *The Hill* online, January 3, 2013, accessed July 17, 2017, http://thehill.com/homenews/house/275527-failed-coup-effort-against-boehner-highlights-divisions-within-house-gop.

3. Alberta, "John Boehner Unchained."

4. David Lester, "Fiscal Cliff Deal Doesn't Solve Nation's Debt Crisis, GOP Representative Says," *Yakima Herald-Republic*, January 3, 2013, A1.

5. Technically, that honor belonged to Democrat Jim McDermott, who represented Washington's Seventh Congressional District from 1989. Doc was the longest-serving Republican in the state's delegation.

6. Susan Page, "Obama's Speech Takes on Divisive Issues," *USA Today* online, January 22, 2013, accessed July 16, 2017, https://www.usatoday.com/story/news/politics/2013/01/21/obama-inaugural-address-analysis/1852081.

7. Doc and Claire Hastings, interview, July 20, 2017.

8. Mark Suppes and Sarah Wheaton, "Analyzing President Obama's State of the Union Address," *New York Times* online, February 13, 2013, accessed July 17, 2013, http://www.nytimes.com/interactive/2013/02/12/us/politics/obama-state-of-the-union-2013.html#/?annotation=280e1219d.

9. Geoff Folsom, "Immigration Reform Protestors 'Occupy' Rep. Hastings' Office," *Tri-City Herald*, June 5, 2014, B2.

10. Alberta, "John Boehner Unchained."

11. Benji Sarlin,"Obama to Take Action after Boehner Kills Immigration Reform," MSNBC, June 30, 2013, accessed August 19, 2017, http://www.msnbc.com/msnbc/obama-take-action-after-boehner-kills-immigration-reform.

12. Doc and Claire Hastings, interview, July 20, 2017.

13. Todd, *The Stranger*, 381.

14. Doc and Claire Hastings, interview, July 20, 2017.

15. Geoff Folsom, "Hastings Downplays Political Tension," *Tri-City Herald*, August 29, 2013, B1.

16. Todd, *The Stranger*, 402-403.

17. Rebecca Kaplan, "Obama: I Will Use My Pen and Phone to Take on Congress," *CBS News* online, January 14, 2014, accessed July 23, 2017, http://www.cbsnews.com/news/obama-i-will-use-my-pen-and-phone-to-take-on-congress.

18. Leslie H. Gelb, "The Mind of the President," *New York Times Magazine* online, October 6, 1985, accessed July 23, 2017, http://www.nytimes.com/1985/10/06/magazine/the-mind-of-the-president.html.

19. Jim Puzzanghera, "Fitch Warns That Debt-Limit Delay Could Hurt U.S. Credit Rating," *Los Angeles Times* online, January 13, 2013, accessed August 15, 2017, http://articles.latimes.com/2013/jan/15/business/la-fi-mo-fitch-ratings-debt-limit-credit-u.s.-20130115.

20. Jonathan Weisman, "House Passes Money Bill and Budget Blueprint," *New York Times* online, March 21 2013, accessed July 17, 2017, http://www.nytimes.com/2013/03/22/us/politics/house-passes-plan-to-avert-federal-shutdown.html.

21. Jonathan Weisman, "Senate Passes $3.7 Trillion Budget, Setting Up Contentious Negotiations," *New York Times* online, March 23, 2013, accessed July 17, 2017, http://www.nytimes.com/2013/03/24/us/politics/senate-passes-3-7-trillion-budget-its-first-in-4-years.html.

22. Alberta, "John Boehner Unchained."

23. Doc and Claire Hastings, interview, July 20, 2017.

24. Ungerecht, email, August 4, 2014.

25. Lisa Desjardins, "The Budget Deal in Plain English," CNN online, December 10, 2013, accessed July 17, 2017, http://politicalticker.blogs.cnn.com/2013/12/10/the-budget-deal-in-plain-english.

26. Lori Montgomery and Rosalind S. Helderman, "Congress Sends Obama Bill to End Shutdown," *Washington Post* online, October 17, 2013, accessed July 17, 2017, https://www.washingtonpost.com/politics/house-effort-to-end-fiscal-crisis-collapses-leaving-senate-to-forge-last-minute-solution/2013/10/16/1e8bb150-364d-11e3-be86-6aeaa439845b_story.html?utm_term=.64ceaf908eb0.

27. John A. Boehner, letter to Doc Hastings, February 24, 2014. Hastings collection.

28. "Remarks by the President to the White House Press Corps," website for *The White House*, August 20, 2012, accessed July 17, 2017, https://obamawhitehouse.archives.gov/the-press-office/2012/08/20/remarks-president-white-house-press-corps.

29. Todd, *The Stranger*, 433.

30. Rob Hotakainen, "No Rush to Back Obama," *Tri-City Herald*, September 7, 2013, A1.

31. Alter, *The Center Holds*, 121.

32. "Congress and the Public," Gallup, accessed August 9, 2017, http://www.gallup.com/poll/1600/Congress-Public.aspx#1; "Presidential Approval Ratings—Barack Obama," Gallup, accessed August 9, 2017, http://www.gallup.com/poll/116479/barack-obama-presidential-job-approval.aspx.

33. Doc and Claire Hastings, interview, July 20, 2017.

34. "Responsible Helium Administration and Stewardship Act (H.R. 527)," website for House Committee on Natural Resources, accessed on August 1, 2017, https://naturalresources.house.gov/newsroom/documentsingle.aspx?DocumentID=320460.

35. "Peter DeFazio," Wikipedia, accessed July 24, 2017, https://en.wikipedia.org/wiki/Peter_DeFazio.

36. John Nichols, "New Hampshire Results Point to a Notable Democratic Enthusiasm Gap," *The Nation* online, January 12, 2012, accessed July 24, 2017, https://www.thenation.com/article/new-hampshire-results-point-notable-democratic-enthusiasm-gap.

37. Peter DeFazio, interview by the author, July 26, 2017.

38. Ibid.

39. "Remarks of Hon. Peter DeFazio," *A Ceremony Unveiling the Portrait of The Honorable Doc Hastings,* Proceedings before the Committee on Natural Resources, November 19, 2014 (Washington, DC: US Government Printing Office, 2015).

40. DeFazio, interview.

41. Annette Cary, "B Reactor Bill Introduced in House," *Tri-City Herald*, March 16, 2013, C1.

42. Annette Carry, "Decision Awaits on B Reactor's Future," *Tri-City Herald*, December 10, 2013, A1.

43. Tim Peckinpaugh, email to the author, December 4, 2017.

44. DeFazio, interview.

45. Joel Connelly, "Alpine Lakes: In the Hands of a Hostile House," *Seattle-Post Intelligencer* online, July 23, 2013, accessed July 31, 2017, https://www.cantwell.senate.gov/news/news-about-maria/alpine-lakes-in-the-hands-of-a-hostile-house.

46. Kyung M. Song, "Odds Grow in Congress to Enlarge Alpine Lakes Wilderness," *Seattle Times* online, December 4, 2014, accessed July 31, 2017, http://www.seattletimes.com/seattle-news/odds-grow-in-congress-to-enlarge-alpine-lakes-wilderness.

47. Geoff Folsom, "Hastings Discusses Capitol Hill Gridlock," *Tri-City Herald*, March 18, 2014, B1.

48. Doc and Claire Hastings, interview, August 10, 2017.

49. Geoff Folsom, "Bladderpod Protected on Federally-Owned Land Only," *Tri-City Herald*, December 20, 2013, A1.

50. Doc and Claire Hastings, interview by the author, August 17, 2017.

51. Staff and news services, "Hastings Leads GOP Effort to Revise Endangered Species Act," *Yakima Herald-Republic*, February 5, 2014, B1.

52. Ungerecht, email, August 4, 2014.

53. Geoff Folsom, "Some Seek Fixes for Columbia River Treaty," *Tri-City Herald*, December 10, 2013, A1.

54. "Benghazi: Exposing Failure and Recognizing Courage," Hearing before the Committee on Oversight and Government Reform, May 8, 2013, https://www.gpo.gov/fdsys/pkg/CHRG-113hhrg81563/pdf/CHRG-113hhrg81563.pdf.

55. "Finding Lois Lerner in Contempt of Congress," Wikipedia, accessed July 26, 2017, https://en.wikipedia.org/wiki/Finding_Lois_Lerner_in_contempt_of_Congress.

56. Doc and Claire Hastings, interview, July 13, 2017.

57. Ibid.

58. Ibid.

59. Doc and Claire Hastings, interview, August 17, 2017.

60. Annette Cary, "DOE Report Calls for Phased Vit Plant Start," *Tri-City Herald*, September 23, 2013, A1.

61. Annette Cary, "Court: Work on Repository Must Resume," *Tri-City Herald*, August 14, 2013, A1.

62. Annette Cary, "Hastings Proposes Money for Water Storage," *Tri-City Herald*, February 5, 2014, B1.

63. Michael Doyle and Annette Cary, "House Passes Low-Cal Farm Bill," *Tri-City Herald*, July 12, 2013, A1.

64. Courtney Ross, "Farm Bill to Fund Research, Crops in the Yakima Valley," *Yakima Herald-Republic*, February 5, 2014, A1.

65. Geoff Folsom, "Hastings Won't Seek Re-election," *Tri-City Herald*, February 14, 2014.

66. Doc and Claire Hastings, interview, August 10, 2017.

67. Doc and Claire Hastings, interview, July 13, 2017.

68. Ibid.

69. Jessica Gleason, email to the author, August 3, 2017.

70. Ibid.; Jenny Gorski, email to the author, August 2, 2017.

71. Folsom, "Hastings Won't Seek Re-election."

72. Ibid.

73. Mike Faulk, "Pasco Republican Hastings, Who Has Served the 4th Congressional District for 20 Terms, Will Retire at the End of the Year: 'It's Been a Great Privilege,'" *Yakima Herald-Republic*, February 14, 2014, A1.

74. DeVaney, email, May 7, 2017.

75. Jeff Markey, interview by the author, January 13, 2017.

76. Annette Cary, "Hastings Not Swayed by Whims of Party," *Tri-City Herald*, February 24, 2014, A1.

77. "Remarks of Hon. John Boehner," *A Ceremony Unveiling the Portrait of The Honorable Doc Hastings*, Proceedings before the Committee on Natural Resources, November 19, 2014 (Washington, DC: US Government Printing Office, 2015).

78. "Remarks of Hon. Cathy McMorris Rodger," *A Ceremony Unveiling the Portrait of The Honorable Doc Hastings*, Proceedings before the Committee on Natural Resources, November 19, 2014 (Washington, DC: US Government Printing Office, 2015).

79. "Remarks of Hon. Doc Hastings," *A Ceremony Unveiling the Portrait of The Honorable Doc Hastings*, Proceedings before the Committee on Natural Resources, November 19, 2014 (Washington, DC: US Government Printing Office, 2015).

80. Congressional Record, 113th Congress, 2nd Session, December 10, 2014. H9036-9038.

81. Congressional Record H3183, April 10, 2014 (Statement of Mr. Ryan).

82. Doc Hastings, interview, March 8, 2016.

Epilogue

1. Geoff Folsom, "Hastings Memorabilia Dedicated at Pasco Museum," *Tri-City Herald*, October 15, 2015, 2A.

2. Cantwell, interview.

3. Annette Cary, "French Firm to Build State's Largest Solar Project North of Richland," *Tri-City Herald*, June 12 2017, 1A.

4. Wendy Culverwell, "Coalition Ready to Lobby Congress, *Tri-City Herald*, April 22, 2016, 1A.

5. Wendy Culverwell, "Critic Gives Army 'I' for Incomplete on Columbia River Shoreline Report," *Tri-City Herald* online, June 14, 2017, accessed August 4, 2017, http://www.tri-cityherald.com/news/local/article156253494.html.

6. Editorial, "Congressional Effort to Blunt Dam Breaching Is Sound," *Walla Walla Union Bulletin*, July 10, 2017.

7. Doc and Claire Hastings, interview, August 17, 2017.

8. Elise Viebeck, "Under-the-Radar Change to Congressional Ethics Watchdog May Weaken It," *Washington Post* online, February 8, 2017, accessed August 3, 2017, https://www.washingtonpost.com/powerpost/under-the-radar-change-to-house-ethics-watchdog-may-weaken-it/2017/02/08/7b066f8e-ee31-11e6-b4ff-ac2cf509efe5_story.html?utm_term=.1390472a142f.

9. Tri-City Herald staff, "Doc Hastings Appointed to Lead Office of Congressional Ethics," *Tri-City Herald* online, February 16, 2017, accessed August 3, 2017, http://www.tri-cityherald.com/news/local/article133277434.html.

10. Will Bunch, "Many Americans think it's worse to vote for a Democrat (or Republican) than for a child molester? Is that a problem?" (ed) *The (Philadelphia) Inquirer*, November 21, 2017, accessed December 8, 2017, http://www.philly.com/philly/columnists/will_bunch/donald-trump-roy-moore-support-doug-jones-20171121.

11. Veronica Stracqualursi, Saisha Talwar, and Dylan Wells, "Trump's Approval Rate at New Low; Slip in Support among Base: Poll," *ABC News*, August 3, 2017, accessed August 4, 2017, http://abcnews.go.com/Politics/trumps-approval-rate-time-low-slip-support-base/story?id=49015043.

12. Del Quentin Wilber and Byron Tau, "Special Counsel Robert Mueller Impanels Washington Grand Jury in Russia Probe," *Wall Street Journal*, August 3, 2017,

accessed August 4, 2017, https://www.wsj.com/articles/special-counsel-mueller-impanels-washington-grand-jury-in-russia-probe-1501788287.

13. Deirdre Walsh, Phil Mattingly, Ashley Killough, Lauren Fox, and Kevin Liptak, "White House, GOP celebrate passing sweeping tax bill," CNN News, December 20, 2017, accessed January 8, 2018, http://www.cnn.com/2017/12/20/politics/house-senate-trump-tax-bill/index.htmlTom Cole, note to Doc Hastings (undated), Hastings collection.

14. Raúl Grijalva, note to Doc Hastings (undated), Hastings collection.

15. Doc and Claire Hastings, interview by the author, August 24, 2017.

BIBLIOGRAPHY

Unpublished Sources

Manuscript Collections
> Smith, C. Mark. Collection of miscellaneous newspaper clippings, letters, and other ephemera in the possession of C. Mark Smith.
> Riggs, Doug. Collection of miscellaneous newspaper clippings, letters, and other ephemera in the possession of Doug Riggs.
> Hastings, Hon. Richard. Collection of miscellaneous digital files, papers, DVDs, and ephemera in the possession of Richard "Doc" Hastings.

Interviews
> Ammons, David
> Atkinson, Linda Yamauchi
> Barnes, Dallas
> Berger, Sharlyn
> Berman, Howard
> Boehner, Hon. John
> Briggs, Jack
> Brown, Donean
> Bullert, Gary
> Cantwell, Senator Maria
> Clauson, Ilene
> Connelly, Joel
> Crider, Bob
> Davis, Jim
> DeFazio, Representative Peter
> DeVaney, Jon
> Dicks, Hon. Norm
> Ehlers, Hon. Wayne
> Eskil, Rick
> Ferguson, Robert
> Fisher, Brad
> Ganders, Larry
> Gerber, Eric

Gleason, Jessica
Graham, Senator Lindsey
Grey, Ron
Gorski, Jenny
Gorton, Hon. Slade
Hankins, Hon Shirley
Hastings, Claire Montmorency
Hastings, Colin
Hastings, Hon. Richard N. "Doc"
Hastings, Roger
Hayward, Allen
Howard, Darryl
Howard, Diahann
Inslee, Governor Jay
Jesernig, Hon. Jim
Kleinknecht, Gary
Lancaster, Kirsten Hastings
Lee, Bill
Ling, George and Janice
Lisk, Barb
McMorris Rogers, Representative Cathy
Markey, Senator Edward
Markey, Jeff
Matheson, Sandy
Moak, Thomas
Morrison, Hon. Sid
Mosebar, Judy
Palmer, LaMar and Joan
Peckinpaugh, Tim
Petersen, Gary
Polk, Hon. William M.
Riggs, Doug
Robertson, Ken
Shepard, Mike
Stewart, Sharon
Taber, Duane
Ungerecht, Todd
Venable, Rick
Ward, Leah
Watts, Jim
Woodward, Scott

Young, Todd

Zusy, Patricia Hastings

*All interviews were conducted in person, on the telephone, or by email. Interview subjects who requested anonymity are not named here.

Recorded Speeches and Interviews:

> *In Focus.* 1992. Yakima, WA: KYVE-TV, 2002. Videotape. Hastings family collection.
>
> Gerber, Eric. *Save the Hanford Reach Timeline.* Boston, MA: Boston Productions, Inc., 2013. Interactive video display. Hanford Reach Interpretive Center (Richland, WA).
>
> Hastings, Hon. Doc. Doc's last speech made on the floor of the Washington legislature. Unknown producer. 1986. Videotape. Hastings family collection.
>
> Hastings, Hon. Doc. Remarks made at a press conference announcing his retirement from serving in the Washington legislature. Unknown producer. 1986. Videotape. Hastings family collection.
>
> Hastings, Hon. Doc. Remarks made at a press conference announcing his candidacy for Congress at the Pasco Red Lion hotel. Unknown producer. 1992. Videotape. Hastings family collection.
>
> Spellman, Hon. John D. *Inside Olympia.* Richland-Pasco-Kennewick, WA: KTNW-TV, 2000. Videotape. Hastings family collection.

Other Unpublished Documents:

> Ehlers, Hon. Wayne. "As the Gavel Falls: Semi-True Confessions of a Part-Time Politician." Unpublished memoir, 2015.
>
> Froistad, Esther M. J. "Family Chronicle." Self-published manuscript, Mukilteo, WA, 1976.
>
> Hales, Marjorie. "A History of Pasco to 1915." Master's thesis, Washington State University, 1964.
>
> Smith, C. Mark. "Reluctant Warrior: DuPont, Hanford and the Bomb." Unpublished manuscript, 2015.

PUBLISHED SOURCES

> Ambrose, Steven. *Nothing Like It in the World: The Men Who Built the Transcontinental Railroad 1863-1869.* New York: Simon & Schuster, 2000.
>
> Baker, Peter. *Obama: The Call of History.* New York: Callaway, 2017.
>
> Brazier, Don. *History of the Washington Legislature 1965-1982.* Olympia, WA: Washington State Senate, 2007. http://leg.wa.gov/History/Legislative/

Documents/HistoftheLeg1965-82.pdf.Buchal, James L. *The Great Salmon Hoax.* Aurora, OR: Iconoclast, 1997.

Bush, George W. *Decision Points.* New York: Crown Publishers, 2010.

Caro, Robert A. *The Years of Lyndon Johnson: The Passage of Power.* New York: Alfred A. Knopf, 2012.

Chasan, Daniel Jack. *Speaker of the House: The Political Career and Times of John L. O'Brien.* Seattle: University of Washington Press, 1990.

Clinton, Bill. *My Life.* New York: Alfred A. Knopf, 2004.

Clinton, Hillary Rodham. *Living History.* New York: Scribner, 2003.

Congressional Record, 113th Congress, 2nd Session, December 10, 2014. Washington, DC.

Davis, Tom, Martin Frost, and Richard Cohen. *The Partisan Divide: Crisis in Congress.* Campbell, CA: Premiere, 2014.

DeFrank, Thomas M. *Write It When I'm Gone: Remarkable Off-the-Record Conversations with Gerald R. Ford.* New York: G. P. Putnam's Sons, 2007.

DeLay, Tom. *No Retreat, No Surrender: One American's Fight.* With Stephen Mansfield. New York: Sentinel, 2007.

Drew, Elizabeth. *On the Edge: The Clinton Presidency.* New York: Simon & Schuster, 1994.

Durham, Nelson Wayne. *History of the City of Spokane and Spokane Country Washington: From Its Earliest Settlement to the Present Time, Volume II.* Spokane, WA: The S. J. Clarke Publishing Company, 1912.

Egan, Timothy. *Breaking Blue.* Seattle: Sasquatch Books, Reprint Edition, 2004.

Faulkner, Susan Davis. *Early Pasco.* Charleston, SC: Arcadia Publishing, 2009.

Findlay, John M., and Bruce Hevly. *Atomic Frontier Days: Hanford and the American West.* Seattle: University of Washington Press, 2011.

Ford, Gerald R. *A Time to Heal.* New York: Harper & Row, 1979.

Gillespie, Ed. *Contract with America: The Bold Plan by Rep. Newt Gingrich, Rep. Dick Armey, and the House Republicans to Change the Nation.* Edited by Bob Schellhas. New York: Time Books, a division of Random House, 1994.

Greenberg, David. *Republic of Spin.* New York: W. W. Norton & Company, 2016.

Halberstam, David. *War in a Time of Peace.* New York: Scribner, 2001.

Harris, John F. *The Survivor: Bill Clinton and the White House.* New York: Random House, 2005.

Hastert, Denny. *Speaker: Lessons from Forty Years in Coaching and Politics.* Washington, DC: Regnery Publishing, 2004.

Hayner, Jeannette. *Jeannette Hayner: An Oral History.* Interviewed and edited by Sharon Boswell. Olympia, WA: Washington State Oral History

Program, Office of Secretary of State, 2007. https://www.sos.wa.gov/lega-cyproject/collection/pdf/hayner.pdf.

Hayward, Allen. *My Ride*. Centralia, WA: Gorham Printing, 2014.

Heffernan, Trova. *Woman First: The Impact of Jennifer Dunn*. Olympia, WA: Washington State Legacy Project, 2012.

House of Representatives. Committee on Natural Resources. *Full Committee Oversight Field Hearing on "California Water Crisis and Its Impacts: The Need for Immediate and Long-Term Solutions."* Republican Briefing Paper, March 19, 2014.

Hughes, John C. *Slade Gorton: A Half Century in Politics*. Olympia, WA: Washington State Legacy Project, 2011.

Johansen, Dorothy O., and Charles M. Gates. *Empire of the Columbia: A History of the Pacific Northwest*. New York: Harper & Brothers, 1957.

Leuchtenburg, William E. *The American President*. New York: Oxford University Press, 2015.

Lewis, Meriwether and William Clark. *The Journals of the Lewis and Clark Expedition, Volume 5: July 28-November 1, 1805*. Edited by Gary E. Moulton. Lincoln, NE: University of Nebraska Press, 1988.

Loeb, Paul Rogat. *Nuclear Culture: Living and Working in the World's Largest Atomic Complex*. Gabriola Island, BC: New Society Publishers, 1986.

Mann, Thomas E., and Norman J. Ornstein. *The Broken Branch: How Congress Is Failing America and How to Get Back on Track*. Oxford, UK: Oxford University Press, 2006.

———*It's Even Worse Than It Looks: How the American Constitutional System Collided with the New Politics of Extremism*. New York: Basic Books, 2013.

Matthews, Chris. *Tip and the Gipper: When Politics Worked*. New York: Simon & Schuster, 2013.

Meacham, Jon. *Destiny and Power: The American Odyssey of George Herbert Walker Bush*. New York: Random House, 2015.

Moore, Ray. *Ray Moore: An Oral History*. Interviewed and edited by Sharon Boswell. Olympia, WA: Washington State Oral History Program, 1999. apps.leg.wa.gov/oralhistory/moore.pdf.

Oberst, Walter A. *Railroads, Reclamation and the River: A History of Pasco*. Pasco, WA: Franklin Country Historical Society, 1978.

Olasky, Marvin. *Compassionate Conservatism: What It Is, What It Does, and How It Can Transform America*. New York: Free Press, 2000.

Oregon Department of Energy. *Hanford Cleanup: The First 25 Years*. Salem, OR: Oregon Department of Energy, 2014.

Relander, Click. *Drummers and Dreamers*. Paperback edition. Seattle: Northwest Interpretive Association, 1986.

Renz, Louis Tuck. *The History of the Northern Pacific Railroad.* Fairfield, WA: Ye Galleon Press, 1980.

Rhodes, Richard. *The Making of the Atomic Bomb.* New York: Simon & Schuster, 1986.

Scott, George W. *A Majority of One: Legislative Life.* Self-published, Xlibris, 2010.

Shirley, Craig. *Reagan Rising.* New York: Broadside Books, 2017.

———*Rendezvous with Destiny.* Greenville, DE: Intercollegiate Studies Institute, 2009.

Smalley, Eugene Virgil. *History of the Northern Pacific Railroad.* New York: G. P. Putnam's Sons, 1883.

Smith, C. Mark. *Community Godfather: How Sam Volpentest Shaped the History of Hanford and the Tri-Cities.* Richland, WA: Etcetera Press, 2013.

———*Raising Cain: The Life and Politics of Harry P. Cain.* Bothell, WA: Book Publishers Network, 2011.

Smith, Sally Bedell. *For Love of Politics: Bill and Hillary Clinton; The White House Years.* New York: Random House, 2007.

Thayer, Harry. *Management of the Hanford Engineering Works in World War II.* New York: ASCE Press, 1996.

Todd, Chuck. *The Stranger.* New York; Little, Brown and Company, 2014.

United States Congress. *Biographical Directory of the United States Congress, 1774–2005.* Washington, DC: US Government Printing Office, 2005.

United States Congress, House of Representatives, Committee on Natural Resources, Committee Print. *A Ceremony Unveiling the Portrait of the Honorable Doc Hastings: Proceedings before the Committee on Natural Resources, November 19, 2014.* Washington, DC: US Government Printing Office, 2015.

United States Congress, House of Representatives, and Committee on Oversight and Public Reform. *Benghazi: Exposing Failure and Recognizing Courage.* Washington, DC: US Government Printing Office, 2013.

United States Congress and House of Representatives. *Referral to the United States House of Representatives pursuant to Title 28, United States Code, Section 595(c), Communication from Kenneth W. Starr, Independent Counsel, September 9, 1998.* 105th Congress, 2nd Session, House Document 105-310. Washington, DC: US Government Printing Office, 1998.

Van Arsdol, Ted. *Tri-Cities: The Mid Columbia Hub.* Chatsworth, CA: Windsor Publications, 1990.

Vance, J. D. *Hillbilly Elegy: A Memoir of a Family and Culture in Crisis.* New York: HarperCollins, 2016.

Wagner, Eileen M. Benitz, and Michele S. Gerber. *Senator Max E. Benitz, Sr.: "Mr. Energy."* Ft. Worth, TX: NorTex Press, 2014.

Washington State Legislature: *Members of the Washington State Legislature 1889-2014*. Olympia, WA: Legislative Information Center. 2014. http://leg.wa.gov/History/Legislative/Documents/MembersOfLeg2014.pdfWood, Charles R. *The Northern Pacific: Main Street of the Northwest*. Seattle: Superior Publishing, 1968.

Woodward, Bob. *Bush at War*. New York: Simon & Schuster, 2002.

———*The Choice*. New York: Simon & Schuster, 2005.

———*Plan of Attack*. New York: Simon & Schuster, 2004.

———*The Price of Politics*. New York: Simon & Schuster, 2012.

———*State of Denial*. New York: Simon & Schuster, 2006.

———*The War Within*. New York: Simon & Schuster, 2008.

Recordings

100 Days: Contract with America Celebration. Washington, DC: National Republican Campaign Committee, 1995. DVD.

INDEX

ABOUT THE TYPE

The text of this book is set in Minion Pro 11.5/16. Minion is the name of a typeface designed by Robert Slimbach in 1990 for Adobe Systems. The name comes from the traditional naming system for type sizes, in which minion is between nonpareil and brevier. It is inspired by late Renaissance-era type. Minion Pro is an update of the original family, released in 2000.